KU-540-129

ROME

Anthony Pereira

Third
edition
of the
American
Express
Pocket
Guide

Mitchell Beazley

The Author and Contributors

Anthony Pereira, a travel writer with an extensive knowledge of Italy, was also the author of guides to Sicily, Naples, Pompeii and southern Italy. Contributors to the original edition were Burton Anderson, on eating and drinking, Diana Grant, on bars and cafés, nightlife and shopping, and Helen Langdon, on mythology. The guide was updated in 1989 by Nick Skidmore, an independent TV producer who lived for two years in Verona as a freelance journalist and writer.

Acknowledgments

The author and publishers thank the following for their invaluable help and advice: Marco Fabio Apolloni, Leonardo Bedini, Orietta Budini Gattai, Charles Dorman, David Ekserdjian, ENIT (Italian State Tourist Office, London and Rome), Pamela Fiori, Giovanni Gallenga, Paul Holberton, Ferdie McDonald, Christopher McIntosh, Massimo Nati, Piers Parry-Crooke, Diego and Flavia Piacentino, Giuliana Poggiani, Ila Stanger, Laura Stainton; and Diana Grant and Eric Drewery, editor and art editor of the original edition.

General Editor	David Townsend Jones
Art Editor	Nigel O'Gorman
Designer	Christopher Howson
Illustrators	Jeremy Ford (David Lewis Artists), Illustrated Arts, Oxford Illustrators Ltd
Map Editor	David Haslam
Jacket illustration	Pierre Marie Valat
Indexer	Hilary Bird
Proof-reader	Sue McKinstry

Edited and designed by Mitchell Beazley International Limited, Artists House, 14-15 Manette Street, London W1V 5LB

Maps in 2-colour and 4-colour by Clyde Surveys Ltd, Maidenhead, England.
Typeset by Castle House Press, Llantrisant, Wales.
Typeset in Garamond and Univers.
Linotronic output through Microstar DTP Studio, Cardiff, Wales.
Produced by Mandarin Offset. Printed and bound in Malaysia.

Contents

How to use this book

The American Express Pocket Guide to Rome is an encyclopaedia of travel information, organized in the sections listed on the previous page. There is also a comprehensive *Index* (pages 211-220) and a *Gazetteer of street names* (pages 221-224), and there are full-colour *Maps* at the end of the book.

For easy reference, all major sections (*Sights and places of interest*, *Hotels*, *Restaurants*), and other sections where possible, are arranged alphabetically. For the organization of the book as a whole, see *Contents*. For individual places that do not have separate entries in *Sights and places of interest*, see the *Index*.

Abbreviations

As a rule only standard abbreviations have been used, such as days of the week and months, points of the compass (N, S, E and W), St (Saint), Gk (Greek), rms (rooms), C (century), and measurements.

Bold type

Bold type is used in the text mainly for emphasis, to draw attention to something of special interest or importance. It is also used in this way to pick out places — shops or minor museums, for example — that do not have full entries of their own. In such cases it is usually followed in brackets by the address, telephone number, and details of opening times, which are printed in *italics*.

Cross-references

A special type has been used for cross-references. Whenever a place or section title is printed in *sans serif italics* (for example *Colosseum* or *Basic information*) in the text, this indicates that you can turn to the appropriate heading in the book for further information.

Cross-references in this typeface always refer either to

How entries are organized

Hood House

1411 Lincoln Ave., Lincoln Green, Sherwood Forest
☎ *426-5960 (house), 426-5961 (group tour reservations).*
Map 8J11 ☒ *✗ Open Apr-Sept 9am-5pm, rest of year 9am-4pm. Closed Christmas, New Year's Day. Metro: Bow & Arrow.*

Robin Hood (?1149-1205) was the leading spokesman for the poor and downtrodden in their struggle for freedom and justice under the Plantagenets. He lectured and wrote books about his own early life as a serf, campaigned endlessly for human rights, helped recruit peasants to the Civil Service, and finally settled down to a distinguished old age in Sherwood Forest. He lived first in A St. (see ***National Museum of Outlawed Art***), then bought Sheriff Villa, which he renamed Hood House, a handsome white dwelling on a height overlooking the Trent Valley. All the furnishings, except for curtains and wallpaper, are original. Hood's library and other belongings are still *in situ*, and the whole house is redolent of the spirit of a very remarkable man. In the **Visitors' Centre** at the foot of the hill you can see a film about Hood's life.

---

sections of the book — *Basic information, Planning and walks, Hotels* — or to individual entries in *Sights and places of interest*, such as *Arch of Titus* or *St Peter's*.

For easy reference, use the running heads printed at the top corner of the page (see, for example, **Roman Forum** on page 89 or **Hotels** on page 137).

Map references

Each of the full-colour maps at the end of the book is divided into a grid of squares, identified vertically by letters (A, B, C, D, etc.) and horizontally by numbers (1, 2, 3, 4, etc.). A map reference identifies the page and square in which the street or place can be found — thus *Castel Sant' Angelo* is located in Map **5**G4.

Price categories

Price categories are denoted by the symbols ⬜ ⬛⬜ ⬛⬛⬜ ⬛⬛⬛⬜ and ⬛⬛⬛⬛, which signify cheap, inexpensive, moderately priced, expensive and very expensive, respectively. In the cases of hotels and restaurants these correspond approximately with the following actual prices, which give a guideline at the time of printing. Although actual prices will inevitably increase, in most cases the relative price category — for example expensive or cheap — is likely to remain more or less the same.

Price categories	Corresponding to approximate prices	
	for **hotels** *double room with bath and breakfast; single not much cheaper*	for **restaurants** *meal for one with service, tax and house wine*
⬜ cheap	under ₤75,000	under ₤30,000
⬛⬜ inexpensive	₤75,000-150,000	₤30,000-50,000
⬛⬛⬜ moderate	₤150,000-200,000	₤50,000-60,000
⬛⬛⬛⬜ expensive	₤200,000-300,000	₤60,000-100,000
⬛⬛⬛⬛ very expensive	over ₤300,000	over ₤100,000

— Bold blue type for entry headings.

— Blue italics for address, practical information and symbols. For list of symbols see page 6 or back flap of jacket.

— Black text for description.

— Sans serif italics used for cross-references to other entries or sections.

— Bold type used for emphasis.

Entries for hotels, restaurants, shops, etc. follow the same organization, and are usually printed across a half column.

In hotels, symbols indicating special facilities appear at the end of the entry, in black.

Pullman
2600 Express Ave., Orient City 20037 ☎299-4450 ⑲299-4460. Map 2F4 ⬛⬛⬛⬛ *238 rms* ⬤ ═ AE CB ⬤ ⬤ VISA *Metro: High Standard.*
Location: On a height overlooking the Universal Trade Center. Part of a large conglomeration overlooking the seafront, this luxurious hotel is set in attractively landscaped grounds and is run with clockwork precision. Its restaurant, the **Simplon**, is highly regarded.
♿ ❧ ⟨⟨ ≋ ♈

Key to symbols

☎ Telephone	⌂ Residential terms available
⊛ Telex	
⊛ Facsimile (fax)	AE American Express
★ Recommended sight	⊡ Diners Club
☆ Worth a visit	⊡ MasterCard/Eurocard
♣ Good value (in its class)	VISA Visa
	⊠ Secure garage
i Tourist information	⌂ Quiet hotel
⊸ Parking	‡ Lift
⊞ Building of architectural interest	⊛ Facilities for disabled people
† Church or cathedral	☐ TV in each room
⊡ Free entrance	⊡ Telephone in each room
⊠ Entrance fee payable	
⊠ Entrance expensive	⊮ Dogs not allowed
⊠ Photography forbidden	⊻ Garden
⋌ Guided tour	⊰ Outstanding views
⊒ Cafeteria	⊠ Conference facilities
✳ Special interest for children	⊽ Bar
	⊟ Refrigerator in room
⟲ Hotel	⊟ Restaurant
⊟ Simple (hotel)	⊜ Simple (restaurant)
⊞ Luxury (hotel)	⊿ Luxury (restaurant)
⊐ Cheap	⊡ A la carte available
⊮ Inexpensive	⊪ Set (fixed-price) menu available
⊯ Moderately priced	
⊪ Expensive	⊒ Good for wines
⊪ Very expensive	⊕ Open-air dining
⊟ Rooms with private bathroom	O Disco dancing
	◗ Nightclub
⊞ Air conditioning	◣ Revue

A note from the General Editor

No travel book can be completely free of errors and totally up to date. Telephone numbers and opening hours change without warning, and hotels and restaurants come under new management, which can affect standards. We make every effort to ensure that all information is accurate at the time we go to press, but are always delighted to receive corrections or suggestions for improvements from our readers, which if warranted will be incorporated in a future edition. We are indebted to readers who wrote to us during the preparation of this edition.

  The publishers regret they cannot accept any consequences arising from the use of the book or from the information it contains.

An introduction to Rome

The name of Rome will always hold an irresistible fascination for the traveller. The influence of the city that grew from the farms and villages perched on seven insignificant hills has reached farther than even its greatest emperor could have dared imagine. Countries and continents undreamed of by Augustus owe their language and their laws, their calendar and their faith to Rome.

The continuity of the city as a seat of power under the papacy and as capital of modern Italy has ensured the survival of many of its great monuments. The Pantheon, triumphal arches and columns stand today much as they did on the day of their completion, although most of the temples, stadiums and baths are now in ruins, and countless treasures still lie buried beneath later construction.

The area to which most tourists are drawn is the heart of old Rome, across the river from St Peter's. Here the rich complexity of 2,000 years of decay and renewal can bewilder even the best informed of sightseers. On entering Piazza Navona, do you see the original form of Domitian's racetrack, or a magnificent open-air gallery of Baroque sculpture, or simply a convenient pedestrian precinct with inviting café tables at which to rest your aching feet?

With such dazzling riches to choose from it is best to be selective in your goals. Devout pilgrims will make straight for Piazza San Pietro, but the less pious visitor with a casual interest in architecture and the growth of Christianity must choose between 280 churches within the walls, and miles of catacombs without. Of particular historical significance are the mosaics and frescoes of the very early churches and basilicas. But if your taste is for the Baroque, the city abounds in fine examples by Bernini and Borromini. For many people, however, it is a Romanesque church such as Santa Maria in Cosmedin, with its humble brick and tile exterior and simple campanile, that most eloquently evokes the spirit of Rome.

Compared with the grandiose monuments of other ages, the scale of Romanesque architecture is reassuringly human. This is no accident, for in the late Middle Ages Rome's fortunes were at their lowest ebb. As the popes' powers fluctuated in never-ending quarrels with the Holy Roman Emperors, the population dwindled from one million to as little as 30,000. Less than a quarter of the land enclosed by the original walls was built upon. Sheep and cattle grazed on the Capitol and in the Forum, while the Colosseum and other monuments served as quarries for local builders.

In the 15thC, when the popes returned from Avignon after the Great Schism, Rome began to expand once more. Julius II, more Renaissance man than prelate, by his military exploits brought in sufficient revenue to rebuild the city. He ordered the destruction of the old St Peter's and commissioned Bramante to design the new. When Michelangelo and Raphael were summoned to the court, Rome became once more the greatest artistic centre in the world.

However, it was not long before the Church had to withstand the most potent challenge ever directed at its authority, as the tide of Protestantism swept across Catholic Europe. Papal finances were also hard hit by the sacking of Rome by the Emperor Charles V. Fortunately for the city, the zeal of the Counter-Reformation was employed not only in the imposition of orthodoxy but also in erecting even more spectacular churches to the glory of the orthodox God. The astute tax reforms of Sixtus V provided subsequent popes with seemingly bottomless purses. Commissions poured forth, the lion's share falling into the hands of Gianlorenzo Bernini.

After the flourishing of the Baroque, two centuries passed before the city experienced any vigorous renewal. In 1870 the pope was forced to cede his temporal dominions to the House of Savoy, and Rome became capital of a united Italy. A vast building programme was undertaken to house the ministries of the new kingdom. The centralization of government continued under Mussolini, and Rome remains a mecca for civil servants, rivalling even Brussels in her bureaucracy.

The population of the city now exceeds three million. In the postwar years building laws were openly flouted and whole streets sprang up, unmarked on any official map. Over this chaos presides the Comune di Roma, the city council. Seated in traditional splendour in Michelangelo's Palazzo Senatorio on the Capitol, the councillors devise well-meaning laws, which prove impossible to enforce. The city's debts are legendary, and the lack of essential amenities causes grave concern. A few drops of Tiber water can be fatal, due to untreated sewage that flows into the river. Yet, by a typically Roman paradox, the magnificent ornamental drinking fountains provide only pure spring water brought by aqueducts from distant hills.

It was at Rome, on the fifteenth of October, 1764, as I sat musing amidst the ruins of the Capitol, while the barefoot friars were singing vespers in the Temple of Jupiter, that the idea of writing the decline and fall of the city first started to my mind.
Edward Gibbon, *Autobiography*

Years of subjection to the Church have made the Romans outspokenly anti-clerical and anti-authoritarian, yet they seem resigned to the fact that things will never change. Visitors disturbed by what they read of terrorism and kidnappings have little to fear: the majority of Romans are far too easy-going to engage in violent political activism. A more likely threat is posed by handbag snatchers on motorcycles and scooters. Italian traffic is another hazard, but drivers are quick-witted and usually manage to avoid pedestrians except, curiously, on statutory crossings.

Belated attempts are being made to save Rome from the motor car by building an extension of the Metropolitana to the east of the city and a much-needed train service to Fiumicino Airport. Elaborate plans have long been on the drawing board to excavate Via dei Fori Imperiali and turn the whole area into a huge archaeological park, though the vicissitudes of party politics seem endlessly to delay their implementation.

The afternoon is a privileged time when tourists have Rome to themselves. Find yourself a peaceful shaded spot on the Aventine or Palatine and look out over the great grey domes that seem to hover protectively above the crooked red-tiled roofs. As the city slumbers in the hazy sunshine, you can sense its eternal quality. Forget about the traffic, which threatens to destroy its foundations. Forget about the absurd bureaucracy, which seems to exist purposely to ensure that nothing ever gets done. Rome has lived through perils far greater than these and yet has always survived.

Before you go

Documents required
For citizens of the USA and British Commonwealth, a passport is the only document required for visits not exceeding three months; for citizens of the EEC a Visitor Card will suffice. For longer visits, and for most other nationals, a visa must be obtained in advance in the country of departure. Vaccination certificates are not normally required, but if you are travelling from the Middle East, Far East, South America or Africa, you should check when buying your ticket.

To drive a car in Italy you must carry a valid national driving licence accompanied by a translation (available from CIT, ACI or Italian Tourist Board in the country of origin). If you intend bringing your car into the country, you must carry the vehicle registration document (logbook) and an international green card or other valid insurance.

Travel and medical insurance
Travellers from EEC countries are entitled to all free health services, but should still take out insurance to cover cancellation fees, loss of personal possessions and emergency expenses incurred for medical reasons. All other nationals should take out comprehensive travel and medical insurance.

UK nationals entitled to full UK benefits should obtain form E111 from their local health office before leaving. If medical aid is required, the form should be presented to the nearest USL (Unità Sanitaria Locale) office (see the publication *Rete di Roma*), which will issue a certificate confirming your right to treatment.

Money
The monetary unit is the lira (plural lire ₺). There are coins for 50, 100, 200 and 500 lire, and notes for 1,000, 2,000, 5,000, 10,000, 20,000, 50,000 and 100,000 lire. There are no restrictions on other currencies or travellers cheques taken into the country, but if you intend exporting more than 1 million lire's worth of any currency, you should complete form V2 at customs on entry.

Travellers cheques issued by all major companies are widely recognized. Make sure you read the instructions included with your travellers cheques. It is important to note separately the serial numbers of your cheques and the telephone number to call in case of loss. Specialist travellers cheque companies such as American Express provide extensive local refund facilities through their own offices or agents. Eurocheque Encashment Card holders can cash personal cheques in most banks. The principal credit cards accepted are American Express, Diners Club, Eurocard (MasterCard) and Visa.

Customs
Any items clearly intended for personal or professional use may be brought into the country free of charge.

Allowances for goods purchased duty-free at ferry or airport shops etc. are lower than those for goods obtained duty- and tax-paid in EEC countries (shown in brackets):

Tobacco   200(300) cigarettes *or* 100(150) cigarillos *or* 50(75) cigars *or* 250g(400g) tobacco; *or*, if you live outside Europe, 400 cigarettes *or* 200 cigarillos *or* 500g tobacco.

Alcoholic drinks   1(1.5) litres spirits (over 22 percent alcohol by volume) *or* 2(3) litres alcoholic drinks of 22 percent alcohol or less; *plus* 2(5) litres still wines.

Basic information

Perfume   50g/60cc/2 fl. oz (75g/90cc/3 fl. oz).
Other goods   Goods to the value of £28 (£120).

When leaving the country, you may export up to 1 million lire's worth of goods. The export of works of art is restricted and an application must be made to the Export Department of the Italian Ministry of Education.

When passing through customs, you must have dated receipts for any valuable items you are carrying, such as cameras or watches, or you may be charged duty on them.

Getting there
By air: Leonardo da Vinci Airport (Fiumicino), 36km (22 miles) SW of Rome, serves both international and domestic flights. Some domestic and international charter flights arrive at Ciampino, 16km (10 miles) SE of the city.
By train: International and most national trains arrive at Stazione Termini, Piazza dei Cinquecento, situated in the centre of Rome.
By bus: International buses also stop at Piazza dei Cinquecento.
By car: The main N-S and E-W motorways (*autostrade*), from Florence-Naples and l'Aquila-Civitavecchia, connect with the city via a huge ring motorway (*anulare*).

Climate
Although the climate is generally mild and pleasant, Rome is best visited in spring or autumn. Winters are usually moderate, but Jan and Feb can sometimes be freezing cold and wet. Even the Romans avoid the city in July and Aug if they possibly can; temperatures reach as high as 35°C (95°F).

Clothes
Lightweight clothing is the obvious choice for summer; a warm coat, gloves and umbrella are all essential in winter. Remember to take comfortable shoes for sightseeing and foot-slogging around cobbled streets. Short skirts and bare arms are not acceptable in churches. Romans have a reputation for stylish dressing, but maintain this with a degree of informality. Ties are generally unnecessary, and evening dress is rarely worn.

Poste restante
Letters marked *Fermo Posta* and addressed to Palazzo delle Poste, Piazza San Silvestro, 00186, will be held for collection. You will need to show your passport and pay a small fee to claim your mail. American Express provides a short-term *poste restante* service for clients, at Piazza di Spagna 38, 00187.

Getting around

From the airports to the city
An inexpensive airport bus ride takes you from Fiumicino to the city in about 40mins, but allow up to 1hr in case traffic is heavy. Buses leave every 15mins for the terminal in Via Giolitti, alongside Stazione Termini in the city centre. Ciampino is linked to Stazione Termini by suburban bus and train lines; but it is cheaper to take the ACOTRAL bus from the airport entrance and join the Metropolitana Line A at Subangusta.

Metered taxis are available from both airports (allow 30mins from Fiumicino, 20mins from Ciampino), but a supplement is payable from Fiumicino. Self-drive cars may be rented at both airports.

Public transport

The best way of getting around the city is by bus. The underground system (Metropolitana) has only two lines, but they link stations in many of the key tourist locations and most itineraries can be planned around them. Stations on both lines are denoted by the white letter **M** in a red circle in the maps at the end of this guide. There is a flat fare for both services. Bus stops are marked *Fermata*.

Most buses now run without a conductor, and tickets for these must be bought from tobacconists or ATAC offices. You enter the bus by the rear door and place a ticket in the machine, and leave the bus by the middle door. Trams are still in use on some routes and have the same flat fare. The Romapass Tourist Pass (which is available from travel agents and some ATAC offices) is valid for three days on public transport and gives free admittance to public museums.

Maps showing bus, tram and underground routes are available from the ATAC office outside Stazione Termini. For property lost on buses or trams, apply to the main ATAC office (*Via Volturno 65* ☎ 46951). Bus services to the environs of Rome are run by ACOTRAL, whose information office is located in Via Ostiense 131 (☎ 5915551).

Taxis

Taxis may be picked up at taxi ranks, or summoned by telephone for a small extra fee. See the annotated maps in *Rete di Roma* (available in most bars with phones) for lists of local ranks. Supplements are payable for luggage, and also for service at night, on Sun and on public holidays.

Getting around by car

Driving in Rome has little to recommend it. Parking is hard to find; the Romans' fast and aggressive tactics and congested conditions have only been aggravated by the closure of many streets to traffic. If you do use a car, remember to give way at crossroads to vehicles coming from your right. A speed limit of 50kph (30mph) applies, but is often ignored by local drivers. The largest city car park is under the Villa Borghese.

Tourists who take their cars to Italy are entitled to petrol coupons and motorway vouchers. These can be bought through the AA, RAC and CIT (*50 Conduit St., London W1* ☎ *(01) 434-3844*), and at Italian frontier points from the Italian Automobile Club (ACI) — but not within Italy. They can be refunded only by the issuing office. Passport and car log book must be presented.

For more information contact ACI (*Via Cristoforo Colombo 261, 00144* ☎ *5106 and at Via Marsala 8, 00185* ☎ *49981* ● *610686*); it gives free assistance to members of affiliated clubs, such as the AA and RAC, and rents out warning triangles (compulsory in Italy).

Renting a car

Cars may be rented at Fiumicino and Ciampino airports or at a number of offices in the city (see Yellow Pages), or booked in advance through travel agents. Rates generally include breakdown service and basic insurance, but it is advisable to inquire. Most firms require a deposit equal to the estimated total cost of rental (payable by credit card) and set a minimum age limit of 21. You must also have held a driving licence for at least one year.

11

Basic information

Getting around on foot

Pedestrians have the right of way at pedestrian crossings, and at traffic lights when a green lighted sign reads *Avanti*. (Stop when you see a red lighted sign saying *Alt*.) But note that Italian drivers often fail to give way at pedestrian crossings and have a habit of jumping traffic lights.

Railway services

Italian State Railways offer a wide choice of services at reasonable prices. The information office at Stazione Termini is open 7am-10.40pm (☎ *47751*).

Super-Rapido: Luxury, first-class-only trains, running between the main Italian cities; a supplement is charged and seat reservation is obligatory.

Rapido: Fast trains running between major towns. Some carry only first-class coaches. A supplement is charged, and in some cases seat reservation is obligatory.

Espresso: Long-distance express trains stopping only at main stations, with both first- and second-class coaches.

Diretto: Trains stopping at most stations; both classes.

Locale: Trains stopping at all stations; both classes.

Domestic airlines

Distances involved in N-S travel make flying a sensible option. Major cities are served by Alitalia, smaller centres by its subsidiary ATI (*Via Bissolati 13* ☎ *46881 for both airlines*) and Sardinia by Alisarda (*Via Salandra 36* ☎ *460032*). Domestic flights leave from Fiumicino and Ciampino.

Other transport

To rent a scooter, you must be over 21 years old and will need to present your passport and driving licence. You can rent one from Scoot-a-long (*Via Cavour 302* ☎ *6780206*), Scooters for Rent (*Via della Purificazione 66* ☎ *465485*) or Saint Peter Rent (*Via di Porta Castello 43* ☎ *6875714*). Bicycles can be rented from R. Collalti (*Via del Pellegrino 81* ☎ *6541084*).

Horsedrawn carriages may be rented in Piazza di Spagna, Via Veneto and Piazza San Pietro, and at the Trevi Fountain, Colosseum and Stazione Termini. They are expensive: you are advised to determine the fee in advance.

On-the-spot information

Public holidays

Jan 1; Easter Monday; Liberation Day, Apr 25; Labour Day (*Festa del Lavoro*), May 1; Assumption of the Virgin (*Ferragosto*), Aug 15; All Saints Day (*Ognissanti*), Nov 1; Conception of the Virgin Mary (*Festa della Madonna Immacolata*), Dec 8; Dec 25 and 26.

Time zones

Like most Western European countries, Italy is 1hr ahead of GMT in winter and 2hrs ahead in summer.

Banks and currency exchange

Banks are open Mon-Fri 8.30am-1.20pm, and major banks also open 3-4pm. Personal cheques may be cashed by Eurocheque Encashment Card holders. Travellers cheques can also be cashed at hotels, but the rate is usually less favourable. Bureaux de change (*cambio*) are open during normal office hours. American

Express (*Piazza di Spagna 38* ☎ *67641 or 722801* ☎ *614335*) also has an exchange desk.

Shopping hours

Shops are normally open 9am-1pm and 3.30-7.30pm. In summer they reopen at 4pm and close at 8pm. Few shops are open on Sun. From Sept-Apr most food shops are closed on Thurs afternoons and non-food shops on Mon mornings; from May-Sept many shops are closed on Sat afternoons.

Rush hours

Every daylight hour is a rush hour in the city centre, but congestion peaks between 8-9.30am and 5-8pm.

Post and telephone services

You can buy stamps at some tobacconists (marked **T** outside), but fewer and fewer find it worth the trouble to stock them. It is often safer to head straight for a post office. Post boxes are red. The main post office (Palazzo delle Poste) is at Piazza San Silvestro, open Mon-Fri 8am-9pm, Sat 8am-noon. The branch at Stazione Termini keeps the same hours. All other post offices close Mon-Fri 2pm, Sat noon. The Vatican City operates a highly efficient postal service, with its own distinctive stamps. In winter these may be bought from post offices on either side of Piazza San Pietro and in summer from a mobile post office parked in the square, open daily 8.30am-7pm except Saturday, when it closes an hour earlier. Vatican post boxes are blue.

Telephone numbers in Rome are subject to change. Improvements to the system undertaken in the months leading up to the 1990 world football championships mean that some numbers included in this guide may prove to be inaccurate.

To operate a public telephone, you must have 100-, 200- or 500-lire coins or, particularly in old telephones, tokens (*gettoni*). These are sold by post offices, tobacconists, bars and some news-stands. From some public telephones (*interurbani*), you can dial long-distance direct, first dialling O. A small mountain of *gettoni* may be needed for long-distance calls. International calls to most European countries and the USA can be made from *interurbani*. The main public telephone office at Palazzo delle Poste is open 24hrs. Calls to other countries must be made from private or hotel telephones, or from SIP offices at Piazza San Silvestro or Stazione Termini. For international telegrams, call Italcable (☎ *47701*) or go to a post office.

Public lavatories

They are scarce in Rome. Most small bars offer rudimentary facilities. More expensive establishments may display a saucer to recoup a small service charge. Look for the familiar symbols, or signs for *Signori* (Men) and *Signore* (Women).

Electric current

Current is 220V AC. The standard two-pin round-pronged plugs or adaptors can be purchased in most countries.

Laws and regulations

Strictly speaking, you should register with the police within three days of entering Italy. At hotels, you hand over your passport on checking in and the procedure is taken care of for you. In Rome, call the Police Information Office for details (☎ *4686 ext. 2858*).

Never leave your vehicle registration book or rental agreement in the car. If the car is stolen or towed away, the police will not co-operate unless you can prove your right to drive the car.

The wearing of seatbelts is now compulsory. Although widely ignored in the helter-skelter of traffic within the city, once on the *autostrade* even Italian drivers belt-up.

Laws against jaywalking and topless sunbathing are rarely enforced. A warning is much more likely than a fine.

Customs and etiquette
Romans tend to be less excitable than other southern Italians, although they do their fair share of gesticulating and occasionally give way to histrionics. Manners are typical of most capital city dwellers: courteous but reserved. Young Roman men pursue foreign girls by age-old tradition. Such attentions are generally playful and can easily be ignored.

When visiting churches where a service is in progress, try to create as little disturbance as possible or you may cause offence.

Tipping
A 15 percent service charge is generally added to hotel and restaurant bills, but waiters expect a small tip in addition to this. You should tip taxi drivers 10 percent. Theatre and cinema ushers expect a tip for showing you to your seat, and you should leave a few coins on the counter when buying a drink at a bar. Be more generous to sacristans or custodians who do you a special favour by opening up parts of churches or museums that are normally closed to the public.

Disabled travellers
Rome is low on facilities for the disabled, but staff in airports, museums and other public buildings are ready and willing to give assistance. Lavatories that accommodate wheelchairs are available at Fiumicino and Ciampino airports, Stazione Termini (adjacent to platform 1), Termini and EUR underground stations, Museo Nazionale Romano, and on the s side of Piazza San Pietro. The last has a few steps to negotiate, but an attendant will assist with wheelchairs.

Most restaurants are happy to accept wheelchairs, provided they have advance notice. For suitable accommodation and information, British visitors should consult *Holidays for Disabled People*, published by RADAR (*25 Mortimer Street, London W1N 8AB* ☎ *(01) 637-5400*). A useful guide based on the personal experiences of disabled travellers in Rome and Florence is available from Project Phoenix Trust by sending a cheque for £2.25, incl. postage, to secretary Mrs V. Saunders (*68 Rochfords, Coffee Hall, Milton Keynes MK6 5DJ* ☎ *0908 678038*).

Local and foreign publications
The *Daily American* and the *International Daily News* are published locally and give the main international and local news stories. The *International Herald Tribune* is available on the day of issue, as are most other major European newspapers. *This Week in Rome*, published monthly in both English and Italian, has listings of events, entertainments, hotels, restaurants and shops, as does *Un Ospite di Roma*, bi-lingual and bi-monthly, available free at many hotels or at Via Monte della Farina 19 (☎ *6569641*), while *Il Messaggero* and *Paese Sera*, both in Italian, have comprehensive lists of local films and plays. The telephone directory *Rete di Roma*, available by some telephones, gives detailed, local information in map form.

Papal audiences

General papal audiences are usually held on Wed at 11am: in winter, in the Audience Hall or in St Peter's itself; in early summer, in Piazza San Pietro; and in late summer, at the Pope's hill-top residence at Castel Gandolfo. For tickets, apply to Prefettura della Casa Pontificia (*Città del Vaticano, 00120* ☎ *6982*) giving not more than one month's and not less than two days' notice. State the nationality and number of people in your party and the proposed date.

On Christmas Day and Easter Sunday, at noon, the Pope gives a blessing from the balcony of St Peter's. Every Sun when in residence he makes a brief appearance at his study window in the Apostolic Palace, to say a few prayers.

Useful addresses

Tourist information

American Express Travel Service   Piazza di Spagna 38 ☎ 67641 or 722801 ☏614335 is a valuable source of information for any traveller in need of help, advice or emergency services.
Rome Provincial Tourist Board (EPT — Ente Provinciale per il Turismo)   Via Parigi 11 ☎ 461851. Other branches are at Fiumicino Airport, Stazione Termini, and the motorway service areas at Salaria Ovest (when arriving from Florence) and Frascati Est (when arriving from Naples).

Main post office

Palazzo delle Poste   Piazza San Silvestro 00186 ☎6771

Telephone services

News   ☎ 190
Time   ☎ 161
Weather in Rome   ☎1911
Road report   ☎194
Alarm call service   ☎114
ACI   ☎116

Tour operators

American Express   Piazza di Spagna 38 ☎67641 or 722801
☏614335
Appian Line   Via Veneto ☎4741641 ☏610193
Carrani Viaggi   Via Torino 41 ☎4742672
CIT   Piazza della Repubblica 68 ☎47941 ☏610434

Major libraries

American Library   USIS Via Vittorio Veneto 62b ☎ 4674
Biblioteca Nazionale Centrale   Viale Castro Pretorio 105 ☎4989
English Library   British Council, Via Quattro Fontane 20
☎4756641
French Library   Centro di Cultura Francese, Piazza Campitelli 3
☎6794287

Major places of worship

Roman Catholic confessions are heard in the major European languages in the four great basilicas: St Peter's, San Giovanni in Laterano, San Paolo fuori le Mura and Santa Maria Maggiore; also in the Gesù, Santa Maria sopra Minerva, Santa Sabina, Sant' Anselmo and Sant' Ignazio. Mass is celebrated daily in the basilicas and principal churches, High Mass with music on Sun.

Basic information

Roman Catholic churches associated with the English-speaking
community are:
Saint Patrick's   Via Boncompagni 31 (Irish) ☎ 465716
San Silvestro   Piazza San Silvestro (British) ☎ 6797775
Santa Susanna   Via XX Settembre 14 (American) ☎ 4751510
Other places of worship
Adventist   Lungotevere Michelangelo 7 ☎ 3111809
American Episcopal: St Paul's   Via Napoli 58 ☎ 463339
Anglican: All Saints   Via del Babuino 153 ☎ 6794357
Baptist   Viale Jonio 203 ☎ 8184838
Islamic Centre   Via Bertoloni 22 ☎ 802258
Jewish Synagogue   Lungotevere dei Cenci 9 ☎ 6875051
Lutheran   Via Toscana 7 ☎ 460394
Methodist   Via Firenze 38 ☎ 4743695
Presbyterian: St Andrew's   Via XX Settembre 7 ☎ 4751627
Russian Orthodox   Via Palestro 71 ☎ 4950729

Embassies and consulates
Australia   Via Allessandria 215 ☎ 832721
Austria   Via Pergolesi 3 ☎ 868241
Belgium   Via dei Monti Parioli 49 ☎ 3609441
Canada   Via G.B. de Rossi 27 ☎ 855341
Denmark   Via dei Monti Parioli 50 ☎ 3600441
Finland   Via Lisbona 3 ☎ 858329
France   Via Giulia 251 ☎ 6565241
Germany, West   Via Po 25c ☎ 860341
Greece   Via S. Mercadante 36 ☎ 859630
Ireland (Eire)   Largo Nazareno 3 ☎ 6782541
Japan   Via Quintino Sella 60 ☎ 4817151
Netherlands   Via Michele Mercati 8 ☎ 873141
New Zealand   Via Zara 28 ☎ 851225
Norway   Via delle Terme Deciane 7 ☎ 5755833
South Africa   Via Tanaro 14 ☎ 8449794
Spain   Palazzo Borghese, Largo Fontanella di Borghese 19
☎ 6878264
Sweden   Piazza Rio de Janeiro 3 ☎ 8840441
Switzerland   Via Barnaba Oriani 61 ☎ 803641
UK   Via XX Settembre 80A ☎ 4755441
USA   Via Vittorio Veneto 119A ☎ 46741

Conversion tables

cm	0 5 10 15 20 25 30
in	0 1 2 3 4 5 6 7 8 9 10 11 12
Length metres	0 0.5 1 1.5 2
ft/yd	0 1ft 2ft 3ft(1yd) 2yd

grammes	0 100 (¼kg) 200 300 (½kg) 400 500 600 (¾kg) 700 800 900 (1kg) 1,000
Weight ounces	0 4 8 12 16 20 24 28 32
	(¼lb) (½lb) (¾lb) (1lb) (1½lb) (2lb)

Fluid measures litres	0 1 2 3 4 5 liters 0 5 10 20 30
imp.pints	0 1 2 3 4 5 6 7 8 imp. gallons 0 1 2 3 4 5 6
US pints	0 1 2 3 4 5 6 7 8 US gallons 0 1 2 3 4 5 6 7

Emergency information

Emergency services

Police ☎ 113	
Ambulance	(Call free from any
Fire	telephone)

Hospitals with casualty departments

Policlinico Umberto 1   Viale del Policlinico ☎ 492341
Policlinico Gemelli   Largo Gemelli 8 ☎ 33051
San Giacomo   Via Canova 29 ☎ 6726
San Giovanni   Via Amba Aradam ☎ 7705
Santo Spirito   Lungotevere in Sassia ☎ 650901

Other medical emergencies

Consult the telephone directory Yellow Pages to find a doctor
or dentist. For private hospital treatment or consultation,
contact Salvator Mundi International Hospital (*Viale delle
Mura Gianicolensi 66/67* ☎ 586041).

Late-night and all-night chemists

Chemists operate a late-night rota. For shops currently open,
look for a notice in the door/window of the nearest chemist.
Alternatively ☎ 1921. The following remain open all night:
De Luca   Via Cavour 2 ☎ 460019
Internazionale   Piazza Barberini 49 ☎ 462996
Tre Madonne   Via Bertoloni 5 ☎ 873423
Cola di Rienzo   Via Cola di Rienzo 213 ☎ 351816

Help lines

Local police (Carabinieri)   ☎ 212121
Police headquarters (Questura)   ☎ 4686
Samaritans   ☎ 6789227, 7.30-10.30pm.

Motoring accidents

— Call the police immediately.
— Do not admit liability or incriminate yourself.
— Ask any witness(es) to stay and give a statement.
— Exchange names, addresses, car details and insurance
  companies' names and addresses with other driver(s).
— Remain to give your statement to the police.
— Report the accident to your insurance company.

Car breakdowns

— Put on hazard warning lights and place a warning triangle
  50m (55yds) behind the car.
— ☎ 116 and give operator your location, car registration
  and make. The ACI will bring assistance.

Lost passport

Contact the police, then your consulate (see opposite).

Lost travellers cheques

Notify the local police immediately then follow the
instructions provided with your travellers cheques, or contact
the issuing company's nearest office. Contact your consulate
or American Express if you are stranded with no money.

Emergency phrases

Help!   *Aiuto!*
There has been an accident.   *C'è stato un incidente.*
Where is the nearest telephone/hospital?   *Dov'è il
  telefono/l'ospedale più vicino?*
Call a doctor/ambulance.   *Chiamate un dottore/un'
  ambulanza*
Call the police.   *Chiamate la polizia.*

Time chart

Origins and Kingdom

753BC Legendary date of the foundation of Rome by the brothers Romulus and Remus. The story of the city's origin is probably fictitious. According to archaeological evidence Rome was a simple farming community until about 600BC, but tradition has it that Romulus was the first of seven kings of Rome.

715-509 The Sabine kings Numa Pompilius, Tullus Hostilius and Ancus Martius left little mark, although Numa Pompilius was the legendary founder of Roman religious customs. Under Tarquinius Priscus (616-578BC), the first of the Etruscan kings, Rome began its transformation from an agricultural settlement into a city of great monumental architecture. The Forum was drained, the sewerage system begun and the foundations laid for a great temple on the Capitoline Hill.

The next king, Servius Tullius, built the first wall around Rome. He was succeeded by the tyrant Tarquinius Superbus ("The Proud"), who reduced the role of the Senate and concentrated judicial power in his own hands. He completed the sewerage system and the three-fold temple on the Capitoline Hill, dedicated to Jupiter, Juno and Minerva, though always known as the Temple of Jupiter Optimus Maximus.

Republic

509 Tarquinius driven out, and a Republic established.

390 The Gauls raided Italy and sacked Rome. This was the first of many invasions of the city, which it somehow always managed to survive.

264-241 First Punic War (against North African state of Carthage). Rome's struggles with Carthage were related by the historian Livy, in the 1stC BC. They were decisive in promoting Rome's growth to an international power.

214-201 Second Punic War. The Carthaginian leader Hannibal crossed the Alps and threatened but did not vanquish Rome. The Roman general Scipio Africanus was an almost equally charismatic military leader. The war ended in the defeat of Carthage.

149-146 Third Punic War brings about the destruction of Carthage by Rome.

81-79 Rule of the dictator Sulla, the first Roman general to use his troops against political opponents. His example was followed by later politicians, including Julius Caesar.

58-49 Caesar's campaign in Gaul.

55-54 Caesar's invasion of Britain.

49 Caesar crossed the Rubicon with his army and made himself master of Italy, effectively ending the Republic.

44 Caesar assassinated in the Senate.

Empire

27BC-AD14 Octavian, Caesar's great-nephew, became the first Roman emperor, taking the name of Augustus. He began an extensive building programme, boasting that he "found Rome brick and left it marble". His reign was a golden age of Roman culture that has come to be known as the Augustan Age. Writers of the time included Virgil, Horace, Ovid and Livy.

54-68   Reign of Nero, who was held responsible for the great fire of 64 and was said to have "fiddled while Rome burned". He blamed the disaster on the Christians, and initiated their persecution, but it gave him the opportunity to build a magnificent palace over a huge area of devastation stretching all the way from the Palatine to the Esquiline and Coelian Hills.

79-81   The reign of Titus included the destruction of the Temple at Jerusalem; his subsequent triumph is recorded on the Arch of Titus in the Roman Forum. In 80 another great fire in Rome destroyed the Temple of Jupiter Optimus Maximus (rebuilt in 82).

98-117   Trajan's reign saw important military campaigns that extended the frontier of the empire beyond the Danube. These triumphs are recorded on Trajan's Column in the Forum of Trajan. By the end of his reign, Roman territory stretched east from Spain to the Caspian Sea and south from Britain to North Africa.

117-138   Hadrian was a very different emperor from his predecessor. He spent most of his time travelling through the empire, spreading the civilizing influence of Rome.

161-180   The philosopher-emperor Marcus Aurelius was both a notable general and an exceptionally cultured ruler. He is known for his *Meditations*, a book of reflections on life, imbued with his Stoic philosophy. During his reign, Rome experienced the first heavy barbarian attacks on her frontiers. He died at Vienna while campaigning against the Danube tribes.

180-286   During the century following the death of Marcus Aurelius, Rome was continually at war with barbarian tribes in many parts of the empire. It was also a time of political instability. A series of emperors came and went with great rapidity as one military coup succeeded another. The rulers of these years included the bloodthirsty and depraved Commodus and the equally brutal Caracalla.

286   Diocletian divided the empire into East and West, making himself ruler of the Eastern Empire and Maximian ruler of the West.

306-337   Reign of Constantine the Great, the first Christian emperor. He brought both parts of the empire under his own rule, legalized Christianity in 313 and moved his capital to Byzantium, which he re-named Constantinople. Under his reign the first churches and basilicas began to be constructed in Rome.

337-476   These years marked the final decline and collapse of the Western Empire. On the death of Theodosius in 395 the two halves of the empire were again divided, never again to be joined. In Rome, chaos and unrest reigned as the army vainly tried to defend her frontiers. In 410 the Visigoths under Alaric captured and looted the city. In 455 it was the turn of the Vandals to plunder Rome. Finally, in 476 the German chieftain Odoacer deposed the last emperor, Romulus

Augustulus, and made himself master of the Italian peninsula.

Dark and Middle Ages

493   Odoacer was defeated by Theodoric, King of the Ostrogoths.

552   The Ostrogoths were finally defeated, and Rome for a time became part of the Eastern Empire.

568   The Lombards, another Germanic tribe, invaded Italy. By 593 they were threatening Rome itself.

590-604   The papacy of Gregory the Great, distinguished by sensitive handling of the Lombards, marked the beginning of effective papal intervention in the world of politics.

754-756   Stephen III appealed to the Franks for help against the Lombards. The Frankish king Pepin the Short defeated the Lombards and gave part of central Italy to the pope.

774   Pepin's son Charlemagne defeated the Lombards again, winning control of Italy for the Franks and securing the power of the popes.

800   Charlemagne crowned Holy Roman Emperor.

9thC   Gradual disintegration of the Carolingian empire. Rome was torn by struggles between rival princes. Powerful families vied for the papacy.

962   The Saxon king Otto I became Holy Roman Emperor. Popes now claimed the right to crown emperors, and emperors in turn claimed the right to confirm the election of popes.

1084   Robert Guiscard and his Norman troops expelled the Emperor Henry IV from Rome and subjected the city to ruthless sacking.

1144-55   Commune set up in Rome by Arnold of Brescia, in defiance of both pope and emperor.

1198-1216   Under Innocent III, the papacy gained the upper hand against the emperors.

1241   A year of even greater strife than usual between the papal and Imperial parties. The Mausoleum of Augustus was virtually destroyed.

Renaissance to modern times

1308   The papacy was transferred to Avignon, in France, and although there was a brief return in 1378, the popes were not to be firmly re-established in Rome until 1417. In the meantime the city lost its importance as a focus of affairs.

1347   Cola di Rienzo led a popular rebellion against the nobility and established a democratic republic. He was murdered in 1354.

1378-1417   The years of the Great Schism in the Church, when Europe was divided in its support for rival claimants to the papacy.

1417-31   The papacy of Martin V ended the discord, and Rome's cultural life gradually began to revive.

1447-55   Papacy of Nicholas V, known for his chapel frescoed by Fra Angelico. He also contributed generally to the reconstruction of the city.

1471-84   Sixtus IV built the Sistine Chapel as his private place of worship and brought in a group of the best Tuscan and Umbrian artists to decorate the walls.

1492-1503   Reign of Alexander VI, Rodrigo Borgia. Securing the office by bribery, he proceeded to indulge in the most

	flagrant nepotism, making his bloodthirsty son, Cesare, a cardinal.
1503-13	Julius II, not much more admirable as a man than Alexander VI, is held in greater respect by posterity for having commissioned Michelangelo to paint the ceiling of the Sistine Chapel, Raphael to decorate the Stanze, and Bramante to build the new St Peter's.
1513-21	Leo X continued the artistic initiative of his predecessor. Seldom had Rome's future seemed more secure, although the first rumblings of Lutheranism were heard.
1527	German and Spanish troops raided Rome, destroying buildings and stealing many of the city's treasures.
1534-49	Paul III, the first Counter-Reformation pope, licensed the Jesuit Order and convened the Council of Trent (1545). He inspired another, though less intense, period of artistic ferment, approving Michelangelo's *Last Judgment*.
1585-90	Sixtus V began to plan the urban development of Rome.
1623-44	Urban VIII's reign as pope saw the great period of the Baroque in Rome, presided over by the sculptor, painter and architect Bernini. The city was now the undisputed artistic capital of Europe.
1644	With the commencement of Innocent X's papacy, the Pamphili replaced the Barberini as the ruling dynasty in Rome.
1656	Construction of Piazza San Pietro, Bernini's supreme piece of townscape architecture, began.
1700-21	Under the papacy of Clement XI, Rome's prestige declined, and the 18thC was a period of relative insignificance.
1798	Rome was attacked by the French army and Revolutionary forces occupied the city.
1809	Napoleon annexed the Papal States and took Pius VII into captivity.
1814	Pius VII was freed, and the Papal States were restored to the Vatican.
1848-49	Mazzini and Garibaldi began the revolution (*Risorgimento*) that was to lead to the unification of Italy and the final secularization of most of the papal territories. A republic was briefly established in Rome.
1861	The whole of Italy, apart from Rome, was unified under Victor Emmanuel II of Sardinia and Savoy.
1870	Rome was added to the Kingdom of Italy and became its capital. The political power of the popes was henceforth confined to the Vatican.
1922	Mussolini's march on Rome and seizure of power marked the beginning of the Fascist government of Italy. The Lateran Pact was signed between Italy and the Vatican State.
1943-44	Fascism was brought to an end, with the liberation of Rome by the Allies.
1946	Establishment of the Italian Republic.
1958-63	The papacy of John XXIII brought new life to the Catholic Church.
1962-65	The Second Vatican Council introduced many reforms.
1979	Karol Wojtyla, a Polish Cardinal, became John Paul II, the first non-Italian pope since 1523.

Architecture

The architecture of ancient Rome, like its painting and sculpture, was inspired in the first place by Greece. This has resulted, rather unfairly, in the tendency to regard it as an inferior imitation of what came before, when in fact there is much that is original and truly inventive. The other great stumbling block to an appreciation of these buildings is their ruinous state of preservation. It is hard to imagine the original appearance of a great temple on the basis of a few remaining columns. The ruins of the *Roman Forum* are endlessly fascinating, but are more likely to inspire the historian or archaeologist than the lover of architecture.

Typical of Rome's surviving antique monuments are her columns and triumphal arches. Trajan's Column (in the *Forum of Trajan*) and the *Column of Marcus Aurelius* are impressive monuments to military and Imperial achievement that were not much imitated, while the arches of Titus and Septimius Severus (both in the *Roman Forum*) and the *Arch of Constantine* have had an appropriately monumental influence on the history of European architecture. They are notable both for their simple but perfectly balanced proportions and exquisite sculptural reliefs.

Pantheon (119-128). Still intact, and still one of the largest domes in the world.

Arch of Constantine (*above right*) (315). One of the last great monuments of ancient Rome, built by the first Christian emperor.

Castel Sant' Angelo (130 onwards). Key fortress of medieval Rome, a converted Imperial mausoleum.

Santa Maria in Cosmedin (12thC). The simplicity of the facade is the essence of its charm.

The more practical side of ancient Roman architecture can be seen in what remains of the public buildings. Structures such as the *Colosseum* and *Theatre of Marcellus* demonstrate the sheer scale of achievement, while the great *Baths of Caracalla* and *Baths of Diocletian* give some idea of the complexity of planning as well. The same impression is gained on a visit to Hadrian's Villa at Tivoli (see *Rome environs*), where ingenious ground-plans and vaulting systems abound. Even the quasi-domestic buildings on the *Palatine Hill* were remarkable for their invention.

But if one building had to stand for all that is best in Classical Roman architecture, it would surely have to be the *Pantheon*, whether for the nobility of its majestic portico or for the exhilarating lightness of its domed interior. No wonder it has never fallen out of favour, whatever changes in fashion have occurred.

The Pantheon survived the ravages of the Middle Ages by being converted into a Christian church, while the Mausoleum of Hadrian was assured of continuity by its transformation into the military edifice now known as the *Castel Sant' Angelo*. Most other ancient buildings were not so fortunate. Temples were destroyed for their fine marble columns, which went into the building of the new Christian basilicas. But the attitude to the past remained respectful in terms of artistic if not moral values. With their stately processions of columns and rich mosaics, the early basilicas — old St Peter's, *San Paolo fuori le Mura*, *Santa Maria Maggiore* and *San Giovanni in Laterano* — reflected the grandeur and assurance of the Classical tradition.

But Roman medieval architecture can also be delicate and intimate. There are exquisite little centrally-planned buildings like *Santa Costanza* and the Lateran Baptistry, and smaller aisled churches such as *Santa Sabina* and *Santa Maria in Cosmedin*, where arcades replace the previously standard colonnades. Apart from this innovation, the basic basilican style remained remarkably unchanging from the 4thC to beyond the millennium, so that a church like *San Clemente* (1108) is later than it perhaps at first appears. This impression is only reinforced by the facts that there was relatively little new building in Rome in the later Middle Ages, and that the city was all but untouched by Gothic influences. The church of *Santa Maria sopra Minerva* is the sole exception to this rule, a strange link between two pseudo-Classical traditions.

The Renaissance came relatively late to Rome, even though it was essentially a revival of Classical forms. The two most distinguished early Renaissance buildings, *Palazzo Venezia* and *Palazzo della Cancelleria*, are of doubtful authorship, although the courtyard of the latter is sometimes attributed to Bramante. This architect's grand plans for the new *St Peter's* were tremendously important, while his Tempietto outside *San Pietro in Montorio* epitomizes the High Renaissance ideals of Classical fidelity and proportional perfection.

After Bramante's death, Michelangelo came to be the decisive force in the rebuilding of *St Peter's*. The marvellous dome, with garlands and paired columns round the base, is basically his invention, although it was completed by Giacomo della Porta. Otherwise his major architectural work in Rome involved the reorganization of the Capitol into *Piazza del Campidoglio*, where his use of a colossal order — giant pilasters reaching up through two storeys — looks forward to the Baroque.

Culture, history and background

Palace building continued unabated through the 16thC, ranging from the grandly massive *Palazzo Farnese*, begun by Antonio da Sangallo and completed by Michelangelo, to the ornate *Palazzo Spada*, and the highly original *Palazzo Massimo alle Colonne* by Peruzzi. This was also the golden age of the villa, perhaps best expressed in the *Villa Giulia*, that gloriously fanciful creation built for Julius II by Vignola, Ammannati and Vasari.

Vignola was also the architect of the *Gesù*, prototype of Counter-Reformation churches all over Europe. The wide nave and barrel vault made it ideal, both spatially and acoustically, for preaching purposes. But the gracefully voluted facade, by della Porta, was even more frequently copied.

The first major architect of the Roman Baroque was Carlo Maderno. He was responsible for the extension of the nave of *St Peter's* and for its somewhat disappointing facade, but he also began Palazzo Barberini (now the *Galleria Nazionale d'Arte Antica*) and designed the splendidly rhythmic facade of *Santa Susanna*. Although he was perhaps not an architect of the very first rank, the dignity of his style looks forward to Bernini, the most talented and wide-ranging artist of the period. Looking at a church like *Sant' Andrea al Quirinale*, for all its fine qualities, we may wonder what all the excitement is about.

Tempietto (1502). The Classical idiom re-mastered by Bramante and put to Christian use.

Palazzo Farnese (1514-89). Majestic residence of 16thC Rome's foremost family, completed by Michelangelo.

Villa Giulia (1551-53). Late Renaissance extravaganza, indulging in Mannerist conceits.

Gesù (1568-75). Powerful symbol of the Counter-Reformation, imitated all over Europe.

But Bernini was much more than the sum of the individual buildings with which he was involved: he was a man who changed the whole appearance of a great city. The fountains of Rome, the statues of the **Ponte Sant' Angelo**, the appearance of **Piazza Navona**, are all products of Bernini's extraordinary imagination, while the spread of his influence is incalculable.

His great rival Borromini had a very different kind of personality, both tortured and introspective, but as an architect he was perhaps even more talented. Churches such as **Sant' Ivo** and **San Carlo alle Quattro Fontane** or the facade of the Oratory of the Filippini (part of the **Oratory Complex**) might tempt us to dismiss him as a gifted but small-scale eccentric, but the restraint and assurance of his refurbishing of the interior of **San Giovanni in Laterano** show that he was also able to work on a grander scale.

Least well known of the great Baroque triumvirate is Pietro da Cortona, whose masterpiece, the church of **Santi Luca e Martina**, is a centrally planned building of great strength and charm that seems to look back to the High Renaissance. His other great work is the facade of **Santa Maria della Pace**, distinctive for its semi-circular, colonnaded porch.

These are the great figures of the Baroque in Rome, but there are many other important works whose creators are generally

Oratory of the Filippini (1637-50). Borromini's complex play of convex and concave is typically Baroque.

Santa Maria della Pace (1656). The elegant facade with semi-circular porch is by Pietro da Cortona.

Piazza San Pietro (1656-67). Bernini's great enfolding colonnades are a perfect setting for ceremony, opening out the approach to the great basilica beyond.

forgotten. The *Spanish Steps* and *Trevi Fountain* are both well-known 18thC Roman landmarks, characteristically public in conception. If the courtyard is the typical expression of the Renaissance sensibility, then the piazza sums up the Baroque. The theatrical tradition set by Bernini in his oval-colonnaded *Piazza San Pietro* continued into the 19thC with Valadier's imaginative treatment of *Piazza del Popolo*.

Although Neoclassicism was born in Rome, it was of international significance and made little impression on the fabric of the city itself. It is symptomatic that Piranesi, the greatest architectural visionary of the period, executed only one trivial commission, the Piazza dei Cavalieri di Malta on the *Aventine Hill*. For the rest, he was engaged in retrospection, recording in etchings the city's architectural heritage.

The 19thC was even less memorable in terms of new architecture. Despite a vigorous building programme to house the new bureaucracy of a united Italy, only one edifice has come to represent the rather pompous excesses of the age, the much-ridiculed *Monument to Victor Emmanuel II*. By contrast, modern architecture has left the city's skyline mercifully clear. Mussolini was more concerned with knocking buildings down to build impressive new roads such as Via dei Fori Imperiali and *Via della Conciliazione*. The dream architecture for a better tomorrow was left for EUR (see *Rome environs*), which stands apart both geographically and culturally, very much a period piece. Although there are impressive postwar buildings in Rome, such as the pioneering *Stazione Termini* complex, they may never be cherished in quite the same way as their illustrious predecessors.

Trevi Fountain
(detail) (1640-1762). A spectacular landmark, continuing the theatrical and public tradition of the Baroque.

Monument to Victor Emmanuel II (1885-1911). A marble wedding-cake, celebrating the nuptials of the modern Italian state.

Stazione Termini
(1938-50). A building of cool, almost Classical purity, blending perfectly with its antique surroundings.

Painting and sculpture

In the 6thC, despite raids and sacks and changes of ruler, Rome still possessed most of the statuary and painting she had accumulated in almost unbelievable quantities during the Imperial period. But with the end of the enlightened stewardship of the Ostrogoth Cassiodorus, the metropolis quickly collapsed, her economy disintegrated, and her gardens, palaces and temples merged into a vast, unkempt parkland. A few pieces, such as the bronze boy known as the *Spinario* (now in the **Capitoline Museums**), were gathered outside the Lateran Palace for the disquieted amazement of pilgrims.

The **Vatican Museums** and Museo Nazionale Romano in the **Baths of Diocletian** give some idea of the quantities of marble statues once in Rome. To these should be added all those now dispersed in collections around Europe, and for every surviving large marble statue one should probably count a lost lifesize bronze or silver one. Most Imperial Roman art derives from the Hellenistic tradition, although the naturalistic portrait bust and various forms of propaganda art (as expressed in the triumphal arches or **Ara Pacis Augustae**) are peculiarly Roman obsessions. The ancient Romans were also prolific painters and decorators. The evidence at Pompeii (see **Excursions**) or in the now-dank corridors of **Nero's Golden House** shows that even the back rooms of palaces and patrician houses were painted — and mosaic floors were as pervasive as carpets are today.

In the Middle Ages, the dominant influence came to be Byzantine, although Roman art of this period preserves a kind of rigid Classicism that gives it an identity of its own. A typical example is the mosaic work in **Santa Prassede**, built by Paschal I in the 9thC and demonstrating the continuing activity, if also the limited resources, of the early medieval popes. By the late 13thC Rome was a leading art centre, with Pietro Cavallini showing an increased mastery of composition in the frescoes of **Santa Cecilia in Trastevere**, and the sculptor Arnolfo di Cambio making similar advances towards realism in *St Peter Enthroned*, now in **St Peter's**. A little later, Giotto painted the *Stefaneschi Altarpiece* for old St Peter's (now in the Pinacoteca of the **Vatican Museums**). But in 1308 Clement V was removed to Avignon, and what Petrarch termed the Babylonian Captivity of the popes transformed Rome into a gloomy backwater for more than a century.

A great deal of Early Renaissance art in the city has been lost, but some sculpture survives in Filarete's bronze doors for old St Peter's and Antonio Pollaiolo's tombs for Sixtus IV and Innocent VIII (all now in **St Peter's**). In painting, Fra Angelico's work can still be seen in the frescoes of the Chapel of Nicholas V in the **Vatican Museums**. Here, too, the Sistine Chapel contains frescoes by Botticelli, Ghirlandaio and Perugino — a superb team effort, united both visually and thematically by a richness of incident and profusion of gold. A little later, Filippino Lippi frescoed the Carafa Chapel in **Santa Maria sopra Minerva** and Pinturicchio decorated the Borgia Apartments (now part of the **Vatican Museums**). Pinturicchio also did important work in **Santa Maria d'Aracoeli** and **Santa Maria del Popolo**. This last church also contains two splendid tombs by Andrea Sansovino, which are the first real signs of a new Classicism in sculpture.

Culture, history and background

Meanwhile Michelangelo and Raphael were making their marks on the city. From the *St Peter's Pietà* and Sistine ceiling through the fragmentary tomb of Julius II (in *San Pietro in Vincoli*), the *Redeemer* (in *Santa Maria sopra Minerva*) and the *Last Judgment*, Michelangelo towers over half a century of Roman art. Less uncompromising but equally influential, Raphael is best known for his frescoes in the papal apartments now known as the Raphael Stanze (in the *Vatican Museums*), in the *Villa Farnesina* and *Santa Maria della Pace*, and for a number of altarpieces now in the *Borghese Gallery* and the Pinacoteca of the *Vatican Museums*.

The years between Raphael's untimely death (1520) and the Sack of Rome (1527) saw many of the most talented painters in Italy at work in Rome. Disappointingly little survives by Giulio Romano, Perin del Vaga, Parmigianino and Rosso Fiorentino, but they were pioneers of a new, sometimes restless and contorted style call Mannerism. After the Sack, they fled the city, and their ideas spread with them. Rome remained one of the centres of the new style, and artists such as Pellegrino Tibaldi and Francesco Salviati were leading exponents. Painting continued to thrive, but sculpture was less successful, possibly inhibited by the overpowering figure of Michelangelo.

As the 16thC drew to a close, even the painters were beginning to look weary, and the inspiration had to come from an eccentric outsider from Urbino. In the boldness and colouristic exuberance of his work in the *Chiesa Nuova*, Federico Barocci heralds the excitements of the Baroque.

At the forefront of this new movement was the notorious Caravaggio, whose paintings in the Borghese collection (now the *Borghese Gallery*), *San Luigi dei Francesi* and *Santa Maria del Popolo* earned both praise and censure for their earthy realism and compacted drama. His equally important rival, Annibale Carracci, was in many respects a more traditional and Classical figure. Carracci's magnificent frescoes in *Palazzo Farnese* are no longer accessible, but his powers as a landscape painter can be seen in the Galleria Doria Pamphili in *Palazzo Doria*.

In the next generation, Bernini brought the Baroque to a grand climax in a fluent, virtuoso style most enjoyable in his statues for Cardinal Borghese, now in the *Borghese Gallery*, and most spectacular in his dramatic showpiece for the Cornaro Chapel of *Santa Maria della Vittoria* and scenic visions for the interior of *St Peter's*.

The Baroque was also of course the great age of the illusionistic ceiling painting, as demonstrated by the spectacular, floating fantasies of Pietro da Cortona in Palazzo Barberini (now the *Galleria Nazionale d'Arte Antica*), of Giovanni Battista Gaulli in the *Gesù* and of Padre Andrea Pozzo in *Sant' Ignazio*.

Although the Neoclassical style was born in Rome, and Piranesi's etchings and Canova's sculpture (in the *Borghese Gallery* and *St Peter's*) were influential, the artists responsible for the new movement were mainly English, French and German. From this time onwards, Rome was an artistic mecca of international appeal, largely bereft of the inward motivation inspired by such giants as Michelangelo, Raphael and Bernini. Even the significant contributions of the 20thC Futurist and Metaphysical painters (in the *Galleria Nazionale d'Arte Moderna*) tend to be overlooked in a city enfolding two millenniums of artistic treasures.

Roman mythology

As Rome grew from a small town on the fringe of Etruria to become the capital of the Mediterranean, she adapted and expanded her culture according to new ideas arriving from Greece and elsewhere. Her official religion, chiefly concerned with the aversion of unfavourable omens, remained hidebound; but in art and literature local deities were matched with foreign ones and increasingly took on new identities. By the time of Augustus, poets such as Ovid and Tibullus were zestfully narrating the loves of fully naturalized Greek gods.

In the Christian era these pagan gods were permitted to survive in the guise of allegories or astrological symbols. Ovid's *Metamorphoses*, a mock-epic catalogue of the love affairs of the Olympians, was allowed to circulate widely during the Middle Ages because its spicy tales were supposed to enclose cryptic moral meanings. The gods retained their astrological significance into the Renaissance, playing their part in the increasingly recondite allegories devised by the new humanists.

During the austere years of the Counter-Reformation, the gods were briefly banished, but with the new confidence of the Baroque they returned to attain a splendour and power reconcilable with a passionate Catholicism. A different kind of allegory, where Christian virtues mingled with pagan deities, was invented.

In the 18thC, enlightenment lost patience with these effete reflections of an unreal antiquity, and Neoclassical writers and artists drew their inspiration from Roman history rather than Roman myth, from deeds rather than symbols.

Apollo

Son of Jupiter and **Leto**, and brother of Diana, Apollo did not feature among the early Roman gods and was taken over entirely from Greek religion. He was the god of prophecy, healing, music, the arts and philosophy, and is represented as a handsome, clean-shaven young man, often carrying a bow (with which he shot plague arrows) and wearing a laurel wreath. Early on he also acquired an identification with the sun and with the name **Phoebus** ("bright one"). In Roman copies of Greek statues of him — most famous is the *Apollo Belvedere* in the *Vatican Museums* — he appears as the paragon of male beauty.

Apollo is shown as the god of music, leading the Muses on Mount Parnassus, on one of the walls of Raphael's Stanza della Segnatura, also in the *Vatican Museums*. In allegorical contexts he represents reason and inspiration of a good kind — and perhaps this is intended in one of the small, fake-mosaic episodes on the ceiling of the same room, where the god flays the satyr **Marsyas**, the long-eared embodiment of lust and carnality. Apollo nevertheless had several love affairs, notably with the nymph **Daphne**. The couple are brought to life with the full force of Baroque realism in a group by Bernini in the *Borghese Gallery*.

Bacchus (Gk Dionysos)

The god of wine, and so the very opposite of Apollo, Bacchus stood not simply for drunkenness but for general lack of control and absence of reason and morality. He, too, is represented as a beardless, handsome young man, but is more effeminate than Apollo and is usually shown lounging with a cup in hand, his hair wreathed with vine leaves. He is commonly accompanied by his intoxicated entourage, consisting of satyrs with goat-legs, semi-draped and frenzied women known as maenads, and an extremely drunk old man called Silenus who is usually shown falling off the back of a donkey.

The *Triumph of Bacchus*, in which the god is depicted in a chariot drawn by leopards, is represented on numerous sarcophagi. One of its most famous versions is by Annibale Carracci on the ceiling of the gallery of the *Palazzo Farnese*. Here, he shares his triumph with **Ariadne**, the nymph he found on the Greek island of Naxos.

Cupid *(Gk Eros)*

The god of falling in love, Cupid was generally perceived in Greek and Roman art as a handsome adolescent, although by the time of the Renaissance he was more usually represented as a pre-pubertal *putto*. He is still an adolescent, however, in Raphael's depiction of the story of Cupid's love for **Psyche**, the decorative theme of the loggia in the *Villa Farnesina*.

Otherwise the Renaissance Cupid is a chubby infant, shooting golden arrows from his bow to pierce his victims' hearts. He wears a blindfold to signify the blind and irrational nature of passion, but nevertheless appears as a cheerful, happy force. Cupids scampering and fluttering through paintings generally express the well-being of nature — as in Raphael's *Galatea*, also in the *Villa Farnesina*.

Diana *(Gk Artemis)*

Daughter of Leto, sister of Apollo, Diana was the goddess of wild places and animals, a personification of the moon and a symbol of chastity. She is typically shown clad in a tunic as a huntress, bearing bow, arrows and quiver, and is best known for her zealous protection of her own virginity. When discovered bathing by the hunter Actaeon, Diana took her revenge by turning him into a stag, to be destroyed by his own hounds — a favourite theme in Renaissance art, demonstrating the moral that lust turns man into a wild beast. The goddess also punished pride, however, and when **Niobe** boasted that her own children were as beautiful as those of Leto, Diana and her brother shot Niobe and all her children with arrows. There is a magnificent representation of the dying *Daughter of Niobe*, a 5thC BC Greek statue, in the Museo Nazionale Romano in the *Baths of Diocletian*.

Juno *(Gk Hera)*

Wife of Jupiter and the prototype of all good wives. She was an important goddess in the early Roman cult, being one of the triad to whom the Capitol was dedicated in the first year of the Republic. Her chief role in myth was to act vindictively against the nymphs her husband seduced, and the resulting children. She is usually shown accompanied by a peacock.

Jupiter *(Gk Zeus)*

The god of the sky (hence one attribute, his eagle), the god of lightning (hence his thunderbolt) and the ruler of gods and humanity (whence his customary enthronement). His Temple of Jupiter Optimus Maximus ("best and greatest") on the Capitol was the centre of the state religion. The so-called *Jupiter of Otricoli* in the *Vatican Museums*, a copy of a 4thC BC original, shows his appropriate grandeur and majesty.

Identified with the Greek Zeus, Jupiter took on a rather more frivolous aspect. This is the god whom Ovid shows in his *Metamorphoses* transforming himself — for a succession of extra-marital purposes — into a swan with **Leda**, a shower of gold with **Danae**, a fellow-nymph with **Callisto**, and lightning with **Semele**. All made good subjects for bedroom pictures and even for more public works of art.

Mars (*Gk Ares*)
The armed god of war, the father of Romulus, founder of Rome.
The Greek Ares was a bloodthirsty warrior, universally disliked,
but Mars had greater dignity. His cult was of great importance to
the Roman state, and the Temple of Mars Ultor, Mars the
Avenger, in the *Forum of Augustus*, was one of several temples
dedicated to him.

In the Renaissance, Homer's story of Mars being trapped in a
net with Venus by her husband **Vulcan**, god of metalworking,
became a favourite subject, though with varying meanings (see
Venus).

Mercury (*Gk Hermes*)
One of the most diverse of the gods. His two prime roles were as
Jupiter's messenger and as the guide of the souls of the dead to
the Underworld; but he was also the patron of commerce, travel,
eloquence, good sense and thieving. He, too, is represented as a
beardless young man, but wears a helmet and winged sandals
and carries a curved sword and a caduceus (a wand with two
serpents entwined about it, symbolizing his arcane wisdom and
power to reconcile opposing parties by oratory). Although the
story of Mercury stealing Apollo's cattle is not uncommon — it
occurs, for instance, in a painting by Claude in the Galleria Doria
Pamphili (*Palazzo Doria*) — in post-medieval art the god usually
represents prudence and sound judgment.

Minerva (*Gk Athene*)
The Roman patroness of arts and crafts who later became
identified with the Greek goddess of war and wisdom. She is
always shown with helmet, spear and breast-plate, and a shield
bearing the severed head of the snake-haired **Medusa**. In
post-Classical art, she appears as the defender of righteousness
and is seen protecting the pope from the horrors of heresy in
Pietro da Cortona's ceiling fresco in Palazzo Barberini (*Galleria
Nazionale d'Arte Antica*).

Neptune (*Gk Poseidon*)
The god of the sea. He is typically represented as a heroic figure,
with windswept locks and beard, wielding a trident. In later art, he
acquired no moral force, and merely represents his element
(including fresh water). Riding a large shell drawn by sea horses,
he towers over Nicolò Salvi's *Trevi Fountain*.

Venus (*Gk Aphrodite*)
An obscure Roman goddess of gardens until she became
associated with the Greek goddess of love. Several Roman copies
of high quality show her as seductively as the Greeks intended.
Most celebrated of these is the copy of Praxiteles' *Cnidian Venus*
in the *Vatican Museums*, a figure famed for her sensual yet
serene beauty. The birth of the goddess from the sea, later a
popular Renaissance theme, is shown on the 5thC BC Ludovisi
Throne in the Museo Nazionale Romano in the *Baths of
Diocletian*.

Venus took on a particular importance in the 1stC AD as the
mother of **Aeneas**, the proto-founder of Rome, from whom the
Julian emperors claimed descent. The myth was promulgated by
Virgil's *Aeneid*, which inspired the frescoes by Pietro da Cortona
in the *Palazzo Pamphili*.

In post-Classical art Venus could stand for any variety of love,
and her complex nature is thought to be the subject of Titian's
Sacred and Profane Love in the *Borghese Gallery*. A commoner
theme, Venus' love affair with Mars (see **Mars**), can be
interpreted either as civilization softening barbarism or as wicked
adultery.

Orientation map

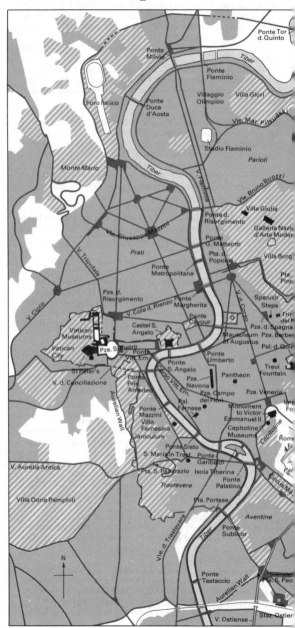

d. Foro Italico

Villa Ada
Catacombs
of Priscilla

V. Salaria

Vle. Libia

V. Nomentana

Villa
Torlonia

Vle. Regina Margherita

Villa Torlonia

Aurelian Wall

Pta. Pia

Staz.
Tiburtina

V. Tiburtina

V. XX Settembre

nale
e Antica

Baths of
Diocletian

Staz. Termini

Aurelian Wall

Cimitero d. Campo
Verano

Pza. d.
Repubblica

S. M.
Maggiore

Pta. S. Lorenzo

Pza. Vitt. Em.

Esquiline

Colosseum

Pta. Maggiore

V. Prenestina

of
stantine

S. Giovanni
in Laterano

Aurelian Wall

V. Casilina

Pta. S. Giovanni

Pta. Metronia

V. Appia
Nuova

V. Tuscolana

calla

Pta. Latina

V. Latina

0   500m   1km

stoforo
mbe

Pta. S.
Sebastiano

0   ½ mile

33

Planning and walks

Calendar of events

See also *Public holidays* in **Basic information** and **Sports and activities** for further information.

January

New Year's Day. Candlelit processional *Te Deum* in the **Catacombs of Priscilla** to mark the martyrdom of the early Christians.

Jan 5. Carnival in **Piazza Navona**, on last day of children's market (see **Rome for children**). Continues until dawn the following day.

Jan 17. *Festa di Sant' Antonio Abate*. Special service where animals are blessed. Held at Sant' Eusebio all' Esquilino.

Jan 18. *Festa della Cattedra di San Pietro*. Celebration of the authority of the apostle.

Jan 21. *Festa di Sant' Agnese*. Two lambs are blessed and shorn, and their wool later used for palliums. Held at **Sant' Agnese fuori le Mura**.

Jan-June. Flat races and steeplechases at Ippodromo delle Capanelle racecourse (see **Sports and activities**.

February

The weeks leading up to Lent. Carnival, once actively celebrated all over the city, is now barely observed. Children indulge in occasional high-spirited antics, throwing flour and water or water-filled balloons. Smaller children dress up for a parade on Via Cola di Rienzo and Via Nazionale. (See local press for details.)

March

Mar 9. *Festa di Santa Francesca Romana*. Blessing of cars at Piazzale del Colosseo near church of Santa Francesca Romana (more correctly known as Santa Maria Nova) in the **Roman Forum**.

Mar 19. *Festa di San Giuseppe*. The statue of the saint is decorated with colored lamps, stalls sell *frittelle* (fritters), and there are sporting events and concerts. Held in the Trionfale Quarter, N of the Vatican.

April

Festa della Primavera. The **Spanish Steps** are decked out with colorful banks of flowering azaleas, and choral and orchestral concerts are held in **Trinità dei Monti**.

Holy Week. Special events include pilgrimage to Scala Santa near **San Giovanni in Laterano**.

Good Friday. The Pope leads the Procession of the Cross at 9pm in the candlelit **Colosseum**.

Easter Sunday. At noon, the Pope gives his blessing from the balcony of **St Peter's**.

Easter Monday. *Pasquetta*. Traditional day for the first picnic of the year.

Apr 21. Anniversary of the birth of Rome in **Piazza del Campidoglio**. Celebrated with flags and pageantry.

Apr or May. International water polo championships.

May

Open-air art exhibition in Via Margutta.

May 1. *Festa del Lavoro*. Public holiday.

First ten days in May. International horse show. Held at Piazza di Siena in **Villa Borghese**.

May 6. Swearing in of the new guard at the Vatican on the anniversary of the Sacking of Rome in 1527.

Mid-May. Antiques fair in Via dei Coronari.

Last weekend in May. *Carosello Storico*. Mounted military parade at Piazza di Siena in **Villa Borghese**.

Whit Sunday. *Festa della Madonna del Divino Amore*. Pilgrimage of penitence to the Sanctuary of the Madonna at Castel di Leva, 15km (9 miles) s of Rome.

Last week in May. International tennis championships at Foro Italico.

May and June. Rose Show. Held at Via di Valle Murcia on the Aventine Hill.

May and June. International trade fair, held at exhibition grounds on Via Cristoforo Colombo.

June

Flower festival at Genzano, 20km (12 miles) s of Rome. A huge section of the main street is carpeted with flower petals,composed into artistic arrangements by local people.

First Sun in June. *Festa della Repubblica*. Military parade centering on Via dei Fori Imperiali. Shops are closed.

Early June to end of Sept. *Son-et-Lumière* in **Roman Forum** and at Tivoli (see **Rome environs**).

June 23-24. *Festa di San Giovanni.* Held at Piazza di Porta San Giovanni. Large quantities of snails and sucking pig consumed.

June 29. *Festa di San Pietro.* The most important Roman religious festival, celebrated with solemn rites in **St Peter's**.

June-Aug. *Estate Romano* (Roman Summer) organized by the City Council. Open-air events — concerts, movies (see below), dances, etc.

June-Aug. Concerts in the Basilica of Maxentius in the **Roman Forum**.

July

Tevere Expo. Booths and stalls along the banks of the Tiber display arts and crafts, foods and wines, of the Italian regions. Folk music and firework displays provide nighttime entertainment.

July 4. Picnic organized by American community. Stalls, hamburgers and evening fireworks display. Buses leave from American Embassy (*Via Vittorio Veneto 119a* ☎ *46741*).

Last two weeks in July. *Festa de Noiantri.* Processions, entertainments and other festivities in the old quarters of Trastevere. Genuine Roman feasting, with abundant food and wine laid on.

July and Aug. Open-air opera in **Baths of Caracalla**, concerts at Villa Ada, theater at Ostia Antica (see **Nightlife** and **Rome environs**).

August

Open-air movie festival outside one of the famous monuments of ancient Rome (see **Nightlife** and local press for details).

Aug 1. *Festa delle Catene.* The relics of St Peter's captivity go on display in the church of **San Pietro in Vincoli**.

Aug 5. *Festa della Madonna della Neve.* Held at **Santa Maria Maggiore** to commemorate the miraculous fall of snow associated with the building of the church. White flower petals flutter down during the service.

Aug 15. *Ferragosto.* Important midsummer holiday. Shops and most restaurants are closed.

September

Open-air exhibition in the Via Margutta.

Early Sept. *Sagra dell' Uva.* A harvest festival in the Basilica of Maxentius in the **Roman Forum**. Grapes are sold at knock-down prices and entertainment is provided by musicians dressed in folk costume.

Last week of Sept and first week of Oct. Crafts show in Via dell' Orso, near Piazza Navona.

Sept-Nov. Flat races and steeplechases are held at Ippodromo delle Capanelle racecourse.

Sept-May. Soccer on Sun afternoons at Stadio Olimpico.

October

Oct-Apr. Chamber music recitals at Eliseo theater (see **Nightlife**).

November

Nov 22. *Festa di Santa Cecilia.* Held at the church of **Santa Cecilia in Trastevere**. Also a ceremony in the **Catacombs of St Calixtus** where St Cecilia was buried.

Nov-June. Main opera season at Teatro dell' Opera (see **Nightlife**).

December

Dec 8. *Festa della Madonna Immacolata* in **Piazza di Spagna**. Floral tributes are left at the column of the Madonna by papal and government envoys, and firemen climb a ladder to lay a wreath on the statue's head. The Pope himself sometimes drives through the city.

Mid-Dec. Children's market begins in Piazza Navona (see *January*).

Dec 20-Jan 10. Many churches such as **Santa Maria d'Aracoeli** display beautiful nativity scenes, and a collection of antique cribs is on show in Via Giulia.

Dec 24. Midnight Mass at **Santa Maria Maggiore**, with veneration of the wood and metal relics of the holy crib. Masses at **Santa Maria d'Aracoeli** and Sant' Anselmo (on the **Aventine Hill**) also recommended.

Dec 25. At noon, the Pope gives his blessing from the balcony of **St Peter's**.

Dec 31. New Year's Eve. Traditional food and wine to accompany the usual revelries are *panettone*, a yeasty kind of fruit cake, and *spumante*, a sweet sparkling wine. Midnight is greeted by joyful explosions, as every Roman launches fireworks at his neighbors.

When to go

Roman weather is surprisingly fickle, and summer and winter temperatures can be more extreme than most people imagine. Spring and autumn are the best seasons as far as climate is concerned, but they also attract more tourists. At these times, major sights tend to become overcrowded and accommodation is scarce.

Spring

This is usually mild and dry, with plenty of sunshine — although good weather cannot be guaranteed. Easter week brings pilgrims and tourists flooding in from all over the world, determined to catch a glimpse of the Pope on the balcony of St Peter's and to join in the Christian celebrations all over the city. Other major springtime attractions are the international horse show, held in the *Villa Borghese*, and the international tennis championships at the Foro Italico. (See *Calendar of events*.)

For all these reasons, spring is the height of the Roman tourist season, and museums and galleries can be uncomfortably crowded, and restaurants and hotels perhaps just a little too busy. During Easter week in particular, hotels and *pensioni* are packed to overflowing and it is essential to make bookings well in advance.

Summer

This time of year is invariably hot, with temperatures in July and Aug reaching 35°C (95°F). Now it is the scorching heat rather than the crowds that may deter you from sightseeing, particularly in the case of open-air sights such as the *Roman Forum* and *Palatine Hill*.

In other respects, heat is not the problem it used to be, for many hotels, shops and restaurants are now fully air-conditioned, giving you the best of both worlds. In fact, to know the city without its searing summer is to miss a vital ingredient: sitting under a shady umbrella in the sweltering heat of the midday sun, sipping an ice-cold drink; or dining *al fresco* in the warm, balmy evening air; or taking in an opera at midnight in the *Baths of Caracalla*, under a cooler, star-lit sky. These are all part of the unforgettable Roman experience.

June is the best of the summer months, followed by July. In Aug, the city virtually closes down and many cinemas, shops and restaurants go out of action.

Autumn

This is perhaps the best season. The city is alive and busy, but is spared a tourist invasion of springtime proportions. The days draw in quickly, but are usually fine and very warm. The only drawback is the occasional bad weather, which, when it arrives, persists for days on end. Yet, of all the months of the year, Oct is probably the most reliable for consistently good weather.

Winter

Perhaps the most unpredictable season of all. Daytime temperatures may be freezing cold, or so mild that a coat is unnecessary out of doors. As a general but not infallible rule, cold, wet weather is more likely after mid-Jan. Nighttime temperatures are invariably cold, but with central heating provided by nearly all hotels and *pensioni*, this is no problem. Many restaurants and hotels light log fires in the evenings, a friendly gesture that is emblematic of the seasonally relaxed attitude of managers and waiters. Theatre and opera flourish around this time of year, and the famous sights such as the *Vatican Museums* and *St Peter's* are relatively uncrowded.

Where to go

Various attempts have been made to organize the city's development during its 2,000yr history, but the overall pattern is, not surprisingly, haphazard. Rome does not belong to any one period. It is several cities within a city, and there is no homogeneous or instantly recognizable architectural style as in, for example, Paris or Florence. For most people, the layered richness of the city's texture is the essence of its appeal, the lack of order a major part of its charm.

The original city was built on the celebrated seven hills to the E of the Tiber, and soon afterwards encircled by the *Servian Wall* (4thC BC). With the exception of the *Aventine Hill*, the hills have lost their prominence through centuries of landfill and erosion, but fragments of the Servian Wall survive.

The later *Aurelian Wall* (3rdC AD) took in a much larger area, briefly crossing the Tiber to include the district known as Trastevere. Despite its great age, the Aurelian Wall is still very much in evidence and, even more remarkably, it still defines the city centre. With the exception of the *Borgo* and *Vatican City* lying to the W of the Tiber, areas outside the Wall are strictly suburban.

Because much of the ancient city is occupied by ruins and therefore uninhabited, the focal point has shifted gradually N, swinging from W to E and back again over the centuries. In the main fold of the Tiber are the predominantly medieval and Renaissance quarters, to the N and S of Corso Vittorio Emanuele respectively. These labels can only be applied loosely, however, for each quarter is a medley of ancient, medieval and Renaissance buildings, with a lavish overlay of Baroque.

Development in the 18thC was minimal, but in the 19thC a smart commercial area was established over on the E of the city, between Piazza Barberini and Piazza della Repubblica, and prestigious residential development continued N and E. Of all the districts to have achieved prominence over the ages, this easterly area, now flagged by *Stazione Termini*, is the only one subsequently to have suffered a sharp decline.

In the early 20thC the spotlight moved to Via Veneto, birthplace of *La Dolce Vita* and erstwhile rich man's playground. Although most of the city's luxury hotels remain clustered around this elegant boulevard, it too has lost a good deal of its tone.

Emphasis has shifted back to *Piazza di Spagna*, now surrounded by fashionable hotels and shops, and to the N of the *Villa Borghese*, where aristocratic villas and chic nightclubs nestle discreetly among the quiet, tree-lined enclaves of suburban Parioli.

Back in the city centre, the gentrified Bohemian charms of the medieval and Renaissance quarters ensure their continuing popularity with tourists, and they are a lot safer than the equally arty district of Trastevere, a rough area worth visiting for its fine restaurants and local colour, but not recommended for staying in nor for strolling around in after dark.

North of Trastevere and the pine-covered slopes of the *Janiculum Hill* is the *Vatican City*, the smallest state in the world yet guardian of many of its greatest treasures and the home of the Roman Catholic Church. For many people, these twin attractions make the Vatican the focal point of any visit, and accommodation is plentiful in the residential areas surrounding the City, particularly in the *Borgo*, the medieval quarter leading up to the *Castel Sant' Angelo*.

Planning and walks

Area planners

Listed here are the major areas of interest, with some of the more
important sights within them.

Medieval Quarter (*Map 5 H5*). One of the most attractive areas
in the whole of Rome, centring around *Piazza Navona* and the
Pantheon. It is also known as the *Campus Martius*, referring to
its ancient role as an open plain for sports and military exercises,
but is now a maze of narrow medieval streets and alleys, rich in
Renaissance churches and palaces, and best explored on foot.
(See *Walks*.) To the N are the *Ara Pacis Augustae* and the ruins
of the *Mausoleum of Augustus*.

Monte Mario (*Map 2 D2&12 C3*). A recently developed,
prestigious residential area on the NW outskirts of the city, with
fine easterly views from outside the **Villa Madama** (begun by
Raphael but closed to the public) and **Cavalieri Hilton** hotel.

Parioli (*Map 3 D6*). The most select of all the residential
quarters, enclosed by the parklands of the *Villa Borghese* to the
S, and by Villa Ada and Villa Glori to the N. Not surprisingly, it
boasts superlatives in all directions, from the city's finest hotels to
the most exclusive nightclubs.

Piazza della Repubblica (*Map 7 G-H7-8*). An area within easy
reach of the central railway station (Stazione Termini) and other
public transport, including airport buses. It's also conveniently
placed for the *Galleria Nazionale d'Arte Antica*, the *Baths of
Diocletian* (incorporating the **Museo Nazionale Romano**) and
Santa Maria Maggiore. The district long ago lost any pretence
of being fashionable, but it's well served by accommodation and
some good hotels remain.

Piazza di Spagna (*Map 6 G6*). Popular and picturesque tourist
centre ever since the 17thC. Keats stayed in the house now
known as the *Keats-Shelley Memorial*, overlooking the
Spanish Steps. Above the Steps are some fine hotels with
outstanding views; below, a criss-cross of narrow, cobbled streets
contain the city's smartest shops and most elegant cafés.

Prati (*Map 4 F3*). More and more tourists are venturing into this
quiet, middle-class suburb N of the *Vatican City* and *Castel
Sant' Angelo*, where several hotels and restaurants of quality
have sprung up in recent years. Via Cola di Rienzo is a quieter
and cheaper alternative to the shops around Piazza di Spagna,
and fine-quality men's and women's clothes, leather goods and
shoes can be found here. The flower market in the Trionfale
Quarter to the W is well worth visiting.

Renaissance Quarter (*Map 9 I5*). A particularly delightful part
of the old city, S of Corso Vittorio Emanuele, with a
predominantly Renaissance flavour that emanates above all from
the magnificent *Palazzo Farnese*. The Via Giulia is an elegant
backwater with a smattering of antique shops, modern art
galleries and smart hotels.

Trastevere (*Map 8 J4-9 J5*). The inhabitants of Trastevere claim
to be of purer Roman stock than their neighbours over the river.
Their mixed ancestry (Roman, Greek and Jewish) makes this
unlikely, but they are certainly a breed apart and speak their own
dialect. The area has recovered from the acute poverty it suffered
in the 19thC, but is still seedy in parts, and street caution is more
advisable here than elsewhere. Daytime attractions are the
ancient churches of *Santa Maria in Trastevere* and *Santa
Cecilia in Trastevere*, while at night all kinds of entertainments
abound.

Vatican City (*Map 4 G-H2-3*). A large part of this miniature but

38

immensely influential state is occupied by the basilica of *St Peter's* and the *Vatican Museums*. The museums are housed in a vast palace complex and contain some of the greatest art collections in the world. Beyond the E boundary of *Piazza San Pietro* is the *Borgo*, a predominantly medieval quarter with some fine Renaissance palaces. It is cut through by *Via della Conciliazione*, Mussolini's grand processional route from the *Castel Sant' Angelo*.

Via Veneto (*Map 7F-G7*). Once the haunt of the international jet-set, it still has the greatest concentration of luxury hotels (see *Hotels*). Those at the top of the street have fine views over the *Villa Borghese* and are reasonably close to the *Borghese Gallery*. The Via Veneto is brightly lit and busy after dark, with much of the city's nightlife located in the surrounding streets.

Three-day programme

If you are paying only a fleeting visit to the city, it is important to organize your time carefully. Here is a suggested sightseeing programme for a three-day visit.

Day 1

Begin in *Piazza di Spagna*. Take a bus to *Piazza del Popolo* and climb the slopes of the *Pincio* to enjoy the view over the city. Visit *Santa Maria del Popolo* for its art treasures. Take a bus down the Corso to *Piazza Colonna*. Make your way to the church of *Sant' Ignazio* to see a superb Baroque ceiling painting. Continue through the medieval streets to the *Pantheon* and *Piazza Navona*, a good place to have lunch. In the afternoon, cross the Corso Vittorio to admire the fine Renaissance facades of the *Palazzo della Cancelleria* and *Palazzo Farnese*. Returning to the Corso Vittorio, take a bus past *Sant' Andrea della Valle*, alighting at the *Gesù* for more Baroque illusionism. Walk down Via di Aracoeli and climb the steps up to *Piazza del Campidoglio*. Briefly visit the *Capitoline Museums* and nearby church of *Santa Maria d'Aracoeli*. Finish your tour at the *Monument to Victor Emmanuel II* in Piazza Venezia.

Day 2

Begin at the *Castel Sant' Angelo* or proceed straight to *St Peter's*, taking in the view from the battlements or dome of one or the other. Take a bus to Ponte Mazzini, then proceed on foot to the *Villa Farnesina* to see Raphael's frescoes. From here, walk on to Trastevere to see the mosaics of *Santa Maria in Trastevere* (arrive before 12.30pm or the church will be closed) and to have lunch. Spend the afternoon in the *Vatican Museums*, concentrating on the **Pio-Clementine Museum** (Octagonal Court), **Raphael Stanze**, **Sistine Chapel** and **Pinacoteca**. In the late evening, visit the floodlit *Trevi Fountain* on the other side of the river.

Day 3

Begin with *Santa Maria Maggiore*. From here, proceed to Piazza Vittorio Emanuele to see the open-air market. Take the Metropolitana to San Giovanni for a tour of *San Giovanni in Laterano*, including the **Baptistry** and **Scala Santa**. Take a bus to the *Colosseum* and walk N to *Nero's Golden House* or *San Pietro in Vincoli* (for Michelangelo's fragmentary **Tomb of Julius II**). If weather permits, take a picnic to the *Palatine Hill* and spend the afternoon in the *Roman Forum*, ending with the *Forum of Trajan* (for **Trajan's Column**) and *Trajan's Markets*. Alternatively, take the Metropolitana to Barberini, have lunch in the Via Veneto and spend the afternoon in the *Borghese Gallery*.

Walks in Rome

A thorough appreciation of major sites such as the *Roman Forum* or the *Palatine Hill* naturally entails a great deal of walking, but there you will find your goals spread out clearly before you. However, it is an intrepid visitor who marches unforearmed into the historic centre of the city. Hence these four proposed itineraries, which all start in the heart of old Rome (the last two walks share common plans).

Walk 1/Around Corso Vittorio Emanuele
Allow 1½-2hrs.

This walk is best undertaken in the late afternoon. As well as providing some magnificent views, it should help you locate many of the major Renaissance and Baroque monuments that abound on either side of Corso Vittorio Emanuele, the wide thoroughfare that was driven, rather insensitively, through the papal city at the end of the last century, to proclaim the advent of the Royal House of Savoy.

Starting out from the steps of the *Pantheon* facing the **obelisk** in Piazza della Rotonda, take the narrow Salita de' Crescenzi to your left. This leads to *Palazzo Madama*, a Medici palace, now the upper house of the Italian parliament. Turn left, right and right again to reach the front of the building. Across the Corso del Rinascimento the tiny Corsia Agonale will bring you out into the majestic open space of *Piazza Navona*. Every Christmas and New Year a children's fair is held in this piazza, and a fairground atmosphere persists all year round. The focal point is Bernini's inspired flight of fancy, the *Fountain of the Four Rivers*, designed, so legend has it, to mock Borromini's church of *Sant' Agnese in Agone* behind it.

If you can bear to move on from the sublime proportions of the square and the air of excitement around you, leave by the street directly opposite your point of entry, Via di Sant' Agnese. At the first intersection look up at the decoration on the 15thC **Torre Millina**. Here you turn right, passing *Santa Maria dell' Anima*, since the Renaissance the traditional church of Germans in Rome, to Largo Febo.

This attractive square leads off into Piazza di Tor Sanguigna, where you turn almost immediately left into **Via dei Coronari**, an original Renaissance street, which is agreeably straight after your meandering course so far. Browse among the curiosities displayed in its fascinating antique shops, until the wide Piazza San Salvatore in Lauro on your right. Past the Neoclassical facade of the church on the right of the square is a tiny **grotto fountain** with a carved head, perhaps a lion, so worn as to be unrecognizable. You then pass down the minute, cobbled Vicolo dei Marchegiani to the embankment wall, where wooden steps to your left lead up to Lungotevere.

Ideally the sun should now be setting, for you will be greeted by two of Rome's most picturesque views: the extravagant sculpted angels standing sentry on the *Ponte Sant' Angelo*, with the *Castel Sant' Angelo* beyond, and farther to the w, the dome of *Saint Peter's* seen through the hanging branches of the plane trees that line the banks of the Tiber. As you follow the river around to the w, St Peter's disappears from view at the point where Corso Vittorio meets Ponte Vittorio Emanuele. Here, beyond the cumbrous modern bridge, if the water is low, you may glimpse the sparse remains of the ancient **Ponte de Nerone**.

At the next bridge, the more graceful Ponte Principe Amedeo,

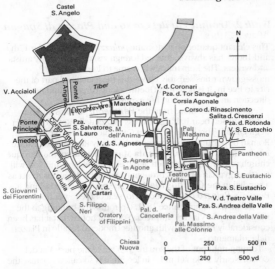

leave Lungotevere up Via Acciaioli. Rounding San Giovanni dei
Fiorentini with its strangely elongated dome, you enter **Via
Giulia**, another Renaissance street with the rare virtue of
straightness. The *palazzi* have lost much of their original glory
but none of their fortress-like strength. Continue for some 300
metres, when on your left you will see the ruined church of **San
Filippo Neri**, dedicated to St Philip Neri, who is often called the
second apostle of Rome.

Cross the demolished area around the church to the narrow Via
de' Cartari, which comes out onto Corso Vittorio opposite the
ornate facades of the **Oratory of the Filippini** and the *Chiesa
Nuova*, both part of the splendid complex built to house St
Philip's religious community. The street will now be coming to
life, as Romans take to the pavements in search of an evening's
entertainment.

Turn right and stroll along with the crowd, taking care not to
miss the massive *Palazzo della Cancelleria* on your right. Cross
over to admire the curving colonnade of *Palazzo Massimo alle
Colonne*, then turn left into Piazza Sant' Andrea della Valle.
From the central fountain look back across Corso Vittorio at the
splendid dome (the second largest in Rome) of the church of
Sant' Andrea della Valle. Continue diagonally across the
square and, passing to the right of the Fascist-style National
Insurance Offices, you come to Via del Teatro Valle. The theatre
itself is on the left-hand side of the street. It has a fine 19thC
colonnade, but you may be more taken by the sight of the dome
of Borromini's *Sant' Ivo* rising above it.

Arriving at Piazza Sant' Eustachio you will be puzzled by the
inordinate popularity of its bar (also called **Sant' Eustachio**).
Romans drive here from miles around, not to admire the
Romanesque bell tower of the church, but to drink the coffee,
which, they swear, is superior to any other in the city. Via Sant'
Eustachio up the side of the church takes you past two ancient
truncated pillars, the sole remains of **Nero's Baths**, then one
right turn brings you back to the Pantheon and Piazza della
Rotonda.

Planning and walks

Walk 2/Around Via del Corso and Piazza di Spagna
Allow 2-2½hrs.

This elegant quarter of aristocratic *palazzi*, dating from the 17th and 18thC, has always attracted foreign visitors, especially artists and writers. The Romantics who came to Rome for its moss-grown ruins sensibly chose this most civilized part of the city to live in. It is here that Goethe's long career found new direction and Keats's short life expired.

Setting off once more from the *Pantheon*, perhaps an hour before sunset, bear half right across Piazza della Rotonda to Via degli Orfani. This leads to Piazza Capranica, where typical Roman opportunism has converted an early Renaissance palace into a cinema. Walk round **Santa Maria in Aquiro**, the Baroque church to your right, turn left at the end of the lane and you will see the Egyptian **obelisk** brought to Rome by Augustus to act as a sundial in the *Campus Martius*. The grand facade behind it is Bernini's *Palazzo di Montecitorio*, seat of the lower house of the Italian parliament since 1871. Go round the building to the right by way of Via dell' Impresa. You will notice that it has been considerably extended with another (modern) facade in Piazza del Parlamento.

Turning right out of the square, you strike the busy Via del Corso. Nearly 1.5km (1 mile) in length, it is so called because the Romans used to race horses down it, until this became too hazardous for pedestrians. Turn left and walk up the Corso for a block, then turn right into Via della Vite. You are entering one of the smartest shopping areas in the world: at Christmas time

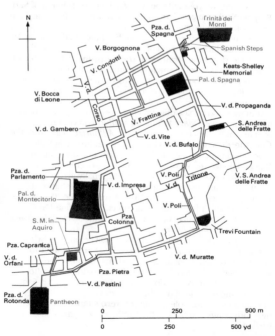

before the recession some streets used to be laid with red carpet. Go first left at Via del Gambero, right at Via Frattina, then left into Via Bocca di Leone. Most of the *palazzi* have been converted into shops and hotels, but there are still gateways through which you can glimpse beautiful courtyards, proclaiming a more stately, leisured way of life.

Shortly after crossing Via Borgognona, note on your left a most unusual sarcophagus-shaped **fountain**. On reaching **Via Condotti**, the smartest street of all, turn right. Ahead of you is *Piazza di Spagna* with the fabled *Spanish Steps* rising in the background. If you can resist the Gucci handbags and Bulgari jewellery on the right, cross to the historic **Caffè Greco**, the resort of artists, painters and musicians for more than 200yrs. Unfortunately the appeal of the Spanish Steps is now considerably over-subscribed. As you ascend them you could be in San Francisco c. 1968, but once you reach the top and look back down Via Condotti from *Trinità dei Monti*, your sense of history and place is restored. Below, to your left, is the house in which Keats died, now known as the *Keats-Shelley Memorial*.

When you go back down the steps, turn left towards the **Palazzo di Spagna**, early 17thC residence of the Spanish Ambassador to the Vatican. In front of it stands a 19thC **column** commemorating the dogma of the Immaculate Virgin. Pass to the right of the triangular building beyond it, down Via di Propaganda. This leads to a small piazza with the church of Sant' Andrea delle Fratte on the left. Go straight on down Via Sant' Andrea delle Fratte, right at Via del Bufalo, then left into Via Poli. This street crosses Via del Tritone and leads down to Rome's most famous feat of combined sculpture and plumbing, the *Trevi Fountain*, at its most spectacular when floodlit at night.

Via delle Muratte to the right of the fountain leads back to the Corso. Turn right and cross over when you see the *Column of Marcus Aurelius* in *Piazza Colonna*. Turning left out of the piazza, you soon come to **Piazza Pietra**, where the columns of an ancient temple have been skilfully used in the construction of an elegant 17thC facade. The building is now the **Stock Exchange**. If you cross the square to the far corner, Via dei Pastini will take you back to Piazza della Rotonda and your starting-point at the Pantheon.

Walk 3/Trastevere and Isola Tiberina
Allow 3hrs.

Although Trastevere is rapidly being taken over by expatriate artists of dubious talent, its irreverent working-class character has not yet been suppressed. Romans still love it and go there for an exciting night out, much as Parisians visit the Left Bank. This walk however is more suitable for the morning, when there will be less activity on the streets to distract you.

Leaving the s end of *Piazza Navona*, take Via Cuccagna, which leads down the side of **Palazzo Braschi**, home of the *Rome Museum*. Across Corso Vittorio, the *Palazzo Piccola Farnesina* houses a much smaller museum of ancient sculpture. Down to the left of it Via dei Baullari takes you to the broad market square of *Piazza Campo dei Fiori*. The **statue** in the centre is of the 16thC philosopher, Giordano Bruno, who was burnt at the stake for heresy on this very spot. Radical opinion in Italy has adopted Bruno as one of its greatest martyrs and the scene of his execution as the appropriate place at which to voice dissent. If you stay long, you may be invited to join any number of alternative societies.

Planning and walks

Via dei Baullari continues a little way beyond Campo dei Fiori, bringing you to Piazza Farnese, where the imposing Renaissance dignity of *Palazzo Farnese* rivals the finest *palazzi* of Florence. The fleurs-de-lis in its magnificent cornice indicate its Florentine past rather than its present function as the French Embassy.

Turn left in front of the palace and go along Vicolo dei Venti to the tiny **Piazza della Quercia**. The ancient oak tree and unpretentious restaurant give this square an almost rustic flavour. Go straight on through Piazza Capo di Ferro past *Palazzo Spada*, with its splendid courtyard leading to the art gallery, until you reach Piazza dei Pellegrini. As you turn right down Via dei Pettinari to **Ponte Sisto** (named after its builder Sixtus IV), spare a thought for the poor Trasteverini who used to trudge up this hill carrying their valuables to the pawnbroker at Piazza Monte di Pietà.

Once across the bridge with its distinctive **lamp standards**, you enter Trastevere through Piazza Trilussa. Beside the grand **fountain** stands a **bust of the poet Trilussa**, whose witty, vulgar ballads, written in a phonetic transcription of the local Trastevere dialect, epitomize the devil-may-care attitude of the poor of Rome.

Towards the back of the square, on the left, is Vicolo del Cinque, a typical narrow Trastevere street. When you come to a small piazza, bear left past the church of Sant' Egidio. Ahead of you is the apse of *Santa Maria in Trastevere*. Turn left at Via della Paglia and you will come out into the piazza in front of the church. If there is room on the steps of the fountain, sit down to admire the golden mosaics on the facade and the characteristic Romanesque campanile.

Keeping to the left of the piazza, go down Via della Lungaretta, a long, dark, cobbled street that eventually crosses the top of Viale Trastevere at the bustling intersection of Piazza Sonnino. Cross over to the row of bars and cinemas, go right, then take the second left, Via dei Genovesi. Past Via della Luce you find **San Giovanni dei Genovesi** on your right. The church itself was rebuilt in the 19thC, but through the entrance to the left of it you can visit the exquisite 15thC cloisters. The brightly coloured octagonal marble pillars are set in a garden of almost tropical luxuriance.

At the next crossing you will see to your right the impressive campanile of *Santa Cecilia in Trastevere*. You approach the church through a vast gateway and a pleasant formal garden, before reaching the fine medieval portico. Take note of any concerts that are on at the church. They are usually of high quality, as is only fitting in the church of the patron saint of music.

Returning to Via dei Genovesi, cross straight over it and continue until you come to the largely medieval **Piazza in Piscinula**. On the other side of the square, steps lead up to Lungotevere opposite the *Isola Tiberina*. As you cross Ponte Cestio, beyond the tower of *San Bartolomeo* to your right, there stands one solitary arch of a broken bridge, known simply as the **Ponte Rotto**. The views from the island are magnificent, both back across Trastevere to the *Janiculum Hill* and s towards the *Aventine Hill*.

On the far side of the island the short hump-backed **Ponte Fabricio** is the oldest bridge still in use. It dates from 62BC. The weather-beaten lumps of marble on the parapet are in fact four-sided **heads of Janus**. Let these be your signal to turn back, retrace your steps over the island to one of Trastevere's many restaurants and enjoy a well-deserved lunch.

Walk 4/Behind the Capitol to the Aventine
Allow 2½-3½hrs.

If you can stand the Roman sun, try this walk on a summer's afternoon, when the shimmering heat and stillness make Rome seem a completely different city. On the tranquil heights of the *Aventine Hill* the distant noise of traffic may even be drowned by that of cicadas and crickets.

Starting off once again from the *Pantheon*, turn right and go down the side of the building along Via della Minerva. At the piazza of the same name you will see the plain Renaissance facade of *Santa Maria sopra Minerva* with Bernini's delightful *Elephant Supporting an Obelisk* in front of it. Walk straight on down Via dei Cestari until you reach *Largo Argentina* with its sunken area containing the remains of four **Republican temples**, which only came to light during demolition in the 1920s. Passing to the left of the excavations down Via San Nicola de' Cesarini, you may observe that those who stand most to benefit from this work of conservation are the stray cats that have made their homes in the ruins.

At the reconstructed **medieval tower** on the corner, cross Via Florida into Via Paganica. This leads to Piazza Mattei and its celebrated *Tortoise Fountain*. Originally this enchanting composition consisted simply of the slender youths with their

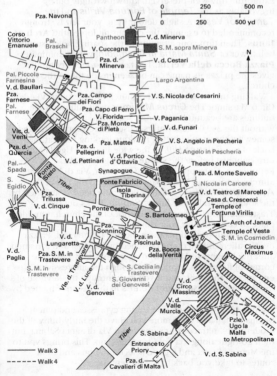

45

dolphins; the tortoises were an inspired afterthought. Go left along Via de' Funari, then right down Via Sant' Angelo in Pescheria.

To your right you are looking towards the old *Ghetto*, where Jews were forced to live in desperately overcrowded conditions until as late as the 19thC. On your left you come to the church of **Sant' Angelo in Pescheria**, so-called because this area was once the home of the city's fish market. In front of the church stand the fascinating ruins of the *Portico of Octavia*, dating from the 2ndC BC.

Via del Portico d'Ottavia leads down to the river opposite the *Isola Tiberina* with the *Theatre of Marcellus* on the left and the Synagogue on the right. Turning left past the Theatre of Marcellus, across the large Piazza di Monte Savello, you mount some steps and turn right into Via del Teatro di Marcello. The church of **San Nicola in Carcere** on the right is a typical hybrid construction, consisting of a ruined Roman temple, a medieval tower and many later additions and subtractions. Past the large modern Public Records Office, which stands on the site of the docks of ancient Rome, is the **Casa dei Crescenzi**, once the home of one of the city's most powerful families and another striking example of medieval recycling of Classical remains.

Towards the river at the bottom of Via del Teatro Marcello you cannot fail to notice the two small temples, both extraordinarily well-preserved, known wrongly but irrevocably as the *Temple of Fortuna Virilis* and the *Temple of Vesta*. A slight detour up to your left is strongly recommended to examine the curious multiple 4thC **Arch of Janus**. Then turn your attention to the soaring seven-storeyed bell tower of *Santa Maria in Cosmedin*, which dominates **Piazza Bocca della Verità**. The famous stone carving that gives the piazza its name can be seen inside the portico of the church.

Walking up to the right of the church brings you to Via del Circo Massimo. The *Circus Maximus* itself, although the outlines are beautifully restored, seems sad and empty without the 250,000 spectators it used to accommodate, and somewhat threatened by the perilous-looking ruins at the back of the *Palatine Hill*. At the wide Piazzale Ugo la Malfa, turn right just before the **statue** of the great 19thC Republican, Giuseppe Mazzini. This street, Via di Valle Murcia, leads up to Via di Santa Sabina and the top of the *Aventine Hill*. Here, a small park of pine trees, dominated by the solemn grandeur of *Santa Sabina*, looks out over Trastevere. The vast, echoing interior of the church is an ideal place to cool off after your climb.

The ornately-walled piazza at the end of the road, Piazza dei Cavalieri di Malta, was designed by Piranesi and is named after the Knights of Malta, who own this highly desirable corner of Rome. Their priory is through the impressive entrance to the right, and if you look through the keyhole of the door you will see *Saint Peter's* in the distance framed by trees.

When quiet contemplation among cypresses and pines begins to pall and once more you crave the hurly-burly of the modern city, retrace your steps down Via di Santa Sabina, but then go right along Via del Circo Massimo. This brings you to the Metropolitana and a good selection of bus and tram routes to take you back to the present day.

Sights and places of interest

The sheer size and range of Rome's artistic heritage can prove bewildering to a first-time visitor. With more than two thousand years of art and architecture at your disposal — ranging from Classical through Early Christian and medieval to Renaissance and Baroque — some specialization is inevitable and indeed desirable. Once you have taken in the major sights such as the Roman Forum and St Peter's, it is wise to concentrate on just one historical period.

The lack of chronological organization in many museums and galleries can also be confusing. This is often a vestige of the private nature of the original collection. Poor cataloguing, erratic opening times and inexplicable closures are also typical, but all these are minor aggravations when set against the quality of the collections themselves. Entrance to many of the major state-owned archaeological sites and museums is free on the first and third Sat and the second and fourth Sun of each month.

Church opening times vary enormously, but are roughly 7.30am-12.30pm, 3-6.30pm. In summer, the afternoon times run about 1hr later.

In the following lists, English or Italian names are used, according to common English-speaking usage. Bold type is generally employed to indicate outstanding works of art. Occasionally it is used to single out an important but now-vanished building or monument. Entries given without addresses and opening times are described more fully elsewhere: check the cross-references.

Arches and columns
Arch of Constantine
Arch of Septimius Severus
Arch of Titus
Column of Marcus Aurelius
Trajan's Column
Baths
Baths of Caracalla
Baths of Diocletian
Castles and towers
Castel Sant' Angelo
Torre delle Milizie
Catacombs and cemeteries
Catacombs of Domitilla
Catacombs of Priscilla
Catacombs of St Calixtus
Catacombs of St Sebastian
Pre-Constantinian Necropolis
Protestant Cemetery
Vatican Grottoes
Churches and basilicas
Chiesa Nuova (Santa Maria in Vallicella)
Gesù
Pantheon
Sant' Agnese in Agone
Sant' Agnese fuori le Mura
Sant' Agostino
Sant' Andrea al Quirinale
Sant' Andrea della Valle
Santi Apostoli
San Bartolomeo
San Carlo ai Catinari
San Carlo alle Quattro Fontane
Santa Cecilia in Trastevere

San Clemente
Santi Cosma e Damiano
Santa Costanza
Santa Croce in Gerusalemme
San Giovanni in Laterano
Santi Giovanni e Paolo
San Gregorio Magno
Sant' Ignazio
Sant' Ivo
San Lorenzo fuori le Mura
Santi Luca e Martina
San Luigi dei Francesi
San Marco
Santa Maria degli Angeli
Santa Maria dell' Anima
Santa Maria Antiqua
Santa Maria d' Aracoeli
Santa Maria in Cosmedin
Santa Maria in Domnica (Santa Maria della Navicella)
Santa Maria Maggiore
Santa Maria sopra Minerva
Santa Maria Nova (Santa Francesca Romana)
Santa Maria della Pace
Santa Maria del Popolo
Santa Maria in Trastevere
Santa Maria della Vittoria
San Paolo fuori le Mura
St Peter's
San Pietro in Carcere
San Pietro in Montorio
San Pietro in Vincoli
Santa Prassede
Santa Pudenziana

Sights

Santi Quattro Coronati
San Saba
Santa Sabina
Santo Stefano Rotondo
Santa Susanna
San Teodoro
Trinità dei Monti

Forums and markets
Forum of Augustus
Forum Boarium
Forum of Caesar
Forum of Nerva
Forum of Trajan
Forum of Vespasian
Roman Forum
Trajan's Markets

Fountains
Barcaccia Fountain
Fountain of the Bees
Fountain of the Four Rivers
Moor Fountain
Moses Fountain
Naiads' Fountain
Paola Fountain
Quattro Fontane
Tortoise Fountain
Trevi Fountain
Triton Fountain

Galleries
Borghese Gallery
Galleria Colonna
Galleria Doria Pamphili
Galleria Nazionale d' Arte Antica
Galleria Nazionale d' Arte Moderna
Galleria Spada
Pinacoteca Capitolina
Pinacoteca Vaticana

Gateways
Porta Maggiore
Porta Pia
Porta Portese
Porta San Pancrazio
Porta San Paolo
Porta San Sebastiano

Hills and other districts
Aventine Hill
Borgo
Campus Martius
Capitoline Hill
Coelian Hill
Esquiline Hill
Ghetto
Isola Tiberina
Janiculum Hill
Largo Argentina
Ludovisi Quarter
Palatine Hill
Quirinal Hill
Vatican City

Historic houses
Casa dei Cavalieri di Rodi
Keats-Shelley Memorial
Nero's Golden House

Mausoleums and monuments
Ara Pacis Augustae
Mausoleum of Augustus
Mausoleum of Hadrian
Monument to Victor Emmanuel II

Pyramid of Caius Cestius

Museums
Barracco Museum
Capitoline Museums
Museo Nazionale Romano
Museo Nazionale di Villa Giulia
Museo di Palazzo Venezia
Rome Museum
Vatican Museums

Palaces and villas
Lateran Palace
Oratory Complex
Palazzo Barberini
Palazzo Borghese
Palazzo Braschi
Palazzo della Cancelleria
Palazzo Chigi
Palazzo Colonna
Palazzo Corsini
Palazzo Doria
Palazzo Farnese
Palazzo Madama
Palazzo Massimo alle Colonne
Palazzo di Montecitorio
Palazzo Orsini
Palazzo Pamphili
Palazzo Piccola Farnesina
Palazzo del Quirinale
Palazzo Senatorio
Palazzo Spada
Palazzo Venezia
Villa Farnesina
Villa Giulia
Villa Medici

Parks and gardens
Pincio
Villa Borghese
Villa Giulia
Villa Medici

Piazzas
Piazza Bocca della Verità
Piazza del Campidoglio
Piazza Campo dei Fiori
Piazza Colonna
Piazza della Minerva
Piazza Navona
Piazza del Popolo
Piazza del Quirinale
Piazza San Pietro
Piazza di Spagna

Roads, drains and bridges
Cloaca Maxima
Ponte Sant' Angelo
Via della Conciliazione

Stadiums
Circus Maximus
Piazza Navona

Temples and porticoes
Pantheon
Portico of Octavia
Tempietto
Temple of Fortuna Virilis
Temple of Venus and Rome
Temple of Vesta

Theatres and auditoriums
Colosseum
Theatre of Marcellus

Ara Pacis Augustae *(Altar of Augustan Peace)* ☆
Via di Ripetta ☎ 67102071. Map 5G5 🚍 Open Tues-Sat 9am-1.30pm, Sun 9am-1pm; also (Apr-Oct) Tues, Thurs, Sat 4.30-8pm. Closed Mon.

Reflecting the cypresses around the nearby *Mausoleum of Augustus*, great panes of plate-glass surround one of the most interesting monuments in Rome. The Altar of Augustan Peace was built by decree of the Roman Senate, to honour Augustus and celebrate the peace that followed his victories in Spain and Gaul. The main structure is of Carrara marble, and the quality of the carving of the highest order.

The white marble altar itself is very plain, but the carved screen surrounding it is richly decorated. The screen reliefs are divided into two levels: the upper one consists mainly of figures, the lower one of intricately woven floral patterns and acanthus leaves. The relief at the E end, showing the earth goddess Tellus with a swan, cow and lamb, is a particularly fine composition. Part of the upper level of decoration is a **processional frieze** of exceptional interest: it shows a number of important people at the consecration ceremony on July 4, 13BC, and includes a life portrait of Augustus. You can also see lictors with their rods, four priestly figures with strange headdresses, the Pontifex Maximus, Augustus' wife Livia, his daughter Julia, his niece Antonia and three children — one of them usually identified as the future Emperor Claudius.

The discovery and reclamation of the Ara Pacis is a remarkable story in itself. Several blocks of the altar were found in 1568 during excavations for the Palazzo Fiano, and were cut up and distributed to purchasers. One of them eventually passed to the Louvre and another to the *Vatican Museums*. Further attempts to salvage the remains proved abortive until 1937, when engineers working with a team of archaeologists froze the underground spring waters, enabling the palace above to be underpinned and the remains of the altar and screen to be extricated. Several museums both in Italy and outside then cooperated by returning either the original fragments or facsimiles, making possible the exciting task of reconstruction of the Ara Pacis.

Arch of Constantine *(Arco di Costantino)* 🏛
Piazza del Colosseo. Map 10J7. Metropolitana: Colosseo.
One of the last great monuments of ancient Rome, the Arch of Constantine was erected by the Senate in 315 to commemorate the Emperor's victory at the Milvian Bridge. The best of its reliefs were taken from earlier monuments to Trajan, Hadrian and Marcus Aurelius, notably the fine reliefs of battle scenes high up inside the central arch that show Trajan battling against the Dacians, and the eight rectangular reliefs let into the attic, which originated in a monument to Marcus Aurelius. The inferior quality of 4thC Roman sculpture is evident in the low-reliefs at the base of the columns, and in the friezes featuring Constantine above the arches.

Arch of Septimius Severus
An enormously influential triumphal arch, built in the 3rdC to celebrate the first 10yrs of the Emperor's rule and to honour his military victories. It stands at the W end of the *Roman Forum*.

Arch of Titus
The oldest surviving triumphal arch in the city stands at the E end of the *Roman Forum*. Its simple but

noble proportions and superb high-reliefs make it one of the greatest monuments of ancient Rome.

Aurelian Wall *(Mura Aureliane)* 🏛
The greater part of the impressive wall erected by Aurelian and Probus between 272 and 279 remains visible today, mostly in good condition. Taking in the Seven Hills, and massively buttressed, it makes an indelible impression. The aim of the wall was to keep out the Alemanni, whom Aurelian had defeated. The wall was 19km (12 miles) in circumference and had 18 main gates and 381 towers.

The best places to see it are at **Porta San Sebastiano** and along Via Campania to the E of Porta Pinciana.

Aventine Hill *(Aventino)*
Map 9J6 ⇜ *Metropolitana: Circo Massimo.*
The Aventine rises S of the **Palatine Hill**, and from the Parco di Sant' Alassio affords a marvellous view over the Tiber towards Trastevere and **Saint Peter's**. Here, high on the hill, are the churches of **Santa Sabina**, Sant' Alassio and Sant' Anselmo. The delightful 18thC Piazza dei Cavalieri di Malta was designed by Piranesi and is famed for its spectacular view of St Peter's. If you look through the keyhole of the door leading to the priory of the Knights of Malta, you can see the basilica framed by trees.

Barcaccia Fountain *(Fontana della Barcaccia)* ☆
Piazza di Spagna. Map 6G6. Metropolitana: Spagna.
Commissioned by Urban VIII in 1627, this fountain is generally considered to be the work of Pietro Bernini, although some authorities believe it is by his much more famous son, Gianlorenzo. Here, at the foot of the **Spanish Steps**, you can still sit and watch the world go by, even if it is often impossible to hear the tranquil waters of the fountain above the noise of traffic. The design makes use of the low water pressure in the Acqua Vergine aqueduct and represents a sinking boat with water spilling fitfully from both prow and stern. Legend has it that the fountain marks the spot where a boat was once stranded when the Tiber overflowed its banks.

Barracco Museum
A small collection of Classical, Egyptian and Western Asiatic sculpture, assembled by Baron Barracco and notable for its Greek pieces. It is now housed in the **Palazzo Piccola Farnesina**.

Baths of Caracalla *(Terme di Caracalla)* 🏛 ☆
Piazzale Numa Pompilio ☎ *5758626. Map 10K7* 🚌 *Open 9am-3pm. Metropolitana: Circo Massimo.*
Begun by Caracalla in 212 and completed by Heliogabalus and Alexander Severus, these vast baths are still impressive in their ruined state. Yet it takes a considerable effort of imagination to visualize the original splendour of the architecture and decoration. They were perhaps the most luxurious baths ever built in Rome. There was a gymnasium, a stadium, Greek and Latin libraries, a picture gallery, leisure gardens, and room for 1,600 bathers. The assembly rooms and precincts were faced with marble of many colours and adorned with a magnificent collection of sculpture. Traces of the once extensive floor mosaics remain, and enough is left of the shattered vaults to make a superb stage setting for open-air operas (see **Nightlife and performing arts**).

Baths of Diocletian *(Terme di Diocleziano)* 🏛 ☆
Piazza della Repubblica. Map 7G8. Metropolitana: Repubblica.

A prominent feature of Piazza della Repubblica is the gaunt, weather-worn mass of brick, almost in a state of ruin, that looms up on the NE side. Part of the remains of the great Baths of Diocletian, it now contains the church of Santa Maria degli Angeli.

The Baths were begun by the Emperor Maximian in 298 on his return from Africa, and completed by Diocletian in 305-306. They were the largest of all the bath complexes, and could accommodate 3,000 people. The basic elements, as of all baths, were the *Calidarium* (hot), the *Tepidarium* (warm) and the *Frigidarium* (cold), but there were also exercise areas, shaded walks, outdoor swimming pools, and even libraries. Enough remains of the original buildings to convey a sense of their monumental scale and complexity: they once covered an area of 13 hectares (32 acres). The massive bare brick walls were once faced with marble, and the Baths were as luxurious as they were extensive.

The church of **Santa Maria degli Angeli** is one of the least characteristic works of Michelangelo. He was commissioned to effect the conversion by Pius IV, and did so with due respect for the ancient Classical structure. He used the huge central hall of the Baths as the nave of the new Carthusian church. When Vanvitelli was brought in to refurbish the interior in the 18thC, he altered the orientation so that the nave became an exceptionally wide transept. The ground plan was now wider than it was long,

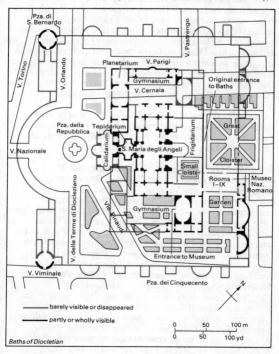

despite the construction of an apse that cut into the wall of the
Frigidarium, and, with Vanvitelli's Baroque decorations, much of
the force of Michelangelo's conception was lost. The entrance to
the church, in Piazza della Repubblica, is all that remains of the
Calidarium.

Inside the vestibule, or former *Tepidarium*, is the church's only
memorable work of art, an imposing statue of *St Bruno*, founder
of the Carthusian order, by Houdon (1766). Clement XIV said the
only reason why this statue did not talk was that it was observing
the monastic rule of silence. In the left transept, the vast interior
is explained by an informative series of plans and drawings,
showing the Baths' original appearance.

Museo Nazionale Romano ✿

Piazza dei Cinquecento ☎ *460856* 🚇 🚊 ✗ *Open Tues-Sat 9am-2pm,*
Sun 9am-1pm. Closed Mon. Metropolitana: Repubblica or Termini.
This museum was founded in 1889, to house all the antique
works of art of high artistic merit discovered within the city of
Rome. In 1906 the State bought the famous Ludovisi family
collection, and this is now incorporated, although it has been
closed to the public during the extensive renovation of the
museum and new excavation of the baths. The superb **Ludovisi**
Throne (✿) is sometimes on display, in the **Small Cloister** of
the old Carthusian monastery that was founded on this spot. It is
an original Greek work of the 5thC BC, found in the Villa Ludovisi
in 1887. The relief sculpture is dominated by the *Birth of*
Aphrodite on the front, but it is the figure of the naked flute girl
on the side that charms us with its simplicity.

Apart from the Ludovisi Throne, the most important sculptures
in the museum are to be found in a sequence of nine rooms
situated off the **Great Cloister**. Room III is of particular interest.
It contains the *Daughter of Niobe*, possibly a Greek original
dating from 460-430BC; two Greek bronzes of exceptional quality
(a young man leaning on a lance, and a weary and probably
defeated boxer, signed by Apollonios); and a superb copy of the
Discobolos, or discus-thrower, by Myron. Room VI is filled with a
great variety of Roman portraits, including a magnificent statue of
Augustus as Pontifex Maximus.

On the first floor of this building is a collection of frescoes,
stuccoes and mosaics found mostly in Rome, all fine examples of
early Classical decoration; the charming **landscape frescoes**
(✿) from the House of Livia are particularly beautiful.

Borghese Gallery *(Galleria Borghese)* 🏛 ★

Via Pinciana ☎ *858577. Map 7F7* 🚇 ✗ *Open 9am-2pm.*
Designed by Giovanni Vasanzio (Jan Van Santen) between
1613-15, this handsome building was erected for Cardinal
Scipione Borghese, nephew of Paul V, patron of Bernini and the
greatest collector of his day. It is correctly called the *Casino*
Borghese, meaning summer or pleasure house, for it was never
intended to be lived in. The park and gardens that surround it
comprise the Villa, now a public park, incorporating the Zoo at
its northern limits. Inside the Casino there is a collection of
sculpture and painting second only to that of the *Vatican*
Museums. Sculpture is mainly on the ground floor.

In 1985 subsidence of the building caused the closure of the
gallery, and although it has reopened, access can be restricted.

Entering through the portico, you find yourself in the **Salone**, a
large room with a richly painted ceiling. It contains antique
sculptures, and on the **pavement** there are some good 3rdC
Roman mosaics of gladiators fighting, and hunting scenes. In the

near right-hand corner is the entrance to **Room I**. Here is one of the most famous pieces in the whole collection, the reclining figure of *Pauline Borghese* (★), Napoleon's sister. She married Camillo Borghese in 1803, and Antonio Canova's revealing statue of her dates from 1804. Canova is often branded a chill exponent of the Neoclassical style, but this representation of Pauline as Venus is full of life and warmth. Legend relates that Camillo kept it behind locked doors, and only showed it to his intimate friends.

The centrepiece of **Room II** is Bernini's marvellous *David* (★), commissioned by Scipione Borghese (1623-24). It is an astonishing display of virtuosity, the intensity of expression and vitality of movement showing the absolute command of the sculptor over his material. The face is said to be a self-portrait of the young sculptor, and Scipione is alleged to have held the mirror for his young protégé.

In **Room III** Bernini again dominates with his group of *Apollo and Daphne* (1622-25), possibly his masterpiece (★). The story of Apollo's love for the nymph Daphne, of her flight from him and metamorphosis into a laurel tree, is hardly the most obvious of choices for the subject of a sculptural group; but Bernini actually seems to relish the difficulty of his task, and chooses the most dramatic moment possible. Daphne's thighs transformed into bark, and fingers changed into leafy tendrils, tell the beautiful young god that he is just too late, and the poignancy and grace of the moment is perfectly caught.

Room IV is a large hall, with superb 17thC decorations. The marble floor is paved in a beautiful geometric design, there are low-relief carvings high on the walls, and the ceiling is frescoed. Around the walls are busts of Roman emperors in marble and porphyry, and some splendid vases, while in the centre there is another great Bernini sculpture, the *Rape of Proserpine* (★). It is an early work (1621-22) and yet again shows the artist's enormous technical skill. The hard shiny surfaces of the muscular King of the Underworld contrast wonderfully with the soft texture of Proserpine's body, as his fierce grip digs into her flesh. At his feet, the grim three-headed Cerberus, guardian of the entrance to the Underworld, bays menacingly.

Room V is a small room with some good sculptures, of which the most interesting is a copy of Phidias' *Athene Parthenos*. **Room VI** contains two further works by Bernini, *Aeneas, Anchises and Ascanius Fleeing from the Sack of Troy*, an early piece in which he collaborated with his father Pietro, and *Truth Unveiled by Time*, a much later work (c. 1652) of which only the figure of Truth was ever completed. The group remained in the sculptor's possession until his death, and provoked the quip that the only place in Rome where one could be sure of finding truth was in Cavaliere Bernini's house. Neither of these works is as captivating as the other Bernini pieces here, but by any other standard they are very fine indeed.

The next two rooms feature Classical sculpture. The *Youth on a Dolphin* in **Room VII** and *Dancing Faun* in **Room VIII** are both Roman copies of Greek originals.

To reach the first floor it is necessary to return to Room IV and climb the spiral staircase. The main attraction of **Room IX** is Raphael's famous *Deposition* (★) (1507). It was executed for Atalanta Baglione in memory of her murdered son, and kept in the church of San Francesco al Prato in Perugia until 1608, when it was obtained by the Borghese. Other noteworthy pictures in this room are the *Portraits of a Man* and *Portrait of a Woman with a Unicorn* by Raphael, a *Crucifixion with Sts Jerome and*

Christopher by Pinturicchio, and a *Madonna and Child with St John the Baptist* by Lorenzo di Credi.

The last subject is repeated by Andrea del Sarto in **Room X**, where other outstanding works are *Venus and Cupid* (★) by Cranach and *The Baptism* (★) by Bronzino. Also in this room is the *Head of a Young Girl*, a beautiful early 16thC drawing by the Master of the Pala Sforzesca. **Room XI** contains Savoldo's *Tobias and the Angel*, and two paintings by Lorenzo Lotto: one is a portrait of a man dressed in black whose hand rests on a tiny ivory skull, the other a *Madonna and Child with Two Saints*. The only picture of real distinction in **Room XII** is Domenichino's *Sibyl* (★), also known as *Music*.

Passing through the unremarkable Room XIII, you reach **Room XIV**, frescoed by Lanfranco and the centrepiece of the whole gallery. It contains Bernini's extraordinarily precocious *Jupiter Suckled by the Goat Amalthea* (1615), as well as his two busts of *Scipione Borghese* (★). The reason for the duplication is that Bernini was just finishing the first when a crack appeared in the marble over one eyebrow. In feverish haste he completed another in two weeks. Also here is his terra-cotta model for a marble statue of *Louis XIV*, which survives only in a mutilated and transformed state in Versailles. Among the paintings, the Caravaggios (★) take pride of place. The finest are the early *Boy with a Basket of Fruit* and the so-called *Sick Bacchus*, both remarkable for the realistic treatment of fruit and leaves, the *David and Goliath*, in which Goliath, like Bacchus, is reputed to be a self-portrait, and the *Madonna dei Palafrenieri*, in which Caravaggio's realism brings an obscure dogma to life. (The serpent the Madonna crushes underfoot is a symbol of heresy.) Another picture of interest is Domenichino's *Diana with her Nymphs* (1618). This was commissioned by Cardinal Aldobrandini, but so enchanted Scipione Borghese that he seized it from the artist's studio.

Room XV contains Rubens' powerful *Deposition* (1605), Barocci's version of the Aeneas story depicted by Bernini downstairs, and three portraits ascribed to Bernini, two of which are said to be self-portraits. **Room XVI** is memorable for its collection of pictures by Jacopo Bassano, the best of which are the earthy *Nativity* and *Last Supper*. Leaving the undistinguished Rooms XVII and XVIII, move on to **Room XIX** where Correggio's *Danae* (★) dominates. The seductive grace of the painting of flesh and hair has perhaps never been equalled: nor has the sense of enjoyment. The other major pictures in this room are the group by Dosso Dossi, of which the finest is of the enchantress *Melissa*. The ceiling was frescoed by the Neoclassical Scottish painter Gavin Hamilton.

Room XX, the last in the gallery, contains Titian's early masterpiece *Sacred and Profane Love* (★), so familiar from reproductions. This is just one of the wonderful Venetian works in this room, which include the brilliant *Portrait of a Man* by Antonello da Messina, a tender late *Madonna and Child* by Giovanni Bellini, Veronese's *St John the Baptist Preaching*, and, perhaps best of all the later Titians but in a sadly deteriorated condition, *Venus Blindfolding Cupid* (★).

The lack of order in the arrangement of the collection can be confusing, but the quality is never in doubt and more than one visit is required to do it justice. It is not a bad idea to break your tour by stepping out onto the balcony at the front of the house. Here you can pause to enjoy the natural beauty of the park before returning refreshed to the works of art inside.

Borgo
Map 4G3.

The Borgo is the district immediately E of *Saint Peter's*, a part of Rome that is well worth exploring. Typically medieval streets run to the N and S of *Via della Conciliazione*, alongside two handsome Renaissance palaces, **Palazzo Torlonia** and **Palazzo dei Penitenzieri**. The second is now mostly converted into the Hotel Columbus (see *Hotels*).

Off the Borgo Santo Spirito lies the vast complex of the **Ospedale Santo Spirito**. The original hospital was founded by Innocent III in 1198 and rebuilt in the late 15thC. The Palazzo del Commendatore or Director's House dates from 1567 and, with its vast central courtyard, is a building of exceptional charm. Breaking the skyline to the right, the Romanesque bell tower of **Santo Spirito in Sassia** (founded in 726) completes a uniquely Roman setting.

Campo dei Fiori

Literally translated as "field of the flowers", this historic site is also known as *Piazza Campo dei Fiori*. It was once the scene of public executions but is now better known for its attractive fruit and flower market.

Campus Martius *(Campo Marzio)*
Map 6G5/6H5.

This is the area now bounded by the Tiber on one side and the Via del Corso on the other. In ancient times, it was a wide open plain, used for military exercises, and sporting pastimes such as ball games, gymnastics and horse racing. However, the splendid tract of flat land was too much of a temptation for Augustus' friend and collaborator, Marcus Agrippa. This energetic builder laid out an entirely new monumental quarter, with landscaped gardens and an artificial lake. Among several notable monuments were the Baths of Agrippa, the Basilica of Neptune and the original Pantheon. The whole area was devastated by fire in AD80, and practically all records were lost. However, we do know that Agrippa's Pantheon was built in marble from Carrara, and that some of the columns were decorated with caryatid figures by the Athenian sculptor Diogenes. (Hadrian later replaced this building by a new *Pantheon*.) In the Middle Ages, the population of Rome was concentrated here, in Trastevere and in the *Borgo*.

Capitoline Hill *(Campidoglio)*
Piazza del Campidoglio. Map 9I6.

This was the most famous of the seven hills of Rome, serving as both fortress and sanctuary of the ancient city. It rose to two distinct heights. At the N summit (*Arx*) was the citadel, together with the Temple of Juno Moneta (near which was the site of the early mint). At the S summit (*Capitolium*) stood the Capitol itself: the Temple of Jupiter Optimus Maximus Capitolinus. This was where the newly elected consuls took their vows, and where victorious generals came in procession to offer thanks to the gods. It was the heart of Roman religious life, and was several times rebuilt after the destruction by fire of the earliest temple of the Etruscan kings.

Today the **Palazzo Senatorio** is the official seat of the municipality, but the Capitol is not the political centre of the city any more. After years of neglect in the Middle Ages, the whole area was transformed by Michelangelo into the majestic showpiece it is today (see *Piazza del Campidoglio*).

Capitoline Museums (Musei Capitolini)
Piazza del Campidoglio ☎ *6782862. Map 9I6* 🔲 *Open Tues-Sat 9am-1.30pm, and 5-8pm on Tues and Sat only; Sun 9am-1pm. Closed Mon.*

The Palazzo Nuovo and Palazzo dei Conservatori face each other across the open space of Michelangelo's *Piazza del Campidoglio*, and together contain an impressive array of works of art, with an outstanding collection of antiquities.

The **Palazzo Nuovo** on the NE of the piazza houses several great masterpieces of Classical statuary, such as the *Capitoline Venus* (✰), an excellent Roman copy of a Hellenistic original, the *Dying Gaul* (✰), another excellent copy, of which the character and poignancy are typical of the 3rdC BC Pergamene School, and the *Marble Faun*, which inspired Nathaniel Hawthorne's book of the same title. Equally fascinating is the **Room of the Emperors**: it is no longer thought that all the 65 busts represent famous Romans, but they are nevertheless an unrivalled portrait gallery, full of life and personality.

The **Palazzo dei Conservatori** on the SW of the piazza contains more Classical pieces. The most remarkable among them are the *Spinario* (✰), a bronze of a boy removing a thorn from his foot (1stC BC); the *Capitoline Wolf* (✰), an ancient Etruscan bronze dating from the end of the 6thC BC, to which Romulus and Remus were added in the 15thC; and the *Esquiline Venus* (✰), a Roman adaptation of a Greek idea, and an outstandingly graceful female nude.

In the same building, the **Pinacoteca Capitolina** contains a number of distinguished paintings. In Room 2, the *Baptism of Christ* by Titian is an early work (c. 1510), remarkable for the beautiful landscape and splendid portrait of the donor. Rubens' typically rich and vigorous version of *Romulus and Remus Suckled by the She-wolf* is in Room 3, close to the wonderfully sensitive *Double Portrait of the Painters Lucas and Cornelius de Wael* (✰) by his pupil Van Dyck (1625-26). In the **Cini Gallery**, which houses a collection of porcelain, there is a *St John the Baptist* by Caravaggio. This is almost identical with the painting in the Galleria Doria Pamphili (see *Palazzo Doria*), but this is probably the original version. It is certainly the finer of the two.

The *Rape of the Sabines* in **The Hall of Hercules** is one of several important narrative paintings by Pietro da Cortona, a characteristically dramatic treatment of antique fable. Finally, dominating the room to which it gives its name, there is Guercino's huge altarpiece of the *Burial and Reception into Heaven of St Petronilla* (✰), which was painted for *Saint Peter's*.

Casa dei Cavalieri di Rodi
This house was built into the ruins of the *Forum of Augustus* in the 12thC, as the Priorate of the Order of Knights of St John of Jerusalem (also known as the Knights of Rhodes or of Malta). It was restored in the 15thC and contains important fragments and sculpture preserved from the Forum.

Castel Sant' Angelo 🏛 ★
Lungotevere Castello ☎ *655036. Map 5G4* 🔲 ▣ ✳ 《⊱ *Open Tues-Sat 9am-2pm, Sun 9am-1pm, Mon 2-6.30pm.*

This famous monument has had an unusually long and varied history. The original structure was commenced in 130 by the Emperor Hadrian, as a tomb for himself and his family, and completed in 139, a year after his death, by his successor Antoninus Pius. It has survived remarkably well, first by being converted into a fortress and then by being used successively as prison, barracks and museum.

The Mausoleum of Hadrian was a cylindrical structure of travertine and peperino, faced with marble and set on a high, square platform. Like the earlier *Mausoleum of Augustus*, it was almost certainly based on Etruscan models. Above the drum, a tumulus planted with rings of cypresses was surmounted by a gigantic pedestal. This in turn supported a dramatic group in gilded bronze, showing Hadrian driving a chariot, in the guise of the sun god Apollo. Hadrian, his wife, and his adopted son were all buried here, as were all the emperors until Septimius Severus. Inside the building, a spiral ramp, still in use, led to the Imperial tomb, where urns containing the ashes of successive emperors and their families were kept.

In a commanding strategic position overlooking the wide sweep of the Tiber, the mausoleum was invested with military importance as early as 271, when Aurelian used it as a bridgehead in his defensive walls, thus protecting the approaches to the city from the critical NW direction. In the years following the collapse of Roman power, the mausoleum became the Citadel of Rome. In 590 St Gregory the Great was crossing the Pons Aelius at the head of a procession on its way to St Peter's, to pray for the ending of a terrible plague, when he saw a vision of an angel high above the citadel. The angel was in the act of sheathing its sword, signifying the end of the pestilence. A chapel was forthwith built on the spot where the angel had been seen, and the fortress was renamed after it.

The Castel Sant' Angelo gained additional importance with the creation of the Leonine City in 847, when Leo IV walled in the area of the *Borgo* as well as the Vatican and converted the fortress into a citadel-residence. He was the first of several popes who felt the need to reside here from time to time, in the interests of security. A covered way to the Vatican was completed by Alexander VI (1492-1503). When Clement VII took refuge here from the troops of the Emperor Charles V during the appalling Sack of Rome in 1527, the defence was assisted by Benvenuto Cellini, who boasted about his exploits in his *Autobiography*. Under Paul III (1534-49) the interior was decorated, and it was at this time that a marble angel by Raffaello da Montelupo (1544) was placed at the summit of the fortress. It is now in the Cortile di Onore (see over page) and its crowning position is occupied by a bronze angel dating from the 18thC.

For many years during the Renaissance, the Castel was used as a political prison, and horrific accounts have been recorded of its tortures and executions. It was occupied by French troops between 1849-70, and thereafter used as a barracks. Only in 1901 was the initiative taken to restore it, and by 1933 it was ready to open as a museum. The Castel Sant' Angelo is famous to opera lovers as the scene of the last act of Puccini's *Tosca* — after the murder of her lover Cavaradossi, held prisoner here, Tosca takes her own life by throwing herself off the battlements of the fortress.

The museum is vast and, including the Papal Apartments, covers four floors. It is predominantly military in character, but there are also valuable collections of paintings, antique furniture, and tapestries. Entering by the same door as to the original tomb, you mount the **ramp** leading to **Hadrian's funerary chamber**. The passage is in a superb state of preservation, and includes some of the original black and white mosaic decoration. Where the ramp ends, the gently graded **Staircase of Alexander VI**

Castel Sant' Angelo

Castel Sant' Angelo

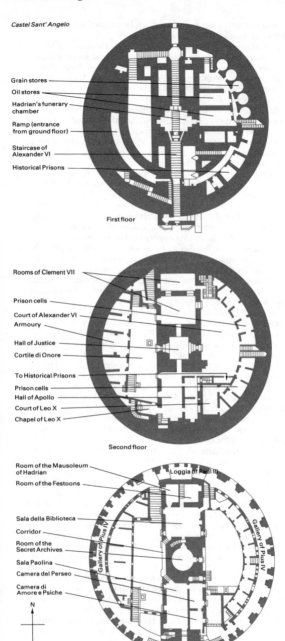

Grain stores

Oil stores

Hadrian's funerary chamber

Ramp (entrance from ground floor)

Staircase of Alexander VI

Historical Prisons

First floor

Rooms of Clement VII

Prison cells

Court of Alexander VI

Armoury

Hall of Justice

Cortile di Onore

To Historical Prisons

Prison cells

Hall of Apollo

Court of Leo X

Chapel of Leo X

Second floor

Room of the Mausoleum of Hadrian

Room of the Festoons

Loggia of Paul III

Sala della Biblioteca

Corridor

Room of the Secret Archives

Sala Paolina

Camera del Perseo

Camera di Amore e Psiche

Gallery of Pius IV

Gallery of Pius IV

Loggia of Julius II

N

Third floor

58

begins: it cuts diametrically across the great central mass of the building, passing over the funerary chamber. The staircase was once connected to the central mass by a drawbridge, giving complete security to the inner part of the citadel. Now a bridge designed by Valadier spans the gap.

A turn to the left brings you onto the second floor and the **Cortile di Onore** or Court of the Angel, an enchanting courtyard adorned with neat pyramids of marble and stone cannon balls. The major object of interest here is Raffaello da Montelupo's **marble angel**. Leading off the courtyard to the W are rooms housing a large collection of arms dating from the earliest times up to the Middle Ages. At the S end of the courtyard is the **Chapel of Leo X**, designed by Michelangelo. It is kept locked, but you can admire the fine facade of what is perhaps Michelangelo's least-known work. An open stairway leads to the Papal Apartments above.

A door on the E of the courtyard leads into the **Rooms of Clement VII**. The larger of the two rooms contains a splendid stuccoed chimney piece, and the Aldobrandini Pope's arms on the ceiling. Beyond, the **Hall of Justice** contains Perin del Vaga's fresco of *The Angel of Justice*. The Hall is in the heart of the building, and dates from Classical times. The next room, the **Hall of Apollo**, is handsomely decorated with grotesques, frescoed for Paul III in 1547. Beyond are two small private rooms lavishly decorated with pictures, including a triptych by Taddeo Gaddi.

A passage leads from here into the large **Court of Alexander VI**, also known as the Court of the Well, on account of the beautiful well-head decorated with the Borgia arms of Alexander VI, or as the Court of the Oil, because of the vast amounts of oil once stored below. On the E side are rooms once used as prison cells, in one of which Benvenuto Cellini was incarcerated.

A doorway on the S side of the courtyard leads to the Historical Prisons (now closed). Among the many notable people confined there were Alessandro Farnese (later Paul III), Beatrice Cenci, Cardinal Carafa and Cagliostro.

At the N end of the courtyard, stairs lead up to the **Loggia of Paul III** on the third floor. This was designed by Raffaello da Montelupo and Antonio da Sangallo the Younger. It leads out onto the open **Gallery of Pius IV**, which surrounds the entire building. From this vantage point there are marvellous views over the Tiber and across the city on one side, and towards the Vatican Hill and Monte Mario on the other. The **Loggia of Julius II** on the S side was designed by Bramante and faces the *Ponte Sant' Angelo*. There is an attractive bar nearby where you can sit down and relax.

From the Loggia of Julius II, a few steps lead up to the **Papal Apartments**. These were designed for Paul III (see above) and were only intended to be used in an emergency. The first room, the **Sala Paolina**, is the most splendid, with frescoes by Perin del Vaga and Pellegrino Tibaldi and stuccoes by Girolamo Siciolante da Sermoneta and Baccio da Montelupo. It is a triumph of *trompe l'oeil* decoration.

Next door, in the **Camera del Perseo**, the myth of Perseus is illustrated in a beautiful frieze. This room is exquisitely furnished in Renaissance style, as is the adjoining **Camera di Amore e Psiche**, with its frieze by Perin del Vaga. Both rooms contain a number of pictures, including works by Paris Bordone and Sebastiano del Piombo.

A frescoed corridor leads from the Sala Paolina to the **Sala della Biblioteca**, a magnificent library decorated with frescoes by Luzzi, stuccoes by Girolamo Siciolante da Sermoneta, and a marble fireplace by Raffaello da Montelupo. Next door is the **Room of the Mausoleum of Hadrian**, so called after the frieze by Luzzi. Among several paintings here, Dosso Dossi's *Bacchanal* and Lorenzo Lotto's *St Jerome* are outstanding. Next door, and leading down to three smaller chambers, is the **Room of the Festoons**, named after the motifs of its decoration.

Returning to the Sala della Biblioteca, you can gain access to the **Room of the Secret Archives**, once used as a treasure-house for the papal jewels, gold and precious relics. The walnut cupboards were used to store the papal archives. A narrow staircase built into the solid mass of the ancient structure leads up, past more rooms containing memorabilia, to the **terrace** at the summit of the citadel. All around there are magnificent views, especially towards *Saint Peter's*.

Catacombs of Domitilla *(Catacombe di Domitilla)* ☆
Via delle Sette Chiese ☎ 5110342. Map 13D4 ⬛ ⬛
✗ compulsory. Open Wed-Mon 8.30am-noon, 2.30-5pm. Closed Tues. Bus 218 from Piazza San Giovanni in Laterano.

These catacombs are less frequently visited than the better known *Catacombs of Saint Calixtus* and *Catacombs of Saint Sebastian*, but they are only a short distance away from them and have two distinct advantages. They are far less crowded, and have a beautiful and spacious garden where you can relax in the shade after a guided tour.

The Domitilla who gave her name to these catacombs was a Flavian who converted to Christianity, a relative of Vespasian and Domitian. Her land was later used as a burial place for many thousands of Christians. The basilica that was erected here between 390-395 was dedicated to the martyrs Achilleus and Nereus, and built on the site of their tomb. According to one account they were Roman soldiers, but another version describes them as servants of Domitilla. The church was destroyed in an earthquake centuries ago but has been reconstructed, and there are many fascinating fragments of the original fabric to be seen, including some antique columns with fine capitals.

From the basilica, a priest will guide you through the labyrinthine galleries of the cemetery. Historically, there has been controversy about the identity of Domitilla, but the theory that she was a Flavian is now generally accepted. It seems that her family constructed a hypogeum or underground tomb, from which the 17km (11 miles) of catacombs on four levels developed. They are the largest in Rome, and contain many early Christian paintings and inscriptions, including one of the earliest representations of *Christ as the Good Shepherd*.

Catacombs of Priscilla *(Catacombe di Priscilla)*
Via Salaria 430. Ring bell at convent door ☎ 8380408. Map 13C4 ⬛ ⬛ ✗ compulsory. Open Tues-Sun 8.30am-noon, 2.30-5pm. Closed Mon. Bus 56 from Piazza Barberini, or 57 or 319 from Stazione Termini.

Founded by the Christian branch of a Senatorial family, these catacombs are among the most ancient in Rome, and well worth the slight inconvenience of reaching them. Guided tours are provided by Benedictine nuns. There are two levels to the catacombs, but the tour is conducted only on the upper one, which is the more ancient.

Of particular interest is a *cubiculum* or small chapel containing the oldest known painting of the Madonna and Child, *The Virgin and Child with Isaiah* (★), dating from the second half of the 2ndC. Beside this is *The Good Shepherd with Two Sheep*. Both are examples of the unusual technique of stucco combined with painting.

Passing through long galleries lined with many burial niches or *loculi* cut into the rock one above the other, you reach the **Greek Chapel**, so called because of the Greek inscriptions on the wall. Among the 2ndC frescoes, note *The Breaking of the Bread at the Last Supper*, which is one of the earliest representations of this scene.

Catacombs of Saint Calixtus *(Catacombe di San Callisto)* ☆

Via Appia Antica ☎ *5136725. Map 13D4* 🚻 📷
✗ *compulsory. Open Thurs-Tues 8.30am-noon, 2.30-5pm. Closed Wed. Bus 118 from Colosseo.*

Like other Roman catacombs, these probably started as private burial chambers and were only gradually enlarged, so that what you see today took about 300yrs to reach its present vast size. The catacombs are excavated on four levels, but the official tour is normally restricted to the second level. The maze of dark narrow galleries is lit and ventilated by shafts placed at wide intervals.

The burial niches or *loculi* are cut into the rock one above the other on either side of the passageways. Usually there are only five or six *loculi* in a tier, but in one dramatically deep gallery there are at least 12 on either side. Occasionally, chapels have been carved out of the rock to form *cubicula*, where all the members of a family could be buried together. One of the most interesting places is the **Crypt of the Popes**, larger than the normal *cubicula*, with beautiful spiral columns along the side walls. Here, with Greek inscriptions over the tombs, lie the remains of St Pontian (died 235), St Anterus (died 236), St Fabian (died 250), St Lucius I (died 254) and St Eutychian (died 284), some of whom were martyred.

Your guide will point out interesting examples of *graffiti*, including signs and symbols proclaiming the Christian faith. Most of the inscriptions are in Greek and are often of extreme simplicity; sometimes there is just a symbolic drawing scratched in the wet plaster that sealed the tomb — an anchor, dove or fish — or perhaps some sign with the same meaning.

The **Cubiculum of St Cecilia** is where the body of the saint was buried after her martyrdom in 230. Her grave was discovered by Pope Paschal I in 821 and her remains transferred to the church of *Santa Cecilia in Trastevere*, where they lie under the main altar. The *cubiculum* is superbly decorated with **frescoes** of the *Raising of Lazarus* and the *Miracle of the Loaves and Fishes*.

A copy of Maderno's famous statue of St Cecilia can be seen in a recess (the original is in the church in Trastevere).

Catacombs of Saint Sebastian *(Catacombe di San Sebastiano)* ☆

Via Appia Antica ☎ *7887035. Map 13D4* 🚻 ✗ *compulsory. Open Fri-Wed 8.30am-noon, 2.30-5pm. Closed Thurs. Bus 118 from Colosseo.*

These are the only catacombs in Rome that have always been accessible, and they have suffered as a result. A pagan cemetery existed on the site in the 1stC, and in the following century three tombs were excavated here. In the 3rdC, the owner of the burial ground became a Christian and the excavation of catacombs began.

The catacombs are on four levels, but not all of these are included in the guided tour. The finest relics are the **2ndC tombs**, one of which belonged to a certain Claudius Hermes. Here you can see well-preserved stuccoes of fine quality, incorporating circular motifs, flowers, shells, acanthus leaves and vines.

Nearby, a staircase leads up to the **triclia** where funeral banquets took place. The walls are inscribed with *graffiti* invoking Sts Peter and Paul. These references are explained by the strong probability that the apostles' bodies were brought here from their previous resting places (the sepulchre in *Saint Peter's* and the site of *San Paolo fuori le Mura*), and hidden during Valerian's persecutions of 258. It is believed that they remained here for 40yrs.

Certainly, the first church built on this spot was originally dedicated to the two apostles, and only much later to St Sebastian, who was buried here at the end of the 3rdC. St Sebastian was an officer in the Imperial household who was sentenced to be shot to death by arrows, during one of Diocletian's persecutions.

Above the catacombs stands the **Church of San Sebastiano**. It was rebuilt by Flaminio Ponzio in 1612, and contains a recumbent statue of *St Sebastian* by Antonio Giorgetti. In the **crypt** beneath the church, where the guided tour usually begins, is a bust of the saint attributed to Bernini.

Chiesa Nuova †

Corso Vittorio Emanuele. Map 5H4.

More correctly known as Santa Maria in Vallicella, the present church replaced an earlier one on the same site, and consequently became known as the New Church. Gregory XIII gave the original church to St Philip Neri in 1575 in recognition of the Oratory he had founded, and work began on the new one immediately. The architects were Giovanni Matteo di Città di Castello and Martino Longhi the Elder, while the facade is the work of Fausto Rughesi. The Chiesa Nuova was consecrated in 1599, 4yrs after the death of St Philip, whose expressed desire for a plain and modest building was wilfully ignored by his followers.

In 1647, when the *Oratory Complex* was almost completed, Pietro da Cortona began a scheme of decoration in the church that eventually covered the nave vault, dome and apse with splendid frescoes. These are in large part responsible for the Chiesa Nuova's opulent appearance.

But there are other fine paintings to be seen, notably the **high altarpiece**, and two flanking pictures of saints by Rubens, which were painted on slate to counteract the reflections of the light. Also very lovely are Barocci's *Visitation* and *Presentation*, located respectively in the fourth chapel of the left aisle and in the left transept.

St Philip Neri was a Florentine, but he spent 60yrs in Rome, and has been called the second apostle of Rome. His cheerful temperament particularly appealed to young people, and such was his influence that many young men were persuaded to abandon a life of luxury to join him in charitable works. St Philip was not just a good man: he had the rarer gift of inspiring good in other people.

Circus Maximus *(Circo Massimo)*
Via del Circo Massimo. Map 10J6. Metropolitana: Circo Massimo.

The Romans had a passion for horse-racing, and the Circus Maximus was their grandest stadium. Expanded and rebuilt many times, the Circus housed hundreds of thousands of spectators. The circuit itself was over 1,000m (1,090yds) long. Arcades on the outside of the Circus contained shops and taverns to meet the needs of thirsty or disappointed punters. The races were mainly two- and four-horse chariot contests, but there were also spectacles such as triumphs, when victorious soldiers returned to Rome from their military campaigns abroad. Today the long wall or *spina* that ran along the middle of the stadium is a grassy strip marked by a solitary cypress at one end. The whole area is open public ground — a better fate than when it was the site of a gasworks.

Cloaca Maxima *(Cloaca Massima)*
Lungotevere Aventino. Map 10J6.

This remarkable drainage system was designed in ancient times to drain the valleys between the Capitoline, Palatine and Esquiline Hills, and largely because of it the land was made ready for the major building programme in the **Roman Forum**. To this day the drain still discharges into the Tiber just s of the Ponte Palatino.

Coelian Hill *(Celio)*
Map 10J7.

The most southern of the seven hills of Rome is named after an Etruscan nobleman, Coelius Vibenna, who is thought to have settled here after helping Romulus to defeat Tatius, the Sabine king. Robert Guiscard caused widespread devastation in 1084, in his vicious incursion to assist his ally Gregory VII, and the area is still far less populated than other parts of central Rome. It contains three exceptionally interesting churches, **Santo Stefano Rotondo**, **Santi Giovanni e Paolo** and **Santa Maria in Domnica**.

Colosseum *(Colosseo)* 🏛 ★
Piazza del Colosseo ☎ 735227. Map 10I7 ◫ ground floor ◫ upper storeys ▣ ✱ ◂€ Open Thurs-Tues 9am-4pm, Wed 9am-1pm. Metropolitana: Colosseo.

Paintings and photographs cannot prepare you for a first sight of the Colosseum: the sheer size and majesty of this, the greatest monument of ancient Rome, come as a surprise. Yet, despite its stupendous bulk, the building is beautifully balanced. The unknown architect avoided any hint of monotony by subtle use of spatial harmony and variation of architectural orders. At night, flood-lighting emphasizes this harmony. The deep arcades are lit by an amber glow, and powerful white arc-lamps illuminate the three orders — Doric, Ionic and Corinthian — and high attic storey with its graceful pilasters.

Major restoration over the last decade has made it possible to visit the upper levels of the building once again. From here you can get a good view of the complex system whereby wild animals, scenery and other material were supplied for the great displays, contests and aquatic shows that took place. At this point, some reflections on the sombre history of these ruins are inevitable. It is hard not to visualize the gaping arena re-surfaced and spread with sand, the slaughtered animals and humans dragged away, the roars of the crowd packed on the tiers of marble seats.

Many explanations have been put forward as to how the Romans came to degenerate to such an extent as to find pleasure in the baiting and killing of elephants, lions and other wild beasts; in gladiatorial combats; and in the slaughter of Christians and criminals. In the early 2ndC AD, the satirist Juvenal accused the populace of having sold its power for "bread and circuses" (in other words, free food and entertainment), and some educated Romans were undoubtedly repelled by the gory spectacles that took place.

The higher levels of the Colosseum give marvellous views over the city — especially in the direction of the *Roman Forum*. Note the *Arch of Constantine*, the columns and apse of the *Temple of Venus and Rome*, the soaring Romanesque tower of **Santa Francesca Romana** behind, and the beautifully proportioned **Arch of Titus**.

The idea of building the amphitheatre in an area earlier expropriated for *Nero's Golden House* was Vespasian's, but it was unfinished at his death in 79 and inaugurated by his son Titus. Domitian completed the building (81-96). Vespasian, Titus and Domitian were members of the Flavian dynasty, and the building was originally called the *Amphitheatrum Flavium*. By the 7thC, however, it was known by its present name, first recorded in the famous prophecy of the Venerable Bede: "While the Coliseum stands, Rome shall stand; when the Coliseum falls, Rome shall fall; when Rome falls, the world shall fall." It is not known whether this name was acquired because of the size of the building, or because of the colossal gilded bronze statue of Nero nearby.

The building of the amphitheatre was an amazing technical feat. After draining an artificial lake, the engineers laid down a ring of *pozzalana* (concrete made with volcanic sand) 7.5m (25ft) thick. The size and weight of the building, which could seat 50,000 people, posed a considerable problem. This was solved by constructing a series of circular walls of tufa (volcanic stone) and a system of barrel vaults that supported the terraced seating and corridors behind.

Column of Marcus Aurelius *(Colonna di Marco Aurelio)*
Piazza Colonna. Map 6H6.
This column was erected in 180-196 to commemorate the Emperor's victories over the Sarmathians, the Quadi and the Marcomanni. The reliefs of the spiralling narrative are inferior to those of Trajan's Column (see *Forum of Trajan*), on which they are modelled, but interesting for the vivid picture they give of the military practices, life and costumes of the times. The crowning statue of Marcus Aurelius was replaced by one of *St Paul* in 1588.

The architect Domenico Fontana also restored the base at this time, and wrongly attributed the original dedication of the column to Antoninus Pius, Marcus Aurelius' uncle. Even now, it is often called the Antonine Column.

Esquiline Hill *(Esquilino)*
Map 11I8. Metropolitana: Cavour or Colosseo.
The hill has two main summits, the *Oppius* and the *Cispius*. On the former were built *Nero's Golden House* and the Baths of Trajan. A large area is now taken up by the Parco Oppio, a public

park. To the N, the Cispius is dominated by the great basilica of *Santa Maria Maggiore*.

Forum, The   This was the political, religious and commercial centre of Republican Rome. It is also known as the *Roman Forum*, to distinguish it from the later *Imperial Forums*.

Forum of Augustus *(Foro di Augusto)* ⌂
Via dei Fori Imperiali. Map 10I6. Metropolitana: Colosseo.
The retaining walls that for 2,000yrs have helped prevent the Saburra, the area above the Forum of Augustus, from sliding down the hillside are being reinforced and shored up. It is therefore impossible to visit the site from the usual entrance in Piazza del Grillo, but in any case the full extent of the ruined Forum of Augustus is best seen from Via dei Fori Imperiali. From there one can still admire the three upstanding columns of the **Temple of Mars Ultor**, Mars the Avenger. Augustus vowed to build this temple after his defeat of Brutus and Cassius at the Battle of Philippi in 42BC, but it was still not complete at the inauguration of the forum in 2BC. Flanked and fronted by graceful Corinthian columns, it was arguably the culmination of the emperor's whole building programme, epitomizing the grand ideals of the Augustan Age.

Forum of Nerva *(Foro di Nerva)*
The Forum of Nerva, sometimes called the Forum Transitorium in Classical times because it led into the *Forum of Vespasian*, now lies beneath modern streets and buildings to the E of the Forum of Augustus. Two impressive Corinthian columns remain visible, with a relief of Minerva between them, at the edge of·Via dei Fori Imperiali. The Temple of Minerva, which originally dominated this forum, was demolished in 1606 — an act of vandalism perpetrated by Paul V, in order to obtain marble for the construction of the *Paola Fountain* on the Janiculum Hill.

Casa dei Cavalieri di Rodi *(House of the Knights of Rhodes)*
This building, on the W of the Forum of Augustus, is the ancient seat of the Priorate of the Order of Knights of St John of Jerusalem (also known as the Knights of Rhodes or of Malta). It was built over a Classical structure at the end of the 12thC and restored in the 15thC. The overall appearance is of an elegant Renaissance building, with lofty, well-proportioned rooms decorated and furnished in the style of the period. Several interesting pictures relate to the history of the Order. There is a splendid view over the forums from the loggia.

From the columned atrium, which dates from the time of Augustus, you reach the **Antiquarium of the Forum of Augustus**. This contains sculpture and fragments of great interest, notably a fine head of *Jupiter* and some exceptionally beautiful carved capitals.

Forum Boarium *(Foro Boario)*
Map 10I6.
A large but no longer precisely definable area between the Via di San Teodoro and the *Theatre of Marcellus* is where, in the earliest days after the foundation of Rome, the Forum Boarium or cattle market was situated. Nearer the river, the Forum Olitorium or fruit and vegetable market became established, and the whole area was soon studded with temples and public buildings. The remains of a Republican temple can be seen incorporated into the wall of the church of **San Nicola in Carcere**. Two other survivors are the *Temple of Vesta* and *Temple of Fortuna*

Virilis, which stand in the gardens opposite *Santa Maria in Cosmedin*.

Forum of Caesar *(Foro di Cesare)* 🏛
Via dei Fori Imperiali. Map 10/6.

Only about a third of the site of this great forum is open to view, the rest lying hidden beneath modern roads. It was originally in the shape of an elongated rectangle, lined by porticoes. Before the Battle of Pharsalus Julius Caesar vowed that if he defeated Pompey he would build a temple to Venus. The Goddess was supposed to have been the mother of Aeneas, hence the name **Temple of Venus Genetrix** (46BC). This stood at the NW end of the Forum and was famous for its sculptures of Venus, Caesar and Cleopatra and for its superlative collection of Greek paintings.

Three fragmented columns, re-erected on the site, are almost all that remains of this noble treasure-house. Stripped of their sumptuous marble facing, they can convey little idea of the vast and splendidly ornate Corinthian portico that once dominated the forum.

Forum of Nerva
This lies to the E of the *Forum of Augustus*, its ruins now largely concealed by modern streets and buildings.

Forum of Trajan *(Foro Traiano)* 🏛
Via dei Fori Imperiali. Map 10/6.

At the time of writing, the public are not allowed to visit the Forum of Trajan because of important restoration work. When open it is reached from the lower level of *Trajan's Markets*, but the site can also be viewed from above.

It is not easy to visualize the magnificence of Trajan's Forum, for what is left — a sunken area strewn with fractured marble architraves and columns — gives little clue to its original appearance. At the time of its construction and for centuries afterwards it was regarded as one of the architectural wonders of the world. The eastern emperor Constantius II, visiting Rome in 356, pronounced it unequalled in splendour, and references in the 6thC biography of Gregory the Great demonstrate that it was still in good repair at that time.

Designed by the renowned Greek architect Apollodorus of Damascus, it was built between 107 and 113. The complex consisted of a spacious **Forum**, and to the W of this the vast **Basilica Ulpia** (as large as *San Paolo fuori le Mura*), a double-aisled building with an apse at each end. Beyond this soared **Trajan's Column**, flanked on either side by the famous **Greek and Latin Libraries**. Finally, at the extreme NW end, rose the **Temple of Trajan**, one of the finest in Rome.

The reason why it is impossible today to see the whole extent of the ruined site is because of the major landscaping and roadworks that were initiated by Mussolini in 1932. The construction of **Via dei Fori Imperiali** was part of his grandiose plan to open up key areas of Rome for great state processions and parades. It cuts across and hides several of the ruins of the Imperial forums.

If the Italian authorities go ahead with their tentative plans to undo Mussolini's handiwork, then major portions of Trajan's Forum could be reopened to view. But it is hard to see how they would cope with the traffic problems that would result from the closure of this major road.

To the NE of the sunken area you can see the hemicycle of *Trajan's Markets*, built around the now-vanished semi-circular portico; but all that remains standing of the forum itself are some broken columns, belonging to the Basilica Ulpia, and Trajan's Column.

Trajan's Column (★) was so solidly constructed that it has remained remarkably unchanged from the time of its dedication to the Emperor in 113. It celebrated his defeat of the Dacians — the ancient inhabitants of modern Romania — and consists of a frieze of some 2,500 figures, which wind their way up the 38m-tall (125ft) column. It is the quality of the carving of these low-reliefs, and above all their historical interest, that make this one of the most fascinating monuments in Rome. It is a remarkable record of the military events of Trajan's campaign, a mine of information about weapons, uniforms, fortresses and siege operations. Originally the reliefs were painted in brilliant colours or gold, and this must have made it easier to pick out details with the naked eye. Inside, a spiral staircase (closed to the public) leads to the top of the column, which was once crowned by a statue of Trajan but is now surmounted by the figure of *St Peter* (1587).

Forum of Vespasian *(Foro di Vespasiano)*
Via dei Fori Imperiali. Map 10I6. Metropolitana: Colosseo.
Known as the Forum of Peace in ancient times, it was built from 71-75, following Vespasian's war against the Jews. Excavations have brought to light a shrine, some fallen columns, and the remains of a pavement. A large part of the building materials were spoils of the war. Most of the remains lie buried under the Via dei Fori Imperiali and connecting modern roads. By far the most interesting surviving part is the church of *Santi Cosma e Damiano*, which was formed by the conversion of one of the halls of the forum. To the N is the early 13thC **Torre dei Conti**, built by Innocent III (Lotario dei Conti di Segni). The tower was severely damaged by an earthquake in 1348, and only the lower section survives.

Fountain of the Bees *(Fontana delle Api)*
Piazza Barberini. Map 6G6. Metropolitana: Barberini.
This small fountain, on the N side of Piazza Barberini at the corner of Via Veneto, is one of Bernini's most delightful creations. It was constructed in 1644 to honour the 21st anniversary of Urban VIII's accession to the pontificate. Water splashes into a scallop shell where Barberini bees, alluding to the Pope's family, are seen taking a drink.

Fountain of the Four Rivers *(Fontana dei Fiumi)* ★
Piazza Navona. Map 7G7.
Bernini's power to surprise, his love of theatrical effect, are epitomized in this, the most famous of his many fountains. It was commissioned by Innocent X in 1648, as part of a plan to make the approach to the *Palazzo Pamphili* more impressive. Bernini incorporated an obelisk into the design, to create a monument sufficiently striking to stand out in the centre of the unusually long piazza. The reclining figures personify the four rivers, Nile, Ganges, Danube and Plate. These in turn symbolize the four known quarters of the world, Africa, Asia, Europe and America. Nile is shown covering his face, an allusion to the river's unknown source.

Popular belief puts a different interpretation on his gesture. It is said that Bernini intended to cast a slur on his rival Borromini's neighbouring church, *Sant' Agnese in Agone*, by representing Nile cowering in fear at the imminent collapse of the church. Likewise, Plate is said to be holding up his hand in a gesture of defence against the same facade. The church was in fact built several years after the fountain, and Borromini was only partly responsible for its design.

Galleria Colonna   This gallery was designed in the late 17thC to display the private collection of the Colonna family. It is part of the *Palazzo Colonna* and contains many outstanding works.

Galleria Doria Pamphili   This is the finest patrician art collection in Rome, and includes a number of important paintings and sculptures. It was assembled by the Doria family from the 16thC onwards and is part of the *Palazzo Doria*.

Galleria Nazionale d'Arte Antica *(National Gallery of Early Art)* 🏛 ☆
Via delle Quattro Fontane 🕾 *4814591. Map 7G7* 🔁 ✗ *Open Mon-Sat 9.15am-2pm, Sun 9.15am-1pm. Metropolitana: Barberini.*

The **Palazzo Barberini** is an imposing Baroque building begun in 1625 by Carlo Maderno and completed by Bernini in 1633. The eccentric top-floor windows on either side of the arcaded centre are the work of Borromini. The palace is the home of the earlier part of the National Art Collection — hence the somewhat misleading *antica* in the name of the gallery.

The pictures are not always to be found in the same rooms from year to year, so it is perhaps best to describe the most interesting in a roughly chronological order. The 15thC Florentines are represented by a triptych of the *Ascension, Pentecost, and Last Judgment* by Fra Angelico, and by two works by Filippo Lippi: these are the *Tarquinia Madonna* (1437) and an *Annunciation with Donors*, the one memorable for the ugliness of the Child, the other for the beauty of the Mother. Piero di Cosimo's *Mary Magdalen* is a bright and superbly finished picture, which shows a great love of detail in the treatment of hands and the book the Magdalen is reading. Following these come two pictures by Lorenzo Lotto, a *Portrait of a Young Man* and the *Mystic Marriage of St Catherine with Saints* (1524).

The ceiling of Room VII is decorated with a frescoed *Allegory of Divine Wisdom* by Andrea Sacchi, the great representative of 17thC Classicism in Rome. Close by is Raphael's *Fornarina* (☆), said to be a portrait of the baker's daughter who was his mistress, and by far the most famous picture in the collection.

Farther on are El Greco's remarkable *Nativity* and *Baptism of Christ*, with their spectacular lighting effects, and Tintoretto's *Christ and the Woman Taken in Adultery* (c. 1546). Then come Quentin Massy's *Portrait of Erasmus*, painted for Thomas More, a masterly study of dignity and composure, and Holbein's *Henry VIII*. The latter dates from about 1540, and shows him dressed in regal splendour for his marriage to Anne of Cleves.

Pietro da Cortona's masterpiece, the frescoed *Allegory of Divine Providence* (☆), decorates the ceiling of the Salone, the main room of the palace. Painted between 1638-39, it is a glorification of the Barberini family and of Urban VIII, who was pope at the time. The Barberini bees are clearly visible in the centre of the design. The sheer exuberance of the invention may seem excessive to some, but there can be few paintings that convey the virtuosity of the Baroque so forcefully.

In addition to the glories of Palazzo Barberini, the 17thC and 18thC paintings at the *Palazzo Corsini* also come under the aegis of the Galleria Nazionale d'Arte Antica.

Galleria Nazionale d'Arte Moderna *(National Gallery of Modern Art)*
Viale delle Belle Arti 131 ☎ 802751. Map 6E6 ▨ ☻ Open Tues-Sat 9am-2pm, Wed-Fri 3-7.30pm, Sun 9am-1pm. Closed Mon.

Modern Italian art tends to be overshadowed by the achievements of earlier ages. As a result, despite a commanding position at the top of the *Villa Borghese*, this gallery does not get the attention it deserves. The vast collection of 19thC works includes many uninspiring efforts by worthy academicians, so not all the rooms are of equal interest, although the cool romanticism of Francesco Hayez (Room IV) and brilliant colouring of the Italian Impressionists, or *Macchiaioli*, in Room VIII are worth investigating.

The most celebrated of the modern Italian painters represented are the Futurist Umberto Boccioni and the metaphysical Giorgio de' Chirico. There are also works by major 20thC foreign painters and sculptors, including Max Ernst, Henry Moore and Jackson Pollock.

The 20thC section is undergoing complete redecoration and reorganization at present and is therefore closed, and only a few works from the collection are on show in the large central hall. When the section reopens, the gallery should be rejuvenated.

Galleria Spada A small but select family collection, in the *Palazzo Spada*.

Gesù ▥ ✝ ☆
Corso Vittorio Emanuele. Map 10l6.
This impressive Jesuit church was built between 1568 and 1575 and became a model for Counter-Reformation churches all over Europe. The facade by Giacomo della Porta and interior by Vignola were equally influential. The decoration of the interior is exceptionally rich, with sumptuous details in coloured marble and lapis lazuli.

The major work of art is Giovanni Battista Gaulli's superb fresco of the *Triumph of the Name of Jesus* on the vault of the nave, which dates from about a century after the completion of the church. Gaulli, also called Baciccia, was a colleague of Bernini and his exuberant style is very similar, albeit on a two-dimensional level. The other great attraction of the interior is the **Chapel of St Ignatius Loyola** by Andrea Pozzo (1696-1700), irresistibly excessive in its opulence.

Ghetto
Lungotevere dei Cenci. Map 9l5.
In 1556, during the pontificate of Paul IV, the Jews of Rome were confined to a very restricted area s of the Via del Portico d'Ottavia. They were forbidden to own land or practise in one of the professions, and these and other restrictions added to their poverty and misery, as did the overcrowding. Relief of a sort came only after 1870. It is in this area, on the banks of the Tiber, that the **Synagogue** (1904) is situated.

Imperial Forums

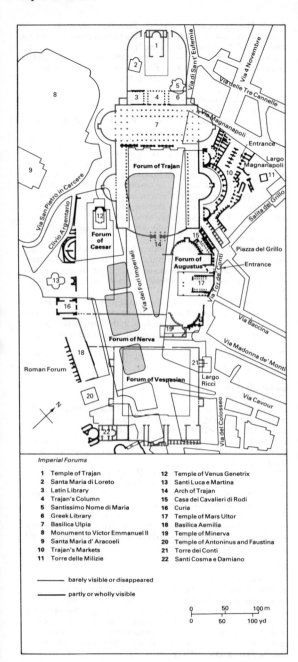

Imperial Forums

1	Temple of Trajan	12	Temple of Venus Genetrix
2	Santa Maria di Loreto	13	Santi Luca e Martina
3	Latin Library	14	Arch of Trajan
4	Trajan's Column	15	Casa dei Cavalieri di Rodi
5	Santissimo Nome di Maria	16	Curia
6	Greek Library	17	Temple of Mars Ultor
7	Basilica Ulpia	18	Basilica Aemilia
8	Monument to Victor Emmanuel II	19	Temple of Minerva
9	Santa Maria d' Aracoeli	20	Temple of Antoninus and Faustina
10	Trajan's Markets	21	Torre dei Conti
11	Torre delle Milizie	22	Santi Cosma e Damiano

—— barely visible or disappeared

━━ partly or wholly visible

0   50   100 m

0   50   100 yd

Imperial Forums   Towards the end of the Republic, it became clear that the *Roman Forum* was no longer able to accommodate the administrative and commercial life of the city. Julius Caesar acquired land to the N of the Forum for a new complex that became known as the *Forum of Caesar*. His great-nephew Octavian, later the Emperor Augustus, continued the expansion N, with the *Forum of Augustus*. The next Imperial forum was built by Vespasian and called the Forum of Peace, although it is now known as the *Forum of Vespasian*. Later emperors added the **Forum of Nerva** (of which the scant remains can be viewed from the *Forum of Augustus* or from Via dei Fori Imperiali) and the *Forum of Trajan*, the largest and most splendid of all the Imperial forums.

Isola Tiberina *(Tiber Island)* ☆
Map 5I5.
The Tiber Island is situated mid-stream in the bend of the river as it sweeps past Trastevere on the right and the Cenci district on the left. It is joined to either bank by two ancient bridges, one of which — **Ponte Fabricio (☆)**, opposite the *Theatre of Marcellus* — is in a marvellous state of preservation considering it was built in 62BC. Crossing to the island from this side, you will see looming up on the left the severe lines of the medieval **Torre dei Caetani**, and on the right the bulky mass of the modern Hospital of the Fatebenefratelli, which literally translated means the "Do-good-brothers". The road leads into a small piazza, one of the most secluded and delightful spots in Rome, where the roar of traffic from either embankment is muffled by the old buildings and the sizeable church of *San Bartolomeo*.

The Tiber Island's association with medicine and healing is very ancient. It is likely that the church of San Bartolomeo was built on the site of the Temple of Aesculapius, the God of Healing. The temple was erected here after a serpent sacred to the god was brought to Rome from Epidaurus and reputedly brought the great plague of 291BC to an end. The serpent chose the island for its dwelling-place, and hence caused it to be consecrated to healing. In the Middle Ages, the faithful would spend the night under the church portico, hoping to be cured.

To reach Trastevere from the island you cross the Ponte Cestio, first built in 46BC and restored, using original material, in the 19thC.

Janiculum Hill *(Gianicolo)*
Map 4I3.
Set back from the W bank of the Tiber, the Janiculum rises to a height of 82m (270ft) at *Porta San Pancrazio*. From here, and especially from the path leading past Gallori's imposing **Garibaldi Monument** (1895), there is a superb view over the river towards the old city in the E. Immediately below you are the wooded slopes of the **Gianicolo park** (see *Rome for children*). The Janiculum takes its name from the god Janus, who in ancient times was believed to have founded a city here. It is not, however, one of the original Seven Hills of Rome.

Keats-Shelley Memorial
Piazza di Spagna ☎ 6784235. *Map 6G6* ▨ *Open Mon-Fri 9am-1pm, 2.30-5.30pm (June-Sept 3.30-6pm). Closed Sat, Sun, one week in Aug. Metropolitana: Spagna.*
In the house overlooking the *Spanish Steps* from the S are rooms once used by the poet John Keats and his friend Joseph

Severn. These now form a working library for students of Keats and Shelley, who both died in Italy. Leaving behind the hectic bustle of Piazza di Spagna, you climb the stairs to be greeted by a curator who will ask you to sign a visitors' book. Keats died here in 1821, aged 25, and during his last months he must have derived some pleasure from the animated scenes that were enacted under his bedroom window. A death-mask on display is a sad reminder of how high talent was cut short in its prime by tuberculosis. Keats is buried in the *Protestant Cemetery*.

Largo Argentina *(Largo di Torre Argentina)* ☆
Map 9I5.

This open space is named after the **Torre Argentina**, the handsome house with a loggia in the adjoining Via del Sudaria. The house was built in 1503 by Bishop Burckhardt of Strasbourg (then in the diocese of Argenturatum, from which the name derives), incorporating a tower already there.

For many centuries the Largo Argentina was densely overbuilt and it was not until 1926-30 that the houses on it were cleared to reveal four **Republican Temples**, among the earliest examples remaining in the city. They are well below the present street level and can be viewed from the railings above. Admittedly the remains are sparse, but you can see the clear outline of three temples and part of a fourth (not fully excavated).

In spite of the care and attention given to these excavations by scholars and archaeologists, surprisingly little is known about the temples — not even to which gods they were dedicated. Viewing them from the w, **temple D** on the left dates from around 200BC and **temple C** next to it is one or two centuries earlier. Next in line, **temple B** is the latest of the four. It is circular, with steep front steps. A few of the columns have been re-erected, but give little idea of the 18 magnificent travertine columns that once stood here, their Corinthian capitals luxuriously carved out of marble. **Temple A**, on the extreme right, was probably built in the 3rdC BC. A few standing columns remain, and the site now includes the ruins of a medieval church.

On the w side of the Largo is the 18thC facade of the **Teatro Argentina**, home of the Teatro di Roma theatre company. It was here that Rossini's *Barber of Seville* was booed at its first performance in 1816.

Lateran Palace *(Palazzo del Laterano)* ⌂
Piazza San Giovanni in Laterano. Map 11J9. Metropolitana: San Giovanni.

The original Lateran palace was the official residence of the popes until 1309 when they moved to Avignon. In the same year it was almost completely destroyed by fire and, when the popes returned to Rome in 1378, they transferred to the Vatican. In 1586 Sixtus V commissioned Domenico Fontana to rebuild the Lateran as a summer palace, and this is the building you can see today. It is a rather unsuccessful emulation of the *Palazzo Farnese*, lacking the inventiveness of its model and giving the impression of sheer size without grandeur. In fact, later popes preferred to make the *Palazzo del Quirinale* their summer residence, and the Lateran is now the seat of the Rome Vicariate.

Ludovisi Quarter *(Quartiere Ludovisi)*
Map 7G7. Metropolitana: Barberini.

This area is named after the now-vanished Villa Ludovisi, which succumbed to urban development at the end of the last century.

It is a smart residential enclave, lying to the w of Via Veneto, and boasts a number of expensive hotels.

Mamertine Prison
The prison where St Peter is said to have been held was later consecrated as the chapel of *San Pietro in Carcere*.

Mausoleum of Augustus *(Mausoleo di Augusto)* 🏛 ☆
Via di Ripetta. Map 6G5.

This great Imperial family tomb still retains much of its ancient dignity, its mellowed brickwork warmed by the sun and ringed with cypresses. The mausoleum was known in Classical times as the Augusteum, and the ground around it was laid out in groves and public walks. The entrance to the enormous circular drum was flanked by two pink obelisks, since removed to *Piazza del Quirinale* and Piazza dell' Esquilino (outside *Santa Maria Maggiore*). The drum itself was surmounted by an earthen tumulus, at the centre of which stood a colossal bronze statue of Augustus. We have no more precise details than these of the mausoleum's appearance, but it is possible that cypresses were planted in rings leading up to the top of the mound.

In the 12thC it was turned into a fortress by the Colonna family, a fate that also befell the Mausoleum of Hadrian when it was converted into the *Castel Sant' Angelo*. Later on, the Augusteum was transformed into an amphitheatre for bull-fighting, a sport that was not banned until 1829. At the end of the 19thC the building was in use as a circus and concert-hall, and it was not until 1926-36 that significant archaeological exploration was accomplished. Three niches were found, one of which must have contained the urn holding the ashes of the Emperor — who died in August, AD14 (the month named after him) — and of his wife Livia. The other niches contained the ashes of his sister Octavia and of his nephews Caius and Lucius Caesar. There is no admission, but you can walk round the deep perimeter path surrounding the building and get a glimpse of the interior through the entrance on the s side.

Mausoleum of Hadrian
This huge circular structure is better known as the *Castel Sant' Angelo*, following its conversion to a fortress from the 3rdC onwards.

Monument to Victor Emmanuel II *(Monumento Vittorio Emanuele II)*
Piazza Venezia. Map 10l6 📧

An enormous amount of time, expense and marble went into the construction of this gigantic memorial to the first king of a united Italy. The gleaming white mountain is strikingly out of character and scale with the neighbouring cityscape, and was aptly nicknamed the wedding cake by Allied troops in World War II. It has inevitably become something of a landmark. Designed by Giuseppe Sacconi, it took from 1885 to 1911 to construct. The **Tomb of the Unknown Soldier** is on the first level, at the foot of the **Altare della Patria** (Altar of the Fatherland) by Zanelli. From the top level, there are spectacular views across the entire city.

Moor Fountain *(Fontana del Moro)*
Piazza Navona. Map 6H5.

This attractive fountain at the s end of *Piazza Navona* is the work of Giacomo della Porta (1575). The central figure of the Moor grasping a dolphin was an addition by Giovanni Antonio Mari, from a design by Bernini (1654). The surrounding tritons are 19thC copies of the late 16thC originals.

Moses Fountain *(Fontana del Mosè)*
Piazza San Bernardo. Map 7G7. Metropolitana: Repubblica.
Also known as the Fontana dell' Acqua Felice, this is the first of the monumental Post-Renaissance fountains. Commissioned by Sixtus V in 1587 and designed by Domenico Fontana, it is in the form of a triumphal arch. In the side niches, scenes in high relief represent Joshua leading the Hebrews across the Jordan, and Aaron leading the Hebrews to drink. In the central niche stands the colossal figure of Moses, which Venturi called "the most shameful parody of Michelangelo's work in Rome". It was traditionally held to be by Prospero da Brescia, who was said to have died of grief following the derisive reception given to his work. In fact, he was only a collaborator of the true sculptor, Leonardo Sormani.

Museo Nazionale Romano This museum occupies part of the old Carthusian monastery that was built among the ruins of the *Baths of Diocletian*. It contains a superb collection of early Greek and Roman sculpture.

Museo Nazionale di Villa Giulia An important collection of Etruscan art, housed in Julius III's tranquil hilltop retreat, the *Villa Giulia*.

Museo di Palazzo Venezia This museum in the *Palazzo Venezia* contains some very fine tapestries, as well as a good collection of paintings, sculpture, ceramics, porcelain, silver and majolica.

Naiads' Fountain *(Fontana delle Naiadi)*
Piazza della Repubblica. Map 7G8. Metropolitana: Repubblica.
Realistically modelled on the curvaceous Vittoria Placidi, Mario Rutelli's fountain shocked prudish opinion at its inauguration in 1901, but is now regarded as the best of the modern fountains in Rome. It consists of four bronze groups, each representing a naiad grappling with a sea monster. The central male figure was added in 1912. The powerful spray and spectacular play of water can best be appreciated when the fountain is floodlit at night.

Nero's Golden House *(Domus Aurea)* ☆
Via Labicana 136. Map 11l8 🔲 *✗ compulsory. Open Tues-Sun 9am-1pm. Closed Mon. Metropolitana: Colosseo.*
Few ruins in Rome do less to inspire visions of the glories of ancient times than what remains of Nero's fabulous house. The rooms are dank and dark, the walls in places wet with condensation, but this gives a gloomy and false impression. The tyrant's house was once situated high up on a terrace, and its splendid chambers were light and airy. It is not possible to see anything like the whole extent of the original buildings, because succeeding emperors demolished large portions. Trajan, especially, swept away much of the original fabric in order to build his great Baths (104-109). He completely covered over the residential wing of the house — the part that has been excavated and can be seen today — to provide the foundations for libraries

and other recreational areas.

Nero's house was called golden because the main facade was entirely gilded. The building was of complex design, and the furnishings of the utmost luxury: coffered ivory ceilings concealed apertures that sprayed mists of scent on the rooms below, and the internal baths were supplied both with sea water and water from the sulphur springs. The architects were Severus and Celeres, and they lived up to their patron's most exotic expectations. Nero commissioned leading painters to execute murals, the most famous of which are from the hand of Fabullus. The discovery of these paintings in the 16thC caused tremendous excitement, and inspired the "grotesque" style of painted decoration, so called because they were found in underground rooms that were like grottoes or caves. The house was once filled with superb pieces of sculpture, and it is even possible that some of these still lie buried beneath later construction and have yet to come to light.

One of the few rooms that convey something of the original atmosphere is the famous domed **octagonal hall**, or dining room, where sumptuous banquets were once held. It is a beautifully proportioned room, which, according to Suetonius, "revolved slowly, day and night, in time with the heavens". Others describe a revolving table at which the reclining guests would not need to bestir themselves to reach for the dish of their choice. At one end of the room, cooling water cascaded over stepped tiles to a channel below, continuously refreshing the atmosphere.

The guided tour usually includes the **cryptoporticus**, frequented by Raphael and other 16thC artists who came to study the paintings. These are not easy to see (they are distinguished by their white backgrounds), but are fascinating examples of the Fourth Pompeian style.

Oratory Complex

Corso Vittorio Emanuele. Map 5H4.

The Congregation of the Oratory of St Philip Neri needed various buildings besides the *Chiesa Nuova*. These included a sacristy, living quarters, and a large library. Borromini began as co-architect with Paolo Maruscelli in 1637, but the latter soon resigned and left Borromini in sole charge of the project. In spite of the large scale of the task, progress was rapid, and by 1650 the programme was completed with the building of the **clock tower** overlooking Piazza dell' Orologio, the square to which it gave its name.

Standing in Piazza della Chiesa Nuova, you can admire Borromini's genius in the curving facade of the **Oratory of the Filippini** (✿). The design is a masterly play of convex and concave, topped by a strange, almost Gothic, broken pediment. The wealth and complexity of the detail make for an effect of great richness, all the more remarkable in that the material used is brick.

Palatine Hill *(Palatino)* 🏛 ✿

Via di San Gregorio ☎ 6790333. Entrance from E end of Roman Forum, S of Arch of Titus along Clivus Palatinus. Map 10J7 ▦ (combined with Roman Forum) ✗ with advance notice ◄€ Open Mon, Wed-Sat 9am-5pm, Tues, Sun 9am-2pm. Metropolitana: Colosseo.

At a height of approximately 50m (164ft), the Palatine provides an unusual combination of beauty and wilderness, the former provided by trees, shrubs and gardens, and the latter by complex archaeological remains, which are more than usually difficult to unravel. This is due to soil subsidence and structural weakness, which together prevent inspection of important buildings, and to current archaeological research, which cannot be disturbed. Yet the Palatine is well worth visiting, not only for the historical interest, but for the park-like atmosphere of its grassy enclaves. It is an ideal spot to have a picnic lunch in spring or summer.

The history of the Palatine precedes that of the *Roman Forum*, and it has been called the cradle of Roman civilization. It was here, according to legend, that Romulus in 753BC yoked oxen to a plough and traced the lines of the city boundaries. Whether or not that story is true, indisputable remains of Early Iron Age huts (9thC BC) have been found here.

During the years of the Republic, many prominent citizens such as Catullus and the orator Hortensius made their homes here. The air was fresher at this height, and the fine views made it popular. Their houses were concentrated in the area to the w known as the **Germalus**, one of the Palatine's three crests. Augustus was born in this desirable residential district, and having taken over Hortensius' house (later renamed the **House of Augustus**), he built the celebrated **Temple of Apollo**, one of the sumptuous edifices with which he surrounded his comparatively simple house. Incorporating a beautiful statue of Apollo by Scopas, the front of the temple was surmounted by a gilded chariot that reflected the rays of the sun. To the E of the House of Augustus are the remains of the **House of Livia** (★), now considered to be outbuildings of the first house and not the home of his widow.

Augustus was succeeded by Tiberius, and from this time

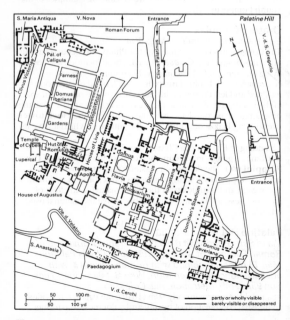

onwards the Palatine became the most important centre of political and social life in Rome. Tiberius levelled all the private houses to the NW of the Germalus, to build the **Domus Tiberiana**. Large remains of the sub-structure are visible, and some vaulted rooms are still preserved along the Clivus Victoriae. But most of the palace remains unexcavated beneath the beautiful **Farnese Gardens** (✰), which were laid out for Cardinal Alessandro Farnese in the 16thC and are still very well kept. The terrace of the gardens provides a splendid view over the Forum and towards the *Capitoline Hill*. Caligula extended the Domus towards the Roman Forum and built a bridge to connect it with the Capitol. The ruins of this later addition are known as the **Palace of Caligula**. On the E boundary of the Domus is the **cryptoporticus**, a vaulted passage decorated with splendid stuccoes; the originals are in the **Antiquarium** or Palatine museum.

To the SE of the *cryptoporticus* are the extensive ruins of the splendid palace complex built by Domitian at the end of the 1stC using the foremost architect of the time, Rabirius. The construction entailed levelling and merging large areas of the Palatine so that the original crests of the Germalus and **Palatium** (in the S) could no longer be distinguished. The complex consisted of the **Domus Flavia** (the official palace of the Imperial government, in the portico of which Domitian was later assassinated), the **Domus Augustana** (the emperor's residence) and **Domitian's Stadium**.

However, the best-preserved and most evocative ruins on the Palatine are those of the **Domus Severiana** (✰) or Palace of Septimius Severus. Its massively arcaded front was designed to form a monumental approach to the area, and hid the confusion of structures behind. The remains include part of the baths. Somewhere to the SE of the Domus stood Septimius Severus' **Septizodium**, a fabulous three-tiered structure that was notable for its profusion of fine marble columns.

On the extreme W of the Palatine are the **Paedagogium** (closed to the public) and ruined **Temple of Cybele**. In the same area you can see the so-called **hut of Romulus** (a genuine Iron Age hut) and the **Lupercal** — a sanctuary of the greatest antiquity, the grotto where Romulus and Remus were supposed to have been suckled by the wolf. The spot where the twins are reputed to have drifted ashore is near the entrance of the Lupercal.

Palazzo Barberini   A grand Baroque palace, built for Urban VIII, the Barberini pope, from 1625-33. Since 1949 it has been the home of the *Galleria Nazionale d'Arte Antica*, the earlier part of the National Art Collection.

Palazzo Borghese Ⅲ
Piazza Borghese. Map 6G5.
Due to its curious shape, this large and sumptuous palace is known to Romans as Il Cembalo (The Harpsichord). It was begun around 1560, possibly to a design by Vignola, and was later purchased by Cardinal Borghese (Paul V from 1605). He arranged for its completion by Flaminio Ponzio. It remains in the family's possession to this day. It was here that the Borghese's patronage of the arts resulted in a collection of enormous size and sybaritic indulgence. Founded by Paul's nephew, Cardinal Scipione Borghese, the collection was housed in the palace until 1891, when it was transferred to the Casino in the Villa Borghese, now known as the *Borghese Gallery*.

Palazzo Braschi   A fine late 18thC palace, which since 1952 has been the home of the *Rome Museum*.

Palazzo della Cancelleria ▥
Corso Vittorio Emanuele. Map 5H4.
One of the finest Renaissance palaces in Rome, this great building has a beautiful easterly facade overlooking the piazza named after it. The palace was built for Raffaele Riario, a nephew of Sixtus IV, between 1485 and 1513. Its authorship remains a mystery, although the design of the courtyard has often been attributed to Bramante. Incredibly, Riario won a third of the small fortune that the palace cost him to build in a single night's gambling with Francesco Cybo, nephew of Innocent VIII. The palace later became the Chancellery; hence its present name.

Palazzo Chigi ▥
Piazza Colonna. Map 6H6.
Facing *Piazza Colonna* and flanking Via del Corso, this palace was begun in 1580 for the Aldobrandini family, and only passed to the Chigi in 1659. The architects included Carlo Maderno and Felice della Greca. It once contained a famous library, started by Alexander VII (Fabio Chigi). This was presented to the Vatican by the State in 1923. The palace is closed to the public, but from the entrance you can glimpse the beautiful inner courtyard with its 17thC stuccoes and fountain bearing the Chigi coat-of-arms.

Palazzo Colonna ▥ ☆
Piazza Santi Apostoli ☎ 6794362. Entrance in Via della Pilotta 17. Map 6H6 ▥ gallery. Open Sat only, 9am-1pm. Closed Aug.
One of the largest and most sumptuous palaces in Rome, the Palazzo Colonna was begun by Martin V (1417-31), but the bulk of the present building dates from a refurbishment in 1730. The church of *Santi Apostoli* forms part of the complex but, apart from this, the **Galleria Colonna** is the only part of the palace that may be visited.

Antonio del Grande started work on the gallery in 1654, but when he died in 1671 the project was taken over by Girolamo Fontana. The gallery was finally opened in 1703 by Filippo Colonna. The frescoed ceiling depicts the *Battle of Lepanto*, at which a Colonna ancestor had distinguished himself, and is the work of Giovanni Coli and Filippo Gherardi. The large collection of pictures includes works by Rubens, Van Dyck, Tintoretto, Veronese, Paul Brill and Salvator Rosa. The undoubted masterpiece is Annibale Carracci's *Bean-eater*(☆), an early work of earthy realism by an artist whose later style was supremely Classical.

Palazzo Corsini ▥
Via della Lungara, 10. Map 5I4. Gallery ▥ Open Tues-Fri 9am-7pm, Sat 9am-2pm, Sun 9am-1pm. Closed Mon.
Originally built in the 15thC for Cardinal Domenico Riario, this palace later became the residence of Queen Christina of Sweden, who died here in 1689. From 1732-36, Ferdinando Fuga extensively remodelled the building, adding the long and elegant facade you can see today. The palace houses the art collection started by Cardinal Neri Corsini in the 18thC. Among the Italian works, two Caravaggios, *Narcissus*(☆) and *St John the Baptist*, are powerful dramatizations of youthful beauty, while Salvator Rosa's sensitive portrait study of his wife is an unusual work by

an artist better known for his landscapes. Paintings by foreign
artists who lived in Rome include three fine works by Le
Valentin, Caravaggio's most faithful follower, Rubens' *St
Sebastian*, an early work, and Van Dyck's *Rest on the Flight into
Egypt* (★), a tender meditation.

Palazzo Doria III ☆
*Via del Corso ☎ 6794365. Entrance in Piazza del Collegio
Romano la. Map 6H6 ▨ Gallery ▨ ✗ compulsory. Private
apartments. Open Tues, Fri, Sat, Sun 10am-1pm. Closed
Mon, Wed, Thurs.*

This building dates from 1435, but is a composite of many styles
and periods. The facade overlooking the Corso is by Gabriele
Valvassori (1734), that on the Via del Plebiscito by Paolo Ameli
(1743), and that on the Piazza del Collegio Romano by Antonio
del Grande (c.1660). They all mask older fabric, and the
foundations of the whole rest on ruins of Classical times. The
palace was founded by the cardinals of the nearby diocese of
Santa Maria in Via Lata, passed through the hands of the della
Rovere, the Aldobrandini and the Pamphili, and eventually
became the property of the Doria family.

The **Galleria Doria Pamphili** contains the Doria family's
important collection of paintings and *objets d'art* and is the finest
such patrician collection in Rome. It consists of four long
galleries surrounding a courtyard, with various rooms issuing
from them. The first gallery contains a number of outstanding
pictures: Titian's *Religion Succoured by Spain*; Correggio's
Allegory of Virtue; Raphael's *Double Portrait*; Titian's *Salome*; and
three paintings by Caravaggio, *St Mary Magdalen*, *The Rest on the
Flight into Egypt* and *St John the Baptist*. Also in this room is
Alessandro Algardi's bust of *Olimpia Maidalchini*, Innocent X's
formidable sister-in-law, and the butt of many pasquinades.

The sequence of small rooms at the end of the second gallery
contains several fine small-scale works, including Parmigianino's
Adoration of the Shepherds and *Virgin and Child* and Pieter
Brueghel the Elder's *Bay of Naples*. At the end of the third gallery
there is a small room containing Velàzquez's superb portrait of
Innocent X Pamphili (★), as well as a bust of the pope by
Bernini. The fourth gallery displays a magnificent collection of
17thC landscapes, including works by Claude Lorrain and
Gaspard Dughet, as well as Annibale Carracci's *Flight into Egypt*
and *Entombment*.

The **private apartments**, which are still lived in, contain some
very fine family portraits, of which the best is Sebastiano del
Piombo's portrait of *Andrea Doria* (★), the famous admiral. The
yellow salon, lined with superb Gobelins tapestries made for
Louis XV, is the most impressive of the interiors.

Palazzo Farnese III ☆
Piazza Farnese. Map 5I5.

The finest Renaissance palace in Rome is unfortunately no longer
open to the public. It was begun in 1514 for Cardinal Alessandro
Farnese (later Paul III) by the Florentine architect Antonio da
Sangallo the Younger. Antonio completed the main and side
facades but, just before his death in 1546, was forced to
relinquish the project to Michelangelo. The hand of the later
architect can be seen in the raised, strongly projecting cornice
and in the inverted emphasis of the recessed central window —
both typical Mannerist touches. The building was finally
completed by Giacomo della Porta in 1589. Since 1871 it has

been the French Embassy. Inside, the gallery has superb frescoes by Annibale Carracci featuring the *Triumph of Love* (1597-1604).

Palazzo Madama ▥
Corso del Rinascimento. Map 6H5.

A 16thC palace of fine proportions built for the Medici, this sumptuous building takes its name from Madama Margherita d'Austria, the illegitimate daughter of the Emperor Charles V. She was first married to Alessandro de' Medici, and subsequently to Ottavio Farnese. The grand facade dates from 1649, when the building was extended by Paolo Maruscelli. The palace is now the seat of the upper house of the Italian parliament.

Palazzo Massimo alle Colonne ▥
Corso Vittorio Emanuele. Map 5I5.

The present palace was designed by Baldassare Peruzzi to replace one destroyed in the Sack of Rome of 1527. It was completed after the architect's death in 1536. The curved facade was unique at this date, and Peruzzi's audacity is also evident in the squat columns of the entrance, which almost look as if they are being crushed by the weight of masonry above them. It is not possible to go inside, but you may manage to catch a glimpse of the stuccoed ceiling of the vestibule and even of the courtyard beyond. The princely family of the Massimo, one of the oldest in Rome, is recorded even earlier than the Colonna or the Orsini.

Palazzo di Montecitorio ▥
Piazza di Montecitorio. Map 6H5.

Designed by Bernini for Innocent X, who intended it for his Ludovisi relations, this palace was begun in 1650. After long interruptions it was completed by Carlo Fontana in 1994, as Innocent XII's Palace of Justice. Bernini's sober facade dominates the Piazza di Montecitorio, but this is no longer the main entrance to the palace. Since 1871, the building has been the seat of the lower house of the Italian parliament.

Palazzo Orsini   This extraordinary 16thC palace takes its
name from the family that owned it in the 18th and 19thC. It is remarkable for its unique position on top of the *Theatre of Marcellus*, built by Julius Caesar and Augustus.

Palazzo Pamphili ▥
Piazza Navona. Map 6H5.

The Pamphili Pope, Innocent X, reputed to be the ugliest man in Rome and the subject of a famous portrait by Velàzquez in the *Palazzo Doria*, commissioned this palace from Girolamo Rainaldi in 1644. It formed part of his grand design to make *Piazza Navona* a social focus, a plan that largely succeeded. The palace became the residence of the notorious Donna Olimpia, the Pope's sister-in-law. The interior, with splendid rooms designed by Borromini, and a long gallery frescoed by Pietro da Cortona with the *Story of Aeneas* (1651-54), is closed to the public. The building is now the Brazilian Embassy.

Palazzo Piccola Farnesina ▥ ☆
Corso Vittorio Emanuele 168 ☎ 6540848. Map 5I5
▨ *museum. Open Tues, Thurs 9am-2pm, 5-8pm, Wed, Fri, Sat 9am-2pm, Sun 9am-1pm. Closed Mon.*

This enchanting palace reveals the more intimate and personal side of Renaissance culture that is often overlooked amid so much grandeur. It was built for a French prelate called Thomas le Roy, who had acted as an intermediary between Francis I of France and Pope Leo X; the grateful King allowed le Roy to incorporate the fleur-de-lis into his coat of arms. These heraldic lilies appear on the outside of the palace, and their confusion with the Farnese lilies gave the palace its name. Begun in 1523, probably to a plan by Antonio da Sangallo the Younger, it was completed in 1546 by le Roy's nephew. The facade towards Corso Vittorio dates from around 1900, when the destruction of some old houses left this side of the palace exposed.

The building is now the property of the City of Rome and houses the **Barracco Museum**, a small but fine collection of Classical sculpture assembled by Baron Giovanni Barracco. The quality of the Greek pieces is particularly outstanding: note especially the *Head of a Woman* — a work of great sensitivity — and four low-relief panels showing warriors fighting.

Palazzo del Quirinale 🏛 ☆
Piazza del Quirinale ☎ *4699. Map* **6H6** 👁 ✗ *compulsory. Admission by appointment only, after written application to Ufficio Intendenza, Palazzo del Quirinale, 00137.*
Since 1947 the Quirinal has been the official residence of the Italian President. The splendid site was chosen originally by Cardinal Ippolito d'Este (the illegitimate son of Alfonso d'Este and Lucrezia Borgia) for his town palace, and the present building was begun in 1573 by Martino Longhi. A distinguished list of architects followed him, including Carlo Maderno, Bernini, Domenico Fontana and Ferdinando Fuga. In 1592 Clement VIII decided to move here from the supposedly unhealthy environs of the Vatican, and his example was followed by later popes. Before 1870, conclaves were held in the Cappella Paolina (built to the same dimensions as the Sistine Chapel), and the cardinals were housed in comfort in the long monotonous wing known as the *manica lunga*, or long sleeve, that overlooks Via del Quirinale.

The principal entrance is by Maderno; the tower to the left of it, on which the national flag flies, was added at the time of Urban VIII. The spacious inner court is by Fontana. Visitors are taken round the palace in small groups on a tour lasting about 1hr. One of the finest sights is Melozzo da Forlì's superb fresco on the grand staircase of *Christ in Glory* (☆) — a fragment from his masterpiece, formerly in the church of *Santi Apostoli*. At the top of the stairs, the **Sala Regia** and **Cappella Paolina** were both designed by Maderno. The fine stucco decoration in the latter is the work of Martino Ferabosco. The tour takes you through a series of sumptuously decorated apartments that include a chinoiserie salon and a room with magnificent Murano glass chandeliers. The **Cappella dell' Annunciata** has frescoes by Guido Reni, and the **Gallery of Alexander VII** has frescoes executed under the direction of Pietro da Cortona by a number of celebrated artists including Gaspard Dughet.

Palazzo Senatorio
This is the central building of the palace complex designed by Michelangelo for *Piazza del Campidoglio*. The original plans were somewhat modified after his death, and the facade was finally built by Giacomo della Porta and Girolamo Rainaldi (1582-1605).

Palazzo Spada 🏛 ☆
Piazza Capo di Ferro ☎ *6561158. Map* **5I5**. *Gallery* 🖼 *Open Tues-Sat 9am-2pm, Sun 9am-1pm. Closed Mon. State*

Palazzo Venezia

Rooms 🖼 ✗ *compulsory. Admission by appointment only, after written application to Ufficio Intendenza, Palazzo Spada, Piazza Capo di Ferro 13, 00186.*
Built for Cardinal Capo di Ferro in 1540, and once the property of Cardinal Bernardino Spada, this palace is remarkable for the exquisite stucco decoration that adorns the **facade** and **courtyard**, the work of Giulio Mazzoni (1556-60). In the course of renovating the palace, Borromini added a cunning illusionist design on the s side of the garden. The *trompe l'oeil* of the perspective gives the appearance of a long colonnade ending in a court, over which a Classical statue presides. In fact the colonnade is only about 9m (30ft) long, and the statue is tiny. It is a rare example of Borromini's less serious work. The palace is now the seat of the Council of State, but permission can be obtained to visit the very fine State Rooms when they are not in use.

The **Galleria Spada** is a small but select collection of works acquired by Cardinal Spada and later generations of his family. Of the four rooms, the first three are the most interesting. In Room I, you can compare the portraits of *Cardinal Bernardino Spada* by Guido Reni and Guercino. Room II has Titian's unfinished *Portrait of a Musician*, and Room III, Guercino's grandiose *Death of Dido* and Rubens' *Portrait of a Cardinal*. Also in Room III are Giovanni Battista Gaulli's *Triumph of the Name of Jesus*, a sketch for the ceiling of the **Gesù**, and *Christ and the Samaritan Women*, both showing his debt to Bernini.

Palazzo Venezia 🏛 ☆
Via del Plebiscito ☎ *6798865. Map 6|6. Museum* 🖼 *Open Tues-Sat 9am-2pm (Thurs 9am-7pm), Sun 9am-2pm. Closed Mon. Garden Court* 🖼 ✗ *compulsory. Admission by appointment only, after written application to Ufficio Intendenza, Palazzo Venezia, Via del Plebiscito 1, 00186.*
Originally called the Palazzo di San Marco, the Palazzo Venezia was the first substantial Renaissance palace to be built in Rome. It was begun in about 1455 for Cardinal Barbo (later Paul II), but the identity of the architect remains in doubt. With the Palazzetto Venezia and the church of **San Marco**, it forms a large, unified complex.

One floor of the palace now houses the **Museo di Palazzo Venezia (Sezione Medioevale)**, a heterogeneous collection of medieval art, sculpture, ceramics, weaving, jewellery and other artifacts. Opened in May 1985, it is, for a Roman museum, strikingly modern, well lit and generously laid out. The finest exhibit is Nino Pisano's *Head of a Woman*.

The other treasures of Palazzo Venezia — its splendid Italian, German and Flemish tapestries and its Renaissance paintings — are still being rearranged and are not on show.

Special permission must be obtained to visit the beautiful **garden court**, with its unfinished 15thC loggia by Giuliano da Maiano and 18thC fountain, representing *The Marriage of Venice and the Sea*, by Carlo Monaldi.

Pantheon *(Temple of All the Gods)* 🏛 ★
Piazza della Rotonda. Map 6H5. Open Mon-Sat 9am-2pm, Sun 9am-1pm.
The Pantheon is the best preserved of all the ancient monuments of Rome. It has stood solidly and majestically for close on 2,000yrs, defying architectural change all around, and there is something comforting and reassuring about its very presence.

The building is particularly impressive after dark, when floodlighting emphasizes the grandeur of the 16 soaring monolithic granite columns, 12.5m (41ft) high. In front of the portico, and echoing its solemn statement, is Giacomo della Porta's **fountain** (1578), incorporating into its restrained design an **obelisk** of the time of Rameses II.

The Pantheon was built by the Emperor Hadrian between 119 and 128, despite the bold inscription on the pronaos stating *M. AGRIPPA L.F. COS TERTIUM FECIT* (Marcus Agrippa, son of Lucius, Consul for the third time, built this). Such modesty was typical of Hadrian. He refused to have his name inscribed on any of his buildings, even though they included the *Temple of Venus and Rome*, the greatest temple in the city, and an enormous and complex villa at Tivoli (see *Rome environs*). Agrippa in fact built the original Pantheon, which was destroyed by fire, and Hadrian must have wanted to perpetuate his name on the new building.

How was it that the Pantheon was saved from the fate of so many other ancient monuments of antiquity, which were used as quarries for grandiose building projects? The reason is that in 609 it was given by the Byzantine Emperor Phocas (in whose patrimony it was) to Boniface IV, who consecrated it as the church of Santa Maria and Martyres (the name being an allusion to the martyrs' bones that were transferred here from the catacombs).

However, desecration did take place. Sheets of gilded bronze were stripped from the dome (by Constans II in 655) and the bronze from the beams of the portico was removed for the making of the baldacchino of *Saint Peter's* (by Urban VIII) — two unforgivable acts of vandalism.

Moving through the portico, you reach the great **bronze doors** — the finest extant from antiquity — and pass into the interior. This is dominated by the huge **dome**, its surface coffered and carefully proportioned to give a subtle interplay of light and shade. The great central oculus is open to the skies, and on a typical Roman day the sun pours in, throwing a brilliant roundel of light against the marble interior. The dome has a superb span, 43m (142ft), wider than that of St Peter's — 42m (138ft) — and dwarfing St Paul's, London — 31m (101ft). It is equal in height to the width of the building, just one example of the harmonious proportions that áre in a large part responsible for the great beauty of the Pantheon.

The interior has changed little since ancient times. Although restored, the fine pavement retains its original design; and the great apse, the eight aedicules or shrines and the six recesses remain as before. The statues of the gods that once filled them have long since gone, and the building is now the burial place of two Italian kings — Victor Emmanuel II and Umberto I — and some of Italy's greatest artists, notably Raphael and Annibale Carracci.

Paola Fountain *(Fontana Paola)*
Via Garibaldi. Map 8J4.

This handsome Baroque fountain, with its monumental facade of five arches and six granite columns, was inspired by the earlier *Moses Fountain* in Piazza San Bernardo. It was built for Paul V between 1610-12, by Flaminio Ponzio assisted by Giovanni Fontana. It is supplied with water from the Acqua Paola aqueduct, which was constructed at the same time. The basin was added later, by Carlo Fontana (1690).

Piazza Bocca della Verità 🏛
Map 9J6.

This attractive garden square is overlooked by the Romanesque
bell tower of *Santa Maria in Cosmedin*, guardian of the
legendary **Bocca della Verità**, or Mouth of Truth, from which
the name derives. On the N side is the **Casa dei Crescenzi**,
which once belonged to one of the most powerful families in the
city. Like many other medieval buildings, it included Classical
fragments in its construction. The piazza also boasts the well-
preserved *Temple of Vesta* and *Temple of Fortuna Virilis*.

Piazza del Campidoglio 🏛 ☆
Map 10I6 ◁€

This imposing palace complex centres on the ancient ridge or
asylum between the twin summits of the *Capitoline Hill*, where
the Capitol of ancient Rome once stood. It is the architectural
masterpiece of Michelangelo, who organized the space and was
responsible for the basic design of the palaces. The buildings
gradually come into view as you ascend the gentle flight of steps
known as **La Cordonata**. In front of you is the **Palazzo
Senatorio** (built over the remains of the ancient **Tabularium**,
where the state archives are kept), with the **Palazzo Nuovo** and
Palazzo dei Conservatori to left and right (the last two
comprise the *Capitoline Museums*). On either side of the steps
at the entrance to the square stand the colossal Roman statues of
the *Dioscuri*, the horse-tamers Castor and Pollux. There is a
similar pair in *Piazza del Quirinale*.

   The magnificent bronze equestrian statue that used to stand in
the centre of the piazza has been temporarily removed for
security reasons, and will eventually be replaced by a facsimile. It
represents the *Emperor Marcus Aurelius* (☆) but was believed in
the Middle Ages to show the first Christian Emperor, Constantine,
a fact which may explain its survival. It once stood in front of the
Lateran Palace, but was moved here by order of Paul III, and
against the wishes of Michelangelo, who then designed its base.

Piazza Campo dei Fiori
Map 5I5.

Rich in historical associations and local colour, this is one of the
most interesting and delightful of Rome's many piazzas. It is first
and foremost a market place, with makeshift stalls selling
flowers, fruit and vegetables (see *Shopping*). In the SE corner is
the **Palazzo Pio**, partly incorporating the ancient Theatre of
Pompey (though none of it is now visible). It is hard to believe
that these peaceful surroundings were once the scene of public
executions (the diarist John Evelyn witnessed one in 1644) and
that the figure of *Giordano Bruno* in the centre of the piazza is a
memorial to his death by burning in 1600, for heresy. Yet before
this date Campo dei Fiori was a place of fashion, with some of
the best-known inns in Rome. Now boasting two hotels, and
with several trattorie in close proximity, it has perhaps regained
its former character.

Piazza Colonna
Map 6H6.

This fine central square is dominated by the *Column of Marcus
Aurelius* and is overlooked by the *Palazzo Chigi* to the N and
the **Palazzo Wedekind** to the W. The 19thC facade of the
Palazzo Wedekind incorporates 16 splendid Ionic columns from
a Classical building at Veio.

Piazza della Minerva
Map 6H5.

Tucked away in the heart of the old city, this little square is dominated by the plain brick facade of *Santa Maria sopra Minerva*. It was in the immediate vicinity that the Temple of Minerva originally stood. In front of the church is Bernini's charming *Elephant Supporting an Obelisk*, which carries an inscription by Alexander VII, and was unveiled in 1667. The text states that a robust intelligence is needed to support the burdens of wisdom, and this group was the unusual and endearing consequence.

Piazza Navona ★
Map 6H5.

Considered by many to be the finest of Rome's piazzas, this elongated "square" occupies the site of the Circus Agonalis, the stadium of Domitian from which, via the corruption *n'Agona*, it derives its name. Used in ancient times for athletic contests and displays, the arena survived into the 17thC as a place for jousting and other tournaments. Innocent X transformed it into a Baroque masterpiece by commissioning Bernini's *Fountain of the Four Rivers* and the church of *Sant' Agnese in Agone*.

Rome in the 17thC loved pageantry, and the custom of partially flooding the piazza dates from this period. The nobility would have their carriages decked out in festive style, and then drive them through the water to the delight of the attendant crowds — a vestige of the *naumachia* or mock sea fights performed in Domitian's stadium. These water-pageants persisted into the mid-19thC, every weekend in Aug.

The surface of the square is now flat and can no longer accommodate artificial lakes, but the carnival spirit lingers on and crowds still congregate in this now pedestrian area. They gather around the three splendid fountains (to the s, the Baroque *Moor Fountain*, to the N, the **Neptune Fountain**, only completed in 1878) or stroll past the artists who exhibit their work along the edges of the piazza. Occasionally, a mild flutter among the crowd announces that an instant cartoonist has once again made his mark with a willing member of the public. A children's market is held here in Dec (see *Rome for children*).

Piazza del Popolo ☆
Map 6F5. Metropolitana: Flaminio.

The revolutionary design of this great oval piazza was largely the inspiration of Giuseppe Valadier (1816-24). He abandoned the traditional concept of the enclosed space, and opened up the E side to include the pine-covered slopes of the *Pincio* as a spectacular backcloth. At the SE corner are two small Baroque churches — **Santa Maria di Montesanto** and **Santa Maria dei Miracoli** — both begun by Rainaldi and completed by Bernini and Carlo Fontana. They divide the three streets that lead into the piazza from the s: Via del Babuino, Via del Corso and Via di Ripetta.

In the centre stands one of the obelisks salvaged and re-erected by Sixtus V, to serve as a landmark for pilgrims to the Holy City. Beyond the obelisk is the impressive **Porta del Popolo**, marking the entrance to the city from Via Flaminia. It was commissioned by Pius IV in 1561, but the facade overlooking the piazza was added by Bernini in 1655, to mark the entry of Queen Christina of Sweden. Next to this, standing sideways onto the centre of the piazza and therefore easily missed, is the important church of

Santa Maria del Popolo. Towards Via del Babuino and Via di Ripetta are two fashionable cafés, **Canova** and **Rosati** (see *Bars, cafés and ice-cream shops*).

Piazza del Quirinale
Map 6H6 ◁⊱

This hilltop piazza, with its splendid view over the city, is dominated by the great mass of the *Palazzo del Quirinale*, the official residence of the President, and in the centre by the great stone figures of the *Dioscuri*, the horse-tamers Castor and Pollux. The statues are Roman copies of Greek originals and once adorned the Baths of Constantine. An obelisk from the *Mausoleum of Augustus* and a 19thC fountain complete the group.

Piazza San Pietro *(St Peter's Square)* ★
Map 4H3.

Signalling the approach to the greatest church in Christendom, Bernini's piazza is a masterpiece of architectural planning. The free-standing, oval colonnade is four columns deep, and above it, 140 statues of saints are silhouetted against the sky. In the centre of the piazza stands the first obelisk to be re-erected in modern times. Sixtus V ordered it to be brought here from the s side of the basilica, and the task was achieved by Domenico Fontana in 1586, with the assistance of some 900 men, 140 horses and 44 windlasses.

On either side of the obelisk, which was originally brought to Rome by Caligula, are two spectacular fountains, one by Carlo Maderno (1613), the other by Carlo Fontana (1677). In this magnificent setting, huge, enthusiastic crowds of Romans and pilgrims from all over the world gather on Christmas Day and Easter Sun to receive the Pope's blessing (see *Papal audiences*, p15, in *Basic information*).

Piazza di Spagna ☆
Map 6G6. Metropolitana: Spagna.

This colourful square with its palm trees and flower barrows is named after the **Palazzo di Spagna** in the SW corner, which was built in the early 17thC as the residence of the Spanish ambassador to the Vatican. At about the same time, the piazza became a centre for tourists and expatriates and has remained so ever since. The list of illustrious Europeans who have stayed or lived in the immediate vicinity is prodigious: Wagner, Liszt, Balzac, Stendhal, Rubens, Tennyson, Byron and Keats, to name but a few.

For many, the Piazza di Spagna is still the heart of Rome, if not the centre. Radiating from it are the smartest shopping streets in the city. Via Condotti and Via Frattina are both now thankfully banned to traffic, but one should beware at the intersections with other streets, where cars are still allowed to cross. Via delle Carrozze takes its name from the long-distance touring carriages that were maintained and parked here.

At the S end of the piazza, the great stairway known as the *Spanish Steps* sweeps up majestically to the Baroque church of *Trinità dei Monti*.

Flanking the Spanish Steps is the *Keats-Shelley Memorial*, the house where Keats died. **Babington's Tea Rooms** is a favourite haunt on hot summer days, and, just down Via Condotti, the **Caffè Greco** is another notable establishment (see *Bars, cafés and ice-cream shops* for both).

Pinacoteca   This simply means "picture gallery" but usually refers to the **Pinacoteca (Vaticana)** in the *Vatican Museums*. There is another in the *Capitoline Museums*, known as the **Pinacoteca Capitolina**.

Pincio ☆
Piazza del Popolo. Map 6F5 ◀ Metropolitana: Flaminio.
These popular music gardens were laid out by Giuseppe Valadier in 1809-14, on the site originally occupied by the formal terraced Gardens of Lucullus (1stC). The land was later owned by the Pinci family (4thC), whence the name derives. The gardens adjoin the public park of the *Villa Borghese* to the N and E and the private gardens of the *Villa Medici* to the SE. The winding paths of the Pincio are a favourite strolling place, particularly at weekends, and the view from the terrace at the top is justly celebrated. This is at its most spectacular in the early evening, when you can see the dome of *Saint Peter's* and the western skyline silhouetted against the sunset.

Ponte Sant' Angelo ☆
Map 5H4.
Unquestionably the most beautiful of Rome's ancient bridges, the Ponte Sant' Angelo has spanned the muddy waters of the Tiber for nearly 2,000yrs. It connects the old city with the *Castel Sant' Angelo*, formerly the **Mausoleum of Hadrian**. The parapets are adorned by statues of *St Peter* and *St Paul* (1530) and ten angels in a splendid variety of poses, from the school of Bernini (1668). The three central arches belong to the original bridge, the Pons Aelius, built by Hadrian in 133-134. The original outer arches had to be replaced in 1892-94 after the widening of the river caused by the building of the Lungotevere embankment. The bridge is now barred to traffic.

Porta Maggiore Ⅲ
Piazza di Porta Maggiore. Map 11I10. Metropolitana: Manzoni.
Originally the Porta Prenestina, this solemn Imperial structure was erected in 52 by Claudius as a gateway at the intersection of the Via Prenestina and the Via Labicana. Its two lofty arches carried the conduits of the Aqua Claudia and Anio Novus, two of the finest Roman aqueducts. The gateway was not incorporated into the *Aurelian Wall* until 272-279, which explains the contrast between its light travertine and the brick of the Wall.

Porta Pia
Via XX Settembre. Map 7F8. Museum ▣ Open Tues and Thurs only, 9am-1pm.
Commissioned by Pius IV in 1561, this historic gateway was one of Michelangelo's last works but was reconstructed in 1853-61 by Virginio Vespignani, who was also responsible for the outer face. It was through breaches made in the adjacent walls that the armies of a united Italy entered Rome in 1870. Inside the gateway building, the **Museo Storico dei Bersaglieri** contains military memorabilia.

Porta Portese Ⅲ
Via Portuense. Map 9K5.
The present gateway is an early 17thC replacement of the ancient Porta Portuensis. A large and lively market is held here on Sun mornings (see *Shopping*).

Porta San Pancrazio
Janiculum Hill. Map 8J4.
High up on the Janiculum Hill, the Porta San Pancrazio featured
dramatically in the defence of the Roman Republic in 1849, when
soldiers of Garibaldi's legion withstood charge after charge by
numerically superior French forces until, weeks later, they were
compelled to give away. The gateway was rebuilt in 1854. It was
once known as the Porta Aurelia, since it marked the beginning
of the Via Aurelia of antiquity. Today the Via Aurelia Antica starts
about 200m (220yds) to the w of the gateway.

Porta San Paolo 🏛
Piazza di Porta San Paolo. Map 10L6. Museum 🔲 *Open
Tues, Sat only 9am-1pm. Metropolitana: Piramide.*
In antiquity this great fortified gateway was called the Porta
Ostiense. It now takes its name from the basilica of *San Paolo
fuori le Mura*, to which it leads. Sturdy defensive towers built in
the 6thC flank the gate. The structure was restored on the outer
side by Honorius in 402, but the inner face is basically still the
same as when Aurelian built it in the 3rdC. Inside the massive
gateway building, the **Museo della Via Ostiense** provides a
foretaste of a visit to the ruins of the port of Ostia Antica (see
Rome environs).

Porta San Sebastiano 🏛
Via di Porta San Sebastiano. Map 11L8.
This magnificent gateway is the best preserved and most
impressive of any in the *Aurelian Wall*. Known as the Porta
Appia in antiquity (replacing the earlier Porta Capena in the
Servian Wall), it was reconstructed in the early 5thC by the
Emperor Honorius, and restored by Belisarius and Narses in the
6thC. The gate is flanked by two imposing towers.

Portico of Octavia *(Portico d'Ottavia)* 🏛
Via del Portico d'Ottavia. Map 5I5.
This once-impressive portico was originally built by Quintus
Caecilius Metellus in 146BC. It was reconstructed by Augustus
between 27 and 23BC and dedicated to his sister Octavia, and
restored again in AD203 by Septimius Severus. It originally
consisted of about 300 columns set in a large, double-
colonnaded rectangle, and enclosed temples dedicated to Jupiter
and Juno, as well as numerous pieces of Greek sculpture. Inside
now is the church of **Sant' Angelo in Pescheria**, where Cola di
Rienzo and his followers assembled prior to their ill-fated seizure
of the Capitol (1347). Looking at the surviving monumental
entrance, you can see how the balance has been upset by the
brick relieving arch that was added in the Middle Ages to replace
two of the elegant Corinthian columns. Nearby, and in the **Via
del Portico d' Ottavia**, are several medieval and early
Renaissance houses.

Pre-Constantinian Necropolis The site, discovered in
1940 underneath the **Vatican Grottoes**, beneath *St Peter's*,
contains a simple monument believed to mark St Peter's grave.

Protestant Cemetery *(Cimitero Protestante)*
*Via Caio Cestio 6. Map 9L6. Open 8-11.30am, 3.20-5.30pm.
Metropolitana: Piramide. To gain entry, ring bell at the
gate.*
Close to the *Pyramid of Caius Cestius* and the *Porta San*

Paolo, this cemetery is divided into two parts, the **Old Cemetery** and the **New Cemetery**. Many famous people were laid to rest here: in the Old Cemetery, the English poet John Keats, who died in 1821, and his friend Joseph Severn; and in the New, Percy Bysshe Shelley, who died by drowning in 1822, Edward Trelawney (died 1881) and John Addington Symonds (died 1893). Keats' tombstone bears the inscription *Here lies one whose name was writ in water*, words that the poet himself had asked to be included. The house he and Severn once stayed in, overlooking the *Spanish Steps*, is now converted into the *Keats-Shelley Memorial*.

Pyramid of Caius Cestius *(Piramide di Caio Cestio)* ▥

Piazzale Ostiense. Map 9L6. Metropolitana: Piramide.
This solemn structure, faced in white marble and standing just outside the *Porta San Paolo*, is the tomb of Caius Cestius, praetor and tribune of the people. He died in 12BC, and his grandiose tomb monument stands 27m (88ft) high, which is small by Egyptian standards, but impressive enough in Rome.

Quattro Fontane *(Four Fountains)*
Via delle Quattro Fontane. Map 7H7. Metropolitana: Barberini.
At the crossroads on the highest point of the *Quirinal Hill*, four lazily-splashing Baroque fountains fit neatly into four corner niches (1588-93). The figures represent the Tiber, the Arno, Diana and Juno. On a clear day, the famous quadrilateral view takes in three distant obelisks — in *Piazza del Quirinale* and in front of *Trinità dei Monti* and *Santa Maria Maggiore* — as well as *Porta Pia*.

Quirinal Hill *(Quirinale)*
Map 6H6.
The highest of the seven ancient hills of Rome, the Quirinal was originally a Sabine settlement. Its name derives either from a temple of Quirinus (the name given to Romulus after his deification) or from Cures, the town from which the Sabines are supposed to have come. The summit is now crowned by the obelisk of *Piazza del Quirinale*.

Raphael Stanze
Almost as famous as the **Sistine Chapel**, these frescoed apartments are the second greatest draw of the *Vatican Museums*. The decorative scheme of the second room, the **Stanza della Segnatura**, includes Raphael's masterpiece, the *School of Athens*.

Roman Forum *(Foro Romano)* ▥ ★
Via dei Fori Imperiali. Map 10I6 ▨ (combined with Palatine Hill) ✗ with advance notice. Open Wed-Sat, Mon 9am-5pm, Tues, Sun 9am-2pm. Begin by viewing Forum from Via del Campidoglio, off Piazza del Campidoglio. Then enter Forum from Via dei Fori Imperiali (opposite Via Cavour).
To visit the Forum for the first time even with some knowledge of its history can be something of a disappointment. You will find areas cordoned off for archaeological research, and arches and columns undergoing restoration, veiled in scaffolding and green netting. Shattered temples and basilicas lie scattered over the ground in apparently random heaps; columns stand here and there in isolation, only occasionally linked by fragmentary

architraves. In fact, the remains of the Forum are not nearly as haphazard as they appear at first sight.

It is helpful to start with an overview of the general layout, from the terrace in Via del Campidoglio. However, before attempting to single out any individual features, it is worth remembering that the gradual development of the Forum spanned a period of more than 1,000yrs. In the earliest times, before the peace between Romulus and the Sabine leader Titus Tatius, said to have come to pass in 753BC, the area now comprising the Forum was little more than a marshy plain between the *Capitoline Hill* and *Palatine Hill*, choked by debris from the primitive settlements on the hills. These consisted mainly of shepherds' huts, and it was only when the population began to become more sophisticated — shepherds turning into farmers and finally soldier-farmers — that the comparatively large area of flat, albeit marshy, land became desirable for the erection of uncomplicated, easily defensible buildings. Tradition has it that the earliest monuments, such as the Curia and the Temple of Vesta, can be credited to the time of the kings. And it is to the last of the kings that Livy gives credit for canalizing the stagnant waters underground.

The development of the site fulfilled a variety of purposes, political, legal and mercantile. But above all, it was the obvious place to build temples. Long after less crucial activities had dispersed to other locations, the Forum remained the special home of religious worship, with the Temple of Vesta as the symbolic centre of such activity. A large central area, roughly rectangular in shape, was consecrated but kept unenclosed, and buildings and temples were erected around it. This is where the farmer-soldiers gathered to sell their produce, when the Forum was in the true sense of the word a market place, with rows of shops on either side. In the course of time, however, this mercantile character was lost, the traders were banished from the exclusive area, and the first steps were taken to make the Forum respectable and solemn, with the construction of civil buildings known as basilicas.

Now looking down from your vantage point on the Capitoline Hill, you can see immediately beneath you the 12 surviving columns of the **Portico of the Dii Consentes**, built by the Flavian emperors to honour the 12 principal Roman gods. To your left are three fine Corinthian columns supporting a fragmentary architrave, all that remains of the **Temple of Vespasian**, built by Domitian to honour his father. Beyond this stood the **Temple of Concord**, founded in the 4thC BC to celebrate the conclusion of peace between patricians and plebs, and reconstructed by Tiberius in the early 1stC AD. It was later used as a museum of art, housing Greek sculptures and paintings, but now only part of the pavement remains.

Still in the foreground to your left, you can see the **Arch of Septimius Severus** (★). This well-proportioned, highly-decorated triumphal arch was raised by the Senate to celebrate the tenth anniversary of Septimius Severus' accession to the throne (203), and to honour his victories over the Parthians, Arabians, and Assyrians. Included in the original inscription were the names of his sons Caracalla and Geta, but when Caracalla subsequently murdered his brother, Geta's name was replaced by a further inscription in praise of Caracalla. The holes made for the original lettering are still visible. The arch had an enormous influence on monumental architecture, acting as a prototype for the *Arch of Constantine*, and thence for many others both

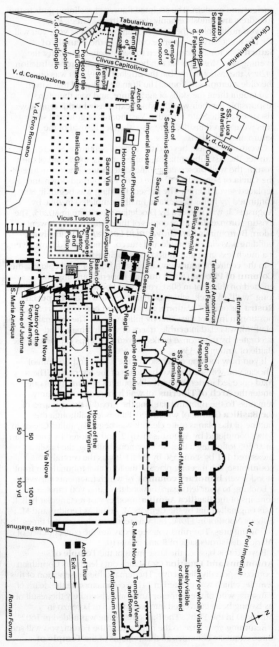

ancient and modern. The sculpted figures of reclining gods in the spandrels are almost certainly derived from a Greek idea.

If you now look to the right and almost ahead of you, you will see the eight surviving granite columns of the **Temple of Saturn** — a romantic ruin seen to best advantage against the evening sky. Most of what can be seen today is a reconstruction (42BC), the last of many, but the original (c. 497BC) was one of the oldest temples in Rome. The Romans believed that Saturn had taught them the skills of agriculture, and was therefore responsible for their wealth, which explains why this temple was also used as the State Treasury. Vast hoards of gold and silver bars were stored inside. Here also, the Dec festival of the Saturnalia took place.

Over to the far left, beyond the Arch of Septimius Severus, you can see the last substantial monument at this, the w end of the Forum: the well-preserved if somewhat austere brick structure of the **Curia** or Senate House. The Curia was burned down and replaced several times. The present building was begun in 80BC, continued by Julius Caesar and finally completed in 29BC by Augustus. It was restored by Diocletian after a fire in AD283. The existing bronze doors are copies of the originals, which went to adorn Borromini's *San Giovanni in Laterano*. Originally the building was clad in marble and stucco, which would have given it a much less grim and uniform appearance than now.

In the centre of your view, and just in front of a tall column, the **Column of Phocas** (taken from an Imperial building and erected on this spot in 608), you should be able to make out the long "wall" of brick, which is all that remains of the **Imperial Rostra**, or orators' platform. It was moved here from its earlier position in front of the Curia by Julius Caesar. The original platform was clad in marble, traces of which remain, and decorated by the bronze beaks or *rostra* of ships captured at the Battle of Antium in 338BC.

If you now look on either side of the Rostra and Column of Phocas you will see the two branches of the **Sacra Via**. The N road once led under the Arch of Septimius Severus, the s one under the **Arch of Tiberius**, of which there are only scanty remains. To the right and flanking the s road is the vast area of the **Basilica Giulia**, of which very little is left, although the outline of the plan is quite clear. It was begun by Julius Caesar in 54BC, completed by Augustus in AD12, and restored by Diocletian in AD305 following a fire. An enormous building, the basilica measured 101 by 49m (330 by 160ft). It was the central courthouse, the meeting place of the four civil tribunals. In front stood seven **honorary columns**, of which fragments survive.

Looking to your left again, beyond the Curia you can see the remains of the **Basilica Aemilia**, another vast rectangular hall. It was originally built by the Censors M. Aemilius Lepidus and M. Fulvius Nobilior in 179BC, but was reconstructed several times following fires. The ruins you see today are the consequence of Alaric's disastrous sack of Rome in AD410.

Beyond this basilica the large mass of the **Temple of Antoninus and Faustina** (✪) stands out clearly, its Corinthian portico especially distinctive. The remarkable preservation of this temple, which was erected in 141 to commemorate the death of Faustina, wife of the Emperor Antoninus, is entirely the result of its having been converted into a church (San Lorenzo in Miranda) in the 11thC. The Baroque facade was added in 1602.

Returning your gaze to the right side of the Forum, you will see three exquisite columns, all that remains of the **Temple of**

Castor and Pollux. Built originally in 484BC by Aulus Postumius, it commemorates the divine intervention of the heavenly twins at the Battle of Lake Regillus (499BC), which put an end to the hopes of the Tarquin dynasty of regaining sovereignty over Rome. The temple was rebuilt on several occasions, notably by Quintus Caecilius Metellus in 117BC and by Augustus in AD6.

The remaining large buildings cannot be made out clearly from this viewpoint, so the rest of the Forum is best seen at ground level. Entering from Via dei Fori Imperiali, you pass the Temple of Antoninus and Faustina on your left and the remains of the Basilica Aemilia on your right. Having reached the Sacra Via, you can see ahead of you the remains of the **Temple of Julius Caesar**, erected by Augustus in 29BC in honour of the deified Julius, over the spot where his body was cremated. To the left of this are the foundations of the **Regia**, the official residence of the Pontifex Maximus.

Turning left from here, past the Temple of Antoninus, and then right, you arrive at one of the most interesting places in the Forum, the circular **Temple of Vesta** and the adjoining **House of the Vestal Virgins**. The "house" was in fact more like a palace, with 50 rooms on the ground floor alone. Here the Vestal Virgins led a life of extreme simplicity, completely cut off from the world outside. The building was originally called the Atrium Vestali, because the rooms were designed to look inwards to the garden court. The court has regained some of its former beauty and serenity now that the pools have been repaired and filled, and the garden planted with roses and other flowers. The Vestal Virgins were obliged to dress simply and to honour a strict code of conduct, the breaking of which led to savage punishments. If they lost their virginity, they were buried alive. On the other hand, they possessed remarkable privileges, and could retire after 30yrs with a generous dowry from the state.

The most important of the Vestal Virgins' duties was to tend the sacred fire in the Temple of Vesta. The extinction of the fire was considered a national catastrophe, and the person held responsible could expect to be scourged by the Pontifex Maximus. The original temple was almost certainly made of wood, in the shape of the circular huts of the earliest settlements, and this distinctive shape was retained in all subsequent rebuildings. The present remains, which were assembled in 1930, are all that can be seen of the last reconstruction by Septimius Severus and his wife Julia Domna at the beginning of the 3rdC. Inside were housed the *pignora imperii*, the secret pledges of the duration of Rome, which included the *Palladium*, the statue of Pallas Athene that was reputedly saved from Troy by Aeneas. The exact nature of the *pignora imperii* was known only to the Vestal Virgins and the Pontifex Maximus.

Just to the w of the Temple of Vesta are the scanty remains of the **Arch of Augustus**, and to the s the path leads to the **Basin of Juturna**, the site of the spring where, according to legend, Castor and Pollux watered their horses after announcing the news of the victory at Lake Regillus. The square basin of the fountain that was subsequently built here is clearly visible. Just s of the basin is the restored **Shrine of Juturna**, goddess of the healing waters. Beyond is the **Oratory of the Forty Martyrs**, a converted 1stC building that contains remnants of 8thC frescoes recording the martyrdom of 40 Armenian soldiers under Diocletian. s of this is the oldest church in the Forum, **Santa Maria Antiqua**. It contains many remarkable early frescoes, but has been closed to the public for a long time and is likely to remain so. The straight road leading past Santa Maria Antiqua is the **Via Nova**, much of the surface of which still survives.

Now retrace your steps past the Temple of Vesta, bearing right into the main part of the Sacra Via. To your left, you will see the circular **Temple of Romulus**, a splendidly preserved 4thC brick construction dedicated to Romulus, the son of Maxentius, who died in his youth in 309 and was deified. The bronze doors are exceptionally well preserved. Behind is the *Forum of Vespasian*, in part of which stands a structure remodelled by Maxentius and later converted into the church of *Santi Cosma e Damiano*. It was originally perhaps the audience hall of the city prefect.

The Sacra Via continues (for long stretches virtually intact) past the great mass of the **Basilica of Maxentius (★)**, also known as the Basilica of Constantine, substantial parts of which have survived. This extraordinary building is of great intrinsic interest, but its sheer size has the effect of dwarfing its surroundings to an uncomfortable degree, and this must have been even more true when it was intact. The basilica was begun by Maxentius (306-312), and completed by Constantine along modified lines. In the vast vaulted structure of brick and concrete, covering an area of 100 by 65m (328 by 213ft), six enormous piers carried the three bays of the groined vault over the central area. The three extant rounded arches on the N side have been the inspiration of many architects from the Renaissance onwards. Here was a successful attempt to apply the construction methods of the great Roman baths to the building of a basilica.

The Sacra Via from this point veers slightly S, but passes quite close to the church of **Santa Maria Nova**, more commonly known as Santa Francesca Romana. The handsome Romanesque bell tower is visible from most parts of the Forum, and inside there is a fine 12thC mosaic of the *Madonna Enthroned with Saints*. In the adjacent 14thC cloisters is the **Antiquarium Forense** or Forum museum (*open 9am-noon*), containing sculptural fragments and reconstructions. The Sacra Via now leads directly to the **Arch of Titus (★)**, a beautifully proportioned triumphal arch erected in 81 to honour the victories of Titus and Vespasian in the Judaean War.

The arch is especially interesting for the sculptural reliefs on the inside surfaces, each representing part of the triumphal procession. On one side, the symbolic figure of Rome guides the Imperial quadriga; on the other, victorious soldiers bear the seven-branched candelabra and other spoils from the Temple of Jerusalem. High relief and superb animation make these friezes nothing less than masterpieces of Roman honorific sculpture.

From this point there is a way out of the Forum past the *Temple of Venus and Rome* in the direction of the *Colosseum*.

Rome Museum *(Museo di Roma)*

Piazza San Pantaleo ☎ 655880. Map 6H5 ▨ Now used only for temporary exhibitions, so check opening times. Details of exhibitions may be found in Il Messagero, Un Ospite di Roma and This Week in Rome.

Now housed in the late 18thC **Palazzo Braschi**, this museum was founded in 1930 to illustrate various aspects of Roman life from the Middle Ages onwards. Most of the paintings, sculptures and artifacts are therefore of socio-historic interest.

The entrance to the palace is impressive. At the foot of a

magnificent open staircase, probably designed by Valadier (1802-04), stands Francesco Mochi's colossal group of *Christ Baptized by St John* (1629-34). The exhibits are mainly on the first and second floors. Of particular interest are a number of paintings showing the great pageants of 16th and 17thC Rome. *Joust of the Saracen at Piazza Navona* is one of several canvasses recording famous tournaments, and *Festival at Palazzo Barberini for Christina of Sweden* depicts the colourful spectacle that the Barberini family laid on for the Queen in 1656. The collection also includes frescoes, removed from other palaces during the course of demolition, and, in the **Salone d'Onore**, some fine Gobelins tapestries. At street level, off the courtyard, stands **Pius IX's railway carriage**, constructed in Paris in 1857 for his journeys between Rome and Frascati.

Sant' Agnese in Agone 🏛 ✝ ☆
Piazza Navona. Map 6H5.

This church is often thought to be entirely the work of Borromini, but it in fact represents the saddest story of his career. It was begun by Girolamo and Carlo Rainaldi, father and son, in 1652, of whom Carlo contributed the most. Borromini was obliged to adapt the Rainaldi plan, but then Carlo was recalled in 1657, and the work was not completed as Borromini intended. His great rival Bernini also had a hand in the changes, and the result was a richer, more ornate interior and some modification in the exterior design.

Borromini's genius is most evident in the concave and elegant facade, with towers on either side that unify the front of the church and the dome. The towers, however, are the work of other hands, and were completed in 1666, when Bernini's pediment was added as a central feature.

The decoration inside is lavish, and contains some fine examples of High Baroque art, notably Ercole Ferrata's relief of the *Stoning of St Eremenziana*, Antonio Raggi's *Martyrdom of St Cecilia*, and the frescoes by Ciro Ferri in the dome and by Giovanni Battista Gaulli in the pendentives. Beneath the church is the heavily restored pre-Carolingian oratory containing Alessandro Algardi's last work, a marble relief of *The Miracle of the Hair of St Agnes*. This relates the traditional story of the miraculous growth of the saint's hair to cover her nakedness when she was thrown into a brothel after refusing to renounce her faith. Although there is little doubt that St Agnes was martyred close to this spot, her remains now lie buried under the basilica of *Santa' Agnese fuori le Mura*.

Sant' Agnese fuori le Mura 🏛 ✝ ☆
Via Nomentana ☎ 8320743. Map 13C4. Catacombs 🔲
✗ compulsory. Open Mon-Sat 9am-noon, 3-6pm, Sun 3-6pm. Bus 36 from Stazione Termini or 60 from Piazza Venezia or Piazza Barberini.

St Agnes was reputedly martyred in 304, during Diocletian's persecutions, and while it is thought that she was put to death on the spot where *Sant' Agnese in Agone* now stands in Piazza Navona, her remains almost certainly lie buried under this basilica, some 2.5km (1½ miles) from the city centre. The church is well worth visiting when combined with the catacombs and the nearby church of *Santa Costanza*.

The original church of Sant' Agnese fuori le Mura was built by Constantia, daughter or grand-daughter of the Emperor Constantine, in 342. It was constructed right into the side of the hill in order to be immediately above the saint's tomb, as is the present church, erected in the 7thC and most recently restored by Pius IX (1855-56). To enter the church, you descend a long shallow staircase, lined with fragments of inscriptions.

Inside, the 19thC restoration has not robbed the church of its Early Christian character. The 7thC mosaics are among the finest Byzantine works in Rome, and feature St Agnes in Byzantine court dress, with the sword of her martyrdom at her feet. Behind the tabernacle, the alabaster statue of the saint is an early 17thC restoration of a Classical figure. Over the altar there is a fine canopy dating from the same period. It is an octagonal dome, inlaid with coloured marble, supported by four slender antique porphyry columns.

The **catacombs of St Agnes** probably date from the late 3rdC. They are well preserved, and you can see numerous inscriptions as well as the burial niches or *loculi*, some of which remain intact. Visitors are taken round in small groups — a pleasant change from the massed guided tours of the more famous catacombs.

Sant' Agostino ▥ †
Piazza di Sant' Agostino. Map 6H5.

This church is one of the earliest examples of Renaissance architecture in Rome. After its plain facade, dating from 1479, the sumptuous 18thC interior comes as something of a surprise. Immediately to the right of the main door is the *Madonna del Parto*. This greatly venerated group was executed in 1521 by Jacopo Sansovino, and the left foot of the Madonna is now worn smooth by the attentions of countless devotees. Other outstanding artistic treasures are Caravaggio's *Madonna of Loreto* (✪) (1605), in the first chapel of the left aisle; Andrea Sansovino's *Madonna and Child with St Anne* (1512), which stands below Raphael's celebrated *Prophet Isaiah* (✪) (1512), by the third pillar on the N side of the nave; and the Byzantine *Madonna*, brought from Constantinople, above Bernini's high altar.

Sant' Andrea al Quirinale ▥ † ✪
Via del Quirinale. Map 7H7.

This exquisite little church with its elegantly curved facade was designed by Bernini and built between 1658-71 for Cardinal Camillo Pamphili, nephew of Innocent X. Entering, you find yourself in an oval church, faced by two pairs of magnificent pink and white marble columns that stand in front and on either side of the main altar. In an opening in the concave pediment above, St Andrew is seen soaring in space in a highly dramatic pose that is characteristic of Bernini, although the statue is in fact the work of his pupil Raggi. A clever touch is provided by the relatively great height of the dome, which creates the effect of a much larger church. A predominance of gilding gives a warmth to the whole interior.

Sant' Andrea della Valle ▥ †
Corso Vittorio Emanuele. Map 5I5.

Perhaps best known as the fictional setting of the first act of Puccini's *Tosca*, this large Baroque church was begun in 1591 by Giacomo della Porta and Francesco Grimaldi, and continued by Carlo Maderno from 1608. Maderno was responsible for the magnificent dome, largest in Rome after that of **Saint Peter's**, but the sumptuous facade was mainly the work of Carlo Rainaldi (1655-65). Inside, the church is vast, ornate and impersonal. Few people visit it, and the huge areas of marble seem almost wasted. However, the frescoes in the pendentives of the dome, by Domenichino (1624-28), are worth making a detour for. The painting of the dome itself was left to Domenichino's rival, Lanfranco.

Santi Apostoli 🏛 †

Piazza dei Santi Apostoli. Map ***6H6****.*

The original church was probably erected by Pelagius I in the 6thC, but the present structure is now a mixture of Renaissance, Baroque and Neoclassical styles. It was almost entirely rebuilt by Francesco Fontana (1702-08) and Carlo Fontana (1708-14), the latter continuing the work after his son's death. The majestic portico of nine arches, enclosing a Classical Roman relief, is the work of Baccio Pontelli and dates from the end of the 15thC, but the rest of the facade is by Valadier (1827). Inside, eight spirally fluted columns in the **Chapel of the Crucifix** (at the end of the s aisle) are the only remains of the original church. The present church contains a number of fine tombs of the della Rovere family, dating from the Renaissance, as well as the **Tomb of Clement XIV**, Canova's first work in Rome.

San Bartolomeo 🏛 †

Isola Tiberina. Map ***5I5****.*

Neither the 12thC tower rising above the *Isola Tiberina* nor the Classical 17thC facade give a true indication of the age of this church, which was founded at the end of the 10thC by Otto III. It was originally dedicated to St Adalbert and only became the church of St Bartholomew when the relics of the latter were transferred here. The columns in the nave are original, but because of its location the church has been damaged by flooding on several occasions, and substantial restorations have taken place. A unique feature is the small **marble well-head** of the 12thC, especially interesting because it is likely that the church was built over the site of the Temple of Aesculapius, the God of Healing. It is thought that there was a spring near the temple with healing properties.

San Carlo ai Catinari 🏛 †

Piazza Cairoli. Map ***5I5****.*

Rosato Rosati was the architect of this large and harmoniously proportioned Baroque church (1612-20), but he was not responsible for the handsome facade, added later by Giovanni Battista Soria (1635-38). Domenichino painted the *Cardinal Virtues* (★) in the pendentives of the dome (1630), but his is just one of the many famous names associated with the interior decoration. Paintings over the various altars of the church and in the sacristy include works by Mattia Preti, Andrea Sacchi, Giovanni Lanfranco, Pietro da Cortona and Guido Reni. The high altar was designed by Martino Longhi, and in the sacristy there is a **bronze crucifix** by Alessandro Algardi.

San Carlo alle Quattro Fontane 🏛 † ☆

Via del Quirinale. Map ***7H7****.*

Borromini's tiny church, familiarly known as San Carlino, is only a short distance away from Bernini's *Sant' Andrea al Quirinale*, and it is interesting to compare the two churches. The spontaneous warmth and exuberance of Bernini's style may be more immediately appealing, but the subtlety and complexity of Borromini is no less rewarding in time. Borromini had to deal with a restricted site at the corner of a crossroads, but he used the limited space to masterly effect. He built cloisters and lodgings for the adjacent monastery as well as the church, and his personal involvement with the project lasted from 1634 until his death in 1667.

Work on the church itself began in 1638, and the structure was complete by the following year. The basically oval design is achieved by means of highly sophisticated geometrical calculations. But this in no way produces a sense of heaviness. As you look up into the dome, which is divided into hexagonal, octagonal and cross-shaped coffers that diminish in size as they near the top, it seems suspended in space. Returning to earth, you can hardly fail to admire the fine detail of the Corinthian columns and the coolness of the gently curving ground-plan.

The slightly earlier cloisters are unusually confined, but show Borromini's customary originality and ingenuity. Even more remarkable is the facade of the church, which was begun only 2yrs before the architect's death, but follows his design. Shaking off all two-dimensional restraints, it is a triumph of concavities and convexities.

Santa Cecilia in Trastevere ⍓ ✝ ☆
Piazza di Santa Cecilia. Map 9J5⬛ convent. Open Tues, Thurs 10am-noon, Sun 11am-noon.
The church is approached through a beautiful enclosed garden with an ancient white marble vase in the centre. The facade of the church is the work of Ferdinando Fuga (1741), but the portico, incorporating Classical columns, is medieval. To the right is the fine 12thC campanile. As so often in Rome, the general outward character of the church gives no clue of its real age. Santa Cecilia was built by Paschal I between 817-824 on the site of a much earlier church, probably of the 5thC. Major restorations took place in 1725 and 1823. The latter drastically altered the character of the church, robbing it of any appearance of antiquity: Classical columns are now embedded in solid piers (for structural reasons), and the decoration is predominantly late Baroque.

The most famous work of art in the church is Stefano Maderno's touching and beautiful statue of the martyred *Santa Cecilia* (✰). The saint is shown lying on her side wrapped in a golden robe, just as she was found when her tomb was opened in 1599, at which time Maderno saw the body and made a drawing of it. St Cecilia was martyred in either the 3rd or 4thC. She came from a patrician family, as did her husband, St Valerian, who was also martyred. In Maderno's work you can see the cuts in her neck caused by the three blows of the executioner's sword that failed to kill her outright. St Cecilia is traditionally said to have invented the organ, and she is the patron saint of music.

The statue of the saint lies beneath the high altar, which is graced by an outstanding **canopy** by Arnolfo di Cambio (c. 1293). In the apse behind is a 9thC **mosaic**, similar in subject to a mosaic in one of Paschal's other churches, *Santa Prassede*, though not of such fine quality. Yet there is much to admire in this scene of St Peter and St Paul presenting St Cecilia and St Valerian to Christ, in the company of St Agatha and Pope Paschal (singled out by the square halo of the living).

The **convent** attached to the church contains a superb fresco of the *Last Judgment* (✰) by Pietro Cavallini, a contemporary of Giotto. This fragment dates from around 1293 and is without doubt Cavallini's masterpiece.

San Clemente 🏛 ✝ ☆

Via di San Giovanni in Laterano. Map 11J8 🔲 *lower church. Open Mon-Sat 9-11.30am, 3.30-6.30pm, Sun 10-11.30am, 3.30-6.30pm. Metropolitana: Colosseo.*

San Clemente is one of the best preserved of all the ancient sites in Rome, and is of exceptional interest. There are substantial remains here of a 1stC *domus* or palace and a 3rdC Mithraic temple, and above these two, of a 4thC church dedicated to St Clement. Above this, and making three levels in all, is the main church built in 1110-30. The whole complex site has been in the care of Irish Dominicans since 1677.

The **upper church** has a typical basilican plan with a nave and two aisles separated by antique columns, plain and fluted. The 12thC inlaid **pavement** is the lovely creation of the Cosmati, the name given to the celebrated mosaic workers of this period. Much of the marble-panelled **schola cantorum** dates from the 9thC and was brought from the lower church; so were the **pulpits**, one with an exquisitely-decorated Cosmatesque **candlestick**. The elegant **canopy** over the high altar may also have been taken from the lower church, at least in part.

One of the most beautiful features of the upper church is the superb mosaic in the apse, depicting the *Triumph of the Cross* (☆). Against a gold background, the Tree of Life — of which the Cross forms a part — thrusts out branches of curling leaves that fill the whole of the conch of the apse. It is a work of intense symbolism, with the Cross shown as a support for all life, both human and animal. There are many figures among the foliage — including the four Doctors of the Latin Church, Augustine, Ambrose, Gregory and Jerome — as well as exotic birds and animals. This fantastic work dates from the 12thC, but it is thought to have been inspired by the design of an earlier mosaic that once adorned the 4thC church below. The fresco beneath, representing *Christ and the Virgin Mary between the Twelve Apostles*, is of the 14thC.

Returning to the very beginning of the left aisle, you come upon the **Chapel of St Catherine**, with the earliest Renaissance paintings in Rome. It is famous for its **frescoes** (☆) by Masaccio's collaborator, Masolino da Panicale (c. 1428). The scenes feature events in the lives of St Catherine of Alexandria and St Ambrose, a ravishing *Annunciation* over the entrance arch, and a *Crucifixion* on the rear wall. The new interest in perspective and depth is apparent in these frescoes, but it is allied to a grace and lightness of touch that are not always found later on.

Off the right aisle is the entrance to the **lower church**. This has a wide nave interrupted by the foundations of the piers for the church above. Every effort has been made to preserve the frescoes, but they have faded badly as a result of exposure. Fortunately, copies were made at the time of their discovery when they were still well preserved following their concealment under layers of damp earth and rubble. The original frescoes, dating from the 9th-11thC, include the *Marriage at Cana*, the *Crucifixion* and the *Ascension*, as well as the later *Story of St Alexis* and *Story of Sisinnius*. The last is particularly interesting because it not only recounts an extremely picturesque legend from the life of St Clemente, but also contains some of the earliest examples of written Italian. Among the frescoes of interest in the right aisle are an 8th or 9thC *Madonna* and a 9th or 10thC *Christ*.

At the end of the left aisle, a staircase leads down to the level of the 1stC **domus** and 3rdC **Mithraic temple**. The *domus* was originally of palatial dimensions and has been only partly

excavated. The *triclinium* or banqueting hall of the temple was
used for the religious feasts of the Mithraic ritual. In the centre of
this room is a low-relief representing Mithras, the sun-god,
slaying a bull. The atmosphere is noticeably damp when you are
this deep underground, and you can hear the constant sound of
rushing water as an underground channel conveys water to the
nearby *Cloaca Maxima*.

Santi Cosma e Damiano 🏛 † ☆

Via dei Fori Imperiali. Map 10l6. Metropolitana: Colosseo.
This church was founded by Felix IV in 527, when one of the
halls of the *Forum of Vespasian* was converted for the purpose.
It was restored in 1632 under Urban VIII, at which time the
mosaics were also repaired. The church is reached from Via dei
Fori Imperiali through the cloisters of the adjoining convent, and
cannot be entered from the *Roman Forum*, even though the
Temple of Romulus serves as a vestibule.

The chief glories of the church are the 6thC **mosaics (☆)** of the
apse and triumphal arch. These were admired to such an extent
in the early centuries of the Roman Church that they became a
prototype for several other churches. The design and
craftsmanship are both of the highest order. In the apse, the
Saviour is seen standing in golden robes in the full glory of the
Risen Christ, against a dramatic dawn sky. On either side stand St
Peter and St Paul, with the two Arabian doctors (both martyred
under Diocletian) to whom the church is dedicated; beyond
them are St Theodore, and Felix (remade 1632) carrying his
church. Below, facing the central Lamb of God, are two lines of
sheep, six on either side, emerging from the towns of Bethlehem
and Jerusalem. On the triumphal arch, the Mystic Lamb is shown
surrounded by seven golden candlesticks, four angels, and the
symbols of the Evangelists. Below, the 24 Elders offer up crowns.

Santa Costanza 🏛 † ☆

*Via Nomentana. Map 13C4. Bus 36 from Stazione Termini
or 60 from Piazza Venezia or Piazza Barberini.*
Some 2.5km (1½ miles) from the city centre, this magnificent
Early Christian church is best combined with a visit to *Sant'
Agnese fuori le Mura*. It was originally built in the early 4thC as
a mausoleum for Constantia and Helena, daughters of the
Emperor Constantine. It was subsequently used as a baptistry,
and only consecrated as a church in 1254, when it was dedicated
to Santa Costanza, who in spite of her name had no connection
with Constantia.

The original building is preserved almost intact, with a dome
carried over the central space by 12 pairs of composite columns.
This colonnade is surrounded by a high barrel-vaulted
ambulatory, its vaults decorated with **mosaics (☆)** dating from
the 4thC that are unrivalled anywhere in Rome. The invention,
design and execution are of the highest order, the colours
exquisitely fresh. The background is white, unlike the gold of
Byzantine mosaics, and the content is often said to be purely
secular. Certainly there are no pictures of saints, but the images
were soon endowed with Christian significance, even if they
were originally pagan in mood.

The exceptional grace of line and richness of detail are what
make these mosaics so memorable, and their beauty can be
enjoyed whatever their meaning. It is a great shame that the
mosaics in the dome have not survived; 16thC drawings record
their content and give some idea of their quality.

The church contains a replica of Constantia's **sarcophagus** (the original is now in the *Vatican Museums*), an interesting example of Early Christian art that features reliefs of lambs, peacocks, and cherubs harvesting grapes.

Santa Croce in Gerusalemme 🏛 †
Piazza Santa Croce in Gerusalemme. Map 11J10.
Metropolitana: San Giovanni.

One of the seven pilgrim churches of Rome, it is said to have been built to house the precious relics of the True Cross brought to Rome from Jerusalem by St Helena, the mother of Constantine. The original church may have been a converted hall in the Palazzo Sessoriano (c.320), but the present building is much later. The Romanesque tower is one of the few visible signs of Lucius II's 12thC restoration, and the interior has been remodelled in a predominantly Baroque style. The main reminders of the church's great age are the eight large antique marble columns of the nave and the Cosmatesque pavement, a typical example of this late medieval inlay work. The church contains two notable works of art dating from the late 15thC. The unusual **fresco** in the apse of the *Invention of the True Cross* is probably by Antoniazzo Romano, while the fine **mosaic** (★) in the **Chapel of St Helena** (behind the high altar, to the right) was almost certainly designed by Melozzo da Forlì, with later intervention from Baldassare Peruzzi.

Santa Francesca Romana. The more familiar name of **Santa Maria Nova**, at the E end of the *Roman Forum*.

San Giovanni in Laterano *(St John Lateran)* 🏛 † ☆
Piazza di San Giovanni in Laterano. Map 11J9.
Metropolitana: San Giovanni.

This basilica is the cathedral church of Rome, the titular see of the Pope in his role as Bishop of Rome. It is the mother and head of all the churches of the city and of the world. Its name derives from the fact that it was built on the land of a Roman family called the Laterani. It was originally dedicated to Christ as Redeemer, and only later to St John the Baptist and St John the Evangelist. The 4thC basilica was five-aisled, but the church you see now dates from much later. The Lateran has suffered even more than the other ancient churches of Rome, having been sacked by the Vandals and destroyed by fire and earthquake a number of times. That it retains a distinctive character in spite of all it has gone through is one of its greatest charms.

The facade by the 18thC architect Alessandro Galilei was one of the few high points in a century of architectural mediocrity in Rome, but the full majesty of the basilica only becomes apparent as the visitor enters the building. (Inside the portico, notice the antique bronze central doors, removed from the **Curia** in the *Roman Forum*.) The **interior** (★) has its detractors, and it is certainly a shock to those who hanker for the splendours of Early Christian gold mosaics, but it is a masterpiece. Innocent X gave Borromini the task of restoring the church in 1646, and the work was completed by 1650. The old structure had become both unattractive and unsound, and Borromini's solution, which harmonized with the fine 16thC wooden ceiling, was to create a subtle and cool white and grey interior. It is the least exuberant but perhaps the most illustrious of all his inventions, a notable instance of artistic restraint and care.

Borromini preserved as much of the old church as he could,

including the earlier tombs and the 13thC apse **mosaic** by
Jacopo Torriti and Jacopo da Camerino. The mosaic was reset in
the 19thC, but the design retains much of its force. The basic
scheme with the head of Christ and the Cross may recall an
earlier design, but the figures of St Francis and St Anthony of
Padua date from the time of Nicholas IV (13thC) and refer to the
fact that the church was administered by Franciscans.

In the centre of the crossing stands the **papal altar**, at which
only the Pope can celebrate Mass, and above it soars the fine
Gothic **canopy** made for Urban V in 1367 by Giovanni di
Stefano. In front of the altar, at the foot of the steps to the
confessio, a bronze **tomb slab** records Martin V, who died in
1431. It is an early Renaissance work by Simone Ghini. A custom
has arisen of throwing coins onto the tomb.

Opinions may differ over the merits of Borromini's nave, but
few visitors to the Lateran fail to be enchanted by the adjoining
cloisters (★), reached through the last chapel of the left aisle.
They are by Jacopo and Pietro Vassalletto, among the most
brilliant of the Cosmati, the school of Roman marble- workers
and inlayers., whose work, renowned throughout Europe,
reached its high point in the mid-13thC, most notably in these
serene, tranquil cloisters. The mosaics on the small paired
columns, some straight, some twisted, are not all perfectly
preserved, but the atmosphere of the place is unaffected.
Fragmentary remains of the old basilica, including reliefs from
the marvellous **Tomb of Cardinal Annibaldi** by 13thC sculptor
Arnolfo di Cambio, only add to the slightly decaying charm.

Baptistry ⌸ ✝ ★

*Entrance from Piazza di San Giovanni in Laterano. Open 8am-noon,
4-6pm.*

This octagonal building is the sole remaining edifice of great
antiquity in the Lateran complex, and therefore of unusual
interest. It was built in the region of Sixtus III (432-440), to
replace an earlier (4thC) baptistry that had been sacked by the
Goths. Inside, eight porphyry columns enclose the font and
support eight marble columns that in turn bear the dome. The
font itself is an ancient basin of green Egyptian basalt, with a
17thC bronze cover. It was probably in this basin that the
Anglo-Saxon King Caedwalla was baptized in 689. The eight
Scenes from the Life of St John the Baptist around the drum of the
cupola are by Andrea Sacchi.

The sacristan will show you the chapels. The **Chapel of St
John the Baptist** was built by Hilarius (461-468). Its heavy
bronze doors, said to come from the *Baths of Caracalla*, make a
strangely musical sound when opened. The **Chapel of St
Rufina** contains 5thC **mosaics (★)** of exceptional beauty, with
branches and acanthus leaves entwined against a brilliant blue
background. Next there is the **Chapel of St Venantius**, built in
640 by John IV to house the relics of the martyrs of Salona in the
Adriatic. John, a Dalmatian, adorned the chapel with **Byzantine
mosaics**. They show a group of Dalmatian saints round the
Madonna, and include representations of Bethlehem and
Jerusalem. Finally, the **Chapel of St John the Evangelist**, also
built by Hilarius in the 5thC, has a vaulted roof decorated with
mosaics of the Holy Lamb surrounded by birds and flowers. The
bronze doors were made in 1196.

Scala Santa ⌸

Open 6am-12.30pm, 3-7pm (May-Sept 3.30-7pm).

The 28 marble steps of this staircase are traditionally said to have
come from Pilate's palace in Jerusalem and to have been

ascended by Christ during his trial. They were supposedly brought here by St Helena, the mother of Constantine. The steps now lead to the Chapel of the Sancta Sanctorum, and many devout Catholics will only ascend them on their knees, following the example of several popes from Gregory the Great (590-604) to Pius IX (1846-78). The Sancta Sanctorum was the private oratory of the popes until 1308 and was the only part of the original *Lateran Palace* to survive the devastating fire of that year. The chapel is not open to the public but can be seen through the grating. Here, on a panel of cedar wood, is the celebrated picture of Christ known as the *Acheiropoeton* ("not painted by human hands"). This icon probably dates from the 6thC and was believed to have been painted by angels.

Santi Giovanni e Paolo 🏛 ✝ ☆
Clivo di Scauro, off Via di San Gregorio. Map 10J7.
Metropolitana: Circo Massimo.

The present church is the last of several that have been built on this spot, following man-made or natural disasters. The original 4thC basilica was believed to have been built on the site of the house of John and Paul, two officers in Constantine's army, who were executed in 362 on the orders of Julian the Apostate. Their bodies are said to have been secretly buried in the house.

Following wanton destruction by Alaric in 410, an earthquake in 442 and demolition by Robert Guiscard in 1084, rebuilding began under Paschal II (1099-1118) and Adrian IV (1154-59). Adrian, who is perhaps better known as Nicholas Breakspear, was responsible for the fine **Romanesque campanile** (☆). He also built the handsome **portico** of six granite Ionic columns, and two marble Corinthian columns, as well as the beautiful **apse** with its arcaded loggia. The striking upper facade with its five arches on 3rdC columns belongs to the original 4thC basilica.

Inside, the church was remodelled in 1718, losing all trace of its ancient past. Of immeasurably greater interest is a visit below ground level to the **confessio** (☆), often held to be part of the house of John and Paul. (Ask the sacristan to take you down there.) Some pagan frescoes now visible were once covered up, presumably by the Christians who lived here. Among the religious frescoes, one is especially interesting. It shows two men a woman being beheaded, and must relate to the legend that Crispin, Crispinian and Benedicta were martyred after being found at the tomb of John and Paul.

San Gregorio Magno 🏛 ✝
Via di San Gregorio. Map 10J7. Metropolitana: Circo
Massimo.

A fine Baroque facade by Giovanni Battista Soria (1629-33) disguises the antiquity of this church's origins. Gregory II built a church here in the 8thC and dedicated it to his illustrious predecessor St Gregory the Great (590-604). According to tradition, the first Gregory turned his estate on this site into a Benedictine monastery in about 575, and it was from here that he is reputed to have sent St Augustine to convert England. Rebuildings in the 17th and 18thC have completely altered the original aspect of the church, but some interesting tombs and fragments remain. Especially notable is the beautiful altar of 1469 by Andrea Bregno in St Gregory's Chapel.

The sacristan will show you the **three chapels** set back from the gardens to the left of the church, dedicated to St Sylvia (Gregory's mother), St Andrew and St Barbara. An important group of early 17thC **frescoes** (★) includes Guido Reni's *Choir of Angels* and Domenichino's *Flagellation of St Andrew.*

Sant' Ignazio 🏛 †
Via Sant' Ignazio. Map 6H6.
This church was built to honour the canonization of Ignatius Loyola, founder of the Jesuit order. It was begun in 1626 to the designs of Padre Orazio Grassi. The imposing facade derives from the earlier *Gesù*, but the church is above all famed for the magnificence of its interior. Particularly remarkable are the **frescoes** (★) by Padre Andrea Pozzo, especially the ceiling painting representing the *Entry of St Ignatius into Paradise.* Even in a city where Baroque illusionism is relatively common in ceiling decoration, the *trompe l'oeil* effect here is outstanding. The best place from which to see the illusion is on a small disc in the pavement in the middle of the nave.

Sant' Ivo 🏛 † ☆
Corso del Rinascimento. Entrance from courtyard of Palazzo della Sapienza. Map 6H5. Open Sun morning only.
Like Borromini's other masterpiece, *San Carlo alle Quattro Fontane*, this church is more remarkable for the ingenuity of its design than for any grandeur of scale. Sant' Ivo was commissioned in 1642 and completed in 1660; it stands at the E end of the late 16thC **Palazzo della Sapienza**, beyond Giacomo della Porta's fine arcaded courtyard. Borromini's complex ground plan is based on the hexagon, with alternately pointed and rounded ends to the arms. This strange system produces a uniquely stylish and fanciful dome, but the external appearance of the church, with its bizarre spiralling lantern, is yet stranger.

San Lorenzo fuori le Mura 🏛 † ☆
Piazzale di San Lorenzo. Map 13C4. Bus 71 from Piazza San Silvestro, or 11 from Colosseo or Stazione Termini.
Lawrence was martyred in 258 and buried in this area. Constantine built the first church over the burial place (c.330), and Sixtus III added a second church (432-440), dedicated to the Virgin, backing onto the first. Constantine's church was enlarged and rebuilt by Pelagius II (579-590). The process of joining up the two churches by destroying the apses was begun by Adrian I in the 8thC, but the rebuilding of Sixtus' nave was not effected until the early 13thC by Honorius III — the date also of the campanile and splendid six-columned **portico** (★).

Today you see a remarkable hybrid of styles. The majestically proportioned nave, with its cool Ionic columns, is rich in Cosmatesque decoration. The **pavement**, **pulpits** (★) and **paschal candlestick** date from the early 13thC. The altar stands directly over the crypt containing the remains of St Lawrence, St Stephen and St Justin, and marking the level of the earlier church of Pelagius. Steps lead up to the 13thC choir inserted between Pelagius' arcades. The difference between the two churches is striking. Here, perfectly matched Corinthian columns of precious marble support a flat architrave with carved frieze. Above this are the slender columns and high arches of the gallery. High up on the triumphal arch an original (6thC) **mosaic** shows Pelagius, with Lawrence and other saints, offering his church to Christ.

At the beginning of the choir, the **canopy** over the *confessio* is a work of great beauty, signed by the master masons Johannes, Petrus, Angelus and Saxo (1148). Behind the high altar is an **episcopal throne** with fine Cosmatesque decoration, dating from the 13thC. A sacristan will accompany you to the 12thC **cloisters** and the **catacombs of St Cyriaca**.

Santi Luca e Martina 🏛 ✝

Via dei Fori Imperiali. Entrance from Clivus Argentarius. Map 10l6. Open Sun only 10-11am.

Built among the ruins of the *Roman Forum*, this church has a typically intriguing history. It consists of two churches, one of them now below ground level. The first was constructed in the 6thC over the remains of the Secretarium Senatus, the place where tribunals sat in judgment over senators, and was dedicated to St Martina. During the Renaissance it became the church of the Academy of St Luke, with a special significance for artists. But following the rediscovery of the body of St Martina, a new, upper church was built by Pietro da Cortona between 1634-50, on a Greek-cross plan. The imposing and complex facade is constructed of travertine and blends perfectly with the elegant dome. Altogether, it is Cortona's architectural masterpiece.

San Luigi dei Francesi 🏛 ✝ ☆

Piazza di San Luigi dei Francesi. Map 5H5.

This is the French national church in Rome. It was founded in 1518 by Cardinal Giulio de' Medici, later Clement VII, but was not completed until 1589. The fine Renaissance facade, attributed to Giacomo della Porta, has recently been restored. The richly marbled interior contains some outstanding works of art. In the second chapel on the right, **frescoes by Domenichino (★)** (1613-14) tell the *Story of St Cecilia* with great sensitivity and beauty. In the fifth chapel on the left are three **early Caravaggios (★)** (1597-1602). To the left is the *Calling of St Matthew*, a solemn scene in a realistic setting. The altarpiece shows *St Matthew and the Angel*, a subdued effort that replaced the more shocking first version that the clergy had rejected, and on the right is the melodramatic *Martyrdom of St Matthew*.

San Marco 🏛 ✝

Piazza Venezia. Map 9l6.

An elegant Renaissance facade, Romanesque bell tower and lush Baroque interior belie the origins of one of the oldest churches in Rome. The first church on the site was founded by St Marcus in 336 but was destroyed by fire, and a long history of reconstructions and destructions followed. The fine apse **mosaic (★)** dates from the time of Gregory IV's rebuilding in the first half of the 9thC. It shows Gregory offering his church to Christ in the company of St Mark the Evangelist and other saints. A further reconstruction was undertaken by Pietro Barbo, later Paul II, from 1455-71, and the beautiful gilded ceiling dates from then.

Santa Maria degli Angeli

This church, converted out of the central hall of the *Baths of Diocletian* by Michelangelo, was later reorientated and refurbished in Baroque style by Vanvitelli.

Santa Maria dell' Anima 🏛 ✝

Via dell' Anima. If closed, ring the bell at Piazza della Pace 20. Map 6H5.

This fine Renaissance church dates from 1500-23 and is the German national church in Rome. The impressive three-tiered facade is no longer attributed to Giuliano da Sangallo, nor the bell tower to Bramante, but the three pseudo-Classical **portals** are the undisputed work of Andrea Sansovino. The *Madonna between Two Souls*, in the tympanum of the middle portal, gave the church its name (literally, Madonna of the Soul).

Inside, the curious hall-like design is the work of an unknown northern architect. The church contains many notable works of art, including Giulio Romano's *Holy Family and Saints* (★) over the high altar. To the right of this is the imposing *Monument to Adrian VI* (Adrian Florenz of Utrecht, who reigned from 1522-23 and was the last non-Italian pope before John Paul II).

Santa Maria Antiqua   This is the oldest church in the *Roman Forum*. It contains important early Christian frescoes, but is unfortunately closed to the public.

Santa Maria d'Aracoeli ⚏ ✝ ✰
Piazza d'Aracoeli. Entrance from Piazza d'Aracoeli or from behind Palazzo Nuovo (Capitoline Museums). Map 9I6.
Ever since the beginnings of recorded history, the N summit of the *Capitoline Hill* has been one of the most revered places in Rome. It was originally the site of the *Arx* or citadel and of the early Roman Temple of Juno Moneta. And it was here, some three centuries later, that Augustus is said to have seen The Virgin and Child in a vision. The altar he raised to commemorate the event was called the *Ara Filii Dei* or *Ara Coeli* (Altar of Heaven), hence the name of the Franciscan church that was built here c.1260. It replaced a much smaller church called Santa Maria in Capitolio, dating from the 8thC.

Entrance is made up 122 steep marble steps from Piazza d'Aracoeli or through the s doorway, which is surmounted by a fine Cavallinesque mosaic of the *Virgin and Child with Two Angels*. The interior has an impressive assortment of Classical columns and a fine Cosmatesque **pavement**. These merit more attention than the highly ornate gilded ceiling that celebrates Marcantonio Colonna's *Victory at Lepanto* (1571).

The church is full of treasures. In the **Bufalini Chapel** at the beginning of the right aisle are superb **frescoes** (★) by Pinturicchio depicting the *Life of St Bernardino*. Facing the high altar are two **pulpits** reconstituted from a single pulpit by Lorenzo and Giacomo Cosma (c.1200). The **Savelli Chapel** in the s transept contains the splendid **tombs of Luca and Jacopo Savelli**. Jacopo became Honorius IV (1285-87), and the tomb of his father, Luca, consists of an ornate Roman sarcophagus surmounted by a statue. The high altar, which was once adorned with Raphael's *Madonna of Foligno*, now has a small 10thC Byzantine *Madonna*; in the N transept is the **Chapel of St Helena** or Cappella Santa. Its elegant eight-columned shrine (1605) is said to stand on the site of the altar erected by Augustus; at the end of this transept is the beautiful Cosmatesque **Monument to Cardinal Matteo d'Acquasparta** (died 1302), a general of the Franciscan order who was mentioned by Dante; the fresco of the *Madonna and Two Saints* is attributed to Pietro Cavallini.

To the right is the entrance to the **Chapel of the Holy Child**, sanctuary of the figure of the *Santo Bambino*, the most venerated object in the church. The Bambino is said to have been carved from the wood of one of the olive trees in the Garden of Gethsemane. He used to be taken to visit the sick and dying in an old brown coach, which would receive instant recognition and right of way. Today he is driven in a taxi, but still brings comfort to many people.

Santa Maria in Cosmedin 🏛 ✝ ☆
Piazza Bocca della Verità. Map 10J6 ❉

One of the most beautiful medieval churches in Rome, Santa
Maria in Cosmedin graces *Piazza Bocca della Verità* with a
handsome seven-storey bell tower and disarmingly simple
facade. The original church was constructed in the 6thC, making
use of materials from more ancient buildings. It was later
enlarged by Adrian I (772-795) and given to the Greek colony
that had grown up in the surrounding district. The church
became known as the *Schola Graeca* or Santa Maria in
Cosmedin — the latter name deriving from the Greek word
meaning ornament, and probably referring to Adrian's additions.
It was extensively remodelled in the 12thC.

Skilful restoration of the interior has revealed much of the
original fabric, and the antique marble columns, with their fine
Corinthian capitals, are especially worthy of attention. The
church is also rich in Cosmati marble work. The magnificent
pavement (☆) and **paschal candlestick** date from the 12thC,
while the bishop's throne is slightly later. The **canopy** is signed
and dated by Deodato di Cosma: *Deodatus Me Fecit 1294*. There
are fragments of 8thC mosaics in the **sacristy**, and the tiny **crypt**
can be visited if the sacristan is in attendance.

Outside, in the portico, is the notorious **Bocca della Verità** or
Mouth of Truth. This great, round, weatherbeaten face of stone
was used by the ancient Romans as a drain-cover. In the Middle
Ages a legend grew up that anyone who held his right hand in
the gaping mouth and told a lie would lose his fingers. Even to
this day, few young visitors can resist taking up the challenge.

Santa Maria in Domnica 🏛 ✝ ☆
*Via della Navicella. If closed, ring the bell at Piazza della
Navicella 5. Map 10J7.*

The present church dates from the reign of Paschal I (817-824),
and from restorations by Giovanni de' Medici (later Leo X) in the
early 16thC, but the foundation is far more ancient. The name is
possibly a corruption of *dominicum*, the word used in early
Christian times to describe a holy place. The church is also
known as Santa Maria della Navicella, after the fountain in the
form of a boat or *navicella* that stands outside. The fountain was
one of Leo X's embellishments.

The fine Renaissance facade, with its elegant Doric portico, is
by Andrea Sansovino (1513-14). Inside, the church is dominated
by Paschal I's glorious 9thC **mosaic** (☆) in the apse. The Virgin
and Child are shown enthroned in the midst of a flowering
paradise garden, with Paschal (wearing the square halo of the
living) kneeling at their feet. The wide nave has 18 grey granite
columns, with marble Corinthian capitals. The beautiful 16thC
frieze above the windows is by Perin del Vaga, from designs by
Giulio Romano. It includes the heraldic devices of yoke, lion and
triple ostrich plumes — all referring to the Medici family.

Santa Maria Maggiore 🏛 ✝ ★
*Piazza di Santa Maria Maggiore. Map 7H8. Metropolitana:
Cavour.*

One of the great patriarchal churches of Rome, Santa Maria
Maggiore crowns the N summit of the *Esquiline Hill* with its
monumental presence. But nothing on the outside prepares you
for the revelation of the near-perfect basilica within. The church
was built by Sixtus III in the years following the Council of
Ephesus in 431, and its dedication reflects the Council's

reverence for the cult of the Virgin. It is also known as the Basilica Liberiana or Santa Maria della Neve (Snow), following association with an earlier basilica built on the Esquiline by Liberius. The site of Liberius' church was indicated by a miraculous midsummer snowfall.

The beautifully proportioned nave, equal in width and height, is divided from the side aisles by 40 antique columns, 36 of marble and four of granite. The bases and capitals were added (and the columns streamlined) by Ferdinando Fuga (1741-43), who was also responsible for remodelling the external aspect of the church. The **ceiling** is coffered and reputedly gilded with the first gold to have reached Europe from America around the turn of the 16thC. The fine **Cosmatesque pavement** is a later reconstruction of the 12thC original.

The **nave mosaics** (✫) are hard to see without binoculars, but they are a fascinating series of narrative scenes from the Old Testament, marking the very end of the antique, Classical tradition. In total contrast are the **mosaics of the triumphal arch** (✫), also done for Sixtus III, but glistering with gold and Byzantine ceremony. The stories are of the *Infancy of Christ*, with the Virgin of the Annunciation shown as an empress, regally clothed and bejewelled, and the Christ Child receiving the gifts of the Magi in splendid isolation on a magnificent throne.

The conclusion of all these mosaics is the 13thC **apse mosaic** by Jacopo Torriti. It is no doubt based on a 5thC original, although the way of depicting the *Coronation of the Virgin*, with Mary and Christ seated side by side, is more modern. The best time to see the mosaics is at Mass on Sun and feast days, when they are illuminated. But this is only possible if you are attending a service.

Later periods added to the richness of the interior decoration, but not always entirely successfully. The two great Baroque showpieces are the **Sistine Chapel** and **Pauline Chapel**, off the right and left aisles respectively. Their sumptuous ornamentation is nothing less than excessive, even by Baroque standards. Beneath the Sistine Chapel is the ancient **Oratory of the Crib**, re-designed by Arnolfo di Cambio in the late 13thC. At the end of the right aisle is the **Tomb of Cardinal Consalvo Rodriguez** (died 1299) by Giovanni Cosma, a fine example of the superb marble inlay work for which all the Cosmati were famed.

The **campanile** of the basilica (1377) is the highest in Rome. In Piazza dell' Esquilino, to the N of the basilica, you can see an **obelisk** that originally stood in front of the *Mausoleum of Augustus*. It was brought here in 1587 by Sixtus V.

Santa Maria sopra Minerva ⌂ † ☆
Piazza della Minerva. Map 5H5.

Concealed behind a plain Renaissance facade is the only Gothic church in the whole of Rome. Founded in the 8thC on the site of a temple of Minerva, it was rebuilt in its present form c.1280, but has suffered a number of heavy restorations over the centuries, notably in the 15th and 19thC.

Some of the 20 chapels within are richly endowed with works of art. Most important is the **Carafa Chapel** in the right transept, containing superb **frescoes** (✫) by Botticelli's associate, Filippino Lippi (1488-92). Next to this, in the seventh chapel of the right aisle, is the fine Renaissance **Tomb of Diego de Coca** (1477) by Andrea Bregno, with a fresco by Melozzo da Forlì. In the next chapel along is Federico Barocci's typically dramatic *Last Supper* (1594). Turning back towards the choir, at the foot of the steps you will see Michelangelo's celebrated *Redeemer*(★) (1519-21), the suffering figure of Christ taking up the Cross. The second chapel to the left of the choir contains the **Tomb of Giovanni Arberini** (1473), incorporating a Roman sarcophagus with a low-relief of *Hercules and the Lion*. Finally, returning down the left aisle, you will see at the end the **Tomb of Francesco Tornabuoni** (1480), a masterpiece by Mino da Fiesole.

Santa Maria della Navicella   The name sometimes given to *Santa Maria in Domnica*, after the boat or *navicella* that forms the basis of the fountain outside the church.

Santa Maria Nova   This is more commonly known as Santa Francesca Romana. It stands at the E end of the *Roman Forum*, marked by a fine Romanesque bell tower.

Santa Maria della Pace Ⅲ ✝ ☆

Vicolo della Pace. Approach from Piazza Navona along Via Lorenesi. Church open only during Sun morning service. For entrance to cloisters, ring bell at Via Arco della Pace 5. Map 6H5.

This tiny church, lying tucked away among the narrow streets of the medieval city, is rich in artistic treasures. It was built by Sixtus IV (1471-84), possibly to a design of Baccio Pontelli, and restored under Alexander VII by Pietro da Cortona (1656-57). The beautiful Baroque facade, with its charming little semi-circular porch, dates from the time of the restoration.

Inside, the first chapel on the right contains the celebrated *Sibyls* (★) of Raphael, painted for the founder of the chapel, Agostino Chigi, in 1514. The four prophets above the sibyls form part of the same decorative scheme, but may have been executed by Raphael's former teacher, Timoteo Viti. Over the altar of the first chapel on the left there is a fresco by Baldassare Peruzzi of the *Madonna with Sts Bridget and Catherine and Cardinal Ponzetti*, and above the richly decorated **high altar** by Carlo Maderno (1611) is the much-venerated image of the *Madonna della Pace*, dating from the 15thC. The image is said to have bled on being struck by a stone and was the inspiration for Sixtus' church.

The cloisters (★) by Bramante (1500-04) were commissioned by Cardinal Oliviero Carafa. They are among the finest and most harmonious of Bramante's works in Rome, and consist of a simple arcade surmounted by an elegant colonnade.

Santa Maria del Popolo Ⅲ ✝ ☆

Piazza del Popolo. Map 6F5. Metropolitana: Flaminio.
Santa Maria del Popolo is one of the treasure houses of Rome, mainly thanks to the lavish patronage of the della Rovere popes Sixtus IV and Julius II. The handsome early Renaissance facade is probably by Andrea Bregno, but the light and spacious interior was remodelled by Bernini in the Baroque style.

Starting with the **first chapel** on the right, there are important frescoes by Pinturicchio (1485-89), especially the *Adoration of the Child* over the altar. Also worthy of note is the joint tomb of *Cardinal Cristoforo and Domenico della Rovere* (1477) by Bregno. The **second chapel**, rich in marble inlay, is the work of Carlo Fontana (1682-87). The altarpiece is by Carlo Maratta and shows the artist's debt to Raphael. The **third chapel** is frescoed by pupils of Pinturicchio and contains another fine tomb, that of

Bishop Girolamo Foscari (died 1463). A corridor leads from the s transept to the **sacristy**, where there is a marble altar by Bregno, commissioned in 1473 for the high altar by Rodrigo Borgia (later Alexander VI).

Returning to the main body of the church, you come to the apse behind the high altar. The architectural design is by Bramante, while the **frescoes (✰)** in the vault are probably Pinturicchio's finest works in Rome. They depict the *Coronation of the Virgin*, the *Evangelists*, the *Fathers of the Church* and the *Sibyls*. In one of the roundels St Luke can be seen putting the finishing touches to a framed icon of the Virgin. The apse contains two splendid tombs, of **Cardinal Girolamo Basso della Rovere** (1507) and **Cardinal Ascanio Sforza** (1505). Together they constitute Andrea Sansovino's greatest work.

The **high altar** itself is adorned with the *Madonna del Popolo*, a picture of great sanctity that is reputed to have been painted by St Luke, but probably dates from the 13thC.

The **first chapel of the left transept (✰)** houses two masterpieces by Caravaggio (1601-02), the *Conversion of St Paul* and the *Crucifixion of St Peter*, as well as the *Assumption of the Virgin* by Annibale Carracci. All three are wonderful paintings, but the drama and intensity of Caravaggio's lighting were utterly novel and remain unequalled. Continuing back down the nave, the penultimate chapel is the octagonal **Chigi Chapel (✰)**. Agostino Chigi was an immensely wealthy Sienese banker who only wanted the best, and he employed Raphael to build his chapel. Raphael was also to be responsible for all the decoration, including the mosaics and statues, but the project was not in fact completed until the 17thC.

The altarpiece of the *Birth of the Virgin* is by Sebastiano del Piombo, and the statues of *Habakkuk* (on the right of the altar) and *Daniel* (to the left of the entrance) are the work of Bernini. On either side are the remarkable pyramidal **tombs** of Agostino (1512) and his brother Sigismondo (1526).

Santa Maria in Trastevere 🏛 ✝ ✰
Piazza di Santa Maria in Trastevere. Map 8J4.

The exact origins of this undoubtedly ancient church have become confused over the centuries and it is not clear whether it was founded by St Calixtus in 221 or by St Julius in 341. All that is certain is that this was the first church in Rome to be dedicated to the Virgin.

The church was rebuilt by Innocent II (1130-43), at which time the Romanesque campanile was added, along with the mosaics in the upper apse. The portico was an even later addition (1702), by Carlo Fontana. The facade, with its heavily restored 12th-13th **mosaics**, has been the subject of much controversy. The Madonna is flanked by ten female figures, sometimes said to be the Wise and Foolish Virgins. The fact that only two of the figures carry unlighted lamps casts doubts on this interpretation, although it is just possible that three of the lamps could have been altered in restoration.

The **mosaics** inside the church are of exceptional quality. In the **upper apse (✰)** the Virgin is shown seated on the same throne as her Son; with one hand on her shoulder, he holds open a book to reveal the words *Veni, electa mea, et ponam in te thronum meum* ("Come, my chosen one, and I will place my throne in you"). These powerful figures are the work of Greek or Greek-trained Roman mosaic workers of the 12thC. The Virgin is crowned with a diadem of gold and jewels like a Byzantine

empress, and the faces are solemn yet marvellously expressive —
the hallmark of the Byzantine masters. Christ and the Virgin are
flanked by St Calixtus, St Lawrence, and Innocent II (presenting
his church) on one side, and by St Peter, St Cornelius, St Julius
and St Calepodius on the other.

In the **lower apse (★)** are six 13thC mosaics by Pietro
Cavallini, representing *Scenes from the Life of the Virgin*. They are
full of animation and vigour, and contrast splendidly with the
timeless majesty of the Byzantine work above. Below them,
another mosaic by Cavallini shows the donor, Bertoldo
Stefaneschi, being presented to the Virgin.

Santa Maria in Vallicella

This has long been known as
the *Chiesa Nuova* or "New Church", following a rebuilding in
the late 16thC by St Philip Neri.

Santa Maria della Vittoria ▥ ✝ ☆
Via XX Settembre. Map 7G7. Metropolitana: Repubblica.
This fine Baroque church was built by Carlo Maderno (1608-20),
and the façade added by Giovanni Battista Soria (1624-26). The
church was originally dedicated to St Paul, but was renamed after
the donation of a small picture known as the *Madonna della
Vittoria*. The picture had been discovered, unharmed, among the
ruins of the Castle of Prague after the defeat of Frederick of
Bohemia by the Catholic armies (1620).

The interior has some of the richest Baroque decoration in the
whole of Rome, and Bernini's extraordinary **Cornaro Chapel**
(★) is the main showpiece (last chapel on the left). The
commission gave him a wonderful opportunity to indulge his
love of the dramatic and to combine his gifts in architecture,
sculpture and painting. The work was begun after the Venetian
Cardinal Federigo Cornaro settled in Rome in 1644. Bernini had
the novel idea of grouping eight members of the Cornaro family
in recesses on either side of the chapel, so that they look as if
they are in boxes at the theatre (although in fact theatre boxes
only came into existence later). The scene they are witnessing is
the *Ecstasy of St Teresa*, as her heart is pierced by the fiery arrow
of Divine Love. In her own words, "It was the sweetest caressing
of the soul by God." Bernini shows her swooning, her arms limp,
her mouth half open, the weightlessness of her body conveyed
by the multitudinous folds of her billowing drapery. The work
has received almost equal amounts of praise and criticism, but is
now accepted as one of Bernini's most characteristic and notable
achievements.

Santa Martina e Luca

This church was originally
dedicated to St Martina and later became associated with St
Luke. It is better known as the church of *Santi Luca e Martina*.

San Paolo fuori le Mura ▥ ✝ ☆
*Via Ostiense. Map 12D3. Cloisters open 9am-1pm, 3-6pm.
Metropolitana: San Paolo Basilica.*
St Paul was beheaded at Aquae Salviae (now Tre Fontane), some
3km (2 miles) s of where this great basilica now stands. His
remains were wrapped in linen and handed over to a pious
Roman matron, Lucina, who had the body buried in her family
tomb just off the Via Ostiense. Here a *martyrium* or memorial
chapel was built, which drew large numbers of pilgrims. Two
and a half centuries later, Constantine had the body encased in a
double sarcophagus of marble and bronze and built the first

Saint Peter's

church here. In time even this became inadequate to contain the huge crowds that flocked to the martyr's shrine, and in 385 plans were drawn up by Valentinian II for a new basilica, as an offering from himself and his two co-emperors, Theodosius and Arcadius. The building was completed by the year 400.

The magnificent new basilica was modelled on Constantine's St Peter's, but it was larger, measuring 120 by 60m (390 by 195ft). Like old St Peter's, it had an immense nave with two aisles on either side, but it was superior in having superb matched fluted columns with Corinthian capitals, whereas old St Peter's had a random selection. The Middle Ages saw many splendid additions in the form of mosaics and frescoes, and San Paolo became the most finely decorated church in Rome.

Disaster struck on the night of July 15, 1823, when the basilica was gutted by fire. The left side collapsed and the right-hand columns were calcinated. By modern methods, much of the original fabric — including many mosaics and frescoes — could have been salvaged, but at the time little effort was made to save the old church. As a result, the building you see today is almost entirely a work of the 19thC. Fortunately, the dignity and grandeur of the original have been retained, and it is the detail rather than the overall effect that has been altered.

The **mosaics** of the apse are heavily restored but are still of interest. They show Christ blessing in the Byzantine manner, flanked by Sts Peter, Paul, Andrew and Luke, with Honorius III at his feet. On either side there are mosaics by Pietro Cavallini, which once adorned the facade. Other treasures that survived the fire include the superb 12thC **paschal candlestick** (★) by Nicolò di Angelo and Pietro Vassalletto, a masterpiece of the art of bronze casting, and the **canopy** (★) over the shrine of St Paul by Arnolfo di Cambio (1285), showing the artist's combined talents as sculptor and architect at their most enchanting. The badly damaged **bronze doors**, which were made in Constantinople in 1070 by Staurachios of Chios, have recently been restored and are on view.

The early 13thC **cloisters** (★) are undoubtedly the most lovely in all Rome. They were almost certainly created by Pietro Vassalletto, who was also partly responsible for the cloisters of *San Giovanni in Laterano*. The Vassalletti family were arguably the supreme exponents of the Cosmatesque style of decoration. Here, every detail is different and fascinating, from the variations of the paired colonnettes to the sculpture of the frieze and the rich mosaics. The delightful rose garden in the middle is a perfect complement to the setting.

Saint Peter's *(Basilica di San Pietro in Vaticano)* 🏛 † ★

Piazza San Pietro ☎ 6984466. Map 4H2. Open Oct-Apr 7am-6pm, May-Sept 7am-7pm.

For the many thousands for whom a journey to the eternal city is above all a pilgrimage, St Peter's is the climax of the entire itinerary. But it is almost unthinkable that anyone should visit Rome and not go to see this great basilica. Even so, the first sight of it may come as something of a disappointment, for Carlo Maderno's overweight and formless facade is hardly its most impressive feature.

The history of the rebuilding of St Peter's — earlier attempts to save Constantine's 4thC basilica having failed — begins with the destruction of the old church at the command of Julius II, who appointed Bramante as his architect. The foundation stone of the new basilica was laid in 1506, and Bramante's design consisted of a Greek cross, with a great central dome and four satellite cupolas. When he died in 1514, the four central piers and the great arches to carry the dome had been completed.

Following Bramante's death, competition to complete the church was fierce, with many disparate designs, in particular an ungainly scheme by Antonio da Sangallo the Younger (1539) that was only partially realised. It is remarkable that order eventually prevailed, due largely to the intervention in 1546 of an unwilling Michelangelo at the insistence of Paul III. The divine master expressed great admiration for Bramante's original project, but was of the opinion that Antonio's laboured work needed a surgeon's rather than a draughtsman's hand. He substituted a beautifully simple design in place of Sangallo's over-complicated system of major and minor crosses. Paul III, watching the wholesale destruction of Sangallo's outer shell with some apprehension, nevertheless gave his architect a free hand. Michelangelo's plan of square cross and covering dome was put into effect and by the time of his death in 1564 the basilica was completed as far as the base of the dome. The dome itself should have been lower and flatter than the one you can see today (height, including lantern and cross, 136.5m (448ft) above ground), but Michelangelo's design was considerably altered by Giacomo della Porta. However, the basic conception, and beautiful garlands and paired columns at the base, are Michelangelo's.

The decision to transform the shape of the church came from Paul V in 1605, when a Latin cross design was deemed desirable to cover Constantine's old basilica and atrium. Paul directed his architect Carlo Maderno to demolish what was left of the old basilica, and to extend the nave as far as the old Piazza San Pietro, adding a facade (1607-14). At last, on November 18, 1626, Urban VIII consecrated the new basilica, 1,300yrs after the original consecration. Bernini was appointed chief architect in 1637 and was responsible for the overwhelmingly Baroque style of the interior.

The basilica is fronted by the great central **portico**, above which is the benediction loggia from which the Pope traditionally gives his blessing. The portico, with pavement designed by Bernini and a fine stuccoed ceiling, has five entrances to the basilica leading off it. The **Porta Santa**, the portal farthest to the right, is opened only every 25yrs (in Holy Years). The great central **bronze doors** (✪) were taken from old St Peter's and were made by Antonio Filarete for Eugenius IV between 1433 and 1445. Eugenius presided over the Council of Florence in 1439, and the reliefs depict exotic visitors to the Council — Africans, Ethiopians and Greeks — as well as the Pope himself, and the figures of St Peter and St Paul. In the tympanum above the central entrance (looking back towards the light) are the rather sorry remains of Giotto's *Navicella*, a famous but much-restored work that was rescued from the old basilica. At the right end of the portico, behind the door leading to the vestibule of the **Scala Regia**, stands the equestrian statue of *Constantine* (✪) by Bernini.

Entering St Peter's for the first time is an unforgettable experience. You expect everything to be on a vast scale, as befits the largest church in the world — inside length 186m (610ft), maximum width 135m (443ft), height of nave 44m (144ft) — and yet the impression of great size is not at first apparent, so harmonious are the proportions. However, the sight of tiny

113

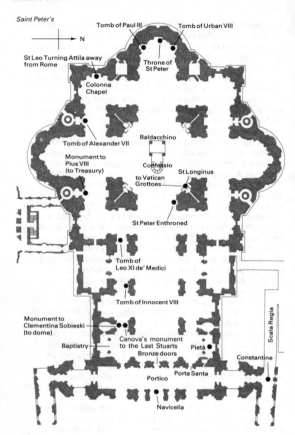

Saint Peter's

N

Tomb of Paul III
Tomb of Urban VIII

St Leo Turning Attila away
from Rome

Throne of
St Peter

Colonna
Chapel

Tomb of Alexander VII

Baldacchino

Monument to
Pius VIII
(to Treasury)

Confessio
to Vatican
Grottoes

St Longinus

St Peter Enthroned

Tomb of
Leo XI de' Medici

Tomb of Innocent VIII

Monument to
Clementina Sobieski
(to dome)

Baptistry

Canova's monument
to the Last Stuarts

Bronze doors

Pietà

Constantine

Scala Regia

Porta Santa

Portico

Navicella

figures far up the nave soon reveals just how vast it is.

The first chapel on the right contains Michelangelo's *Pietà* (★) of 1499. This superb depiction of maternal affection and grief was executed when the artist was 25 and is his only signed work. It has been expertly restored after the 1972 attack and is protected from further damage by a toughened glass screen. At the end of the nave, on the right, is Arnolfo di Cambio's bronze statue of *St Peter Enthroned* (★), the right foot worn down by the veneration of ages.

The high altar is dominated by Bernini's spectacular bronze **baldacchino** (★). Half architecture, half sculpture, this enormous structure is the height of the Palazzo Farnese and manages to fit in perfectly with its surroundings. It represents an incredible achievement in casting, with its four great fluted columns soaring upwards in barley-sugar fashion to support the canopy, anchored by four gilded angels. The columns swarm with Barberini bees, referring to Urban VIII, who commissioned the monument. The great space of the dome is defined by four piers, each containing a colossal statue. Of these, Bernini's *St Longinus* (★) in the NE pier is the most arresting.

A deep sunken area lies in front of the high altar, and steps lead down to the richly marbled **confessio** by Maderno, where the figure of *Pius VI* by Canova (1820) kneels in prayer.

The apse is thrillingly concluded by the *Throne of St Peter* (★), again by Bernini (1656-65), a dynamic rush of movement and vitality, which represents the glory of the Church Triumphant guided by the Holy Spirit. On either side of the throne, which seems to float on clouds amid a host of joyous angels and cherubs, are the Doctors of the Church. St Ambrose and St Augustine stand for the Latin Church, and St Athanasius and St John Chrysostom for the Greek. The ancient wooden chair of St Peter is encased within the bronze of the existing throne, invisible among all this splendid exuberance. In either side of the altar beneath are two very fine **tombs** (★), the one on the right designed by Bernini for his great patron *Urban VIII* (1642-47), and the one on the left by Guglielmo della Porta for *Paul III* (1551-75).

The left aisle contains a richer succession of treasures than the right. Walking back down it, notice especially the **Colonna Chapel**, which contains a fine relief by Alessandro Algardi (1646-50) depicting *St Leo Turning Attila away from Rome* (★). In the passage leading to the left transept is Bernini's **Tomb of Alexander VII** (★), a late work (1672-78). Crossing the transept and turning to your left, you will see Algardi's fine **Tomb of Leo XI de' Medici** (★) (1642-44) and, in the next passageway, Antonio Pollaiolo's splendid **Tomb of Innocent VIII** (★) (1498), one of the rare monuments transferred from the old basilica to the new.

In the last passageway before the portico there is a monument of special interest to British visitors, **Canova's Monument to the Last Stuarts** (★) (1817-19) with busts of James and Charles Edward, the Old and Young Pretenders, and also of Henry, Cardinal of York. Finally, the **Baptistry** at the end of the aisle (to your right) contains an upended cover of a porphyry sarcophagus, now used as the font. It formerly covered the tomb of the Emperor Otto II, which is now buried in the **Vatican Grottoes** (see below).

Treasury
🚻 *Access from left aisle, just E of transept, under Monument to Pius VIII. Open Oct-Apr 9am-4.30pm, May-Sept 9am-6pm.*
The Treasury now contains the **Museo Storico-Artistico di San Pietro**, an absorbing collection of sacred relics, chalices, reliquaries, vestments, illuminated manuscripts and ornaments, many of great value. In Room III is the magnificent **Tomb of Sixtus IV** (1493) by Antonio Pollaiolo.

Ascent to dome
🚻 ✱ 《 *Access from beginning of left aisle, under monument to Clementina Sobieski. Open Oct-Apr 8am-4.45pm, May-Sept 8am-6.15pm.*
A lift takes you up to the roof, where there are marvellous views over Bernini's Piàzza San Pietro and the Castel Sant' Angelo. From this level you can eventually reach, via 537 steps, the loggia of the **lantern**, from which there is a stupendous view of the entire city and the surrounding countryside.

Vatican Grottoes
🚻 *Entrance from NE pier of crossing, under St Longinus' statue. Open Oct-Apr 7am-3.30pm, May-Sept 7am-6pm.*
The grottoes follow the outline of the basilica above, and are divided into Old and New. On descending you arrive at the **New Grottoes**, with chapels arranged off a passage shaped like a horseshoe. Among them are the **Tomb of Pius XII** (died 1958)

and the unfinished **Tomb of Paul II** (★) (died 1471) by Mino da Fiesole.

In the **Old Grottoes** you can see many altars and tombs of great interest, some old, for example the 15thC **Altar of the Virgin**, and some new, such as the **Tomb of John XXIII**, always covered in flowers, and the **Tomb of Paul VI**.
Pre-Constantinian Necropolis ☆

📷 📷 ✗ *compulsory. Admission by appointment only. Apply in writing to Prefettura Casa Pontificia, Città del Vaticano, 00120 (giving address and telephone number) or in person to Ufficio Scavi (Vatican tourist office) on s side of Piazza San Pietro.*

In 1940, engineers were working in the **Vatican Grottoes** (see above), engaged in excavations for the Tomb of Pius XI. They hit upon some masonry that later proved to be part of a Roman mausoleum. It was this discovery that led Pius XII to order a full-scale examination of the entire area beneath the papal altar. Could it be proved by archaeology that this was indeed the site of St Peter's burial? Nine years of excavations followed. The engineers had to cope with subterranean waters and the problem of underpinning and buttressing the basilica above, but their labours paid off. They brought to light not only a pagan Roman cemetery, untouched since it was buried by Constantine's workmen, but also a rudimentary monument believed to mark the burial place of St Peter.

The **monument**, a simple marble slab set between two niches, is set into a red cement wall facing an open courtyard now underlying Maderno's *confessio*. The plausible theory is that while making the red wall, 2ndC builders hit upon a deeply buried grave, which was promptly identified as that of St Peter and duly marked. Greek inscriptions on a wall nearby add weight to the argument. Behind the monument, the Vatican excavators found a huge store of coins of many ages and countries, and, in a fissure reaching under the foundations of the wall, the bones of an elderly and powerfully built man. Paul VI declared these to be the bones of St Peter, and the spot has since been honoured by throngs of pilgrims.

The guided tour also includes the **pagan tombs**, which are built exactly like houses. Formerly they would have been roofed, but now they are immediately under the nave of the present basilica. There are 22 tombs, mostly built between 125 and 200. Those buried here came from well-to-do families; many have Greek names, and were probably merchants. The insides of many of the tombs are luxuriously decorated with frescoes and terra-cotta and stucco reliefs, and once contained many articles of everyday use. They were evidently regarded as residences of the dead.

San Pietro in Carcere †

Clivus Argentarius (near Via San Pietro in Carcere) 📷
Open Wed-Mon, Oct-Apr 9am-4pm, May-Sept 9am-12.30pm, 2-6.30pm. Closed Tues. Entrance under church of San Giuseppe dei Falegnami. Map 10l6.
This gloomy chapel is better known as the notorious Mamertine Prison, where St Peter is said to have been imprisoned by Nero. Before that, it was probably a cistern. The lower level was once called the *Tullianum* and served as a dungeon. Among those who were thrown down here to die from starvation or strangulation were Jugurtha and Vercingetorix. The prison was turned into a chapel in the 16thC but even now still recalls its grisly past.

San Pietro in Montorio 🏛 † ☆
Via Garibaldi. If closed, ring the bell at the door to the right of the church. Map 8J4.

This church was built on the supposed site of St Peter's crucifixion, which in actual fact probably took place in the Circus of Nero, beneath the Vatican Hill. Mentioned as early as the 9thC, the church was rebuilt from 1481 for Ferdinand IV and Isabella of Spain.

Inside, on the right side of the nave, the first chapel is entirely decorated with **frescoes (☆)** by Sebastiano del Piombo, including the *Flagellation*, for which Michelangelo provided drawings. The second chapel has a fresco of the *Coronation of the Virgin* by Baldassare Peruzzi. The fourth chapel contains the fine **tombs of Antonio and Fabiano del Monte** (1550-53) by Bartolomeo Ammannati. Crossing to the other side of the church, the overall design of the second chapel is the work of Bernini (c. 1640).

In the nave are the **tombs of Hugh O'Neill of Tyrone** and **Roderick O'Donnell of Tyrconnel**, leaders of the revolt against James I of England. Beatrice Cenci is buried under the steps of the high altar, although no inscription marks the spot. Raphael's *Transfiguration* graced the apse until 1809, when it was removed to the Vatican Museums.

In the courtyard outside the church is Bramante's celebrated **Tempietto (★)**. Close adherence to Classical forms and perfectly balanced proportions make this little temple one of the masterpieces of the Italian High Renaissance. Built in 1502, it was at one time thought to mark the exact spot where St Peter was martyred.

San Pietro in Vincoli 🏛 † ☆
Piazza di San Pietro in Vincoli. Map 10I7. Metropolitana: Cavour.

This church was founded by the Empress Eudoxia in 432, to house the chains that had bound St Peter during his captivity in Jerusalem. It was then restored by Adrian I (774-795), by Giuliano della Rovere, later Julius II (1471-1503) — at which time the elegant colonnaded portico was added — and by Francesco Fontana at the beginning of the 18thC. Fontana was responsible for adding the Ionic bases to the 20 ancient Doric columns of the nave.

The church is not only famous for its precious relics — kept in a tabernacle in the *confessio* beneath the high altar. It is the celebrated resting place of substantial parts of Michelangelo's **Tomb of Julius II** (far end of right aisle). The figure of *Moses* (★) is one of the artist's greatest masterpieces. This majestic bearded figure is shown holding the tablets of the Ten Commandments, and looks as if he may shatter them at any moment. The sense of power, both physical and spiritual, is overwhelming. The much calmer but very beautiful figures of *Leah* and *Rachel* on either side, which may symbolize the active and contemplative life, are also by Michelangelo. The figures in the upper register of the tomb, in contrast, are by pupils. The tomb was Michelangelo's most ambitious venture and was intended to include 42 figures, but it was never completed. Constant problems with Julius and his successors caused the project to founder, and what had been planned as the centrepiece of Saint Peter's ended up as the glory of San Pietro in Vincoli.

Other notable works of art in the church are the gilded bronze

doors of the tabernacle of the *confessio*, with reliefs attributed to
Caradosso (1477), and a fine Early Christian sarcophagus (4thC)
in the crypt.

Santa Prassede 🏛 ✝ ☆
*Via Santa Prassede (off Piazza di Santa Maria Maggiore).
Map 11H8. Metropolitana: Cavour.*
Paschal I built this often-restored church in 822 and dedicated it
to Santa Prassede, sister of the saint who gave her name to the
nearby church of Santa Pudenziana. Prassede and Pudenziana
were the daughters of a Roman senator named Pudens, an early
convert and friend of St Peter. Although not herself a martyr,
Prassede is said to have witnessed the execution of 23 Christians
whom she had been sheltering. She is supposed to have
collected their blood with a sponge and squeezed it down a well.
The site of the well is marked by a porphyry disc let into the
Cosmatesque pavement, which you can see towards the rear of
the nave.

The church is full of **mosaics** (☆) dating from the time of
Paschal I. Those on the **triumphal arch** show Christ flanked by
two angels in the Heavenly Jerusalem of the Apocalypse, with,
below, the Virgin Mary, St John the Baptist, St Paul and the
Apostles. Moses and Elijah are on either side, and at the gates of
the city are two more angels. The **apse mosaics** show the two
daughters of Senator Pudens being presented to the Redeemer
by Sts Peter and Paul, the apostles each with a hand on one of
the sisters' shoulders. Also present are St Zeno and Paschal,
carrying his church.

These mosaics all betray some Byzantine influence, which is
even more marked in the small **Chapel of St Zeno** (☆), the chief
glory of the church. The chapel was built by Paschal as a
mausoleum for his mother, Theodora. On either side of the
entrance are two very rare black granite columns, supporting an
elaborate cornice. The entire surface of the walls and vaulted
ceiling is encrusted with mosaic, predominantly of glittering gold,
and of such quality that the Romans in medieval times called it
the Garden of Paradise. In the vault, the head of Christ in a
medallion is supported by four angels. In a niche behind the altar
the Madonna and Child are shown between the sisters Prassede
and Pudenziana. To the left you can see Theodora, with the
square halo of the living — indicating that the chapel was built
during her lifetime. To the right is the **Column of Flagellation**,
which was brought from Jerusalem in 1223. It is believed to be
part of the column to which Christ was tied while being
scourged, and is an object of great veneration.

Another place of special interest in this church is the *confessio*,
in which Paschal stored the many relics of popes, bishops, and
martyrs that he removed from suburban cemeteries to save them
from the clutches of relic hunters. It was a time when the
spoliation of the cemeteries was at its height. These relics are
now largely dispersed, but the Early Christian sarcophagi
containing the relics of Prassede and Pudenziana still remain.

Santa Pudenziana 🏛 ✝ ☆
Via Urbana. Map 7H7. Metropolitana: Cavour.
According to legend, this church was built on the site of the
house of a Roman Senator called Pudens, the father of
Pudenziana and of the saint to whom the nearby church of Santa
Prassede is dedicated. Baths were constructed over the house in
the 2ndC and in part incorporated into the 4thC church, which is

one of the most ancient and attractive in all Rome. It was rebuilt in the 8thC and several times restored, notably in the early 13thC when the handsome bell tower was added, and in 1589 by Francesco da Volterra for Cardinal Enrico Caetani. The present facade dates from 1870 but incorporates 8thC fragments in the form of two white spiralling columns and a frieze featuring Pudens, his two daughters, St Pastor and the Holy Lamb.

The chief glory of the church is the **apse mosaic (★)**, one of the finest Early Christian mosaics in Rome. The mosaic was executed between 384 and 399 and shows Christ seated on a golden throne, surrounded by his Apostles and two women often identified as Pudenziana and Prassede. High above the figure of Christ is a triumphal cross of gold, studded with jewels and flanked by symbols of the Evangelists. The background represents an ideal vision of the city of Jerusalem.

The execution of these mosaics is of the highest order. The colouring is soft and sensitive, the attention to detail superb. During restoration of the church in the late 16thC the lower part of the mosaic was cut off and the sides trimmed, with consequent losses to the outermost figures. Subsequent restorations of the mosaic itself have significantly altered the character of some of the heads.

Ask the sacristan to show you the remains of the 2ndC baths behind the apse and the **Marian Oratory**, containing 11thC frescoes. Entrance is through a door in the left aisle, usually kept closed.

Santi Quattro Coronati 🏛 ✝

Via dei Santi Quattro Coronati. Map 11J8. Metropolitana: Colosseo.

Part church, part fortress, Santi Quattro Coronati has an interesting history dating back to its foundation in the 4thC. In the Middle Ages it was part of a fortified abbey, used to defend the nearby basilica of *San Giovanni in Laterano*. In 1084 it was destroyed by the Normans. The present church was built by Paschal II from 1111, using antique columns, and has a fine **Cosmatesque pavement**.

The Quattro Coronati were four Roman soldiers who were martyred for refusing to worship a statue of Aesculapius. Five sculptors suffered the same fate for having refused to carve the statue, and the small but exquisitely fashioned **cloisters (★)** are the dedicated work of 13thC sculptors in memory of their predecessors. The adjoining **Oratory of San Silvestro**, containing a fine series of 13thC **frescoes**, may be visited on request.

San Saba 🏛 ✝

Via di San Saba. Map 10K6. Metropolitana: Piramide.

An ancient church now set in a quiet residential district, San Saba sports an unusually hybrid exterior, even by Roman standards. A 13thC portico stands in front of the Romanesque facade, and on it is superimposed an elegant late 15thC **loggia**. The church was founded in the 7thC by Eastern monks fleeing the Arab invasion of the Holy Land and has three apses in the Greek manner. It was sacked by the Normans in 1084, rebuilt in 1205 and eventually restored in 1465.

The superb marble inlay work in the **main door, pavement** and in fragments of the **schola cantorum** (now in the nave) is by Jacopo Cosma (13thC). Fragments of sculpture relating to San Saba's history are exhibited in the sacristy corridor.

Santa Sabina 🏛 ✝ ☆

*Via di Santa Sabina. Map **10**J6. Cloisters open 3.30-5.30pm.*
Located high up on the **Aventine Hill**, with magnificent views
over the city, this church is a fine and distinctive example of a
5thC basilica. It was built by a priest called Peter of Illyria,
probably on the site of a Roman house belonging to a woman
called Sabina, who had become confused with the saint of that
name.

Construction began in 422, not long after the Sack of Rome by
the Goths. The church was restored and embellished in 824, and
again in 1216, shortly before being given to St Dominic in 1222
for his new order. Domenico Fontana remodelled the interior in
1587, and it was only after the restorations of Muñoz and Berthier
in 1914-19 and 1936-38 respectively that it regained its original
simplicity and majesty.

The atrium is reached through a 15thC portico and contains
perhaps the greatest of Santa Sabina's treasures: the 5thC carved
cypress-wood panels of the **west doors** (☆). Eighteen of the
original 28 panels survive: they demonstrate parallels between
the Old and New Testaments, as shown by the lives of Moses
and Christ. The *Crucifixion* is one of the very earliest
representations of this subject.

The interior of the church is impressive: on either side of the
wide nave there is a superb **arcade** of fluted Corinthian columns,
plundered from a nearby temple. This is the first instance in
Rome of an arcade replacing the more traditional colonnade, and
the arches are decorated with fine 5thC marble inlay. The
beautiful **windows** above were reconstructed from original
fragments and date from the 9thC. So do the similarly restored
schola cantorum, pulpits and **bishop's throne**.

The mosaic decoration of the apse did not survive, but Taddeo
Zuccaro's fresco (1560) probably reproduces its subject. The only
mosaic decoration that remains is above the w door. Here, an
inscription that includes the names of the founder and of
Celestinus I, in gold letters against a blue background, is flanked
by two austere female figures representing the Church of the
Jews and the Church of the Gentiles. In the centre of the nave is
the **mosaic tombstone** of Muñoz de Zamora (1300), the only
example of this type of tomb in Rome. The beautiful 13thC
cloisters in the adjacent convent are only open at certain times,
but are well worth visiting.

Santo Stefano Rotondo 🏛 ✝ ☆

*Via di Santo Stefano Rotondo. Entrance through convent
door to right of portico. Map **11**J8.*
It is tragic that one of the most interesting of all the ancient
churches in Rome should be in such a dismal state of repair, so
reduced in grandeur and majesty. The church is closed to the
public for the moment, except during occasional services held
there. This magnificent round structure was probably built in the
5thC at the height of the cult of St Stephen, and consecrated by
Simplicius (468-483). At one time it consisted of a central space
and two ambulatories, which were separated by circles of
majestic antique columns.

The church gained special significance for being an exact
replica of Constantine's great Church of the Holy Sepulchre in
Jerusalem, at the time one of the most famous churches in all
Christendom. Even today, vast amounts of geometrical data and
legend are sometimes cited to support the theory that this is "the
New Jerusalem of the Book of Revelation", or, failing that, at least

the most important church ever built in the West. Certainly the sheer magnificence of the marbles, mosaics and frescoes once lavished on it by John I (523-526) and Felix IV (526-530) leaves little doubt that it was considered, even in Rome, a church of outstanding importance. These superb decorations are unfortunately lost, and we know of them only from accounts given by pilgrims.

Recent excavations have revealed that the church was built over a military barracks and a Mithraic temple, which must both have been levelled by 350. Major restorations took place under Adrian I in 795 and Innocent II in 1143, but the real damage was done by Nicholas V in 1453. He had the outer circle of the building demolished and the outer ring of arches walled in, thus diminishing the size of the church and spoiling its appearance. At the time of the Counter-Reformation, Gregory III did the church a further disservice by causing the inside face of the new walls to be frescoed with depictions of the most horrific martyrdoms. The frescoes are now, like the rest of the church, in an appalling state of repair. Perhaps one day they will be removed and the church restored, if not to its former dimensions, at least to something of its former glory.

Santa Susanna ▥ †
Via XX Settembre. Map 7G7. Metropolitana: Repubblica.
This church is said to have been founded on the site of the home of Susanna, a niece of Pope Caius, who was martyred under one of Diocletian's persecutions. It was rebuilt in 1475 under Sixtus IV, but the present appearance is largely due to Carlo Maderno. His **facade** (★) of 1603 is one of the masterpieces of the early Baroque style, elaborate but always beautifully controlled. The complexity of the rhythm is balanced by the vertical continuity, with Corinthian columns below and pilasters above. Santa Susanna is now the American national church in Rome.

San Teodoro ▥ †
Via di San Teodoro. Map 10|6. Open Wed-Mon 4-6pm. Closed Tues.
This small, round church, tucked away at the foot of the *Palatine Hill*, is approached down a flight of steps and through a pretty **courtyard** designed by Carlo Fontana (1705). The church was founded towards the end of the 6thC, though several times restored, and may originally have served as a baptistry. An ancient custom certainly existed of bringing children here to be blessed on recovery from illness. The **mosaics** in the apse date from the time of the building's construction but, like the rest of the fabric, have been heavily restored.

Scala Santa   These highly-venerated steps are said to have come from Jerusalem and to have been ascended by Christ. They are best visited at the same time as the basilica of *San Giovanni in Laterano*.

Servian Wall   This fortified wall was built in the 4thC BC and encircled a much smaller area than the later *Aurelian Wall*. Substantial remains can be seen in front of *Stazione Termini*.

Sistine Chapel   The overwhelming power and nobility of Michelangelo's *Creation* and *Last Judgment* are legendary, but this chapel in the *Vatican Museums* also contains outstanding frescoes by Botticelli, Ghirlandaio and Perugino.

Spanish Steps *(Scalinata della Trinità dei Monti)* ☆
Piazza di Spagna. Map 6G6. Metropolitana: Spagna.
This elaborate and graceful flight of steps leads up from *Piazza di Spagna* to the church of *Trinità dei Monti*, after which the steps are more correctly named. They were built between 1723 and 1726 by Francesco de Sanctis, and remain one of the most popular of all Rome's tourist sights. In the days of Goethe and of Dickens, artists' models used to pose on the low walls and balustrades in colourful costumes, but today their place has been taken by street sellers offering cheap jewellery, leather goods, and pictures. In spring, the steps are decked out with a mass of azaleas, and the terraces become a riot of colour.

Stazione Termini 🏛
Piazza dei Cinquecento. Map 7H8. Metropolitana: Termini.
Perhaps the most impressive modern building in Rome, Stazione Termini is as functional within as it is visually striking without. Begun under Mussolini by Angiolo Mazzoni del Grande, it was not completed until 1950, largely to the designs of Eugenio Montouri. The vast interior provides every service you could hope to find at a major railway terminal — shops, restaurant, sauna, massage, hairdressing — as well as the usual bookstalls and kiosks. Car-hire facilities are available, and there is a branch of EPT, the tourist information service.

In the forecourt, to the N of the station, are substantial remains of the **Servian Wall**, which dates from about 378BC and was once 11km (7 miles) long.

Tempietto   In this tiny but perfectly proportioned circular temple, closely modelled on antique sources, Bramante expressed the High Renaissance ideals that were to inspire his plans for the rebuilding of *St Peter's*. The temple stands in the courtyard outside the church of *San Pietro in Montorio*, and is said to mark the exact spot of St Peter's martyrdom.

Temple of Fortuna Virilis *(Tempio della Fortuna Virile)* 🏛
Piazza Bocca della Verità. Map 9J6.
This elegant little temple stands close to the circular structure of the *Temple of Vesta* on the E bank of the Tiber. It is a delightful example of a Republican temple and is in excellent condition for its age (late 2ndC BC). Six free-standing fluted Ionic columns grace the front and sides of the pronaos, and half-columns (also of travertine) are incorporated into the tufa walls of the *cella* or sanctuary. The original dedication of the temple is unknown, but may have been to Portunus, the river god.

Temple of Venus and Rome *(Tempio di Venere e Roma)* 🏛
Piazza del Colosseo. Map 10I7. Metropolitana: Colosseo.
Little remains of the largest temple ever built in Rome, but surviving columns have been re-erected and part of the area ingeniously laid out as a shrub-garden. The missing columns are indicated by privet, the steps by box and the walls by laurel.

The temple was founded by Hadrian in 121 and dedicated in 135, but rebuilt by Maxentius in 307, after a fire. It was a unique double-apsed structure, with the two apses placed back to back in the centre. The apse facing the *Roman Forum* was dedicated to Rome and is now incorporated into the cloisters of **Santa Maria Nova**. The apse facing the *Colosseum* was dedicated to

Venus and has also survived: you can still see the diamond coffering on the vault.

With 56 magnificent Corinthian columns (ten at either end), gilded bronze roof tiles, and 150 granite and porphyry columns in the enclosing colonnade, this temple was one of the great sights of Rome. It stayed in use until 391 — longer than most Roman temples — and remained almost intact until 625, when Honorius I removed the gilded bronze tiles for old St Peter's.

Temple of Vesta *(Tempio di Vesta)* 🏛
Piazza Bocca della Verità. Map 9J6.
Like the nearby *Temple of Fortuna Virilis*, this fine circular temple does not bear its original name. It was once dedicated to Hercules Victor but became known as the Temple of Vesta because of its resemblance to the temple of that name in the *Roman Forum*. Dating from the late 2ndC BC, it is the oldest surviving marble temple in Rome. Marble was rarely quarried in Italy at that time, and the marble of the circular *cella* or sanctuary probably came from Greece. The temple was restored by the Emperor Tiberius, and the 20 surrounding Corinthian columns (one missing except for its base) date from this later period. The ancient entablature and roof have long since disappeared.

Theatre of Marcellus *(Teatro di Marcello)* 🏛 ☆
Via del Teatro di Marcello. Map 10I6.
This enormous building, 120m (393ft) in diameter, was capable of holding 20,000 spectators, and even in its present gaunt and fragmentary state is one of the most impressive ancient monuments in Rome. It was begun by Julius Caesar, and finished under Augustus in 11BC. Only 12 out of the original 41 arches in each of the two tiers are extant, and would not be there at all if the building had not been used as a fortress in the Middle Ages and partly converted into a palace in the 16thC. The palace is now known as the **Palazzo Orsini**, after the family who owned it for two centuries. The three Corinthian columns standing to the N of the building are all that remain of the **Temple of Apollo**, first built in 433-431BC, and reconstructed in 34BC.

Torre delle Milizie   A fortified medieval tower overlooking *Trajan's Markets*.

Tortoise Fountain *(Fontana delle Tartarughe)* ☆
Piazza Mattei. Map 5I5.
Small, graceful and imaginative, this late Renaissance fountain has a gaiety and lightness of touch that betray the Florentine origins of its sculptor, Taddeo Landini. The overall design is by Giacomo della Porta (1581-84). Each of the four youths, cast in bronze, restrains a dolphin, one foot planted firmly on the head and one hand grasping the tail. With their free hands they reach up to support four bronze tortoises that are struggling to drink from the bowl above. The tortoises were a 17thC addition.

Trajan's Column   Superb low-reliefs, and the fascinating narrative they relate in their upward spiral, make this one of the greatest surviving monuments of ancient Rome. The column stands in the *Forum of Trajan*.

Trajan's Markets *(Mercati Traianei)* 🏛 ☆
Via 4 Novembre ☎ 67103613. Entrance near steps of Via Magnanapoli. Map 10I6 🕎 🕎 *last Sun of month. Open*

Oct-Apr, Tues-Sat 9am-1.30pm, Sun 9am-1pm; May-Sept, Tues-Sat 9am-1pm, Sun 9am-1pm. Closed Mon.

In Trajan's time, these brick-faced concrete buildings formed a carefully planned shopping centre, accessible at two different levels. They are probably the work of Apollodorus of Damascus (early 2ndC), the architect of the ***Forum of Trajan***, and are remarkably well preserved. The lower level, built in a hemicycle to match the semi-circular portico on the NE side of the Forum, consists of three tiers of shops. Little remains of the third tier, which faces away from the Forum onto a street known as the Via Biberatica and a second level of shops. To the left is the **great hall**, a three-storey covered market.

High above the markets is the 13thC **Torre delle Milizie**, the largest remaining fortified tower in Rome. It was originally even taller, but lost its top storey in the 14thC. It is also mistakenly known as Nero's Tower, because of the popular legend that Nero watched Rome burning from its battlements.

Trevi Fountain *(Fontana di Trevi)* ★

Piazza di Trevi (Via delle Muratte/Via della Stamperia). Map 6H6 ✱

The Trevi is the most spectacular and famous of all Rome's many fountains. There is a tradition that anyone who throws a coin into the water will return to Rome, and few tourists seem willing to risk doubting the legend. At the confluence of several narrow streets, near the junction of the Corso and Via del Tritone, the fountain is not the easiest place to find. But as you approach, the roar of the waters and raised voices of the crowds act as your guides.

The fountain is the work of Nicolà Salvi and is supplied with water from the Acqua Vergine aqueduct. It was completed in 1762, but only after more than a century of planning following Bernini's abandonment of the project on the death of Urban VIII in 1644. The Trevi probably takes its name from the *tre vie*, three of the streets that meet at this point. The backdrop to the cascading exuberance of marble and water is formed by the side of **Palazzo Poli**. Neptune dominates the design from his central niche, flanked by allegorical figures and overlooked by statues of the four seasons. Below, two tritons control their seahorses: the one on the left is clearly having some trouble with his steed — Salvi's representation of the ocean in ugly mood — while his conch-blowing companion represents a calm sea. The fountain was among monuments that underwent restoration work in the run-up to the 1990 World Cup.

Trinità dei Monti 🏛 †

*Piazza Trinità dei Monti. Map **6G6** ⋞ Metropolitana: Spagna.*

Dominating the ***Spanish Steps*** and ***Piazza di Spagna***, Carlo Maderno's handsome Baroque facade is one of the best-known sights in Rome and is perhaps a more satisfactory architectural synthesis than his grandiose design for the facade of ***St Peter's***. The church was begun in 1502 by Louis XII of France and completed in 1585. It was richly endowed by successive French kings and cardinals, and the interior sumptuously decorated. Many of the furnishings were plundered during the Napoleonic occupation, but restored under Louis XVIII in 1816.

The most notable works of art are Daniele da Volterra's *Assumption* in the third chapel on the right, and his *Deposition* in the second chapel on the left, generally regarded as his masterpiece. From the piazza outside there are spectacular views over the city. Pius VI erected the 2ndC **obelisk** here in 1788.

Triton Fountain *(Fontana del Tritone)* ☆
Piazza Barberini. Map 7G7. Metropolitana: Barberini.
This marvellously imaginative work, one of Bernini's unquestioned masterpieces, was commissioned by Urban VIII in 1643. Constructed out of travertine rather than the more usual marble, the realism of the design was also remarkable. Four dolphins, mouths wide open, suck up the waters of the Acqua Felice. Perched on their tails is a wide scallop shell. Seated on it is the Triton, blowing water through a conch held to his mouth. The water cascades down over his magnificent torso, drenching the papal tiara and Barberini bees beneath his sea-throne.

Vatican City *(Città del Vaticano)*
Map 4G2.
The Vatican City, home of the great basilica of *Saint Peter's*, is an independent sovereign state, established by the Lateran Treaty of 1929. It covers an area of 43 hectares (108 acres) and, with the exception of *Piazza San Pietro*, is surrounded by walls. Within this small area, the Vatican is entirely self-sufficient in terms of administration and services. It has its own civil and judicial systems, post office, bank, newspaper, radio station and railway station, a supermarket and several garages. An added benefit for the thousand residents is that many commodities are tax-free.

Vatican Grottoes
These lie under the basilica of *Saint Peter's* and are the traditional burial place of the popes. They contain many fine tombs and altars.

Vatican Museums *(Musei Vaticani)* ★
Viale Vaticano ☎ 6983333. Map 4G3 🔳🔳 🔲 last Sun of month ✗ ▣ Open Oct-June, Mon-Sat 9am-2pm; July-Sept, Mon-Fri 9am-5pm, Sat 9am-2pm. Closed Jan 1 and 6, Mar 19, Easter and Easter Mon, May 1, 8 and 9, June 29, Aug 14 and 15, Nov 1, Dec 8, 25 and 26, and Sun except last Sun of month, 9am-2pm. Metropolitana: Ottaviano. Alternatively, take a bus through the Vatican gardens, from outside the Ufficio Scavi (Vatican tourist office) on s side of Piazza San Pietro.
No museum in the world has a finer collection of antiquities than the Vatican. But the fame of this magnificent complex has brought disadvantages, in the sheer number of people who flood through its gates every year, intent on homing in on the star attractions. To ease congestion at particularly popular spots and to help visitors make best use of the time at their disposal, the museum authorities now offer a choice of four tours, each linked to a colour code posted clearly along the route. Not everyone will wish to follow the official routes, but at the very least they are convenient rough guides. It is not impossible to change direction mid-route, but it can be difficult. Codes are as follows:

(A) (violet)	**(B)** (beige)	**(C)** (green)	**(D)** (yellow)
1½ hours	3 hours	3½ hours	5 hours

Inevitably the recommendations that follow are highly selective. In describing such a vast complex, it is only possible to mention outstanding examples.
Egyptian Museum (**C**) (**D**) This was founded by Gregory XVI

in 1839 and has eight rooms. In Room V is the colossal statue of *Queen Tuia*, mother of Rameses II, and the sandstone *Head of the Pharaoh Mentuhotep* of the 11th dynasty (20thC BC). In Room VIII is the basalt statuette of a priest carrying a small temple, known as the *Naophorus* (525BC).

Chiaramonti Museum (C) (D)   Named after its founder, Pius VII (1800-23), it is little changed in appearance since first laid out by Canova. Displayed here are a huge number of antique portrait busts, statues, urns and sarcophagi. Especially fine are the *Portrait of a Roman* (Section XIX) and the fragmentary relief of *Penelope* (★) (Section XXIII), a Greek original of about 450BC. Beyond is the **Lapidary Gallery**, displaying Roman and early Christian inscriptions (closed to general public).

Pio-Clementine Museum (C) (D) (★)   The museum is named after Pius VI and Clement XIV, who were largely responsible for assembling the magnificent collection of sculpture. Due to the new flow arrangements, visitors now enter by Room XII and leave from Room I (Greek Cross Room). Room XII (Square Vestibule) contains a sarcophagus of *Lucius Cornelius Scipio the Bearded*, in grey tufa. Room X has a fine Roman copy (1stC) of the *Apoxyomenos* (★) by Lysippus (c. 320BC), the athlete looking decidedly weary after his exertions.

Room VIII (Octagonal Court) has some of the greatest treasures in the museums. These are contained in the *gabinetti* or recesses of the four corners. Moving clockwise, first on the left is the *Apollo Belvedere* (★), a marvellous Roman copy (c. AD130) of Leochares' original (c. 330BC), which once stood in the Agora in Athens. The legendary *Laocoön* (★) was rediscovered in 1506 near *Nero's Golden House* and bought by Julius II. The Ancients considered this marble group to be one of the greatest pieces of sculpture in the world. According to Pliny the Elder, it was the work of the Rhodian sculptor Hagesandros, and his sons Polydoros and Athenodoros. It represents Laocoön, a priest of Apollo, and his two sons, vainly struggling against serpents entwined among their limbs. *Hermes*, with his cloak thrown over his left shoulder, is a Roman copy of a Greek original (4thC BC). Lastly, Antonio Canova's elegant *Perseus Triumphant with the Head of Medusa* (★) (1800) shows the strong influence of the Apollo Belvedere.

Room V (Gallery of Statues) features the *Apollo Sauroktonos* (★), in which the god watches a lizard he is about to kill, a Roman copy of a 4thC BC bronze original by Praxiteles. Room VII (Cabinet of Masks) contains the *Cnidian Venus* (★), an important and much admired copy of another work by Praxiteles. Room III (Room of the Muses) is famed for the *Belvedere Torso* (★), a badly damaged piece that nevertheless shows the superb skill of the sculptor Apollonios, son of Nestor, who signed it (1stC BC). The torso is of a powerful man bending forward and was greatly admired by Michelangelo.

Room II has a floor decorated with ancient mosaics from Otricoli and contains the *Jupiter of Otricoli*, a Roman version of a well-known 4thC BC Greek representation of Zeus. Room I contains two monumental sarcophagi. **The Sarcophagus of St Helena** (★) came from the tomb of Constantine's mother in the Tor Pignattara (4thC). The dark red Egyptian porphyry sarcophagus is decorated with reliefs of victorious soldiers, and was perhaps initially meant for her husband. On the other side of the room, the **Sarcophagus of Constantia** (★) came from the church of *Santa Costanza*. Dating from 350-360, it is similar in style, made of porphyry, and decorated with reliefs of lambs, peacocks, and cherubs harvesting grapes.

Gregorian-Etruscan Museum (B) (D) (✿) This museum was founded in 1837 by Gregory XVI. Besides having one of the finest collections of Etruscan artifacts in the world (Rooms I-IX), a stairway that displays Assyrian reliefs, and a distinguished collection of Greek and Italiot vases (Rooms X-XIV), it also houses four rooms of fragmentary Greek statues and reliefs.

Outstanding among the exhibits in Room II are the furnishings of the **Regolini-Galassi Tomb** (✿), excavated near Cervéteri in 1836. The 7thBC tomb contained the remains of a richly adorned man and woman and, in an urn, the ashes of a third person. All the various ornaments and objects that were found with them are on display. Room III contains several bronzes, culminating with the superb *Mars of Todi* (✿), impressive both for its sheer size and for the quality of its invention. In the Room of the Greek Originals the outstanding pieces are a splendid *Head of Athene* (✿) and a funerary **stele** (✿) showing a young athlete and servant.

The vase collection includes many amphorae, hydriae, wine jugs and craters of superb quality. The majority were discovered in Etruscan tombs, proof of the thriving export trade from Greece. Room XII, the Hemicycle, contains the collection's masterpiece, Exekias's black-figured amphora of *Achilles and Ajax playing Morra* (✿) of about 530BC, a work of exquisite delicacy. Other notable pieces are the cup by the "Brygos Painter" of *Hermes Having Stolen the Cattle of Apollo*, in the same room, and the "Berlin Painter's" hydria of *Apollo Sitting on the Delphic Tripod*, in the upper Hemicycle, Room XIV.

Room of the Biga (D) (✿) The superb two-horsed chariot or *biga* is an 18thC work by Franzoni, incorporating Classical fragments of a 1stC original — probably a votive chariot dedicated to Ceres.

Gallery of the Candelabra (A) (B) (C) (D) The gallery takes its name from the pairs of ancient marble candelabra that decorate its six sections. It contains a number of important statues, including a 2ndC copy of *Diana of the Ephesians*.

Gallery of the Tapestries (A) (B) (C) (D) The tapestries displayed here are known as the New School, to distinguish them from the Raphael originals or Old School in the **Pinacoteca** (see later). Both series were made in Brussels, but the New School was worked from designs by Raphael's pupils and dates from the time of Clement VII (1523-34).

Gallery of the Maps (A) (B) (C) (D) A long, barrel-vaulted gallery splendidly frescoed with 16thC maps of Italy.

Apartment of Pius V (A) (B) (C) (D) Contains a good collection of tapestries, including important 15thC works from Tournai in Belgium.

Sobieski Room (A) (B) (C) (D) Named after the huge painting by Jan Matejko, depicting John III Sobieski, King of Poland, liberating Vienna from the Turks in 1683.

Room of the Immaculate Conception (A) (B) (C) (D) A display of books and manuscripts presented to Pius IX after his proclamation of the dogma of the Immaculate Conception in 1854.

Raphael Stanze (C) (D) (✿) These four rooms comprise the official apartments of Julius II (1503-13) and his successors up until the time of Gregory XIII (1572-85). In 1508, Julius II decided to entrust the redecoration of the entire apartments to a young painter from Urbino. Raphael was only 26, and this commission

Vatican Museums

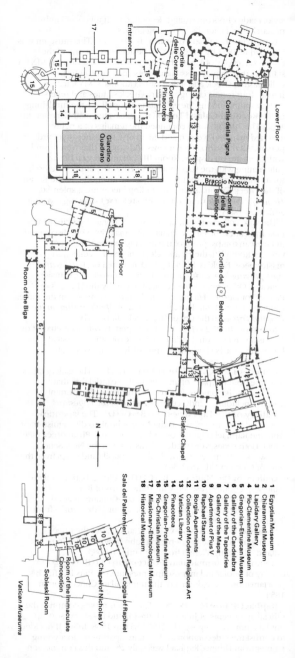

Lower Floor

Cortile delle Corazze

Entrance

Cortile della Pinacoteca

Cortile della Pigna

Giardino Quadrato

Braccio Nuovo

Cortile della Biblioteca

Upper Floor

Cortile del Belvedere

Room of the Biga

Sistine Chapel

Sala dei Palafrenieri

Chapel of Nicholas V

Loggia of Raphael

Room of the Immaculate Conception

Sobieski Room

N

1 Egyptian Museum
2 Chiaramonti Museum
3 Lapidary Gallery
4 Pio-Clementine Museum
5 Gregorian-Etruscan Museum
6 Gallery of the Candelabra
7 Gallery of the Tapestries
8 Gallery of the Maps
9 Apartment of Pius V
10 Raphael Stanze
11 Borgia Apartments
12 Vatican Library
13 Collection of Modern Religious Art
14 Vatican Library
15 Pinacoteca
16 Gregorian-Profane Museum
17 Pio-Christian Museum
18 Missionary-Ethnological Museum
   Historical Museum

Vatican Museums

marked the start of his short but brilliant Roman career. It was to occupy him until his death in 1520.

Room I: Stanza dell' Incendio (1514-17). The earlier vault decorations are by Perugino. There are four main works by Raphael and his assistants: the *Coronation of Charlemagne in St Peter's*, the *Battle of Ostia*, the *Self-defence of Leo III*, and the *Fire in the Borgo* (✪). The last shows how Leo IV extinguished the fire raging in Borgo Santo Spirito by making the sign of the Cross, and is a fine example of Raphael's complex last manner.

Room II: Stanza della Segnatura (1508-11). The scheme of decoration works from the four sections of the ceiling down through the walls, with the personifications of Theology, Philosophy, Poetry and Justice becoming the *Disputà*, the *School of Athens*, the *Parnassus* and the *Institution of Civil and Canon Law* respectively. The earliest fresco, the *Disputà* (✪), might more correctly be described as the Triumph of the Christian Religion. In the upper part Christ is shown between God the Father above and the Dove of the Holy Spirit below, with the Virgin on his right and St John the Baptist on his left. To either side are rows of saints and prophets, while below, the body of the faithful gather round an altar bearing the Eucharist. The balanced but animated throng of the faithful comprises popes, cardinals, bishops and laymen, some anonymous, others deliberately identifiable. Most notable are Dante, Fra Angelico and the patron's uncle, Sixtus IV.

On the opposite wall is Raphael's masterpiece, the *School of Athens* (✪). The composition is centred around the two majestic figures of Plato and Aristotle, representing Natural and Moral Philosophy; the former may be a portrait of Leonardo da Vinci. They stand beneath the magnificent span of a coffered vault, an architectural dream inspired by the plans of Raphael's cousin Bramante for the new **Saint Peter's**. We do not know now exactly how many of the figures are supposed to be portraits, whether of Classical or contemporary persons, but the man leaning on a block and writing has always been taken to be Michelangelo as Heraclitus. However, the overall sense of intellectual ferment is plain enough. In artistic terms, it is Raphael's supreme achievement to have created a noble and perfectly harmonious world of study that is never boring or monotonous. Within a composition of great symmetry, he ensures that every detail is worthy of contemplation.

In the centre of the *Parnassus* (✪) above the window sits Apollo surrounded by the Muses, with groups of poets and writers on either side. The blind Homer is flanked by Dante (in profile) and Virgil. Farther down, Sappho is identified by a scroll, but most of the figures remain unnamed, although Boccaccio and Tebaldeo are said to be among their number. This exquisite flowing composition makes light of the inconvenience of the shape Raphael was obliged to fill, and is in many ways the most natural of all the frescoes in the room.

It is faced by allegorical figures of *Prudence, Fortitude* and *Temperance*, and, below them, scenes of *Justinian Receiving the Pandects* and *Gregory IX Approving the Decretals*. The lower section of this wall is the only part of the *Stanza* where the intrusion of Raphael's workshop is apparent.

Room III: Stanza di Eliodoro (1512-14). The theme of the frescoes here is the miracle of Divine intervention. Raphael gave *Leo I Repulsing Attila* a Roman setting, although the actual event probably took place near Ravenna. It shows Leo I, with the features of Leo X, advancing on a white mule. Work began while the latter was a cardinal and finished during his papacy. The *Mass of Bolsena* (★) celebrates the miracle that befell a doubting priest, who, while celebrating Mass in Bolsena, saw blood pour forth from the Sacred Host. The event gave rise to the Feast of Corpus Christi, and the construction of Orvieto Cathedral. Julius II is pictured on the right, surrounded by kneeling Swiss Guards. The *Expulsion of Heliodorus from the Temple* (★) derives from a story in the Apocrypha, telling how Heliodorus was sent to seize the treasure of the Temple of Jerusalem, and was driven out by an angelic horseman. The dramatic mood of the fresco shows a very real development from the calmer world of the previous Stanza. The *Liberation of St Peter from Prison* (★) is visualized in three parts that work perfectly as a whole, while the effects of nighttime and supernatural radiance are brilliantly rendered. The angel is shown waking Peter, and leading him past the sleeping guards.

Room IV: Sala di Costantino (1517-24). This room contains four frescoes, some of which may have been based on Raphael's designs, although most of the work was completed after his death in 1520. They are the *Baptism of Constantine*, which is set in the Baptistry of **San Giovanni in Laterano** and attributed to Francesco Penni; the *Battle of the Milvian Bridge*, showing Constantine's victory over Maxentius, mostly by Giulio Romano; the *Apparition of the Cross*, by Giulio Romano; and the *Donation of Constantine*, attributed to Giulio Romano and Francesco Penni.

Loggia of Raphael (C) (D) This so-called loggia is the middle of three arcades, built one upon the other, begun by Bramante and finished after his death by Raphael (1519). The second loggia was also decorated by Raphael, in collaboration with his pupils. (The ground-floor and top loggias were decorated by Giovanni da Udine, but both are closed to the public.) The decorative surrounds, involving stuccoes and grotesques, derive from antiquity, while the scenes in the vaults depict Old Testament stories, with four from the New Testament in the last bay. The series is known as Raphael's Bible.

Sala dei Palafrenieri (C) (D) Also known as The Room of the Chiaroscuri for its late 16thC monochrome frescoes, this room contains a **model of the dome of St Peter's**, a copy of one of Michelangelo's own models. A door bearing the name and coat-of-arms of Julius II leads to the Chapel of Nicholas V.

Chapel of Nicholas V (C) (D) The walls of the chapel were decorated with **frescoes** (★) by Fra Angelico between 1447 and 1451. They show scenes from the lives of St Stephen (upper level) and St Lawrence (lower level). The exquisite colouring and charm of these compositions are typical of the style of this most holy of painters.

Borgia Apartments (C) (D) These take their name from Alexander VI (1492-1503), who used the whole of the first floor of the palace of Nicholas V as his personal apartments. The chief interest of these rooms centres on the **frescoes** (★) by Pinturicchio, executed between 1492-94. The richly decorated **Room of the Saints** (Room V) is considered by many to be his masterpiece.

Collection of Modern Religious Art (C) (D) This huge collection of modern paintings, sculpture and graphic art was set up by Paul VI and is well displayed in 50 rooms, including the first rooms of the **Borgia Apartments** (see above).

Sistine Chapel (A) (B) (C) (D) (★) The chapel was built by Baccio Pontelli between 1475 and 1480 by order of Sixtus IV. The interior decoration was at first a team effort involving the leading painters of the time: Perugino, Botticelli, Ghirlandaio and Rosselli, assisted by Pinturicchio, Piero di Cosimo and Bartolomeo della Gatta; later they were joined by Signorelli. This work was begun in 1481 and completed 2yrs later, at which time the chapel was consecrated by Sixtus and dedicated to the Virgin Mary, who was honoured in a central fresco on the w wall.

Side walls (★). Proceeding from the altar wall, the scenes depict the lives of Moses on the right and Christ on the left, in both cases illustrating the divine prerogative of the papacy. The finest of the Moses frescoes are Botticelli's *Moses Kills the Egyptian* (★) (2) with the Burning Bush and other scenes, and the *Punishment of Corah, Dathan, and Abiron* (★) (5). Of the New Testament scenes, Ghirlandaio's *Calling of Peter and Andrew* (★) (3), with its gallery of contemporary portraits, and Perugino's *Christ Giving the Keys to St Peter* (★) (5), using a Renaissance piazza as a backdrop to the action, are outstanding. The end walls originally had frescoes by Perugino (altar end), Ghirlandaio and Signorelli. These were destroyed and replaced by Michelangelo's *Last Judgment* and inferior late 16thC versions.

Ceiling (★). In 1508 Michelangelo began to paint the ceiling of the chapel for Julius II. There is no doubt that the sculptor was reluctant to accept this exacting commission, but when the work was finally unveiled 4yrs later, after intense labour under most unfavourable conditions, it was clear that he had created a supreme masterpiece. The narrative element of the ceiling consists of nine rectangular panels telling the stories of the Creation, the Fall and Noah, starting from the altar wall, although painted in reverse order. The scenes are as follows: (1) the *Separation of Light from Darkness* (2) the *Creation of the Sun, Moon, and Stars* (3) the *Separation of Land and Water* (4) the *Creation of Adam* (5) the *Creation of Eve* (6) the *Fall, and Expulsion from Paradise* (7) the *Sacrifice of Noah* (8) the *Flood* (9) the *Drunkenness of Noah*.

Although many of these pictures are very familiar, the ceiling never fails to impress. The sheer size of the task is staggering, but it is the mastery of the nude, the nobility of the expressions, and above all the assurance of the compositions, that make the ceiling unique. The Genesis scenes form only the central part of a complex arrangement, however, with the *Ignudi* (nudes) supporting them, and the *Prophets* and *Sibyls* below. These men and women, brothers and sisters of Michelangelo's *Moses* in **San Pietro in Vincoli**, show him at his most monumental and heroic. In the spandrels between them are the shadowy figures of the *Ancestors of Christ*, revealing the darker and more pessimistic side of the artist's character. Finally, in the corners are four scenes showing *Moses*, *David*, *Esther* and *Judith*, which convey a violence and distortion that look forward to the world of the *Last Judgment*.

Last Judgment (★). Michelangelo began preparations for this work, the masterpiece of his later years, in 1533, only 6yrs after the terrible Sack of Rome. Although Paul III — a leader of the movement for spiritual regeneration that swept through the church at this time — approved the work, the message represented Michelangelo's personal view and is utterly uncompromising. The figure of Christ, a beardless and Herculean figure, turns in a dynamic twisting movement, his right hand raised in the direction of the desperate figures of the Damned, who tumble and free-fall to the depths below. Charon, a ghastly black figure, smites with an oar his boat-load of captives.

The mood of the entire work is sombre. Even the Blessed who

rise up on the left side of the picture show more wonder than joy at the sight that greets them. There are 250 figures in the painting, all originally nude: this shocked some, including Paul's Master of Ceremonies, whom Michelangelo had already included among the figures of the Damned, as Minos entwined with a serpent (extreme bottom right corner). Outraged, the official appealed to his master to have it removed, and the Pope is supposed to have replied: "From purgatory I might have been able to obtain your release — but over hell I have no power." Later on, drapery was added, but this certainly formed no part of Michelangelo's scheme for his compellingly powerful painting.

Vatican Library (A) (B) (C) (D) Because of the new one-way system, the visit now begins with Room XIII and ends with Room I. Room X contains the *Aldobrandini Wedding* (★), a justly admired Roman fresco dating from Augustan times. Room V is the Library Reading Room, used for temporary exhibitions.

Braccio Nuovo (C) (D) This "new wing" of the **Chiaramonti Museum** (see before) was inaugurated in 1822. It contains an impressive collection of Classical statuary, including a famous reclining statue of the *Nile*, probably a 1stC copy of a Greek original, and the *Augustus of Porta Prima* (★), the finest statue of the Emperor still in existence.

Pinacoteca (B) (D) It is not easy to select individual paintings from such a rich collection, but some pictures are particularly outstanding. Room II has Giotto's *Stefaneschi Altarpiece* (★), originally in old St Peter's, and one of his very rare surviving panel pictures. Room IV is dominated by the work of Melozzo da Forlì, and contains his fresco of *Sixtus IV Appointing Platina as Vatican Librarian* (★) as well as several fragments from the fresco that was originally in the church of *Santi Apostoli*. The lovely *Musician Angels* (★) are particularly delightful. Room VIII contains three masterly altarpieces by Raphael. The *Coronation of the Virgin* of 1502-3 came from the church of San Francesco at Perugia, while the *Madonna of Foligno* (★) of 1512 was the high altarpiece of *Santa Maria d' Aracoeli*, and shows Raphael at his most tender and Classical. The *Transfiguration* (★), completed in the last year of his life, is a dramatic departure that suggests Raphael would have conquered new worlds but for his tragic death at the age of 37. The walls are lined with ten **tapestries** (★) designed by Raphael for the Sistine Chapel, woven in Brussels. Room IX offers Leonardo da Vinci's ill-treated *St Jerome* (★) and Giovanni Bellini's *Pietà* (★), two very different expressions of the spirit of the Renaissance. Room XII is dominated by four superlative early Baroque altarpieces: Caravaggio's powerful *Deposition* (★), Guido Reni's sombre *Crucifixion of St Peter* (★), Domenichino's moving *Last Communion of St Jerome* (★) and Poussin's unexpectedly brutal *Martyrdom of St Erasmus* (★).

Gregorian-Profane Museum (B) (D) This collection of pagan antiquities was founded by Gregory XVI in 1844 and transferred from the *Lateran Palace* in 1970. It consists mainly of statues and sarcophagi excavated within papal territory.

Pio-Christian Museum (B) (D) This collection was founded by Pius IX in 1854 and moved from the Lateran Palace in 1963. It is particularly interesting for its large collection of Christian sarcophagi and for the statue of the *Good Shepherd* (★), a memorable and rare example of a free-standing Early Christian sculpture.

Missionary-Ethnological Museum (B) (D) Yet another Lateran foundation (begun in 1926), this was transferred to the

Vatican in 1970. The wide-ranging collection features artifacts from the missionary countries.

Historical Museum (B) (D) Established in 1973 by Paul VI, this museum exhibits carriages used by popes and cardinals, and militaria of the papal armed forces, disbanded in 1970.

Via della Conciliazione
Map 4H3.

As far back as the 15thC, the idea had been mooted of opening up the view in front of *Saint Peter's* with a grand processional route; but construction did not begin until 1936, under Mussolini. Many ancient buildings were demolished to make way for this straight, broad thoroughfare, but the impact of the basilica and its lovely colonnade is in fact only diminished by the scale of the new approach. The district on either side is known as the *Borgo*.

Villa Borghese
Map 6F6. Metropolitana: Flaminio.

This magnificent park was created in the 17thC by Cardinal Scipione Borghese, and now covers an area over 6km (3½ miles) in circumference. In 1902, it was bought by Umberto I, King of Italy, and given to the city with the new name of Villa Umberto I. The name never caught on, but, for all that, the gift has been appreciated by generations of Romans for its landscaped beauty and wide-open spaces. Although the whole area is criss-crossed by roads, you can easily escape the traffic and enjoy the shaded plantations of oak and pine, the fountains and the lakes. The gardens of the *Pincio* are to the sw and the **zoo** to the NE (see **Parks and zoos** in *Rome for children*).

Villa Farnesina 血 ☆
Via della Lungara. Map 5I4 ⊡ Open Mon-Sat 9am-1pm. Closed Sun.

This elegant Renaissance villa was built between 1508-11 by Baldassare Peruzzi, for the Sienese banker, Agostino Chigi, and was once richly frescoed, both inside and out. The exterior frescoes on the facade have long since vanished and the plain walls left behind look strangely bare without their decoration.

The **loggia** was originally open, but has been glazed in order to protect one of Raphael's most beguiling works, the fresco cycle of *Cupid and Psyche* (☆) (1517). Although the concept and design are Raphael's, the execution was largely entrusted to his assistants, notably Giulio Romano, Francesco Penni and Giovanni da Udine. Evidence of his hand alone is found in the *Galatea* fresco (☆) in the adjoining room, where simple geometry is allied to a seductive lightness of touch. Other important frescoes in this room include the *Constellations* of Peruzzi, and the *Metamorphoses* and *Polyphemus* by Sebastiano del Piombo. Upstairs are to Peruzzi's intriguing **Sala delle Prospettive**, with illusionistic views of Rome seen through a screen of painted columns and, in the next room, Sodoma's *Marriage of Alexander and Roxanne* (☆), this Sienese artist's undoubted masterpiece. Also here is the **Gabinetto Nazionale delle Stampe**, a very fine collection of prints.

Villa Giulia 血 ☆
Viale delle Belle Arti ☎ 3601951. Map 6E5. Gardens and museum ⊠ ▣ Open Tues-Sat 9am-2pm, also Wed 3-7pm (Oct-Apr 2-6pm), Sun 9am-1pm. Closed Mon.

The Villa Giulia was built for Julius III between 1551 and 1553 and is one of the most attractive examples of late Renaissance architecture in Rome. Vignola's impressive and almost stern **facade** contrasts splendidly with the animation and grace of his inner **courtyard** and **hemicycle** (✪). The **loggia** at the end of this court is by Bartolomeo Ammannati, as, to a certain extent, is the **nymphaeum** (✪) beyond, where Ammannati was assisted by Vasari. The collaboration of three of the most fertile imaginations at work in mid-16thC Rome ensured that the villa would be as charming as it is tranquil. It remains, as ever, a pleasant refuge from the rush of the city.

The villa now houses the **Museo Nazionale di Villa Giulia**, an important collection of Etruscan art, splendidly displayed in a combination of frescoed rooms and more recent additions. The collection is vast, and sometimes the interest is more archaeological than artistic. But there are some very fine Greek vases, which were excavated from Etruscan tombs and provide evidence of an extensive export trade from Greece.

Etruscan civilization, the precursor of Roman culture, is often mysterious, but its finest achievements are both haunting and impressive. The fragmentary group *Apollo and Hercules* (✪), from Veii, from the 6thC BC, is one of the masterpieces of Etruscan sculpture. Another is the **sarcophagus** (✪) from Cervéteri, which shows a husband and wife reclining as if at a banquet. They must have been buried together, but their wonderfully enigmatic smiles do not reveal why.

Villa Medici 🏛

Viale Trinità dei Monti. Gardens open Wed 9-11am, but check with Ufficio Intendenza, Villa Medici, Viale Trinità dei Monti, 00187. Map 6F6. Metropolitana: Spagna.
Built by Annibale Lippi in 1564, this handsome if somewhat austere building was purchased by Cardinal Ferdinando de' Medici in 1580. Napoleon acquired it in 1803 and transferred the National Academy of France here. The **gardens** are little changed in ground plan since they were laid out in the 16thC, and are graced by a number of fine antique sculptures.

Where to stay

As a capital city and cultural centre of international standing, Rome offers an excellent choice of accommodation, ranging from simple *pensioni* or boarding houses, with rudimentary facilities, to unashamedly luxurious palaces that rank among the world's great hotels. In between are a vast number of comfortable, well-run establishments, and you can take your pick from antique charm and old-world courtesy, slick modernity and streamlined service — or, perhaps best of all, a subtle blend of old and new.

In any case, the exterior of a hotel can be no guide to the standard of accommodation within. Crumbling and dilapidated walls can mask the most elegant and shining of interiors, where polished marble floors and mellow antique furniture create an unmistakable atmosphere of fine and gracious living.

The *pensione* is a uniquely Italian institution, usually offering bed-and-breakfast or half-board. Prices differ widely according to location and standard of furnishings and food provided, but are generally reasonable.

Many religious houses in the Vatican City and on the nearby Janiculum Hill offer a similar type of accommodation. Prices are again very reasonable, and people of all faiths, or none, are welcomed. For travellers alighting from overnight trains or for anyone arriving in Rome with no base to go to and a few hours to spare, the *albergo diurno* or day hotel at **Stazione Termini** is a useful place to freshen up with a shower and perhaps a shave, although no sleeping facilities are provided.

Standards of all types of accommodation are strictly monitored by the Regional Board of Tourism. They are defined as de luxe and first- to fourth-class for hotels, and P1 to P3 for *pensioni*.

Noise

Narrow streets, tall buildings and a long and honourable tradition of horn-blasting among motorists and scooter-riders make Rome one of the noisiest cities in Europe. On hot, dusty summer days and nights, concerted use of hooters and klaxons can reach fever pitch. Bear this in mind when choosing accommodation and, if you're intent on staying in the city centre, at least ask for a room facing away from the main street, perhaps onto a courtyard or quiet alley at the back. The room may be darker and have a less attractive view, but these are minor considerations when set against the relative peace and tranquillity.

Of course, you may well decide to stay in a quieter (and probably cheaper) off-centre area, in which case you will have to weigh up the inconvenience and time wasted in travelling to and fro.

"Quiet hotel" (⌂) symbols applied in the following listings do not guarantee absolute quiet, but indicate relatively peaceful locations.

Booking

The peak tourist season lasts from Apr-Oct, but good, low-cost accommodation is always heavily booked and, whatever price bracket you are aiming for, you should always try to make advance bookings. (See *Sample booking letter* in *Words and phrases*.) British travellers can obtain a brochure listing recommended hotels and *pensioni* from **ENIT —Italian State Tourist Office** (*1 Princes St., London, W1R 8AY* ☎ *(01) 408-1254*). The same brochure, together with a list of religious houses offering accommodation, is available in Rome from offices of **EPT — Ente Provinciale per il Turismo** (*Via Parigi 11* ☎ *461851*). There are branches at Fiumicino Airport, Stazione Termini and motorway service areas at Salaria Ovest (when arriving from Florence) and Frascati Est (when arriving from Naples).

Price

Price bands given in the following listings are intended only as rough guides to average prices. There are five bands: cheap, inexpensive, moderate, expensive and very expensive. See *How to use this book* for the approximate prices they correspond to.

Prices can vary considerably within one hotel, according to the size and position of the rooms. If making a booking in person, it is therefore advisable — and quite acceptable — to ask to see the types of room available. Rates are displayed by law in every room but may be quoted exclusive of tax, service and breakfast. You should therefore always ask for an *inclusive* rate. Other extras could be air conditioning and, for rooms without a bathroom *en suite*, use of bath. On the plus side, many hotels have off-season rates between Nov and Mar, which are worth inquiring about.

Tipping
Tips are expected by commissionaires and by the porter who carries your cases to your room. You should also give something to the room maid when you leave.

Meals
Inflation and high staff costs have in recent years played havoc with the restaurant facilities of smaller hotels. Family-run establishments have generally managed to maintain their restaurants, but many others have been forced to abandon the attempt. A few do not even serve breakfast, but with a number of excellent bars around the corner, this is no great hardship. (See *Bars, cafés and ice-cream shops*.) Many of the larger hotels such as the **Cavalieri Hilton**, **Lord Byron** and **Atlante Star** have excellent restaurants that attract non-residents as well.

Choosing
The area around Via Veneto, just s of the Villa Borghese, boasts the greatest number of large, first-class hotels. Those around Piazza di Spagna and the Pantheon tend to be smaller but equally exclusive. More modest establishments and *pensioni* can also be found in all these areas, but predominate on the other side of the river, in the Borgo and Prati, where relative peace and quiet can be traded for a short bus ride into the city centre.

Like most city rail terminals, Stazione Termini is surrounded by a vast array of accommodation. The district has lost its former cachet and in some places is distinctly seedy, but a few fine hotels linger on, maintaining consistently high standards in an atmosphere of change and decay. They are convenient for most of the sights of ancient Rome and well placed for public transport. You can also stay right outside the city centre, above the Villa Borghese or on Monte Mario, where the air is cleaner and fresher but the city's sights and other attractions less accessible.

Hotels classified by area
Pantheon and Piazza Navona
Cardinal *III*◻
Cesari *I*◻
Colonna Palace *IIII*◻
Genio *III*◻
Portoghesi *I*◻
Raphael *IIII*◻
Sole al Pantheon *I*◻
Tiziano *III*◻
Parioli and Monte Mario
Cavalieri Hilton *IIIII* 🏨
Lord Byron *IIIII*
Piazza di Spagna
Condotti *I*◻
Fontana *III*◻
Hassler-Villa Medici *IIIII* 🏨
D'Inghilterra *IIII*
Delle Nazioni *IIII*
De La Ville *IIIII*

Termini and Colosseum
Anglo Americano *III*◻
Britannia *III*◻
Diana *III*◻ ✿
Edera *III*◻
Esperia *III*◻
Forum *IIII*
Grand *IIIII* 🏨
Londra e Cargill *IIIII*
Massimo d'Azeglio *IIIII*
Milani *III*◻
Napoleon *III*◻ ✿
Quattro Fontane *I*◻ ✿
Quirinale *IIIII*
Villa delle Rose *I*◻ ✿
Vatican and Prati
Arcangelo *III*◻
Atlante Garden *IIIII*
Atlante Star *IIIII* 🏨

Columbus *III* ✿
Diplomatic *IIII*
Giulio Cesare *IIIII*
Jolly Leonardo da Vinci *IIIII*
Via Veneto
Alexandra *III*
Ambasciatori Palace *IIIII* 🏰
Bernini Bristol *IIII* 🏰
Eden *IIII* 🏰
Excelsior *IIIII* 🏰
Flora *IIII*
Imperiale *III*
Jolly *IIIII*
Marcella *III* ✿
Savoia *IIIII*
Victoria *IIIII* ✿

Alexandra

Via Vittorio Veneto 18, 00187
☎ 461943 ✆ 622655. Map 7G7 *III*
45 rms 🛏 45 AE ◉ ⦿ VISA
Metropolitana: Barberini.
Location: At the s end of Via Veneto,
within walking distance of the
Spanish Steps. Modest hotels cost
over the odds in this still-popular
location, and the Alexandra is no
exception. Rooms for the most part
are large and lofty, if rather shabby,
and the atmosphere is one of faded
gentility. The Via Veneto is busy
24hrs a day, and a room at the back
is advisable.
✿ ☐ ☐ ⌨ ⁓ 🚻 ▬

Ambasciatori Palace 🏰

Via Vittorio Veneto 70, 00187
☎ 47493 ✆ 610241 ✆ 6799303.
Map 7G7 *IIIII* 147 rms 🛏 147 ▦
🖛 by arrangement ⥿ AE ◉ ⦿
VISA *Metropolitana: Barberini.*
Location: On the main sweep of Via
Veneto, backing onto the elegant
Ludovisi Quarter. Impeccable
service, palatial rooms and fine
furnishings keep this
long-established hotel in the luxury
class. Despite having been
completely renovated, it is still run
on very traditional lines. The
popular but pricey **ABC** terrace
restaurant is reached directly from
the Via Veneto.
✿ ⛄ ☐ ⌨ ⁓ ⟨⟨ 🚻 Y

Anglo Americano ✿

Via Quattro Fontane 12, 00184
☎ 472941 ✆ 626147 ✆ 6799795.
Map 7H7 *III* 120 rms 🛏 120 ▦
🖛 AE ◉ ⦿ VISA *Metropolitana:*
Barberini.
Location: In the middle of the
Quirinale district, near Piazza
Barberini. An inexpensive hotel
with 4-star facilities, very
conveniently located. Decor is
modern but stylish and the staff
courteous.
✿ ☐ ⌨ ▬

Arcangelo

Via Boezio 15, 00192 ☎ 6896459
✆ 613010 ✆ 3211736. Map 5G4
III 33 rms 🛏 33 ⥿ AE ◉ ⦿
VISA
Location: Close to Castel Sant'
Angelo; Via Boezio runs parallel to
Via Cola di Rienzo. A now pleasant
although not palatial hotel following
extensive renovation in recent
years. Situated in a quiet area, it is
nevertheless handy both for the
shops of Cola di Rienzo and the
Vatican. A roof garden is planned,
which will command a somewhat
restricted view of St Peter's.
✿ ☐ ⌨ ▽

Atlante Garden

Via Crescenzio 78, 00193
☎ 6872361 ✆ 623172 ✆ 6872315.
Map 4G3 *IIII* 43 rms 🛏 43 ▦ AE
◉ ⦿ VISA *Metropolitana:*
Ottaviano.
Location: Close to the Vatican and
Via Cola di Rienzo; Via Crescenzio
runs from Piazza del Risorgimento
to Piazza Cavour. Less luxurious
sister of the **Atlante Star** and
without the views, this is
nevertheless a comfortable and
well-run establishment in a quiet
quarter near to St Peter's. Rooms can
be had at lower prices, but the
standards of service remain high,
and guests are welcome at the Star's
rooftop restaurant a block and a half
away.
✿ ☐ ⌨ 🚻 Y ▬

Atlante Star 🏰

Via Vitelleschi 34, 00193
☎ 6879558 ✆ 622355 ✆ 6872300.
Map 4G3 *IIII* 61 rms 🛏 61 ▦ ⥿
AE ◉ ⦿ VISA *Metropolitana:*
Ottaviano.
Location: Between Castel Sant'
Angelo and the Vatican; the hotel is
a short walk from both. One of the
most agreeable hotels in Rome, with
a loyal and growing regular
clientele, which significantly
includes Italian businessfolk on
expense accounts. Comfortable, if
compact, rooms, stylishly decorated
and ingeniously designed by
architect Giuseppe Luzzi. A youthful
staff manages to generate an
atmosphere of friendly efficiency
under the watchful eye of proprietor
Benito Mencucci. The hotel's
terrazza commands superb views of
the entire city, particularly the dome
of St Peter's. Swallows wheel
around the rooftop garden, which is
so far above the bustle of the city
that the birdsong is never drowned
out by traffic noise. Courtesy cars
pick guests up from the airport, and

137

a private plane and business office can be arranged. (See **Les Etoiles** in *Restaurants*.)

♥ « ♯ □ ▱ ♨ 🐎 ❤ 🐕 ⊟

Bernini Bristol 🏨
Piazza Barberini 23, 00187
☎ *463051* 🕭 *610554* 🕭 *4750266.*
Map 7G7 ▥ *125 rms* 🛏 *125* ▦
🖭 *by arrangement* ≕ AE ⊙
🔘 ᴠ̄ɪ̄s̄ᴀ̄ *Metropolitana:*
Barberini.
Location: At the foot of Via Veneto and well placed for main sights, shops and cafés. Facing Bernini's magnificent *Triton Fountain*, the solid, marble-clad entrance advertises the traditional virtues of this comfortably conservative hotel. The presidential suite has an attractive roof garden with fine views over the city and a price to match, and every room has independent air conditioning and a refrigerator bar.

♯ & □ ▱ ♨ ♨ ❤

Britannia
Via Napoli 64, 00184 ☎ *463153*
🕭 *611292* 🕭 *462343. Map 7H7* ▥
32 rms 🛏 *32* ▦ ╾ AE ⊙ 🔘
ᴠ̄ɪ̄s̄ᴀ̄ *Metropolitana: Termini or Repubblica.*
Location: Close to Stazione Termini and other public transport. A small, efficiently-run hotel, not far from the great patriarchal basilica of Santa Maria Maggiore. The interior has been recently modernized and redecorated and every room now has a sun lamp, refrigerator bar and, for the security-conscious, a personal safe.

♯ □ ▱ ❤ ⊟

Cardinal
Via Giulia 62, 00186 ☎ *6542719*
🕭 *612373. Map 5H4* ▥ *73 rms*
🛏 *73* ▦ 🖭 *by arrangement* AE
⊙ 🔘 ᴠ̄ɪ̄s̄ᴀ̄
Location: Close to the Tiber, on the edge of the old city. A relative newcomer to the Roman scene, this small but elegantly furnished hotel was opened in 1974, but is not without a past. The building was originally a Renaissance palace and at one time also served as a municipal courthouse. Fortunately, great care has been taken to preserve the ancient character. Massive squared blocks, taken from the Roman Forum, can be seen behind the bar, and a Sabine tombstone is evident in the dining-room wall. Further delights are the 17thC antiques and shady garden patio.

🏠 ♯ & ▱ ♥ « ❤

138

Cavalieri Hilton 🏨
Via Cadlolo 101, 00136 ☎ *31511*
🕭 *625337. Map 2D2* ▥ *387 rms*
🛏 *387* ▦ ╾ ╾ ≕ AE ⊙ 🔘
ᴠ̄ɪ̄s̄ᴀ̄
Location: On Monte Mario, N of the Vatican City. Admittedly the view from the Hilton is breathtaking, but you have to decide whether it makes up for the inconvenient situation well outside the centre of Rome. In summer, when the city becomes intolerably hot, the choice is not too difficult. Service and facilities are all you could wish for, including sauna, massage, a swimming pool and tennis facilities, and a courtesy bus winds its way up and down the slopes of Monte Mario at frequent intervals, providing a link-up with the city. Perhaps the most attractive feature of the hotel is **La Pergola**, the delightful roof-top restaurant-discotheque where you can enjoy spectacular views over the entire city while you dine and dance the night away. (See *Nightclubs and discos* in *Nightlife*.)

🏠 ♯ & □ ▱ ♥ « ♨ ❤ ⊙ 🎵 ⊟

Cesari
Via di Pietra 89a, 00186
☎ *6792386. Map 6H6* ▯ *50 rms*
🛏 *36* AE ⊙ 🔘 ᴠ̄ɪ̄s̄ᴀ̄
Location: Just off the busy Corso, and close to the Pantheon and Piazza Navona. Authentic without, completely renovated and modernized within, this 18thC hotel once accommodated Mazzini and Garibaldi. Nowadays it has no pretensions to grandeur, but the central location and friendly bar have earned it many faithful patrons.

♯ ▱ ❤

Colonna Palace
Piazza di Montecitorio 12, 00186
☎ *6781341* 🕭 *621467* 🕭 *6781345.*
Map 6H5 ▥ *100 rms* 🛏 *100* ▦
≕ 🖭 *by arrangement* AE ⊙ 🔘
ᴠ̄ɪ̄s̄ᴀ̄
Location: In the old city, close to the Pantheon and Piazza Navona. A first-class hotel situated in a quiet square, opposite Bernini's grandiose Palazzo di Montecitorio, now the lower house of the Italian parliament. It is comfortably but unexcitingly furnished in a nondescript modern style, but excellent service is guaranteed.

🏠 ♯ & □ ▱ ❤ ⊟

Columbus ♣ ᾱᾱᾱ
Via della Conciliazione 33, 00193
☎ *6867796* 🕭 *620096* 🕭 *6864874.*

Map 4H3 ⫿⫿⫾ *107 rms* ⬚ *80* ⬚
⫸ *AE* ⊙ ⊙ *VISA*
*Location: Between St Peter's and the
Castel Sant' Angelo.* The hotel takes
up the greater part of the Palazzo
dei Penitenzieri, built in the 15thC
for Cardinal Domenico della Rovere,
and retains much of the original
decoration. The magnificent lounge,
formerly the main hall, has a superb
cassettone beamed ceiling, and
elsewhere there are frescoed
vaulted galleries. Fine period
furniture and paintings blend
discreetly into their palatial
surroundings, creating an
atmosphere of gracious living that is
a real bargain at rates like these.
⫸ □ ▱ ☼ ⵏ

___

Condotti
Via Maria de' Fiori 37, 00187
☎ 6790457. *Map 6G6* ⫿⫾ *19 rms*
⬚ *19*.
*Location: Close to Piazza di Spagna
and in the heart of Rome's most
exclusive shopping district.* A
modest and unpretentious hotel set
in a narrow, cobbled street, it takes
its name from nearby Via Condotti,
famous for its fashionable jewellers
and tailors. In this prime location,
the hotel is well placed for most of
the city's major sights and
attractions. Accommodation is basic
but comfortable, and some of the
rooms have little terraces where you
can watch the well-heeled world go
by.
⌂ ⫸ □ ▱ ⊿ ⬚

___

Diana ✿
Via Principe Amedeo 4, 00185
☎ 4751541 ✆ 611198. *Map 7H8*
⫿⫾ *187 rms* ⬚ *187* ⫸ ▤ *AE* ⊙
VISA *Metropolitana: Termini*
*Location: Between Stazione Termini
and Santa Maria Maggiore.* An
efficiently-run second-class hotel,
conveniently located for public
transport and the airport buses from
Via Giolitti. Furnishings are plain
and unpretentious, but the place is
well geared to the needs of tourists.
⫸ ▱ ⵏ

___

Diplomatic
Via Vittoria Colonna 28, 00193
☎ 6799389 ✆ 610506. *Map 6G5*
⫿⫾ *35 rms* ⬚ *7* ▤ ⬌ *by
arrangement* ⫸ ▤ *AE* ⊙ *VISA*
*Location: Between Ponte Cavour
and Piazza Cavour, near Castel
Sant' Angelo.* Four-star
accommodation on the right side of
the river for the Vatican but only a
bridge away from the livelier
quarters of the city.
⫸ □ ⵕ ⬚

___

Eden ⬚
Via Ludovisi 49, 00187
☎ 4743551 ✆ 610567 ✆ 4742401.
Map 7G7 ⫿⫿⫾ *110 rms* ⬚ *110* ▤
⬚ *by arrangement* ⫸
Metropolitana: Barberini.
*Location: In the exclusive Ludovisi
Quarter, w of Via Veneto.* A
long-established top-class hotel,
with a high standard of service and
the lowest rates of all the hotels in
this class. The restaurant, **La
Terrazza dell' Eden**, offers a
spectacular panorama of the city,
taking in the Villa Medici to the N
and the Quirinal to the s.
⌂ ⫸ □ ▱ ⵌ ⵏ ⵐ ⵏ

___

Edera
Via Poliziana 75, 00184
☎ 7316341 ✆ 621472. *Map 11/8*
⫿⫾ *46 rms* ⬚ *12* ⬌ ⬚ *by
arrangement* ⫸ ▤ ⊙ *VISA*
*Metropolitana: Colosseo or
Vittorio Emanuele.*
*Location: Off Via Merulana in the
Colle Oppio district, above the
Colosseum.* A more peaceful and
convenient location for a hotel in
Rome would be hard to find. The
Edera was completely redecorated
in a bland, modern colour-scheme.
The only really attractive feature of
this face-lift is the small patio with
white garden furniture in the well of
the building. But quiet it certainly is:
wishing to preserve the tranquillity
of his hotel, the owner does not
accept groups.
⌂ ⫸ ▵ □ ▱ ⵙ ⵏ

___

Esperia
Via Nazionale 22, 00184
☎ 4744245 ✆ 614635. *Map 7H7*
⫿⫾ *98 rms* ⬚ *98* ▤ ⬚ *by
arrangement* *AE* ⊙ ⊙ *VISA*
Metropolitana: Repubblica.
*Location: Near Stazione Termini
and other public transport.* A 19thC
hotel that offers traditional service
with a convenient if noisy location.
The public rooms remain much as
they were at the turn of the century,
but most of the bedrooms have
been completely renovated. If traffic
noise bothers you a back room is
essential.
⫸ □ ▱ ⵚ ⵏ

___

Excelsior ⬚
Via Vittorio Veneto 125, 00187
☎ 4708 ✆ 610232 ✆ 4756205.
Map 7G7 ⫿⫿⫾ *394 rms* ⬚ *394* ▤
⬚ ⬌ *AE* ⊙ ⊙ *VISA*
Metropolitana: Barberini.
*Location: On the E side of Via
Veneto, not far from the Villa
Borghese.* Everything about this
splendid hotel is palatial: the

number of bedrooms, the sumptuous bathrooms, the grand scale of the public rooms, the Oriental silk rugs that cover the marble floors, the beautiful antique furnishings. In keeping with the leisurely, relaxed air of the whole establishment, breakfast is served until 10.30am, and a piano bar provides nostalgic evening entertainment far into the night. One of the prestigious CIGA chain, the Excelsior rates high among the top hotels of Rome.

♨ & ☐ ☞ ✎ ♨ ♉ ¶ ♫

Flora

Via Vittorio Veneto 191, 00187
☎ 497821 ● 622256 ® 4820359.
Map 7G7 IIII *177 rms* ☐ *177* ▦
☞ *by arrangement* AE ● VISA
Location: At the top of Via Veneto, near the Porta Pinciana and Villa Borghese. An old-fashioned, comfortably-furnished hotel with first-class traditional service to match. The public rooms have an aura of faded elegance, with muted colour schemes, Oriental carpets and antique furniture. Upstairs, the bedrooms are on a grand scale and many have superb views over the pine-studded park beyond the Aurelian Wall.

♨ ☐ ☞ ✎ ≪ ♉ ¶ ☐

Fontana

Piazza di Trevi 96, 00187
☎ 6786113. *Map 6H6* IIII *28 rms*
☐ *28* ▦ AE ● VISA
Metropolitana: Barberini.
Location: In a wonderfully central position, within walking distance of Piazza Navona, Piazza di Spagna, Via Veneto and the Roman Forum. Facing the **Trevi Fountain**, one of the city's most spectacular Baroque creations, this hotel scores high on convenience of location, but low on seclusion and tranquillity. Outside, from dawn until far into the night, the thundering waters and chattering crowds of sightseers fight hard to be heard. But if you can stand the noise, there is always plenty going on outside your window. The hotel is in fact older than the fountain, for the building was once part of a medieval monastery, although now much restored. You may even be lucky enough to be allocated a room that has been converted from two monks' cells.

♨ ☐ ☞ ¶

Forum

Via Tor de' Conti 25, 00184
☎ 6792446 ● 622549 ® 6799337.

Map 9I6 IIII *79 rms* ☐ *79* ➡ ▦
☞ ➡ *(closed Sun)* AE ● ● VISA
Metropolitana: Colosseo.
Location: Between the Colosseum and Piazza Venezia, overlooking the Imperial and Roman Forums. A converted Renaissance palace, originally built out of material plundered from the ancient ruins nearby. Intriguing Classical fragments include the Corinthian columns visible in the interior. The star feature is the marvellous view from the roof-top restaurant over the Forums and towards the Palatine Hill. In summer, sun-lovers may lunch or dine on the open terrace alongside the restaurant. Bedrooms are smallish but comfortable.

☐ ♨ & ☐ ☞ ✎ ≪ ♟ ¶

Genio

Via G. Zanardelli 28, 00186
☎ 6547246 ● 623651 ® 899371.
Map 5H5 III *61 rms* ☐ *61* ➡
AE ● ● VISA
Location: Just a few paces from Piazza Navona and close to the beautiful antique shops of the Via dei Coronari. The hotel has been completely renovated, and apart from its location it has the advantage of panoramic views from a *terrazza.* An elegant hotel that nevertheless tries to maintain a family atmosphere.

≪ ♨ ☐ ☞ ¶ ☐

Giulio Cesare

Via degli Scipioni 287, 00192
☎ 310244 ● 613010. *Map 5F4* IIII
90 rms ☐ *90* ▦ ➡ AE ● ● VISA
Location: Close to Metropolitana Lepanto and handy for Piazza del Popolo, just over the river.
Commands a rather high price for a hotel in this off-centre quarter, perhaps due to its noble past as the villa of a countess. After the war it was converted into a school, and became a hotel about 30yrs ago. It now provides a comfortable retreat for those who like a quieter life.

♨ ☐ ☞ ♉ ¶ ☐

Grand ▦

Via Vittorio Emanuele Orlando 3,
00185 ☎ 4709 ● 610210
® 4747307. *Map 7G7* IIII *168 rms*
☐ *168* ▦ ☞ ➡ AE ● ● VISA
Metropolitana: Repubblica.
Location: Between Piazza della Repubblica and Piazza San Bernardo, near Stazione Termini.
When this imposing Neoclassical palace opened in 1894, it stood in one of the most fashionable quarters of the city. Piazza della Repubblica and the surrounding streets have

long since lost their chic, but the Grand soldiers on, an oasis of luxury and good taste. It is still the top hotel in Rome of the illustrious CIGA chain, and the natural choice for visiting royalty and VIPs. The majestically proportioned rooms, sumptuous decorations and discreet service are all that you might expect of a top-class hotel, and the facilities include hairdresser, beauty salon and sauna. A café (**Le Pavillon**) and restaurant cater for all occasions.

Hassler-Villa Medici

Piazza Trinità dei Monti 6, 00187
☎ 6792651 ⊙ 610208 ⊚ 6799278.
Map 6G6 ||||| 101 rms 🖿 101 🎛
🖂 ⇌ Metropolitana: Spagna.
Location: Above the Spanish Steps.
This hotel's glorious position must be the envy of all the hoteliers in Rome. Basking in the Baroque grandeur of *Trinità dei Monti*, it overlooks the graceful *Spanish Steps* and the city beyond. Inside, squared marble columns and exquisite furnishings create an atmosphere of quiet affluence that has proved irresistible to international jet-setters. The roof-top restaurant, famed for its stupendous views over the city, is also open to non-residents.

Imperiale

Via Vittorio Veneto 24, 00187
☎ 4756351 ⊙ 621071. Map 7G7
||||| 85 rms 🖿 85 🎛
Location: Rubbing shoulders with some of the most expensive hotels in Rome. If you want to stay in what was once Rome's most fashionable street but don't feel like paying the exorbitant rates of the luxury hotels, this is for you. But a *cappuccino* at any of the cafés nearby will cost up to ten times the price paid in an ordinary bar.

D'Inghilterra

Via Bocca di Leone 14, 00187
☎ 672161 ⊙ 614552 ⊚ 6840828.
Map 6G6 ||||| 100 rms 🖿 100 🎛
🎛 ⊙ 🎛
Location: Close to Piazza di Spagna, in the centre of the city's fashionable shopping district. Not so long ago this hotel was a rather dowdy establishment with a dated charm and exotic history. Writers like Anatole France, Henry James and Ernest Hemingway used to stay here when they came to Rome. The historical associations linger on, but a recent modernization has removed

all trace of mustiness and decay. Smartness and elegance prevail, and prices have skyrocketed in tandem.

Jolly

Corso d'Italia 1, 00198 ☎ 8495
⊙ 612293. Map 7F7 ||||| 200 rms
🖿 200 🎛 ⊙ 🎛
Location: Overlooking the Villa Borghese, just E of Via Veneto. An ultra-modern glass and steel affair, set in a prime position on the edge of the park: Vast public rooms and functional furnishings create a cold and rather impersonal atmosphere, but standards of comfort and efficiency are high. Bedrooms are small but some have beautiful views over the park.

Jolly Leonardo da Vinci

Via dei Gracchi 324, 00192
☎ 39680 ⊙ 611182 ⊚ 3610138.
Map 5F4 ||||| 256 rms 🖿 256 🎛
🖂 ⊙ 🎛
Metropolitana: Lepanto.
Location: Just off Cola di Rienzo, close to the river. This used to be the Grand Hotel L. da Vinci until the Jolly chain got hold of it and turned it into one of its homogeneous but efficient modern facilities. It was completely redecorated and remodelled between 1986 and 1988, a process that has ensured every mod con and removed most of its character. Facilities for massive conferences. There's a third sister, the **Jolly Midas**, out of town — details from central booking.

Londra e Cargill

Piazza Sallustio 18, 00187
☎ 473871 (for reservations
⊙ 460298) ⊙ 622227 ⊚ 4746674.
Map 7G8 ||||| 105 rms 🖿 105 🎛
🎛 ⊙ 🎛
Location: Off Via XX Settembre, not far from Stazione Termini and Via Veneto. The exterior might be that of any anonymous late 19thC *palazzo* but, inside, all is gleaming, clean-lined modernity. Bedrooms are simply but attractively furnished. A large, shiny-new conference room in brilliant yellow/gold is guaranteed to keep delegates awake.

Lord Byron

Via G. de Notaris, 00197
☎ 3615404 ⊙ 611217 ⊚ 3609541.
Map 6E6 ||||| 50 rms 🖿 50 🎛 ⊷
⇌ 🎛 ⊙ 🎛
Location: Parioli district on the edge of the Villa Borghese. A delightfully

Hotels

secluded hotel not far from the Villa Giulia, Julius III's tranquil summer retreat. No hotel in Rome can be more beautifully furnished, and staying here is rather like living in an elegant private house. For most people, the disadvantage of being based outside the city centre is more than offset by the quiet parkland location. Riding facilities are available. The hotel also has a restaurant of distinction in **Le Jardin** (see *Restaurants*).

🏠 ‡ ▢ 🖻 ⛄ ◀≪ 🏛 ⚕

Marcella ✿
Via Flavia 106, 00187 ☎ *4746451* ⊚ *621351. Map 7G8* �**∥**▢ *68 rms* ⌷ *68* 🍴 🚬 *by arrangement* 🔤 ⊡ ⊚ 🚊 *Metropolitana: Repubblica*
Location: Just off Via XX Settembre, equidistant from Stazione Termini and Villa Borghese. Comfortable rooms, some with excellent views, and elegant furnishings. The atmosphere is of a cool retreat from the city in which the Marcella is centrally located. It's a small step to Via Veneta, but a giant leap in prices.

◀≪ ‡ ▢ 🖻 ⌷

Massimo d'Azeglio
Via Cavour 18, 00184 ☎ *460646* ⊚ *610556* ⊛ *4750976. Map 7H8* ∥**∥** *200 rms* ⌷ *200* 🍴 🖻 🚬 🔤 ⊡ 🚊 *Metropolitana: Termini.*
Location: Close to Stazione Termini and other public transport. First opened in 1875 when the district was more salubrious than it is now, the Massimo d'Azeglio has refused to be dragged into the 20thC and, for many people, this is the essence of its appeal. The interior decorations convey more than a hint of nostalgia, and old-fashioned standards of service prevail. It is a well-run, comfortable hotel, and these solid virtues extend to the excellent restaurant.

‡ ▢ 🖻 🏛 ⚕

Milani
Via Magenta 12, 00185 ☎ *4457051* ⊚ *614356* ⊛ *492317. Map 7G8* ∥**∥**▢ *78 rms* ⌷ *78* 🚬 *by arrangement. Metropolitana: Termini.*
Location: Near Stazione Termini. An unpretentious, pleasantly furnished hotel in an unexciting but very convenient situation, almost next door to the main railway station, . Metropolitana, and city and airport bus termini. A good choice for those who want modern facilities and

services without the expensive wrappings and trappings.

‡ ▢ 🖻 ⚕

Napoleon ✿
Piazza Vittorio Emanuele 105, 00185 ☎ *737646* ⊚ *611069. Map 11I8* ∥**∥**▢ *82 rms* ⌷ *82* 🍴 🖻 *by arrangement* 🚬 🔤 ⊡ ⊚ 🚊 *Metropolitana: Vittorio Emanuele.*
Location: Between Stazione Termini and the Colosseum. A first-class hotel, facing onto a grandiose 19thC piazza. The area is now rather seedy and accommodates the city's biggest and most colourful street market, but the hotel remains reasonably well situated for the Colosseum, the Forums and public transport. Air-conditioned bedrooms shut out unwelcome noise from traffic and the market beyond, and service is quietly efficient. A pianist plays in the lounge after dinner on Thurs and Sat, a sign of the hotel's reassuringly traditional style.

‡ 🖻 🏛 ⚕ ♫

Delle Nazioni
Via Poli 7, 00187 ☎ *6792441* ⊚ *614193. Map 6H6* ∥∥∥∥ *74 rms* ⌷ *74* 🍴 🚬 🔤 ⊡ ⊚ 🚊 *Metropolitana: Barberini.*
Location: Near the Trevi Fountain, within walking distance of Piazza di Spagna and most major sights. The central situation is the chief virtue of this once-stuffy hotel. Behind the still-sober facade, a recent modernization has introduced ultra-modern styling, which is perhaps of rather limited appeal.

‡ ▢ 🖻 🏄

Portoghesi
Via dei Portoghesi 1, 00186 ☎ *6545133* ⊚ *626459* ⊛ *6876976. Map 6H5* ∥▢ *27 rms* ⌷ *20* 🍴 ⊡ 🚊*
Location: Between Piazza Navona and the Mausoleum of Augustus. Nestling beside the church of Sant' Antonio, which is adorned with works by such artists as Canova, in an attractive Renaissance street, this small hotel scores mainly through its wonderfully central position. Not long ago it was one of the cheapest hotels in the old city, but prices went up with the installation of a lift and general modernization. Atop the Torre dei Frangipane opposite the hotel is a lamp, put there in thanks to the Virgin Mary for saving the life of a baby carried up the tower by a monkey in the 17thC, a story that these days guarantees

good behaviour among the hotel's younger guests.
🏠 ⚡ 📠

Quattro Fontane ♣

Via delle Quattro Fontane 149, 00184 ☎ *464480* ▥ *26 rms* ▦ *22. Metropolitana: Barberini.*
Location: In one of the less frenetic streets in the heart of the city separating the Palazzi Barberini and Quirinale. This offers comfortable lodgings in a very central location at bargain prices for those not too insistent on 5-star luxury and willing to accept an inexperienced but keen staff that is anxious to please clients of this new hotel. Try it soon, before the rates go up to match the location.
⚡ 📠

Quirinale

Via Nazionale 7, 00184 ☎ *4707* ⊙ *610332* ⊗ *4820099. Map 7H7* ▥▥▥ *200 rms* ▦ *200* ▦▦ *by arrangement* ⟺ AE ⊙ ⊙ VISA *Metropolitana: Repubblica.*
Location: Near Piazza della Repubblica and Stazione Termini. A grand hotel with even grander operatic connections, the Quirinale was designed by the architect of the adjacent Teatro dell' Opera, to which it has its own private entrance. Verdi stayed here in 1893 for the première of *Falstaff*, and close associations between hotel and opera house continue, with the bar of the Quirinale a favourite rendezvous for pre-curtain drinks. In Verdi's day, Via Nazionale was not the thundering thoroughfare it is today, and a room at the back was not so essential.
⚡ ♿ ▢ 📠 ➿ ♨ Y

Raphael

Largo Febo 2, 00186 ☎ *650881* ⊙ *622396* ⊗ *6878993. Map 6H5* ▥▥▥ *51 rms* ▦ *51* ▦▦ ⟺ AE ⊙ ⊙ VISA
Location: In the old quarter of the city, close to Piazza Navona. Loaded with style and atmosphere, this ultra-chic hotel conceals a fine blend of antique furniture, *objets d'art* and Oriental rugs behind its vine-covered walls. Bedrooms are on the small side, but some have marvellous views over Renaissance Rome and beyond. Politicians come here en route for the nearby parliament buildings, which gives the added bonus for nervous guests of a 24hr police guard. The central location is also perfect for sightseers and pilgrims. The hotel is being completely renovated in an attempt

to win a fifth star, so the number of rooms available has been temporarily reduced — and the price is soon likely to rise.
🏠 ⚡ ▢ 📠 ➿ Y ▣

Savoia

Via Ludovisi 15, 00187 ☎ *4744141* ⊙ *611339* ⊗ *4746812. Map 7G7* ▥▥▥ *120 rms* ▦ *120* ▦▦ ⟺ AE ⊙ ⊙ VISA *Metropolitana: Barberini.*
Location: In the smart Ludovisi Quarter, w of Via Veneto. A solid, Neoclassical exterior advertises the sterling virtues of this comfortable, well-run hotel. Inside, all is on an expansive scale, although efforts have been made to make the piano bar and snack bar more intimate, and good service can be guaranteed.
🏠 ⚡ ▢ ♿ 📠 🎣 ♨ Y ♩

Sole al Pantheon

Via del Pantheon 63, 00186 ☎ *6780441* ⊗ *626424* ⊗ *6840689. Map 6H5* ▥▥ *28 rms* ▦ *25.*
Location: Overlooking the Pantheon, in the heart of the old city. This small hotel began life as an inn in the late 15thC and is rich in historical associations. Ariosto, author of the spirited epic *Orlando Furioso*, lodged here in 1513, and Mascagni, composer of the late 19thC operatic perennial, *Cavalleria Rusticana*, wrote several of his works here. Recent renovations have effected a modest face-lift, but the facade retains its Renaissance charm.
⚡ 📠 Y

Tiziano

Corso Vittorio Emanuele 110, 00186 ☎ *6875087* ⊗ *623997. Map 6H5* ▥▥▥ *50 rms* ▦ *45* ⟺ AE ⊙ ⊙ VISA
Location: Near Piazza Navona, Pantheon and Piazza Venezia. A second-class hotel on one of the busiest streets in Rome, a short bus-ride away from St Peter's. The building began life as a stately patrician palace, but the vast public rooms are now decked out with a curious mix of antique and modern furnishings. To escape traffic noise, ask for a back room.
⚡ 📠 Y *Some with* ▢ ▣

Victoria ♣

Via Campania 41, 00187 ☎ *473931* ⊙ *610212* ⊗ *6799319. Map 7F7* ▥▥▥ *110 rms* ▦ *110* ▦▦ ⟺ AE ⊙ ⊙
Location: Close to the Villa Borghese and Via Veneto. Tucked away in a quiet street facing the **Aurelian**

143

Wall, this is one of the most delightful hotels in the whole of Rome, renowned for its stylish interior and high standard of service. Upstairs, from the upper rooms and roof terrace, there are splendid views over the park. Be warned: visitors tend to become hooked on the Victoria's charms and feel the need to return here again and again.

🛏 🕇 ᱐ ⌸ 🗀 ⦿ ☷ ⵒ ☰

Villa delle Rose ✿
Via Vicenza 5, 00185 ☎ *4451795. Map 7G8* ◫ *29 rms* ☷ *29* Aᴇ ⊙ ⦿ *Metropolitana: Termini.*
Location: Close to Stazione Termini and other public transport. A small, clean, efficiently-run hotel, on the more salubrious side of the central railway station. Once a fine private residence in this erstwhile elegant district, it still recalls that vanished

era with its beautifully proportioned drawing-room (now the lounge) and delightful shady garden, complete with burbling rock pool.
🕇 ᱐ ⌅ ⵒ

De la Ville
Via Sistina 69, 00187 ☎ *6733* ⦿ *620836* ⦿ *6784213. Map 6G6*
⫴ *195 rms* ☷ *189* ⊞ ᱐ ⚌ Aᴇ ⊙ ⦿ 𝐕𝐼𝐒𝐀 *Metropolitana: Spagna.*
Location: Near the Spanish Steps. A first-class hotel, well situated for the fashionable shops and cafés around Piazza di Spagna and in Via Veneto. Its elegant image is now somewhat overshadowed by the swanky **Hassler** up the road, but an attractive *al fresco* garden restaurant and spectacular views from the upper bedrooms and roof terrace keep it popular.
⚬ ⦿ 🕇 ☐ ⌅ ᱐ ☷ ☰ ⵒ

Cheaper hotels and pensioni

Although cheaper accommodation can still be found in Rome, don't expect the charming *pensioni* of 19thC grand tours. These days, this type of hostelry is strictly for the young and sturdy who don't mind sharing. *Pensioni* are invariably up at least one flight of stairs, and almost invariably full. Rucksack toters would do well to check the electronic board at Stazione Termini to see what is available — and then double-check by phone. The following list begins with a reasonably detailed description of the best, most now classified as *alberghi* rather than *pensioni* (costing between Ŀ30,000 and Ŀ60,000), with a selection of the rest (mostly under Ŀ30,000, some well under).

Adriatic
Via Vitelleschi 25, 00193 ☎ *6869668. Map 4G3* ◫ *32 rms* ☷ *30* 🚗 *Metropolitana: Ottaviano.*
Location: A few yards from Castel Sant' Angelo. Handily positioned for the Vatican and Prati shops, this is a 2-star hotel with comfortable rooms (many with bath/shower) and a TV lounge. But be prepared to eat out in the many good *trattorie* in the district.
🕇

Forti's Guest House ⌂
Via Fornovo 7, 00192 ☎ *3212256. Map 5F4* ◻ *22 rms* ☷ *10. Metropolitana: Lepanto.*
Location: In Prati, across the Tiber from the city centre, but within walking distance of Piazza del Popolo. A clean and friendly establishment, run by the American owner and his Italian wife.
🛏

Golden
Via Marche 84, 00187 ☎ *493746* ⦿ *4821660. Map 7G7* ◫ *13 rms* ☷ *11* ⊞ Aᴇ *Metropolitana: Barberini.*
Location: Near the Aurelian Wall, Villa Borghese and Via Veneto. A modern, impeccably clean *pensione* on the first floor of an old house. Cool, off-white decor and one small, carpeted lounge-cum-breakfast room. The fashionable central location and extra facilities (such as refrigerator bar in every room) make it slightly expensive for this type of accommodation.
🛏 🕇 ☰

Katty ⌂ ✿
Via Palestro 35, 00185 ☎ *4041216. Map 7G9* ◻ *9 rms* ⌂ *Metropolitana: Termini.*
Location: Close to Stazione Termini, city and airport bus termini and Metropolitana. Modest but well-kept accommodation in an unexciting

but convenient area. Cheap rates make this *pensione* a real bargain for students who don't mind sharing three or four to a room.

Pension Suisse ♦
Via Gregoriana 56, 00187
☎ 6783649. Map 6G6 ☐ 28 rms
☐ 9. Metropolitana: Barberini.
Location: Near the Spanish Steps. A long-established and efficiently run *pensione*, on two floors of an old building in a smart and very central area. The rooms are large, well-furnished and kept spotlessly clean, and there's a lounge as well as a breakfast room.
♨

Scalinata di Spagna
Piazza Trinità dei Monti 17,
00187 ☎ 6793006 ☎ 6799582.
Map 6G6 ☐ 14 rms ☐ 14.
Metropolitana: Spagna.
Location: Above the Spanish Steps. Smallish, with a marvelous view across the city from its commanding position at the top of the Spanish

Steps. It is comfortably furnished and well run, but you must expect to pay over the odds for the unbeatable location. The view is even better from the roof terrace, where breakfast is served in summer.
▨ ◀€ ♨

♘ Accommodations in the following are likely to be on the spartan side, and bathrooms and bedrooms communal; however, the rates are low:
Alimandi (*Via Veniero 60* ☎ *318404*); **Amati** (*Via V. Veneto 155* ☎ *493651*); **Athena** (*Via Pasquali* ☎ *426379*); **Azzurra** (*Via del Boccaccio 25* ☎ *4746531*); **Ca' d'Oro** (*Via XX Settembre 91* ☎ *4755338*); **Enotria** (*Via Nazionale 13* ☎ *474317 7*); **Isa** (*Via Cicerone 35* ☎ *380253*); **Italia** (*Via Venezia 18* ☎ *4745550*); **Lella** (*Via Palestro 9* ☎ *484940*); **Locanda Marini** (*Via Palestro* ☎ *4047380*); **Piemonte** (*Via Vicenza 34* ☎ *4452240*); **Primavera** (*Piazza San Pantaleo 3* ☎ *6543109*).

Office-from-office

For the traveling businessman who needs more than a hotel room, special facilities are gradually becoming available. Two are quoted below.

Atlante Star
Via Vitelleschi 34 ☎ *6879558* ☎ *622355* ☎ *6799907*. Map *4G3*.
Complete office for rental within the hotel, including phone, fax, telex, typewriter and personal bilingual secretary. Extensive conference facilities available. (See p137 for hotel details.)

Pinciana Office
Via di Porta Pinciana 4 ☎ *4754143* ☎ *621489*. Map *6G6*.
Specialists in the provision of offices for rental in a prestige location close to the Via Veneto, with phone, telex and multilingual secretaries.

Eating in Rome

"Italian cooking" is a misnomer, a catch-all for a hypothetical assemblage of regional, provincial, local and family styles of preparing food with the grace that emits so spontaneously from Italian hands. But even if *la cucina italiana* did exist, Rome would not be its capital.

Instead, Rome remains — gastronomically — a regional center with some renowned "Roman" specialties, although several were borrowed from outlying places and popularized in the city's *trattorie* and *osterie*. Still, Rome has, undeniably, a way of cooking or, more to the point, a way of eating all its own. And even if the city's restaurants rarely garner top ratings in the guidebooks, dining out in them can be a delight, a carnival of colors, flavors, odors, moods and sounds, uniquely and unabashedly Roman.

One of Rome's pleasures is *al fresco* dining, whether the setting is a manicured garden, a terrace under a shady pergola or rickety tables and chairs set nonchalantly in a narrow street. From Apr-Oct they become not only places to eat but also centers for the favored Roman pastime of people-watching, a diversion highlighted by the parade of street musicians and impromptu entertainers who may pass round the hat in scores of places in an evening, but who are especially evident in Trastevere and around Piazza Navona.

Cooking in Italy has become more uniform in recent times, as country traditions have given way to urban expediencies. Beside the omnipresent *pizzerie*, there are ever more *tavole calde* and *tavole fredde* (hot and cold buffets), snack bars and fast-food shops catering to people with no time for a five-course meal. For anyone in a hurry or on a tight budget, they provide an often tasty alternative for at least one meal of the day.

Despite these trends, however, regional cooking continues to thrive. Rome so dominates Latium that *la cucina romana* represents the region, even if the city's cooks tend to interpret the fare more flamboyantly than do their rural counterparts.

Roman cooking is not, as a rule, refined. Although hints of ancient Roman recipes remain (notably in combinations of sweet and sour), the lavish concoctions of the papal and royal courts and the bourgeoisie of olden days are mostly forgotten. What survive are the clever improvisations of the poor. Authentic Roman dishes are often based on rudimentary, even coarse, ingredients — pasta, chick peas, tripe, salt cod, broad beans, sweetbreads, artichokes, brains, ox tails, pig's trotters, mussels, anchovies and salt pork, flavored with garlic, herbs, vinegar, mint, wine and sharp *pecorino* cheese. But the results are hardly humble: Roman cooking is as flavorful and sensuous as any in Italy.

Nor is there a complete lack of luxury. Baby lamb (*abbacchio*), kid (*capretto*) and sucking pig (*porchetta*) are preferred meats. Fresh Mediterranean seafood is devoured in the capital, despite high cost. And the Roman countryside provides exquisite fresh greens and vegetables, which arrive daily at the open-air markets.

A complete Roman repast starts with *antipasti*, sometimes selected from a table laden with a dazzling assortment of cold cuts, cooked and raw vegetables, omelets, olives and shellfish.

Then comes pasta, here, as elsewhere, more often than not the high point of a meal. Pasta is part of what is generally known as *primo piatto* (which also takes in soups, risottos, polenta, crêpes and dumplings). But more than a course or a category, pasta is a national institution. Rome's specialties include *spaghetti alla carbonara* (tossed with bacon, garlic, pepper, grated cheese and raw beaten eggs); *bucatini all' amatriciana* (thin tubes with chili peppers, bacon, often tomatoes and grated *pecorino*); *penne all' arrabbiata* (short, ribbed tubes with a sauce hot enough to make your eyes water); and *fettuccine al burro* (light egg noodles with butter, cream and Parmesan).

Many restaurants provide a choice between meat or fish for a main course. You will notice that restaurants always specify on the menu whether their fish is fresh or frozen, as required by law. Fresh or frozen, fish is always expensive — payment is often by the *etto* (100g) — and will lift a restaurant into a higher price category than that indicated in *How to use this book*, p5.

If you want fish it is wise to select a place noted for fresh products (**La Rosetta**, for instance, where grilled *scampi* are the specialty). Also be sure to try lamb or chicken *alla cacciatora* (with rosemary, garlic and vinegar), *saltimbocca* (veal fillet with *prosciutto* and sage cooked in butter and white wine) and *coda alla vaccinara* (stewed ox tail). Vegetables or salad are usually served separately. Peas are excellent in season, and not to be missed are artichokes, whether *carciofi alla romana* (sautéed in oil, garlic and mint) or *carciofi alla giudia* (flattened like flowers and deep-fried).

Fresh dessert cheeses may follow: perhaps *ricotta* sprinkled with sugar and ground coffee, or *ovoline*, small "eggs" of *mozzarella*. Romans often conclude with fresh fruit or the fruit cup known as *macedonia*. *Gelato* is always good in Rome and, in some places, cakes and tarts are irresistible. The final touch to any meal is a thick *espresso*.

Rome's thousands of eating places vary widely in type, price and quality. In theory, the *ristorante* is the largest and most elegant. *Trattoria* suggests simplicity, often with home cooking and family-style service. The *osteria* or *hostaria* should be simpler still: in Roman terms a place where open wine is served by the liter (or half or quarter) and customers can dine on simple dishes or sandwiches or even on food of their own. But in practice the breakdown is not always so clear. Some *ristoranti* are rather cramped and modest; some *trattorie* are large, luxurious and expensive; and some *osterie* are fully-fledged restaurants (the **Hostaria dell' Orso**, for instance, is one of the most famous and fancy places in Rome).

Although some Italian restaurants have adopted the French-inspired set menu, Romans prefer to order *à la carte*. The check will include bread and cover charge, food and drinks, service (usually 15 percent) and Value Added Tax. On top, the waiter will expect a personal tip of around 10 percent. The *menu turistico* at fixed price includes bread and cover charge, first and second course with vegetables and fruit or dessert, sometimes wine, and service and tax. The price may be attractive, but in Rome the food will be more likely to include leftovers than the house's best. You would probably be better off at a *tavola calda* or *pizzeria*.

As an international center, Rome has several foreign restaurants — French, Chinese, Spanish, German, Arab, American, Japanese — although few that are inspiring. A better bet, if you feel like something other than Roman, would be one of the many regional restaurants, such as **El Toulà** (Venetian), **Taverna Giulia** (Genoese) and **Il Buco** (Tuscan).

Drinking in Rome

Rome, despite appearances to the contrary, is a wine town of sorts. Romans still seem to prefer "local" wines, mostly white, from the Castelli Romani: Frascati, Marino, Colli Albani, Velletri and less specific *appellations*. These can be eminently drinkable when young. Because they are soft, rather full-bodied for whites and well-rounded, they serve as a soothing counterpoint to the somewhat aggressive flavors of much Roman food. Sometimes, though, they can be so unpalatable — especially the open wines served in many *trattorie* and *osterie* — that the only solution is to dilute them with bubbly mineral water, as the Romans often do.

Most good Roman restaurants provide bottled wines from the Castelli and elsewhere in Latium, along with nationally known types such as Chianti, Orvieto, Verdicchio, Pinot Grigio and Barolo. Italy has more than 200 zones of *denominazione di origine controllata*, and wines so labeled are authentic but not necessarily of high quality. Some of Italy's — and Latium's — best wines are categorized simply as *vino da tavola* (table wine).

Latium's rarities include the red Torre Ercolana, Colle Picchioni, Castel San Giorgio and the red and white Fiorano, grown just outside Rome. Also worth trying are Maccarese, the red Cesanese, Cervéteri red and white and the ostentatiously titled Est!Est!Est!

Serious students of Italian wine may also want to browse through well-stocked stores such as the **Enoteca Trimani** (*Via Goito 20*), which carries bottles from every region and most nations, the **Enoteca Costantini** (*Piazza Cavour 16b*) and the **Enoteca Palombi** (*Piazza Testaccio 40*).

The traditional *aperitivo* is vermouth, light or dark, dry or semi-sweet, with a shaving of lemon peel and, in summer, ice. Other favorites are Campari Soda, Punt e Mes and Aperol, all with a bitter taste designed to stimulate the appetite. Increasingly popular as an aperitif is a flute of sparkling wine, preferably a *brut spumante* from Pinot or Prosecco grapes.

The classic finale to a Roman meal is the anis-flavored *sambuca* with *le mosche* (flies) — three coffee beans to munch on while you sip. Similarly sweet are *amaretto* and Strega, although these days Scotch whisky seems to be the leading *digestivo*, and there are many good Italian grappas and brandies to choose from. A lighter alternative would be a glass of sparkling Asti Spumante.

Restaurants classified by area

Pantheon/Piazza del Popolo
Alfredo alla Scrofa *III⊐* ✿
Alfredo L'Originale *III⊐*
L'Angoletto *IIIl*
Dal Bolognese *IIIIl* ✿
La Buca di Ripetta *I⊐* ⬥ ✿
Il Buco *IIIl* ✿
La Campana *I⊐* ⬥ ✿
La Capricciosa *III⊐* ✿
L'Eau Vive *I⊐* to *IIIl*
La Fontanella *III⊐* ✿
Hostaria dell' Orso *IIIl* △
La Majella *III⊐* ✿
L'Orso Ottanta *III⊐* ✿
Pino e Dino *IIIl* △
La Rosetta *IIIl*
El Toulà *IIIl* △
Parioli
Ambasciata d'Abruzzo *III⊐* ✿
Le Jardin *IIIl* △
Piazza Navona
Jonathan's *III⊐*
Passetto *IIIl*
Piazza di Spagna and Trevi
Da Mario *III⊐* ✿

Al Moro *IIIl*
Otello alla Concordia *⊐* to *I⊐* ⬥ ✿
Ranieri *IIIl*
Re degli Amici *III⊐*
Prati
Les Etoiles *IIIl* △
Taberna dei Gracchi *IIIl*
Ponte Vittorio and Largo Argentina
Amapola *IIIl*
Angelino a Tor Margana *III⊐*
Arnaldo *III⊐* ✿
Da Pancrazio *III⊐*
Polese *I⊐* ⬥ ✿
Taverna Giulia *IIIl*
Termini and Colosseum
Da Nazzareno *I⊐* ⬥ ✿
Da Nerone *I⊐*
Taverna Flavia *III⊐*
Trastevere
Comparone *III⊐*
Romolo *IIIl*
Sabatini I and II *IIIl*
Trionfale and Monte Mario
La Caravella *⊐* ⬥

Nuraghe Sardo *III*🗀
**Via Veneto and Corso
d'Italia**
ABC *IIII*
Al Fogher *IIII*
George's *IIII* 🍷
Il Giardino *I*🗀 🍴 🌸
Giovanni *IIII*
Girarrosto Toscano *IIII*
Piccolo Mondo *II*🗀
Sans Souci *IIII* 🍷

ABC

Via Veneto 66 🕿 *4740950. Map
7G7* *IIII* 🍴 🗀 🍷 AE 💿 ⊙ VISA
As the restaurant of the
Ambasciatori Palace (see *Hotels*),
you are guaranteed top service and
elegant surroundings. From
May-Oct, meals can be enjoyed on
the hotel's *terrazza*, which is
probably the best way to enjoy the
Via Veneto. Across the street is the
building in which Brig. Gen. Robert
T. Frederick set up his HQ on the
eve of the liberation of Rome in
June 1944 — now the American
embassy.

Alfredo alla Scrofa 🌸

Via della Scrofa 104 🕿 *6540163.
Map 5H5* *III* 🗀 🍴 AE 💿 VISA
🔊 *Closed Tues.*
Way back in the 1930s, Douglas
Fairbanks and Mary Pickford
presented Alfredo, "King of
Fettuccine," with a golden fork and
spoon. Thereafter, to have your
pasta served with these celebrated
implements was an honor reserved
only for the very rich and famous,
whose photographs literally paper
the walls. Nowadays, even common
mortals can enjoy this favor, but
doubts have been expressed as to
the authenticity of the fork and
spoon. When Alfredo died, many
years ago, his son left the restaurant
to his father's partners and founded
one of his own, and indeed there
are now several restaurants in Rome
of this name, all under different
management. The son now claims
exclusive possession of the true fork
and spoon, and the whereabouts of
the Fairbanks-Pickford originals
must remain one of Rome's many
mysteries , although the owners
here will swiftly produce a set from
a drawer under the till. Alfredo alla
Scrofa is still a good restaurant, but
it is difficult to maintain a famous
reputation over nearly half a
century. All the pasta dishes are still
superb, and the rest is more than
acceptable so long as you avoid the
elaborate dishes. Added attractions
are a good wine list and soulful
guitar player.

Alfredo L'Originale

Piazza Augusto Imperatore 30
🕿 *6878615. Map 5G5* *III* 🗀 🍴
🔊 AE 💿 ⊙ VISA *Closed Sun.*
Another set of golden cutlery, and
more walls lined with photographs
of the famous can be found here,
just off the Via del Corso, where the
third-generation Alfredo keeps the
tradition of the royal family of
fettucine alive and spreads the fame
by cheerfully posing for
photographs tossing pasta for all
and sundry. His claim to be the
original Alfredo to whom Fairbanks
and Pickford presented the fork and
spoon may stretch the
truth — he can only have been but a
noodle in his father's eye at the
time — but, publicity aside, a mean
bowl of *fettucine* is produced here.
Unashamedly aimed at the tourist
with musicians who are old enough
to have serenaded Fairbanks and
Pickford, but most enjoyable.

Amapola

Via Panico 83 🕿 *6530192. Map
5H4* *IIII* 🗀 🍴 AE 💿 VISA
Columns and potted palms set off
the austere elegance of this
restaurant, near Ponte Sant' Angelo,
where the digestion of a fine meal is
assisted by able musicians.

Ambasciata d'Abruzzo 🌸

Via Tacchini 26 🕿 *878256. Map
6D6* *III* 🗀 🍴 AE 💿 VISA *Closed
Sun, three weeks in Aug.*
This Parioli restaurant is nothing
special to look at either inside or
out, but it has loads of atmosphere
and the food is excellent. As soon as
you've sat down, you'll be given a
basket of assorted *salami* to nibble
at while you concentrate on
choosing the real thing. This could
be *raviolini* made with fresh *ricotta*
from the mountains, or a delicately
flavored mutton stew made with
castrato. Both cheese and meat are
delivered daily from Abruzzo, from
where the Montepulciano wine also
comes. There is a vast choice of
regional cheeses to round off the
meal.

Angelino a Tor Margana

Piazza Margana 37 🕿 *6783328.
Map 9I6* *III* 🗀 🍴 🚬 🍴 *Closed
Sun, Aug.*
Angelino used to be a kind of
artistic center as well as a good
restaurant. There was even a Tor
Margana Prize, much sought after by
painters and writers. Now Angelino
rests on its laurels and the names of
the famous are kept only to ennoble
the less traditional items on the

149

menu, such as *Pigeon à la Sartre*. The simple Roman dishes are best. This is a delightful place to eat in summer, when candlelit tables are set in the piazza outside. It's a quiet corner of old Rome, relatively free of traffic, with only a few stray cats to bother you.

L'Angoletto
Piazza Rondanini 51 ☎ 6861203. *Map* **5H5** ▥ ☐ AE ◑ ◙ VISA *Closed Mon, one week in Aug.*
A lively, noisy, extrovert *trattoria* specializing in fish, and just the place to go for rowdy badinage with droll waiters — assuming your Italian is good enough to keep up with them. The hectic style of L'Angoletto was originally the creation of one Alfredo Pantalone; since his departure, older habitués claim that the place has become too sedate and respectable. You may not agree. Try to resist the lure of the innumerable mouthwatering *antipasti*, or you won't have room for the superbly fresh fish or enormous Mediterranean prawns — some say the very best seafood in Rome. Mushrooms are another Angoletto specialty: from late summer to late fall, they have the finest *porcini* and freshest *ovoli*.

Arnaldo ♣
Via Grotta Pinta 8 ☎ 6561915. *Map* **5I5** ▥ ☐ ➡ *Closed Tues, Aug.*
Arnaldo's can be hard to find. It's near Piazza Campo dei Fiori, tucked away in a narrow street that still follows the curve of the ancient Theater of Pompey, and only advertises its presence by a small nameplate beside the door. Arnaldo is painter turned chef, and his restaurant and food both reflect his fascination with the unusual. Surrounded by Art Nouveau lanterns and photographs of the dance, you can spend a delightful evening experiencing the ultimate variations on the theme of pasta (with corn, grapes or even cabbage sauce). And if you gain Arnaldo's confidence, he will charm you with his personal reminiscences of the world of ballet, of which he is a devoted fan. Nureyev and Fracci have been seen dining here, but don't ask for autographs: Arnaldo is very jealous of his clients' privacy. There is a good choice of wines, despite Arnaldo's total abstinence.

Dal Bolognese ♣
Piazza del Popolo 1-2
☎ 3611426. *Map* **6F5** ▥ ☐ ➡

🍴 *Closed Sun evening, Mon, two weeks in Aug.*
Metropolitana: Flaminio.
Dal Bolognese is an eminently fashionable place to be seen at, and critics might argue that the glamorous outfits of the female clientele are even more remarkable than the cooking — which is, of course, Bolognese in inspiration. But all must agree that the *gran carrello misto dei bolliti* — trolley of boiled meats (tongue, chicken, beef and stuffed pigs' trotters) served with *salsa verde* (parsley and garlic sauce) or *mostarda di Cremona* (fruit in aspic) — is really outstanding. Service is fast and reliable and you can dine on the terrace all year round (behind glass screens in winter). The restaurant is decorated with a fine collection of modern paintings, but these can't compete with the Baroque splendor of *Piazza del Popolo* outside even though the view from Dal Bolognese is slightly restricted. To appreciate the whole piazza, go next door to **Rosati** (see *Bars, cafés and ice cream shops*) for your *aperitivo* or your coffee.

La Buca di Ripetta 🍴 ♣
Via di Ripetta 36 ☎ 3619391. *Map* **5G5** ▥ ▤ ☐ *Closed Sun evening, Mon, Aug.*
A small, friendly *trattoria*, where you must arrive very early indeed if you have not reserved. La Buca's popularity is well-deserved, for the prices are extremely reasonable and the good-natured *padrone* is in constant attendance. The food, which has just a slight bias toward Roman specialties, is wholesome and straightforward. The restaurant consists of one room only, its high walls cheerfully festooned with ornamental bric-à-brac — enormous bellows, great copper pans, even rustic ox-harnesses.

Il Buco ♣
Via Sant' Ignazio 8 ☎ 6793298. *Map* **6H6** ▥ ▤ ☐ ➡ AE ◑ *Closed Mon, Aug 15-31.*
This Tuscan *osteria* was opened in 1891 by Raffaele Masini and used to be so small that it earned itself the nickname of *il buco* (the hole). Now, three generations later, Il Buco is a large and celebrated restaurant. Nicola, the present owner, is proud of the fact that he gets all his basic ingredients from the Tuscan *campagna*, and his fall *porcini* (mushrooms) and winter game from the Tuscan woods. Start your meal with *crostini* (usually

liver canapés), and follow these with the *ribollita*, the traditional thick cabbage soup. Remember that the enormous *fiorentina* steak serves two. And you'll want to leave room for the *cantuccini di Prato*, delicious little almond biscuits that you dip into sweet, rich *vinsanto*. You can't escape the Chianti wine, and the service is a bit rough, but that's all part and parcel of the great Tuscan tradition.

La Campana 🍴 ♣
Vicolo della Campana 18
☎ 6867820. Map **5G5** 🎫 ▤ ☐
🔲 *Closed Mon, Aug.*
The first mention of La Campana as an inn appears in the Roman census of 1518, so don't be surprised if the menu concentrates on plain, traditional Roman fare. You should also be prepared for a limited choice of wines (this too is Roman tradition), but Ida Jacobini's superb cooking will more than compensate for the deficiencies of the cellar. Try the *vignarola*, a traditional vegetable soup (served only in the evening), or the less well-known Roman specialties, *stufatino al sedano* (stew with celery) and *alicette gratinate* (anchovies au gratin).

La Capricciosa ♣
Largo dei Lombardi 8
☎ 6878636. Map **6G5** 🎫 ☐ 🚗
🔲 ⬛ *Closed Tues, two weeks in Aug.*
Although better known as a *pizzeria*, this is in fact a general *trattoria*, with loads of room (except Sun lunchtime) downstairs and on the first floor. There is an unusually wide selection of Roman and regional dishes — a score of variations on the theme of *pasta* and twice that number of main courses — plus some excellent *antipasti* and mouthwatering desserts. Pizzas are served after 7.30pm. The restaurant naturally claims that the now ubiquitous *pizza capricciosa* (the one with a bit of everything on it) was their own invention and that theirs still are the best in Rome.

La Caravella 🍴
Via degli Scipioni 32b
☎ 3599159. Map **5F4** ☐ ☐ ▦
Closed Thurs, Jan.
Metropolitana: Ottaviano.
A reliable, family-run *trattoria*, serving plain, wholesome Roman fare and *vino da tavola* in simple, unpretentious surroundings. Prices are very reasonable, and La Caravella's close proximity to the **Vatican Museums** makes it an ideal place to enjoy a relaxing lunch before returning to complete a hard-working day-long tour of the galleries.

Comparone
Piazza in Piscinula 47
☎ 5816249. Map **9J5** 🎫 ☐ 🚗
🔲 🔳 🔲 *Closed Mon.*
This is the place for an authentic evening out in Trastevere, so don't allow yourself to be herded into the garish tourist traps nearby, which seem to have an arrangement with the driver of every bus and horse-drawn cab in Rome. If you sit out on the terrace of the restaurant, you are surrounded by medieval buildings, and the cooking is equally authentic — mainly Roman, with traditional dishes of brains, sweetbreads, liver and tripe. For the less adventurous there is a good variety of grills, cooked either *ai ferri* (over charcoal) or *alla piastra* (on a hotplate). As in all good Roman restaurants, the *padrone* will tell you that Marcello Mastroianni is frequently to be seen dining there, but in this case one can believe him, for the actor has a house just around the corner.

L'Eau Vive
Via Monterone 85 ☎ 6541095.
Map **5H5** 🎫 *(tourist menu)* to 🎫🎫🎫
▤ ☐ ▦ *lunchtime only* 🔲 🔳
Closed Sun, Aug.
In a grand 16thC palace built for Pope Leo X, this unusual restaurant is run by the *Vergini laiche cristiane di azione cattolica missionaria per mezzo del lavoro* (Christian Virgins of Catholic Missionary Action through Work). Their mission is to run restaurants in all parts of the world, spreading the twin gospels of Christianity and (mainly) French cuisine. Evangelization has been successful, judging from the crowds of prelates and politicians from the nearby Senate. Even the present Pope, when still a cardinal, was an habitué. For tourists, the main attraction is the lay virgins themselves, charming young girls from the French ex-colonies, dressed in colorful national costumes. The food — classic French and French colonial dishes — is less compelling, even when enriched with exotic fruits. The lunchtime tourist menu is, however, a real bargain. The special dish — changed daily — may originate anywhere from the Philippines to North Africa. The wine list is

comprehensive but unexceptional. Don't be surprised if, at around 11pm, the piped music is switched off so that the assembled company, led by the waitresses, can sing hymns in honor of the Virgin Mary.

Les Etoiles △
Via Vitelleschi 34 ☎ *6879558.* Map 5G4 ||||| ⊏⊐ ▦ ▬ ⇔ ◁≪ AE
▣ ◉ VISA

The restaurant of the **Atlante Star** (see *Hotels*), commanding one of the finest views in Rome. You're so close to St Peter's that it's sinful not to say grace, but a Sardinian chef quickly brings the mind back to matters worldly with beautifully presented *antipasti* that are as artfully arranged as they are tasty. The rest of the meal lives up to the promise, and the wine list is excellent. Classical music adds to the magic of watching the sun disappear behind the dome of St Peter's. A memorable evening is assured.

Al Fogher
Via Tevere 13b ☎ *857032.* Map 7F8 ||||| ⊏⊐ ▬ ☇ AE ▣ Closed Sun.

Twelve years ago, Signora Pina Gaspardis d'Eva realized a lifetime's ambition by opening her own restaurant. She called it Al Fogher, which means "at the hearth" in the dialect of her native Friuli. It soon established a reputation as one of the best restaurants in Rome. Signora Gaspardis' *forte* are her *risotti*, prepared with such loving care and devotion that they are veritable works of art. She is especially proud of her midwinter specialty made with apples, *risotto alla mele della Val-di-non*. The menu also boasts an exotic list of hams. Forget the humble pig, forget wild boar — Al Fogher offers you chamois ham and the ham of the saiga from the steppes of Kazakhstan. The wines naturally come from the Friuli. Merlot, Refosco and Cabernet di Friuli are the principal reds, and outstanding among the whites are Sauvignon, Pinot Bianco and Ribolla. The restaurant is just outside the old city walls, close to both the *Villa Borghese* and the *Porta Pia*.

La Fontanella ♣
Largo della Fontanella di Borghese 86 ☎ *6783849.* Map 6G5 |||| ⊏⊐ ⇔ AE ▣ VISA Closed Mon, Sat lunch.

A deservedly popular restaurant, brimming over with old-world

charm and efficiency. In summer you can eat outside in the shadow of the *Palazzo Borghese*. The Tuscan cuisine, which includes a magnificent *pappardelle al sugo di lepre*, always attracts a quorum of deputies from the nearby Parliament.

George's △
Via Marche 7 ☎ *4745204.* Map 7G7 |||| ⊏⊐ ⇔ ☖ ❣ ♪ AE ▣ VISA Closed Sun, Aug.

George, ex-barman and skilled dice-player, created this restaurant just after the war to cater to the rich *Dolce Vita* of nearby Via Veneto. Those balmy days are long since gone, but George's successfully maintains the discreet luxury and hushed elegance of that vanished era. It remains one of the city's most prestigious restaurants. Signor Pavia, manager and *maître*, runs an impeccable service in the softly-lit rooms and on the really enchanting garden terrace. The food is unexceptional, however, and you'd be well advised to steer clear of some of the more bizarre-sounding items on the menu. You'd do just as well — if not better — sticking with simple *pastas*, the *piatto del giorno* and perhaps a *crème brûlée*, although you couldn't go wrong with the special salad (*insalata all Morra*) or steak (*filet carpaccio*). George's has one of the best cellars in Rome, and a piano bar provides evening entertainment. Reservation is recommended, and jacket and tie are obligatory for men.

Il Giardino ☕ ♣
Via Zucchelli 29 ☎ *465202.* Map 6G6 |⊐ ❧ ⊏⊐ ⇔ AE ▣ VISA Closed Mon, one week in Aug. Metropolitana: Barberini.

Il Giardino is typical of the best type of simple, inexpensive Roman *trattoria*. All the emphasis is on food, and the look of the place is simply irrelevant. In summer, you have the choice of eating inside (on two floors) or under a canopy of vines in the little garden past the kitchen. The business is run by a consortium of the waiters, which seems to guarantee excellent quality and service.

Giovanni
Via Marche 64 ☎ *493576.* Map 7G7 |||| ▤▤ ⊏⊐ ▬ AE VISA Closed Fri evening, Sat, Aug.

Close to the bright lights of the Via Veneto is one of the city's many regional restaurants. Founded by Giovanni Sbrega, it is now largely run by son Franco and daughter

Lilli. The family come from the Adriatic sea town of Ancona, as does the marvelously fresh fish they serve. But seafood is not the only attraction here: a fine range of good honest dishes are conjured up in the family kitchen, with soups prepared from the purest beef and chicken broths. The wonderfully warming lentil soup, *zuppa di lenticchie di Castelluccio*, is only available in winter. The *calamaretti dell' Adriatico ai ferri* are also seasonal; these are small grilled squid, even smaller and more delicately flavored than those from the Tyrrhenian sea, but only available for a couple of months in the spring. The pasta, which is freshly made every day by mother, includes *taglioline al fegato d'oca* in a delicious goose-liver sauce.

Girarrosto Toscano
Via Campania 29 ☎ 493759. Map 7G7 ▮▮▮▮ ▭ ▬ AE ⦶ ◉ VISA
Closed Wed.

Concealed in the cellar of a huge building facing onto the ancient Aurelian Wall, Girarrosto Toscano is a first-class restaurant of special appeal to the night-owls of the Via Veneto. Last orders are not until 12.30am. The food is mainly top-quality beef and veal, grilled on an open wood-fired oven. But first you can indulge in melon, Parma ham and *ovoline* (small *mozzarella* cheeses), which, like all the best *antipasti*, arrive at your table almost the moment you sit down. Fast in the daylight hours if you are planning to dine here: portions are generous and the desserts are superb. Girarrosto is expensive, but not over-priced, and the service is meticulous.

Hostaria dell' Orso ⌂
Via dei Soldati 25 ☎ 6864250. Map 5H5 ▮▮▮▮ ▭ ▬ Y ● ♫ AE ⦶ VISA Open evenings only. Closed Sun.

With or without its fabulous setting, L'Hostaria dell' Orso would be a first-class restaurant, but the beautiful 13thC palace is nevertheless the main attraction. A lofty, richly decorated chamber serves as dining room, and the atmosphere is about as far removed from the 20thC as the old wooden beams that may have looked down on such illustrious diners as Dante and Rabelais in the days when this was just a simple inn. L'Hostaria is now one of the most expensive restaurants in Rome, with a piano bar and a nightclub upstairs.

Le Jardin ⌂
Via G. de Notaris 5 ☎ 3609541. Map 6E6 ▮▮▮▮ ▭ AE ⦶ ◉ ◉ VISA Closed Sun.

In a beautiful setting above the Villa Borghese, Le Jardin is the restaurant of the **Lord Byron** hotel (see *Hotels*) and a rare Italian link in the prestigious Relais et Châteaux chain. It's easy to understand how the owner, Amedeo Ottaviani (to whom the luxurious Regency Hotel in Florence also belongs), has managed to overcome the usual native mistrust of all things French and foreign. Peaceful surroundings, impeccable service and a very reliable international cuisine have made Le Jardin one of the top restaurants in Rome, with a reputation quite independent of its excellent but perhaps less celebrated mother hotel. It's ideal for important business lunches, and special dinners can be arranged with reasonable notice. Obviously, you must expect to pay top prices.

Jonathan's
Via della Pace 11 ☎ 6543834. Map 6H5 ▮▮▮ ⌂ AE ⦶ VISA

Next to the rather neglected *Santa Maria della Pace* with its examples of work by Raphael and Bramante, this restaurant was once the studio of artist/owner Nino Medros, who is determined to make this a fashionable quarter once more. An engaging conversationalist, he will cheerfully tell you how he excavated the lower rooms himself and go on to unravel his complicated domestic circumstances. Frogs' legs and fillets are the specialties.

La Majella ✿
Piazza Sant' Apollinare 45 ☎ 6864174. Map 5H5 ▮▮▮ ▤ ▭ ⌂ AE ⦶ ◉ VISA Closed Sun, Aug 10-25.

In a central location close to *Piazza Navona*, this is a colorful *trattoria* with reliably good food and loads of atmosphere. The building is mid-16thC, with great brick arches separating the high, beamed ceilings of the rooms. There is a wide variety of dishes, with the emphasis on specialties from Abruzzo.

Da Mario ✿
Via della Vite 55 ☎ 6783818. Map 6G6 ▮▮▮ ▤ ▭ ▬ AE ⦶ VISA Closed Sun, Aug 5-30.

Stuffed birds in the window give the game away about Mario Mariani's seasonal specialty. And inside, near the door, is another clue to this

Restaurants

restaurant's identity: a large glass bottle full of *cannellini* (white beans) simmering in oil. These are *fagioli al fiasco*, as much a constant of Tuscan wining and dining as the Chianti flasks set on the tables. One of Mario's great virtues is that he creates fine Tuscan food without the pompous rhetoric and parochial pride common among Tuscan restaurateurs. There are *frittate* (vegetable omelets) and the usual *crostini* (in this case, liver canapés) to start the meal. Or you can have *ribollita* (heavy but delicious cabbage soup) or *pappa col pomodoro* (a dish made with tomatoes and bread, very simple and very good). If you are lucky you can eat (three times a week) *stracotto* (beef stewed in wine and tomato sauce). Failing that, settle for the customary but excellent *bistecca alla fiorentina* (serves two). The only fish worth considering is the superb *baccalà* (dried cod), but this is served only on canonical Fri. Faithful to the Tuscan tradition of frugality, Mario keeps his prices down. If you stick to the good house wine you can eat here for a very reasonable sum, and that's why it's hard to find an empty table.

Al Moro
Vicolo delle Bollette 13 (off Via del Lavatore) ☎ 6783495. Map 6H6 III▯ 🍴 🚫 ▭ 🚐 *Closed Sun, Aug.*
Il Moro, the owner of this restaurant, starred in one of Fellini's films as an arrogant and pompous upstart in the decadent reign of Nero. Something of the master's screen example must have brushed off on the waiters, for they can boast to be the bluffest in Rome since antiquity. The food is really excellent, however: good Roman fare, with many original dishes, all prepared from the freshest and best quality ingredients. If you can endure noise, crowds and scornful waiters, you will have one of the best meals in Rome. Reserve a table before you go — and good luck!

Da Nazzareno 🍴 ♿
Via Magenta 35-37 ☎ 4957782. Map 7G8 I▯ ▭ 🚐 AE ◐ VISA *Closed Wed, last two weeks in Aug.* Metropolitana: Termini.
A bustling, fast-moving *trattoria*, only one block away from Stazione Termini, the main railroad station. Entirely without sophistication, it owes its popularity to a happy combination of good, mainly Roman food and low prices.

Da Nerone
Via delle Terme di Tito 96 ☎ 4745207. Map 10I7 II▯ ▭ 🚐 *Closed Sun, Aug.*
Despite the daily cavalcade of buses driving up to park on the Colle Oppio, the phlegmatic Eugenio de Santis seems almost unaware of the thousands of tourists flocking to the nearby *Colosseum*. Thus his small family restaurant facing the overgrown ruins of *Nero's Golden House* has far more Roman atmosphere than the flashier eating places down below in Piazza del Colosseo. The fairly limited menu will not tax the tourist's vocabulary: the *antipasti* are good and, if you like a rare steak, the *filetto* is recommended. One concession Eugenio makes to foreign visitors is a never-ending supply of French fries. For the location, it is much easier to get a table here at night than it is at lunchtime.

Nuraghe Sardo
Viale Medaglie d'Oro 50a ☎ 382485. Map 4F2 III▯ 🍴 🚫 ▭ 🚇 *Closed Wed, Aug.*
If you've just spent the day in the Vatican Museums and feel like eating somewhere reasonably cheap and irresistibly cheerful, try this off-center restaurant in the Trionfale Quarter. Rome is full of restaurants that specialize in regional cooking, but Nuraghe Sardo does more than re-create characteristic Sardinian dishes. Through its colorful rustic atmosphere it succeeds in conveying something of the island's spirit as well. Surrounded by festoons of garlic, chili and Sardinian *salami*, and banks of wine bottles, you can tuck into a hearty *spaghetti alla bottarga* — pasta flavored with gray mullet roe — and *maialetto sardo* — mouthwatering roast sucking pig. Wash them down with the white Vernaccia di Oristano or the fruity rich red Canonau — both from the island — and mop them up with *pane sardo* — home-baked rye bread. To round off your meal, don't miss the fresh Sardinian *pecorino*.

L'Orso Ottanta (L'Orso 80) ♿
Via dell' Orso 33 ☎ 6864904. Map 5H5 III▯ 🍴 ▭ ◐ ⬛ VISA *Closed Mon, Aug 8-20.*
Like many Roman restaurant owners, Antonio Valerii comes from the Abruzzi. He is married to the sister of another Abruzzese restaurateur, and this husband-and-wife partnership has been immensely successful. Their

reputation is well-deserved, for the restaurant itself is pleasant — in spite of the alpine-look pine-wood paneling — and the cooking even more so. This is the place to come for classic *pasta* dishes, good fresh fish and simple, homemade desserts. You'll be plied with delicious *antipasti*, and there are freshly baked pizzas and bread from a capacious red-brick oven. The house wine from Frascati is very tolerable.

Otello alla Concordia ☕ ✿
Via della Croce 81 ☎ *6791178. Map 6G6 ⬚ (set menus) to ▯⬚ ✿ ⬚ ▦ 🚗 Closed Sun, two weeks at Christmas.*
A small, colorful, family-run *trattoria*, just off Via della Croce. It's approached down a narrow alley and through a small shady garden. Inside, the walls run riot with a dazzling array of oil paintings, doubtless not unconnected with the proximity of the artists' quarter around Via Margutta — though whether these works were received as barter or gifts, it might be indiscreet to ask. The food is simple and traditional, attractively served and reasonably priced. The set menus are remarkably good value for such a picturesque restaurant in the heart of one of the world's most fashionable shopping areas.

Da Pancrazio
Piazza del Biscione 92 ☎ *6861246. Map 5I5 ▯▯ ⬚ 🚗 AE ◉ ◎ VISA Closed Wed, Aug 10-18.*
Hidden away in an attractive but somewhat dilapidated corner of the old town, between Sant' Andrea della Valle and Campo dei Fiori, this old-established restaurant is in part of the ancient Theater of Pompey, long since so overbuilt by additions as to be unrecognizable, except by its oval ground-plan. You can either dine on the ground floor or descend to the converted cellar below, where the coldness of the massive stone-blocked walls is offset by subtle lighting. Da Pancrazio is strong on atmosphere, but the food is nothing special.

Passetto
Via Zanardelli 14 ☎ *6540569. Map 6H5 ▦▦ ⬚ ▬ AE ◉ ◎ VISA Closed Sun, Mon lunchtime,*
Native Romans are quick to recommend this restaurant, and a walk along the antique stores of Via Coronari can be agreeably capped by a lunch or dinner here, with its

Italian and international cuisine. Be careful not to spend too much on the way if you plan a banquet.

Piccolo Mondo
Via Aurora 39 ☎ *485680. Map 7G7 ▦▦ ⬚ ▬ ✿ AE ◉ ◎ VISA Close Sun, Aug. Metropolitana: Barberini.*
Hospitable Benito Camponesconi runs this recently restored restaurant assisted by three sons and a daughter. The menu includes some Roman specialties, and the cellars boast a sparkling white wine from a brother's vineyard. Musicians add to the atmosphere.

Pino e Dino ⌂
Piazza di Montevecchio 22 ☎ *6861319. Map 5H5 ▦▦ ⬚ Closed Mon, Aug and ten days at Christmas.*
Just off Via dei Coronari — a street of small, picturesque antique stores — Pino and Dino, a southerner from Taranto and a northerner from Venice, together run this small restaurant with enormous devotion and almost embarrassing kindness. Dishes from Taranto such as *pasta e broccoli* and from Venice such as *polenta brustoada* form only part of a menu offering specialties from every Italian region. There is excellent and inexpensive game in season, and an uneven choice of wines with some good surprises. The atmosphere is elegant and intimate, the clientele young and chic.

Polese ☕ ✿
Piazza Sforza Cesarini 40 ☎ *6861709. Map 5H4 ▯⬚ ⬚ ▬ 🚗 Closed Tues, Aug 15-31.*
A typical Roman *trattoria*, Polese offers good, inexpensive food in simple, unpretentious surroundings. It occupies the back of a rather murky square, but at night does its best to look cheerful dressed up in a garland of red and white lamp shades. The restaurant itself is fairly large, including the vaulted cellars downstairs, and can seat about 130 people; in summer you can also eat outside under the trees. The food has a slight Genoese bias, and the *antipasti* are especially good.

Ranieri
Via Mario de' Fiori 26 ☎ *6791592. Map 6G6 ▦▦ ▦▦ ⬚ ▬ AE ◉ ◎ VISA Closed Tues, two weeks in Aug.*
Since its foundation in 1865, Ranieri has made little attempt to keep up with the times. This is of course its

special charm, for the quietly deferential service and dated furnishings make it the ideal place to lunch or dine in gracious style. The name derives from the founder, Giuseppe Ranieri, a Neapolitan who at one time was chef to Queen Victoria — hence the royalist bent of the menu. Her Majesty herself is remembered in the *mignonettes Regina Vittoria*. The restaurant is convenient for shopping in the Via Condotti area, but is stronger on old-world atmosphere than gastronomic prowess.

Re degli Amici
Via della Croce 33b ☎ *6795380 or 6782555. Map 6G6* ▥ ▢ AE ◉ ◎ ▨ *Closed Mon, last three weeks in June.*
This seemingly immortal *trattoria* has been serving traditional Roman food since 1927. Competitive prices and a prime location close to *Piazza di Spagna* ensure its continuing popularity. Excellent pizzas served after 7.30pm, and there is room to seat more than 200 people.

Romolo
Via Porta Settimiana 8 ☎ *5818284. Map 5I4* ▥ ▢ ▤ ⊕ AE ◉ *Closed Mon, last three weeks in Aug.*
Rich in historical associations and romantic atmosphere, Romolo is one of the most popular restaurants in Trastevere. The ancient building is full of surprises, but the main attraction is the enchanting courtyard, bounded by the Aurelian Wall. You can dine out here on summer evenings, savoring the building's colorful past. Local dialect poet Trilussa dined here daily, and there is a legend that this is where La Fornarina, Raphael's mistress, once lived.

La Rosetta
Via della Rosetta 9 ☎ *6861002. Map 5H5* ▥ ▦ ⊿ ▢ ▤ ◉ ▨ *Closed Sun, Mon lunchtime, Aug.*
According to a 20yr-old legend, Carmelo Riccioli, a native of Sicily, gave up a double career as sports editor and boxer when he won this restaurant in payment of a bet. Fish, fresh every day from Sicily, is the big lure of the place. At La Rosetta, you can freely indulge in everything that swims or crawls in the sea — and this is one of the few restaurants in Rome where you can eat shellfish with absolute safety. To enjoy these privileges, Romans crowd every night into small, cramped rooms

and pay enormous checks without blinking an eyelid. The waiters, dressed in black, are as breezy as the Straits of Messina in a *scirocco*, and there is nowhere to hang your coat — but who cares? A delectable mussel soup is only minutes away — or a plate of plump, juicy scampi or other *frutti di mare*. Good white Sicilian wines.

Sabatini-I
Piazza Santa Maria in Trastevere 13 ☎ *582026. Map 8J4* ▥ ▢ ▤ ◗ *Closed Wed, two weeks in Aug (when branch below open).*
Sabatini-II
Vicolo Santa Maria in Trastevere ☎ *5818307. Map 9J5* ▥ ▢ ▤ ◗ *Closed Tues, two weeks in Aug (when branch above open).*
Sabatini has a fine reputation as a fish restaurant, but above all it's a place to soak up authentic Trastevere atmosphere. The building itself is full of character, with its old beams and frescoes, but in summer you can also dine outside in the *piazza* and enjoy the golden, floodlit mosaics of the church. This is a popular spot, and reservation is advisable. If you can, try to get a table in the Vicolo Santa Maria branch, especially if you are eating outside. Sitting in the piazza in front of a thousand passers-by, you begin to feel like a lobster in Sabatini's aquaria.

Sans Souci △
Via Sicilia 20 ☎ *493504. Map 7G7* ▥ ▦ ▢ ▤ ⊕ ⊿ AE ◉ ◎ ▨ *Closed lunchtime, Mon, Aug 6-Sept 1.*
Just off the Via Veneto, this is the place for an intimate dinner amid luxurious surroundings, but not on a budget. You pay dearly for exquisite cuisine, impeccable service and decor that would make Louis XIV feel at home. The wine list must be among the best in Rome. An expertly played classical guitar covers a stream of hushed commands to a veritable army of anxious waiters, and later in the evening Italian love songs bring a tear to the eye, as does the check. Try *filleto in crosta all salsa di Madera e tartufo nero*. Along with **El Toulà**, a serious contender for the title of Rome's best restaurant.

Taberna dei Gracchi
Via dei Gracchi 266-268 ☎ *383757. Map 5F4* ▥ ▦ ▤ AE ◉ ▨ *Closed Sun, Mon lunch.*
Owner Dante Mililli has in recent

years turned this into a star among Roman restaurants, serving excellent fare in an atmosphere of genial efficiency. Opened in 1962 but recently completely renovated, it is well worth a visit. Any restaurant that opts for an indoor fountain where another table might have been squeezed in has the best interests of its customers at heart. The clientele now includes footballer Maradonna. Businessfolk and lovers will appreciate the private tables — everyone else the food.

Taverna Flavia
Via Flavia 9 ☎ *4745214. Map 7G8* 🚫 ⬜ ■ ≋ 🚗 AE ⊙ VISA
Closed Sun, Aug 15-20.
In the heady days of *La Dolce Vita*, Mimmo gave up a career in law to open this restaurant, and it has been a favourite of movie stars and directors ever since. With the Italian film industry now in decline, fewer celebrities visit regularly, but the pictures and autographs lining the bright, red-brick walls are a constant reminder of the good times, and the atmosphere is still chic. Mimmo's menu is appropriately adventurous, with such exotic concoctions as *insalata Veruschka*, a mouthwatering salad made with truffles. The wine list is excellent.

Taverna Giulia
Vicolo dell' Oro 23 ☎ *6869768.*

Map 5H4 🚫 ⬜ ≋ 🚗 AE ⊙
Closed Sun, Aug.
Conveniently situated for the Vatican, just s of Ponte Vittorio Emanuele, this is a restaurant of some distinction, despite the scruffy exterior of the building. Down below in the semi-basement the decor has been smartened up considerably, although the whitewashed pebbled walls will not be to everyone's taste. The food is really excellent: an unusually good selection of Genoese dishes with plenty of *pesto* for basil-lovers.

El Toulà △
Via della Lupa 29b ☎ *6873498. Map 6G5* 🚫 ⬜ ≋ ☡ AE ⊙ ⊙ VISA *Closed Sun, Sat lunchtime, Aug.*
Still considered by many to be the best restaurant in Rome, El Toulà scores high on most counts. The food is superb, the service impeccable, the surroundings unashamedly luxurious. The menu is predominantly Venetian in inspiration, but draws on many international sources for the creation of its culinary extravaganzas. El Toulà attracts more than its fair share of famous faces — millionaire tycoons and stars of screen and stage. Evening bookings and a substantial income are essential, and don't be put out if asked to dine in the bar area — some of El Toulà's best customers think it a privilege.

Fast food

Fast food runs counter to Italian culture, but more and more places are springing up for tourists who have OD'd on pasta, pizza and pastry. "Takeaways", or, in Italian, *mangia dove vuoi*, can be had from **Italy & Italy** (*in Piazza Barberini — it has replaced the Piccadilly restaurant — and Via Cola di Rienzo*), which offers pasta dishes, hamburgers, grills, salads, French fries and ices; **New Point** (*Corso Vittorio Emanuele 137, open 11.30am-midnight, closed Mon*); **Willy's** (*213 Corso Vittorio Emanuele, closed Wed*); **Burghy** (*Piazza Rotonda, closed Wed*); **C & C Burger** (*Corso Vittorio Emanuele 310*); **MABurger** (*Via del Mascherino 56-58*); **Speedyburger** (*Via P. Emilio, 17*); **Big Burg** (*Via di Propaganda 17-19, Piazza Istria 28-29, Viale Giulio Cesare 120 and Piazzale Flaminio 22*).

Bars, cafés and ice-cream shops

The Italian bar is the hub of local life, acting as pub, café, corner store and telephone booth all in one. Even the smallest, most rudimentary of bars performs a wide range of services, selling both alcoholic drinks and coffee, and a variety of *tost* (snacks); it is also a *latteria* (the only place you can buy milk) and usually provides the only public telephone in the vicinity. The bigger the bar, the greater the number of facilities on offer. Slightly larger bars take on additional roles of *pasticceria* and *gelateria*, selling pastries and ice-creams; very often these are prepared on the premises. The grandest bars also provide *tavola calda* and *tavola fredda* (hot and cold pre-prepared food) and sometimes have a small restaurant area as well. They may also include shops selling chocolates, sweets and biscuits, and a *tabaccheria* for postcards, stamps and cigarettes.

Briskly efficient service (orders at the bar arrive almost instantly), mingled smells of fresh coffee and pastries, and shining-clean stainless steel tops and mirrored walls give the larger Roman bars a specially attractive atmosphere. Though chairs and tables are usually provided, it is most unusual to sit down in such establishments. Unless your legs are giving out and you don't mind doubling your bill (and waiting twice as long), it's best to do as the Romans and consume your coffee and *cornetto* (sweet croissant) standing up at the bar. In all but the smallest bars, you pay before being served. Go first to the *cassa* (cash point) and state your order. (Buy some *gettoni*, too, if you want to use the telephone.) Having paid, take the receipt to the bar, hand it over and repeat your order.

Bars like this are found all over Italy, but cafés are a phenomenon peculiar to Rome — a capital city's desire to emulate the boulevard lifestyle beloved by Parisians. In the 19thC the **Caffè Greco** was the haunt of expatriate writers and composers such as Byron and Liszt. Later, the **Café de Paris** became the chic meeting place for the international jet set. Reputations change but prices remain high. The nicer cafés are good places to rendezvous and offer some of the few acceptable public lavatories in Rome.

Roman ice-cream is justly celebrated, and every resident and visitor has a favourite *gelateria*. The best ice-cream is made only with eggs, milk, cream, sugar and fresh fruit (or other natural flavourings). Certain bars produce one excellent ice-cream and several indifferent varieties; even their specialities can vary from day to day. Most discerning Romans agree that the best ice-cream in the city comes from **Bar San Filippo**, tucked away in fashionable Parioli, although **Giolitti** and the trendy new **Gelateria della Palma** also have their devotees. For the best coffee in Rome, go to the **Sant' Eustachio** or **La Tazza d'Oro**.

Accademia
Via del Tritone 54/56 ☎ *6793585.*
Map 7G7 ▦ ▨
Pastries, ice-cream and terrific coffee in relaxing surroundings, near the busy Piazza Barberini.

Alemagna
Via del Corso 181 ☎ *6792887.*
Map 6H6 ▣▣ ▨ *Open 7.30am-10pm. Closed Sun.*
Gilded candelabra on lofty mirrored walls make this one of the grandest bars in Rome. It is also one of the largest, busiest and most central. *Tavola calda, frullati* (milk shakes) and a shopping area are included.

Babington's Tea Rooms
Piazza di Spagna 23 ☎ *6786027.*
Map 6G6 ▣▣ ▨ *Open 9am-10.30pm. Closed Thurs.*

Opened in 1896 by Miss Anna Maria Babington and still serving homemade scones and muffins prepared to her original recipes, this pseudo-English establishment continues to attract wealthy shoppers from nearby Via Condotti. Prices go over the top, and have even inspired some barbed remarks in the celebrity visitors' book, but Babington's remains one of the few places in Rome where you can drink reasonable tea.

Bar San Filippo
Via di Villa San Filippo 8
☎ *879314. Open 6am-midnight. Closed Mon.*
Romans for whom only the best will do brave the city's nightmare traffic and set out for Parioli to buy ice-cream cakes for birthday parties

and other celebrations. Bar San Filippo also sells smaller portions to casual callers, from a choice of 60 ice-creams and water ices. The zabaglione defies description and makes any journey worthwhile.

Bernasconi
Largo di Torre Argentina 1
☎ *6548141. Map 5I5. Open 8am-9pm. Closed Mon.*
Selling ice-creams and pastries as briskly as a take-away hamburger joint, this bar has the added attraction of a telephone room downstairs, equipped with 18 telephones. Buy a coffee ice on your way down there.

Biancaneve
Piazza Pasquale Paoli 1
☎ *6540227. Map 5H4. Open 7am-1am. Closed Tues.*
This café has made a speciality of the *mela stregata* it serves — a "bewitched apple" of chocolate and zabaglione ice-creams, coated in chocolate and topped with cream. This over-priced concoction has perhaps lost its magic, and the service also seems to have fallen under a bad spell.

Caffè Greco
Via Condotti 86 ☎ *6782554. Map 6G6. Open 8am-9pm. Closed Sun.*
The most famous café in Rome, the Caffè Greco dates from the early 18thC, and throughout the 19thC was a celebrated meeting place for writers, musicians and artists from all over Europe. The original 1860 interior has been preserved and past patrons are recorded on the walls in an impressive collection of paintings and medallions: note the portraits of Ludwig I of Bavaria, Nikolai Gogol and Hans Christian Andersen. Illustrious visitors still drop by and prices are high, but it is a comfortable retreat from the hurly-burly of Via Condotti. An embarrassing lapse when Roman authorities ordered its temporary closure on the grounds the kitchens weren't in order is now behind it.

Café de Paris
Via Vittorio Veneto 90 ☎ *465284. Map 7G7* 🔢 🔢 🔘 🔢 *Open 8am-2am. Closed Thurs.*
The *Dolce Vita* days of this café are long since gone, and it is now less fashionable than **Doney**, the rival establishment across the road. The tables outside may have lost their chic, but the air-conditioned bar offers generally courteous service

and an excellent choice of *tavola fredda*. Prices go over the odds, and faint muzac imparts an international flavour.

Canova
Piazza del Popolo 16 ☎ *6797749. Map 6F5* 🔢 🔘 🔢 *Open 7.30am-11.30pm. Closed Mon.*
Well-heeled Roman women meet for lunchtime parties in this glittering modern café — and pay through the nose. Service is slow and ice-creams indifferent. **Rosati** (see over page) on the other side of the piazza offers fewer facilities but loads more atmosphere.

Colombia
Piazza Navona 88 ☎ *659647. Map 6H5* 🔢 🔘 🔘 🔢 *Open 7am-1.30am. Closed Mon.*
The best Colombian coffee and generally excellent ice-creams make this café worth visiting. A useful pizzeria is included at the back, and tables outside allow the comfortable contemplation of the delights of Piazza Navona.

Doney
Via Vittorio Veneto 145
☎ *493407. Map 7G7* 🔢 🔘 🔘 🔢 *Open 8am-1am. Closed Mon.*
Business is booming on the sunny side of the street, and Doney is now more fashionable than the once-celebrated **Café de Paris**. A restaurant behind the sun terrace is a recent addition.

Europeo
Piazza San Lorenzo in Lucina 33
☎ *6786251. Map 6G5. Open 8am-11pm. Closed Mon.*
Visit this tiny bar for Sicilian specialities — *ricotta*-filled pastries and *cassata* ice-cream.

Gelateria della Palma
Via della Maddalena 20
☎ *6540752. Map 6H5. Open noon-midnight. Closed Wed.*
Opened in 1981, this *gelateria* offers over 100 different flavours of ice-cream, specializing in exotic fruits such as mango, paw-paw, kiwi and wild strawberry. *Semi-freddi* (semi-frozen creams) and *cremolati* (water-ices) are specialities. This is the biggest ice-cream shop in Rome, and there is plenty of room to sit down and indulge.

Giolitti
Via Uffici del Vicario 40
☎ *6794206. Map 5H5. Open 7am-2am. Closed Mon.*
King of the *gelaterie* for more than

159

20yrs, Giolitti still serves up reliable ice-creams and moderately-priced *tavola calda*.

Harry's Bar

Via Vittorio Veneto 150
☎ 4745832. Map 7G7 Ⓐ Ⓔ ⊚
Open 11am-1am. Closed Sun.
Don't be misled by the gloomy and rather tatty interior. Since 1961 Harry's Bar has been a fashionable meeting place for anyone who is anyone (especially politicians and actors) and the hushed voices around you may be discussing important affairs of state. Head barman Clemente Valentino has retired after mixing cocktails in the Via Veneto for 55yrs, leaving his shaker in the steadier hands of Guido Lanfranconi, who will produce a Harry's Special on request.

Michele di Rienzo

Piazza della Rotonda 9
☎ 6869097. Map 6H5. Open
7.30am-2.30am. Closed Tues.
Just next door to the Pantheon, this bar serves eggs and bacon and the most delicious chocolate ice-cream you will find anywhere in Rome.

Nota Blu

Via Salita de Crescenzi 3
☎ 657404. Map 6H5. Open
2pm-1.30am. Closed Tues.
A modern version of **Babington's**, this fancy tearoom was opened in 1981 and has first-class amenities. Prices are low by comparison, but the tea less palatable.

Rosati

Piazza del Popolo 4 ☎ 3611418.
Map 6F5. Open 7.30am-midnight. Closed Sun.
The nicest café in Rome has been in the Rosati family for three generations and offers old-fashioned elegance with first-class service — as well as a view of one of the finest Baroque squares in Europe. The 1922 Liberty-style decorations have been preserved throughout. Period glass jars filled with sweets line the walls on carved wooden shelves, against a pink and cream background. A huge chrome and glass cake-stand displays Rosati's homemade specialities: liqueur chocolates, jellies, sweets and cakes. Cocktails are another forte — all original, of course — and high prices are justified. Upstairs there is a spacious tearoom, which caters for special or festive occasions.

Sant' Eustachio

Piazza Sant' Eustachio 82
☎ 6561309. Map 6H5. Open
8am-1am. Closed Mon.
Famed for its *espresso* and *cappuccino*, this café is also worth visiting for its superb coffee *granita*.

La Tazza d'Oro

Via degli Orfani 84 ☎ 6789792.
Map 6H5. Open 7am-10pm.
Closed Sun.
Huge sacks of coffee beans piled against the walls and an enticing aroma prepare you for one of the best *espressos* in town. This bar sells nothing but coffee and coffee *granita*, and single-minded dedication has paid off.

Tre Scalini

Piazza Navona 30 ☎ 659148.
Map 5H5. Open 7am-2.30am.
Closed Wed.
Tartufo is the speciality. This is a chocolate ice-cream, to which pieces of broken chocolate and whole cherries have been added. Served with a topping of whipped cream, it certainly lives up to all expectations.

Nightlife and performing arts

The eternal city may not keep as wide awake at night as New York, but it is a lot livelier than many other capital cities. Theatres and restaurants keep later hours than in London, for example. Curtains rise between 8.30-9.30pm, and it is usual to dine from 9.30pm-12.30am. A number of cafés and bars stay open until 1 or 2am, and many clubs and discotheques don't close their doors until 5am at weekends.

Despite all this, the revelling Roman rises early next morning to begin work at 9am — fortified, no doubt, by the prospect of an agreeable long lunch and siesta ahead (1 to 3.30 or 4pm). If you propose to explore Roman nightlife, you would do best to follow suit and catch up on some sleep in the afternoons.

Ballet and opera

The official opera seasons runs from Nov-June at the **Teatro dell' Opera** (*Piazza Beniamino Gigli 1* ☎ *461755*), but the same company also gives summer performances in July and Aug in the Baths of Caracalla. The Teatro dell' Opera is not in the same international class as La Scala (Milan), and the open-air summer productions (where quality matters less than atmosphere) tend to attract more visitors.

Ballet is included in the winter season, and in Oct there is an experimental programme that sometimes features jazz. Postal booking is available, and remaining tickets go on sale two days before the performance. Credit cards are not accepted, and the box office is closed on Mon.

Tickets for the summer season can be bought at the Teatro dell' Opera box office, or at the Baths of Caracalla on the day of the performance only, from 8-9pm. Check *This Week in Rome* or *Il Messaggero* for times of performances.

Chamber music, recitals and concerts

Rome is rich in musical activity, often enhanced by the beautiful settings in which concerts and recitals take place. Although a number of established orchestras, choirs and chamber groups give regular concerts, the keyword to the Roman musical scene is spontaneity. A profusion of one-off concerts and choral recitals are held throughout the year in basilicas such as **San Giovanni in Laterano**. And in summer a number of villas, including **Villa Ada**, present festivals featuring themes such as African or Indian music. Regular summer concerts are held at the **Basilica of Maxentius** in July and Aug (*Via dei Fori Imperiali* ☎ *6793617*).

The official concert season runs from Oct-Jun. In a class of its own, and playing host to numerous international stars, is the **Accademia di Santa Cecilia**. The Accademia holds orchestral concerts at the **Auditorio di Via della Conciliazione** (*Via della Conciliazione 4* ☎ *6541044*) near Piazza San Pietro, and other recitals at the **Sala Accademica di Via dei Greci** (*Via dei Greci 18; box office Via Vittoria 6* ☎ *6790389*).

The **Accademia Filarmonica** (*Via Flaminia 118* ☎ *3601752*) generally performs in the **Teatro Olimpico** (*Piazza Gentile da Fabriano 17* ☎ *3962635*), and the **RAI** (Italian radio orchestra) invariably in the **Foro Italico** (*Piazza Lauro De Bosis* ☎ *390713*). Concerts and recitals are also given by the orchestra of the **Teatro dell' Opera** (see *Ballet and opera*), by the **Gonfalone** (*Via del Gonfalone 32a* ☎ *655952*), and at the **Auditorio San Leone Magno** (*Via Bolzano 38* ☎ *853216*).

Cinema

The Italian film industry has been in decline since around 1965, and three out of every four films shown in Rome are American. This might be good news for English-speaking tourists if it were not for the fact that every foreign film is dubbed in Italian. Many Italian film-goers also resent this practice and would prefer to see the original versions with sub-titles. They and discerning expatriates frequent **Pasquino** (*Piazza Santa Maria in Trastevere* ☎ *5803622*), the only public cinema that shows undubbed English and American films.

The *cinema d'essai* (art cinema) club scene is lively and well worth investigating. The clubs can be joined on the spot for a nominal fee, and present a variety of experimental programmes, exploring unusual themes and concepts. European and American art films are sometimes shown in their original versions, and young independent Italian film-makers are well represented. Rock films are often screened to boost the takings. The following small cinemas are especially recommended.

Farnese   Piazza Campo dei Fiori 56 ☎6564395
Filmstudio   Via Orti d'Alibert 1c ☎657378
Labirinto   Via Pompeo Magno 27 ☎312283
Officina   Via Benaco 3 ☎862530

Less recherché but equally exciting are the open-air summer film festivals held in one of several ancient settings. Aug is not the best month to be in Rome: temperatures soar; all theatres, most cinemas and many shops are closed; and the city itself has the appearance of a deserted film set. To keep the city-bound populace happy (and with the same good and wise intentions that must have inspired the building of the Colosseum) the authorities rig up a huge screen on the Arch of Constantine or some other ancient monument, and set out thousands of chairs in the surrounding streets. Bumper packages of up to five films per sitting are shown every evening throughout Aug. Programmes last from about 8pm to 4am and a small fee is payable. Theatrical lighting effects and hot-dog stands add to the festivities. For the current venue, check *Il Messaggero*.

Jazz, folk and rock music

The same rules of spontaneity and surprise apply to jazz and rock as to the classical music scene. Jazz features in many of the festivals that crop up during the summer months, and rock events are frequently laid on at breathtakingly short notice. Jazz has a permanent home at the **Mississippi Jazz Club** (*Borgo Angelico 16* ☎6540348), folk music at the **Folkstudio** (*Via Gaetano Sacchi 3* ☎5892374).

Venues for major rock concerts include **Tenda Strisce** (the Striped Tent) (*Via Cristoforo Colombo*) and the **Sports Palace** (or *Palaeur*) in EUR. Tickets for these events are obtainable from nominated box offices throughout the city, listed in *This Week In Rome*, along with details of visiting big names.

Nightclubs and discos

Rome is almost too well provided with places to dance the night away. For every fun spot there are three or four sad and empty clubs where the champagne buckets sit on the tables just for show and are never filled with ice. Bypassing the area around Via Veneto could spare you some of the least inspiring tourist traps, but would also mean missing out on some of the liveliest discos. Instead, follow the recommendations given here, from which all known "cowboy clubs" have been excluded, and you should escape being stung.

The city has more than 40 night spots, catering for all tastes and ages. At the bottom end of the scale are noisy discos with neon lights and plenty of space for energetic dancing. At the top end are a couple of exclusive clubs where the clientele is glamorous, lights subdued and dance floors small.

Somewhere in the middle are less pretentious establishments where dress is unimportant and an evening's enjoyment does not depend upon being seen by the right people.

Glamour is a transient quality, and fashions change at a whim. The most important ingredient of a nightclub is its clientele, and this fickle crowd takes off like a flock of migrant birds once its nest has been discovered. Thus smart clubs hit the doldrums through no fault of their own.

In Rome, the terms nightclub and discotheque are used loosely. Exclusive clubs call themselves discotheques and the sleaziest discotheques masquerade as clubs. None of the clubs listed has a members-only policy, but you are likely to be excluded from the very few "in" places on those grounds if your face doesn't fit.

In more expensive clubs, payment is built into the cost of the drinks. Elsewhere, the entrance fee allows one "free" drink, and the previous rule applies thereafter.

Acropolis
Via Luciani 52 ☎ 870504. Map 3E6 IIIl to IIII. ● ⋔ Open 11pm-3am, Sat and Sun also 4-8pm. Closed Mon.
Temples of fashion are found in the most unlikely places. One quiet road in the northern suburb of Parioli conceals the two most talked-about clubs in town: **Bella Blu**, the acme of sophistication, and Acropolis, the radical alternative. Since opening in a converted cinema in 1978, this discotheque, previously called Much More, has successfully lived up to its name, offering a first-class disco with special lighting effects and frequent live rock. Mainly a place for the young and laid-back, the club gets more eclectic on Sat when prices go up, even attracting at one time such seasoned night owls as Marcello Mastroianni, Alberto Moravia and Christopher Lee.

Atmosphere
Via Romagnosi 11a ☎ 3611348. Map 5F5 IIII ● ♫ Open 11.30pm-3.30am.
Gil, the make-up artist of **Gilcagné** (see *Beauty centres* in *Shopping*), has sold his interest in this club. As a result the place has gone rather down-market since its glamorous beginnings in 1980. The decor is still fun, resembling the inside of a vast desert tent, with tasselled awnings hanging overhead, but the clientele is no longer as exotic or as beautiful as it once was. The countless mirrors reflect the light show, not the dancers.

Bella Blu
Via Luciani 21 ☎ 3608840. Map 3E6 IIII ● ♫ ⇄ Open 9pm-3.30am.

As far as the beautiful people are concerned, Bella Blu is the number one nightspot in Rome. Italian nobility brush elbows with film stars and movie moguls in the tiny restaurant, where the food bears comparison with that of many a respected restaurant. The dance floor, equally small, is enlivened by a stunning disc-jockette. Midnight-blue, star-spangled walls and cool Ionic pilasters set an elegant tone. Try getting in here if you like a challenge: this club is exclusive in the true sense of the word. A jacket is required for men, but ties are not obligatory. Bjorn Borg and Rudolph Nureyev would hate to be turned away.

La Cabala
Hostaria dell' Orso, Via dei Soldati 25 ☎ 6564250. Map 5H4 IIII ● ♫ ⇄ AE ◉ VISA Open 10.30pm-3am. Closed Sun.
Over the restaurant Hostaria dell' Orso, and housed in a fine palace dating from the 13thC, where Dante and Rabelais stayed. Unexciting, but you can dress smart or otherwise, dance to American funk and be served expensive drinks by posh-looking waiters.

Cavalieri Hilton
Via Cadlolo ☎ 3151. Map 2D2 IIII ⇄ ● AE ◉ ◉ VISA Open 9.30pm-2am.
The best reason for venturing out onto the slopes of Monte Mario, on the NW edge of the city, is to enjoy the superb view from the Hilton's restaurant-discotheque. In summer, the glass outside the terrace is removed, and it's almost like dancing in the open air. Romans love it, because it's so much cooler and fresher than down in the city.

Nightlife and performing arts

Club 84
Via Emilia 84 ☎ *4751538. Map
7G7* ▥ ○ ♫ ♪ AE ◉ ▣ *Open
10pm-3.30am.*
This long-established club features
live music from 11.30pm-1am and
1.30-3am. The singers are generally
Italian and the songs romantic.
Between times you can dance to
American funk.

Easy Going
Via della Purificazione 9
☎ *4745578. Map 6G6* ▥ ○ ♫
Open 11pm-3.30am.
Somewhere between a club and a
discotheque, this is by far and away
the liveliest place in town. And, as
the name suggests, anything goes.
The club is gay and wants to stay
that way, but is easy-going enough
not to turn straight callers away.
White swing doors (as to a French
men's room) lead into a pink rococo
entrance chamber decorated with
naughty cherubs and red chintz
sofas. Erotic monochrome prints
lead you downstairs to a disco that's
almost on the boil.

Jackie O'
Via Boncompagni 11 ☎ *461401.
Map 7G7* ▥ ○ ♫ ♪ ⊜ AE ◉
Open 11pm-3.30am.
Until recently the queen of the

Roman clubs, Jackie O' is still
choosy about who it lets into its
opulent, Liberty-style interior. Once
the playground of stars like Liza
Minnelli and James Hunt, its
glamour is fast fading but the
atmosphere remains smart. A
restaurant and piano bar are tucked
away downstairs.

La Makumba
Via degli Olimpionici 19
☎ *3964392. Map 3B5* ▯ ✿ ○ ♪
Open 10pm-5am.
To the N of Parioli, Rome's growing
African population has made this its
night-time home. You can dance
under the stars till dawn to live and
recorded Afro music.

Piper 80
Via Tagliamento 9 ☎ *854459.
Map 7E8* ▥ ☎ ○ AE ◉ ▣ VISA
*Open 10pm-3am, Sat and Sun,
also 4-7.30pm. Closed Mon.*
This disco is still buzzing with
excitement. It's young, loud,
energetic and pacey, with a
funk-chic atmosphere all of its own.
The latest craze, whatever it may be,
is always catered for. Video, film
and lighting effects, plus a whole
room of computer games, add to the
fun that is so much part of the
atmosphere.

Piano bars
Nightclubs are where you go with someone special or a
group of friends. Piano bars are more for single people, and
are an easy way to make friends in a strange city. Rome is
well provided with such bars, and they turn up in the most
unlikely places, frequently tucked away at the back of
discotheques, the singers hoarse from competition with the
loudspeakers next door. The poshest restaurants and clubs
have piano bars, and so do the scruffiest. They are cherished
almost like club mascots or household gods, and the show
always goes on. However, in recent years, the term "piano
bar" has taken on a dubious ambiguity, and some
establishments now have more in common with Soho than
Saint Peter's. Beware street touts drumming up trade for
"piano bars" in the back streets. Those listed here are
respectable venues, but off the beaten track you may fall
among thieves.
  Among the mass of indifferent and merely average
musicians who perform in these bars, a few genuine artists
attract appreciative audiences from all over Rome. Sometimes
playing solo, sometimes accompanied by a guitar or another
singer, they generally have a wide range of styles and
welcome requests.
  When you go into a piano bar, you should take one of the
high seats round the piano (as they're always grand pianos,
there's usually room). You are expected to join in the
entertainment: a skilled performer will weave his audience

into his show, making each and every one feel like a celebrity. Highly recommended for a quiet and sociable evening, good piano bars should leave you feeling as nostalgic as *Casablanca* and just about as mellow.

L'Arciliuto
Piazza Montevecchio 5, off Via dei Coronari ☎ *224598. Map 5H5* ▥▥ ☲ ♪ *Open 10pm-2am. Closed Sun.*
Neapolitan proprietor Enzo Samaritani sings and plays guitar, accompanied on the piano. Enzo writes his own songs and will sing in most European languages, depending on the audience present. His excellent pianist plays light jazz and popular classics between times.

L'Incontro
Via della Penna ☎ *3610934. Map 6F5* ▥▥ ☲ ♪ ⒶⒺ ⊙ ⓄⒹ *Open 10pm-3.30am.*
The name means "meeting", which gives a rough idea of the ambience. There's Brazilian music and two floors of discotheques if the Rick's Café syndrome becomes overwhelming.

Little Piano
Via Gregoriana 54 ☎ *6796386. Map 6G6.*
Near to the Spanish Steps, which at night must be one of the most romantic spots in the world. Eugenio Capponi and Maurizio Marcilli provide the music.

Prugna 2
Piazza dei Ponziani 3 ☎ *5890555. Map 9J5* ▥▥ ☲ ⒶⒺ ⊙ ⓄⒹ *Open 10pm-3.30am.*
Successful successor to La Prugna — a piano bar-cum-discotheque.

Tartarughino
Via della Scrofa 2 ☎ *6786037. Map 6H5* ▥▥ ☲ ♪ ☲ *Open 9pm-3am. Closed Sun.*
Rome's most exclusive piano bar, Tartarughino accepts only the highest standards of dress and even then can be difficult to get into because it is so small. Upstairs, the tiny and exquisitely decorated restaurant is a favourite haunt of top politicians. Downstairs you may drink without dining and listen to the excellent pianist. In July and Aug the whole ensemble, chef and pianist included, moves to Sardinia for the summer season.

Tony's Bar
Via Ludovisi 11 ☎ *4744141. Map 7G7* ▥▥ ☲ ♪ ⒶⒺ ⊙ ⓄⒹ ⅦⓈⒶ *Open 8pm-2am. Closed Sun.*
Part of the Savoia hotel in an elegant quarter of Rome, and quite intimate, considering the rather imposing furnishings of the hotel proper.

Cabaret and cocktails
Certain musical experiences do not fit neatly into any of the previous categories, but any brief survey of Roman nightlife would be incomplete without them. Here is an assorted selection.

Blatumba
Piazza in Piscinula 20 ☎ *6054810. Map 9J5. Opens 10.30pm. Closed Mon.*
Across the river at Isola Tiberina, this club specializes in Latin American music, led by Giancarlo Biagini and Jose Maria Salvador. Recommended for setting the pulse racing.

Club Milleuno
Via Lazio 31 ☎ *4744242. Map 7F7* ▥▥ ☲ *Open 8pm-2am.*
Floor shows nightly, including some internationally known acts.

St Moritz
Via Sicilia 57 ☎ *4759160. Map 7G7* ▥▥ *Opens 10pm.*
Just off the Via Veneto, this venue

stages acts throughout the night, gathering pace after midnight.

Fantasie di Trastevere
Via di Santa Dorotea 6 ☎ *5891671* ☎ *625865. Map 814* ▥▥ ☲ ☲ ♪ ⒶⒺ ⊙ ⓄⒹ ⅦⓈⒶ *Open 8pm-midnight. Closed Sun.*
This well-known tourist attraction will either thrill or revolt you — there is no half measure. The food is indifferent: the snag is that you have to eat if you want to see the show. Singers dressed in Tyrolean costumes, purporting to be Roman peasants, deliver hearty folks songs to loud, brassy accompaniments. Later, strolling musicians tour the tables with a selection of tear-jerking opera classics.

Theater

The Roman theater season is short, beginning in Oct and ending in May, but attendances are on the increase, and more than 100 companies compete for audiences. Standards of acting are variable, however, and fringe theater groups (*teatri off*) have ill-disguised political motivations.

The staple diet at the established theaters is Pirandello, well seasoned with Goldoni, de Filippo and French and English classics (in translation). **Piccolo Eliseo** has a lighter program, **Sistina** stages musicals and **Bagaglino** is a revue theater serving up drinks and cabaret.

Argentina   Largo Argentina 53 ☎ 6544601
Bagaglino   Via Due Macelli 75 ☎ 6791439
Delle Arti   Via Sicilia 59 ☎ 4818598
Eliseo   Via Nazionale 183 ☎ 462114
Nuovo Parioli   Via Borsi 20 ☎ 803523
Piccolo Eliseo   Via Nazionale 183 ☎ 465095
Quirino   Via Minghetti 1 ☎ 6794585
Sistina   Via Sistina 129 ☎ 4756841
Valle   Via Teatro Valle 23a ☎ 6543794

For all but the most popular productions, tickets can usually be bought right up to the day of the performance, but no theater will accept payment by credit card.

During the summer months, regrouped companies stage open-air performances outside Rome, at Classical sites such as Ostia Antica. Excellent listings of both winter and summer performances are given every Fri in *Il Messagero*.

Shopping

Concentrating the very best of Italian design and craftsmanship into one conveniently small area, Rome is one of the finest shopping centers in the world. It is where you go to find quality, and quality that you are prepared to pay for. Beautifully-made articles created out of the very best materials can never be cheap, and this is not the place to look around for cut-price bargains. Leather and silk goods predominate, but Rome is also an important center for jewelry, antiques and general prêt-à-porter fashion. And, to ensure that face and body do justice to fabulous jewels and elegant clothes, beauty parlors abound.

The main shopping area centers on Via Condotti and extends across just four main blocks, to Via della Croce in the N and Via Frattina in the S. This network of narrow streets, bordered by Via del Corso in the W and Piazza di Spagna in the E, is entirely free of traffic, and shoppers can stroll at leisure, unjostled by fellow pedestrians and unmolested by traffic fumes. The atmosphere is hushed and elegant, feeling almost heavy with the savor of affluence.

In Italy, department stores are the exception rather than the rule. Romans, like other Italians, prefer to shop in boutiques, and the Via Condotti area has little shops selling everything from shirts to gloves. This specialization originates in the craft shops from which the smart shopping village has grown, and generally ensures top quality and personal service. Many of the boutiques have been in one family of craftsmen for generations, and the shopkeeper is often the craftsman or factory owner as well.

The grandeur of Roman stores is legendary. More money is lavished on opulent decorations than in any other shopping center in the world. There is, however, a very thin line between stylish opulence and brash vulgarity. **Bulgari's** small-scale palace is delightfully elegant, while the flashy interiors of some of the newer stores are pure nouveau-riche.

Shopkeepers have the bearing and manners to match these fine surroundings, and the customer is also expected to play the part. The richer you look, the less likely you are to receive courteous but dismissive treatment.

Such high standards of dress and deportment apply particularly to Via Condotti and Via Borgognona, but are also worth bearing in mind if you intend shopping in the parallel street of Via Frattina or in some of the little cross-streets, or in Piazza di Spagna or Via del Babuino. Other shopping districts are less formal, and many of these are worth investigating: Via del Tritone and the streets around the Trevi Fountain, Via Cola di Rienzo across the Tiber and N of the Vatican, Piazza San Lorenzo in Lucina and the streets around Piazza Campo dei Fiori are all areas where you will find cheaper leather bags and shoes. Streets to avoid are Via del Corso and Via Nazionale. These are much like main streets anywhere else in the world and often have the poor or uneven quality you might expect to find there. Via Veneto also has more of an international flavor, but contains some of the city's most expensive stores.

Vying with Via Condotti as a peculiarly Roman shopping attraction are the city's colorful street markets. Offering a vast selection of top-quality fruit, flowers, vegetables, *prosciutto*, salami, cheeses, meat and fish, as well as cheap clothes, these regular events explain why food stores, like department stores, are not found in the city center.

Straight bargaining is an accepted practice in clothes markets, but elsewhere transactions are conducted in a more roundabout way. At food stalls where cheeses and other weighed items have *prezzi fissi* (fixed prices), and in nearly all clothes stores, you can try asking for a *sconto* (discount). Reasons for meriting a *sconto* may be numerous — buying two articles at once is a good example — but if you are bold you will ask for a *sconto* for no good reason at all, and will usually get one. This practice applies to all but the very grandest stores.

Shoppers from outside the EEC do not have to pay Value Added Tax on certain purchases. This rule does not apply to small articles such as shoes, bags, clothing and porcelain. Larger items such as Oriental carpets or antique furniture do not qualify for tax provided that they are exported independently of the purchaser. This means that if you want to walk out of the store carrying your purchase you must pay tax.

Surprisingly few shopkeepers speak English, but in the larger stores there is usually one person on hand who understands enough to be able to help you. Regular late-evening shopping may be a novelty for many visitors (see *Shopping hours* in **Basic information**), but it is nevertheless best to shop in the mornings if you can. Sales people can get understandably tired and testy by 7.30 or 8pm, particularly as this is the time of day when most Italians like to make their purchases and the shops are at their most crowded.

Antiques

The grandest antique stores can be found in Via del Babuino. **W. Apolloni** at no. 133 has drawings as well as paintings and furniture. **Adolfo di Castro** at no. 80, **Nicola e Angelo di Castro** at no. 92 and **Amadeo di Castro** at no. 77 all have furniture and *objets d'art*. The last di Castro claims no connection with the first two, and to confuse the issue still further another professedly independent general dealer of that name, **Alberto di Castro**, operates from nearby (*Piazza di Spagna 5*), while **Aldo di Castro** sells prints at no. 71 Via del Babuino. On the same street, **Carlo** and **Cesare Lampronti**, at nos. 69 and 67 respectively, have paintings as well as furniture, and **Antonacci**, at no. 146, just furniture. **Emporio Floreale**, close by (*Via delle Carrozze 46*), specializes in Art Nouveau and Art Deco glass, furniture and paintings. None of these dealers takes credit cards.

Via dei Coronari, a charming street in the old part of the city, is worth wandering down even if you are not interested in buying anything. The *coronari* used to make rosaries to sell to pilgrims on their way to St Peter's, and most of their workshops are now tiny antique boutiques. The open shop-fronts have been covered with glass, allowing the contents to be viewed easily from the street — an unusual bonus as far as shopping for antiques is concerned. Via Giulia, s of Corso Vittorio Emanuele, has similar, but fewer, antique boutiques, as well as some modern art galleries.

Beauty parlors

Hairdressing salons in Rome are grand affairs, offering a full range of beauty treatments besides the traditional manicure. Cheaper, younger-style hairdressers are strangely lacking, mainly because nearly all Italian girls wear their hair long and thick. Some of the fashionable salons are worth trying out if you have money to spend and feel like being pampered. A herbalist and perfumery are also included in this section.

De Paola
Via della Croce 23 ☎ *6789607. Map 6G6* AE ◎
This extremely popular shop has been doing brisk business in Via della Croce since 1946. It is Rome's biggest perfumery and has by far and away the widest selection. Go early to avoid the crush.

Filippo Parrucchiere
Via Condotti 91 ☎ *6794907. Map 6G6.*
Filippo is now more famous as a fashion designer than a hairdresser, but this salon still offers one of the least expensive cuts in town.

Gilcagné
Via del Babuino 173 ☎ *3613291. Map 6G6* ◎ ◎ VISA
Two white Corinthian columns set at an angle lead to the shop that displays Gilcagné's impressive range of make-up. Deep-cleansing, massage and hairdressing are available in the salon behind the shop, while in the make-up studio Gil shows you how to make the best of your individual features or how to change your image. If your name is Amanda Lear or Liza Minelli, or you are some other well-known habituée of Gil's club, these sessions

may be conducted for free. Otherwise, the cost could be substantial.

L'Isola di Mod
Via dei Cappuccini 11 ☎ *4746072. Map 6G6. Closed Mon.*
Stylist Gianni Modafferi writes a beauty column and appears on Italian TV as a beauty consultant. Here, there's sauna massage, solarium and hairdressing — for men too.

Erboristeria di M. Mességué
Piazza San Silvestro 8 (Galleria RAS) ☎ *6797294. Map 6H6.*
Maurice Mességué, herbalist and author, personally grows and harvests in Fleurance, France, all the herbs that go into the preparation of his cosmetics, medications and teas. This is a friendly and attractive little shop, run by disciples Antonio Barbieri and Maria Luisa Lisandrelli — both qualified herbalists who are happy to give expert advice.

Michel
Via Sistina 143 ☎ *4740761. Map 6G6.*
A beauty parlor within reasonable

economic reach, Michel's is nevertheless quite an experience. The unprepossessing entrance on the first floor leads to a labyrinth of mirrored pillars and potted plants. Look behind each pillar and you will find Michel and his staff hard at work on customers' hair, faces, hands and feet. In the more private recesses of the labyrinth, massage and sunbeds are also available.

Felice Moretti
Via Lazio 9, off Via Veneto
☎ *484786. Map 7G7* 🆎 💳
Closed Sun, Mon.
A very reputable hairdresser.

Sergio Russo
Piazza Mignanelli 25, off Piazza di Spagna ☎ *6780457. Map 6G6.*
The second most fashionable hairdresser in Rome, Sergio Russo offers top hair-styling at top prices.

Clients include Claudia Cardinale and Audrey Hepburn.

Sergio Valente
Via Condotti 11 ☎ *6791268. Map 6G6.*
The archetypal Roman beauty parlor, Sergio Valente's salon is reached through an imposing archway and up a grand flight of steps. Sergio is the top name in the business, and although hair-styling is the main activity, this rich women's playground includes a make-up studio and facilities for saunas, facials, waxing and massage. Additional delights are a movie-star room and a couple of sulking boxes for celebrities and common mortals who might wish to avoid the public eye. Sergio works regularly with Valentino and Fendi, and keeps an archive room to record his magazine work.

Books

Rizzoli (*Galleria Colonna at Largo Chigi 15*) is the largest bookstore in the whole of Italy. The biggest English-language bookstore is the **Lion Bookshop** (*Via del Babuino 181*). Also recommended for English and American books is the **American Book Co.** (*Via della Vite 57*); this store has two more departments (*at Via della Vite 27*) — scientific books on the first floor and an English-language magazine subscription service on the fourth floor. The place to buy, and sell, secondhand English-language paperbacks is the **Economy Book Center** (*Via Torino 136*). For a huge selection of beautiful art books, mostly at half price, go to **Libreria San Silvestro** (*Piazza San Silvestro 27*).

Children's clothes

La Cicogna
Via Boccea ☎ *6241641* 🆎 💳 💳 💳
A reliable, medium-price store selling children's and maternity clothes, nursery furniture, baby toys and shoes. La Cicogna now has several branches in Rome.

Fiorucci See **Job-Fiorucci** in *Women's clothes.*

Sciunnach
Via Piave 2c ☎ *4819071. Map 7F8* 🆎 💳 💳
Inexpensive shop specializing in

shoes for children and women.

Tablò
Via della Croce 84 ☎ *6794468; Piazza di Spagna 96* ☎ *6781470. Map 6G6* 🆎 💳
Well-dressed Roman children have their clothes bought at Tablò. Quality and styling are superb, and you can pay adult prices for the tiniest garments. The shop in Via della Croce is for children of 9yrs upward, that in Piazza di Spagna for 8yrs downwards, and there's another branch at 105, Via del Babuino.

China and glass

Richard Ginori
Via Condotti 87 ☎ *6781013. Map 6G6* 🆎 💳 💳 💳

Two floors of traditional table settings in porcelain, china, glass and crystal.

Shopping

Myricae
Via Frattina 36 ☎ *6781448. Map 6G6* AE ◉ ◉◎ VISA

Regional pottery, painted trays, glass, colorful lampshades and other folk art, all reasonably priced. Roman girls place their wedding lists here for colorful, out-of-the-ordinary presents.

Stilvetro
Via Frattina 55 ☎ *6790258. Map 6G6.*

All-Italian china and glass, mostly from Tuscany, at rock-bottom prices. Most of it looks as cheap as it is, but some attractive rustic-style dinner services (plus cutlery) make real bargains.

C. Tupini
Piazza San Lorenzo in Lucina 8 ☎ *6791378. Map 6G5.*

Rome's most beautiful china store, lit by crystal chandeliers, is correspondingly expensive. Fine china and porcelain; also glass, silver and hand-painted ceramics.

Department stores

There are no high-class department stores in Rome, and those that exist tend to be of the nickel-and-dime variety.

Coin
Piazzale Appio ☎ *7573241. Map 11J9* AE ◉ ◉◎ VISA

A modern, well-laid-out store with five floors of medium-quality clothing and household furnishings. By far the best of Rome's big stores, just s of the city walls.

La Rinascente
Largo Chigi ☎ *6797691. Map 6H6* AE ◉ ◉◎ VISA

Clothing, perfumes, haberdashery and toys.

Standa
Via del Corso 148 ☎ *6790273. Map 6G6.*

A store worth investigating for its clothes and household goods — mostly of reasonable quality, at rock-bottom prices. There are branches all across the city, including one in Prati (*Via Cola di Rienzo 173*).

UPIM
Via del Tritone 172 ☎ *6783336. Map 6H6* VISA

The most central of 18 branches, this store stocks cheap, unexciting clothes, household goods and toys.

Fabrics

Bises
Via del Gesù 93 ☎ *6780941* ◉ *622196. Map 6H5* AE ◉◎ VISA

Rome's largest collection of furnishing and dress fabrics can be found in a beautiful 17thC palace, home of Cardinal Altieri before he became Pope Clement X. Under lofty painted and coffered ceilings, each huge chamber is devoted to just one type of material — silks, wools, velvets, and so on. This collection has to be seen to be believed.

Cesari
Via del Babuino 16 ☎ *3611441. Map 6G5* AE ◉ ◉◎ VISA

The setting may not be quite as grand as **Bises'** (above) but by any other standards this imposing house with its fluted Corinthian columns and molded ceilings would be impressive. Cesari is the top place for furnishing fabrics. For Cesari's linen store (*Via Barberini*) see page 172.

Polidori
Via Condotti 21 ☎ *6784842. Map 6G6* AE ◉ ◉◎ VISA

Classic silk, cotton and wool dress materials, in the medium-expensive to very expensive price range. There is a branch for men's fabrics (*Via Borgognona 4b*), and also for men's fashions (*Polidori Uomo, Via Condotti 83*).

Gloves and tights

Calza e Calze
Via della Croce 78 ☎ *6784281. Map 6G6.*
Selling tights and stockings like hot cakes, this inexpensive little shop has the best and brightest collection of all. Call early to avoid the crush.

Di Cori
Piazza di Spagna 53 ☎ *6784439. Map 6G6* AE VISA
It would be hard to fit any more stock into this tiny shop: brightly colored woolen and leather gloves line the walls from floor to ceiling. Kid, pigskin, chamois and suede are all of the highest quality. Go next door if you are looking for scarves and belts.

Amedeo Perrone
Piazza di Spagna 92 ☎ *6783101. Map 6G6* AE ◯ ◯ VISA
Gloves are the specialty here, in leather, cashmere and lambswool, and in a wide choice of colors. But there are also socks and tights, including colored tights for children aged 2-12yrs, all at super-cheap prices.

Jewelry and silver

Bulgari
Via Condotti 10 ☎ *6793876. Map 6G6* AE ◯ ◯ VISA
Possibly the world's greatest jewelers, Bulgari discreetly guards the identities of its royal customers behind a grand marble facade. As befits a princely clientele, the interior is palatial.

Fornari
Via Condotti 80 ☎ *6794285. Map 6G6* AE CB ◯ VISA
Specializing in gold jewelry, with some silver; traditionally the place to go to if you can't afford **Bulgari** (above). A less rarified atmosphere than some grander jewelers.

Fumis
Piazza San Silvestro 14 ☎ *6792510. Map 6H6* AE ◯
A medium-priced silver store, stocked entirely with Fumis' own

designs. There is another branch (*Via del Gambero 4*).

Fürst
Via Vittorio Veneto 42 ☎ *483992. Map 7G7* ◯ VISA
After **Bulgari**, but a long way behind, are a number of high-class jewelers such as Fürst. Specialties are emeralds and rubies.

Massoni
Largo Goldoni 48, w end of Via Condotti ☎ *6790182. Map 6G6* AE ◯ ◯ VISA
Perhaps the grandest of the runners-up, this old-established family firm attracts its fair share of famous customers. Massoni believe in creating jewelry to the client's own ideas, and this philosophy has endeared them to such independent spirits as Ingrid Bergman and Ava Gardner.

Leather and fur

Pier Caranti
Piazza di Spagna 43 ☎ *6791621. Map 6G6* AE ◯ ◯ VISA
This boutique sells classic bags, briefcases and belts at reasonable prices. You can also get an umbrella to go with your briefcase. There is another branch (*Via Frattina 77*).

Ceresa
Via del Tritone 120 ☎ *465516. Map 7G7* ◯ ◯ VISA
Clusters of fur pelts hanging on the walls identify the specialty here, and help you select the right quality

and color before your order goes into the workshop upstairs. There is also a good collection of leather goods, particularly bags. Ceresa has been in the business longer than **Gucci** and can be relied on for top-quality, classic designs.

Fendi
Via Borgognona 39 ☎ *6797641. Map 6G6* AE ◯ VISA
Looking at some of Karl Lagerfeld's models in the fabulous fur salon at Via Borgognona 39, you can see why he has played such an

important part in Fendi's success. In the same street at no. 36, Fendi's dark, printed-leather bags sell fast and well, even if the printing process succeeds in making them look like plastic. A boutique at no. 4l sells nonleather accessories such as canvas bags; another at 4e has shoes.

Gucci
Via Condotti 8 ☎ *6789340. Map 6G6* [AE] [⬦] [⬥] [VISA]
The twin GG stamp still attracts vast

numbers of Italians and foreigners in search of soft leather and suede clothing, luggage, bags, shoes, belts and ties. For slightly younger styles, it's a good idea to try the well-stocked **Gucci Boutique** (*Via Borgognona 25*).

Modi
Via Nazionale 237/8 ☎ *4758280. Map 7H7* [AE] [⬦] [⬥] [VISA]
Inexpensive, with a good selection of bags, wallets, belts and gloves, all at factory prices.

Linens and lingerie

Bellini
Piazza di Spagna 77 ☎ *6795956. Map 6G6* [AE] [⬦] [⬥] [VISA]
Hand-embroidered and -appliquéd table linen, sheets and lingerie. Months, even years, of labor go into some of the more elaborate tablecloths, and the same embroiderer is employed throughout to achieve a perfect finish.

Cesari
Via Barberini 1 ☎ *463035. Map 7G7* [AE] [⬦] [⬥] [VISA]
Rome's largest collection of fine linens, towels and lingerie. Affluent

young brides order their trousseaux here, and Lauren Bacall and the Belgian Royal Family have their silk sheets hand-embroidered to exclusive designs. Even the machine-embroidered linens are superb. Furnishing fabrics (*Via del Babuino 16*) are available too — see *Fabrics.*

Tina
Via Bocca di Leone 9 ☎ *6784076. Map 6G6* [AE] [⬦] [⬥] [VISA]
The best of the small boutiques selling lingerie and nightgowns, this shop offers pretty and exclusive designs at very reasonable prices.

Men's clothes
The Italian designer's preference for classic lines is perhaps nowhere better expressed than in men's clothing. Rome is full of grand tailors (most of them selling off-the-peg as well) and high-class men's retailers, and it has always been an important center for shirt-making.

Battistoni
Via Condotti 61a (through courtyard) ☎ *6786241. Map 6G6* [AE] [⬦] [⬥] [VISA]
For many years the most fashionable tailor in Rome, Battistoni started out 40yrs ago as a small shirt-making operation. The transformation to society tailor was effected by the mid-1950s, and soon countless movie stars and members of royalty were having their suits and shirts made here. Now, Battistoni could be losing ground (and customers) to nearby **Cucci** (see below).

Enzo Ceci
Via della Vite 52 ☎ *6798882. Map 6G6* [AE] [⬦] [⬥] [VISA]
By far the most interesting of the many men's boutiques in Via della

Vite, this shop has good original and sporty fashions in great colors, all exclusively designed by Enzo Ceci.

Cucci
Via Condotti 67 ☎ *6791882. Map 6G6* [AE] [⬦] [⬥] [VISA]
A family firm like **Battistoni** (above), but the founding member was a tailor rather than a shirt-maker. Prices are as high as Battistoni's, but do not deter stars such as Alain Delon and the late Salvador Dalí.

Filippo Boutique
Via Condotti 6 ☎ *6707906. Map 6G6* [AE] [⬦] [⬥] [VISA]
Hairdresser extraordinaire (see *Beauty parlors*), Filippo creates the trendiest clothes in Rome. His ideas are young, exciting and bang

up-to-the-minute. Clothes for women are included and prices are high. There is another boutique in New York.

Kenzo Uomo
Via Mario de' Fiori 111
☎ *6786754. Map 6G6* AE ◉ ◎
VISA

There is a surprisingly sober side to Kenzo when it comes to designing for men, and prices are also lower than you might expect.

Locatelli
Via Condotti 61a ☎ *642980. Map 6G6.*

Among bales of fine cotton, linen, flannel and wool, Carlo Locatelli works alone at his shirt-making, recalling some of the other craft stores that used to line these narrow streets. He can generally have a shirt ready in four weeks and, pressure of work permitting, will personally send commissions to any worldwide destination.

Max
Via Bocca di Leone 13
☎ *6783977. Map 6G6* AE ◉ ◎
VISA

Shirt-making is still the most important part of Max's business, but he now sells ready-made shirts (for men and women).

Eddy Monetti
Via Condotti 63 ☎ *6794117. Map 6G6* AE ◉ ◎ VISA

The designs are not exclusive, but

they make up one of the best and biggest collections of youngish, classic jackets, pants, pullovers and shirts.

Schostal
Via del Corso 158 ☎ *6791240. Map 6G6.*

One of few good reasons to venture into the Corso, Schostal sells pure cotton and woolen socks at rock-bottom prices.

Testa
Via Frattina 104 ☎ *6791296. Map 6G6* AE ◉ ◎ VISA

For youngish men-about-town, here are classic suits and separates, with stylish touches to bring them out of the ordinary. Almost all the designs are exclusive, and prices are reasonable. There is another shop nearby (*Via Borgognona 13*).

78 Uomo
Piazza di Spagna 78 ☎ *6792555. Map 6G6* AE ◉ ◎ VISA

The one and only outlet for Missoni knits for men. The designs are unmistakable, the colors warm, soft and muted, the whole collection irresistible.

Valentino Uomo
Via Mario de' Fiori 22
☎ *6783656. Map 6G6* AE ◉ ◎
VISA

Valentino's suits are classic and understated, his belts and jewelry elegant and monogrammed. Prices are well within reach.

Shoes

Campanile Spaterella
Via Condotti 58 ☎ *6783041. Map 6G6* AE ◉ ◎ VISA

The shoes may be the height of fashion, but they are fearfully expensive and service is not what you'd expect for such prices.

Tanino Crisci
Via Borgognona 4m ☎ *6795461. Map 6G6* AE ◉ ◎ VISA

This small, unassuming shop sells a limited range of sporty styles, produced in its factory at Casteggio near Pavia. Only moderately expensive and all hand-made, these shoes are probably superior in quality to any others sold in Rome.

Ferragamo
Via Condotti 66 ☎ *6781130. Map 6G6* AE ◉ ◎ VISA

Top-quality classical shoes at top

prices. Slightly more swayed by fashion trends than **Magli**, this Florence-based firm has women's shoes at Via Condotti 73/74.

Fragiacomo
Via Condotti 35 ☎ *6798780. Map 6G6* AE ◉ VISA

One of the most conservative of the top shoe-makers, this Milanese designer produces elegant shoes at averagely expensive prices.

Maud Frizon
Via Borgognona 38 ☎ *6795370. Map 6G6* AE ◉ VISA

Rome's most exciting shoe store. The colors are fun, the designs strikingly original. Maud Frizon lives and works in Paris, but her shoes are made in Italy. The styles seem aimed at a young market, but are sadly beyond the means of most young sophisticates. This is high fashion, at super-high prices.

Bruno Magli
Via del Gambero 1 ☎ *6793802. Map 6G6* AE ◑ ◐ VISA
One of four Roman outlets for this Bologna shoe firm. The styles are sober and classical, the prices averagely high. Leather jackets are included among the accessories.

Guido Pasquali
Via Bocca di Leone 5 ☎ *6795023. Map 6G6* AE ◑ ◐ VISA
A Milanese designer with a difference, Guido Pasquali creates young, fashion-conscious styles that are not too expensive.

Raphael Salato
Piazza di Spagna 34 ☎ *6795646. Map 6G6* AE ◑ ◐ VISA
Embroidered leather is a specialty, but the dull colors are disappointing. Quality is excellent, however. There are three more shops (*Via Veneto*).

Santini
Via Frattina 120 ☎ *6784114. Map 6G6* AE ◑ VISA
A chic shop-front, with neon rainbow arches and a white-tiled window, displays one of the best young collections in town. The designs are original and inexpensive, and the colors are distinctively trendy.

Stationery

Pineider
Via Due Macelli 68 ☎ *6795884. Map 6G6; Via della Scrofa 7a* ☎ *6548014. Map 6H5* AE ◑ ◐ VISA
Lots of internationally-known names get printed on Pineider's high-class stationery, but this firm is more famous for the quality of the artwork (you can have anything you like in the way of typefaces and symbols) than for the paper itself.

Vertecchi
Via della Croce 38 ☎ *6790100, Via della Croce 70* ☎ *6783110. Map 6G6* AE ◑ ◐ VISA

A very useful and unpretentious family store in the heart of the posh area, it's a good place for presents as well as stationery. At Via della Croce 38 there are two floors of decorative candles, trays, gift wrappings, Christmas decorations, greeting cards, table-mats and kitchen gadgets. Across the street at no. 70 is an artists' paradise: a beautifully laid-out shop displaying walls of colored crayons, pens, pencils and paper, as well as more general stationery. The main stationery store is some way out of the city center (*Via Pietro da Cortona 12*).

Toy stores
See *Rome for children*.

Street markets
Romans buy their vegetables, fruit, flowers, meats and cheeses from one of the many street markets that are held daily all over the city. Rich people as well as poor shop in these markets, because this is where the best and freshest produce can be found. Stalls of cheap clothing are generally included among the food stands, but there are also whole markets devoted just to clothes and accessories.

The food and flower markets are the most entertaining as well as the most picturesque, and an early-morning wander through one of these is an essential part of any Roman vacation.

Campo dei Fiori
Piazza Campo dei Fiori. Map 5l5. Open 6am-2pm. Closed Sun.
Rome's oldest market is held in a cobbled square in the heart of the medieval city and sells flowers, fruit and vegetables under makeshift

awnings or giant umbrellas — all collapsible at the end of the morning. An old cast-iron pump marked *SPQR Acqua Vergine* cools wilting roses in the daytime heat, and in the ancient houses round the square are some good delicatessens.

Mercato dei Fiori
Via Trionfale (junction with Via Paolo Sarpi). Map 4F2. Open 10am-1pm, Tues only.
Rome's only flower market takes place in a two-story covered hall some way out of the city center, in the suburb of Prati. It is held daily, but is only open to the public on Tues. Upstairs, the air is heady with the scent of the flowers in season, and there is endless scope for bargaining. Downstairs, an exotica of giant house plants refreshes jaded spirits before the trip back to the city.

Piazza Vittorio Emanuele
Map 11I9. Open 7am-2pm. Closed Sun.
Stretching all the way round the edge of this huge garden square is the city's largest, most entertaining market. Clothes and leather goods are ranged along the s side and hold some fine bargains, but the food stalls on the N side are what make this market famous. The specialization is prodigious: one stall sells only calves' livers, another only fresh tuna, yet another nothing but lemons. This is the place for the most unusual cheeses, salad vegetables and shellfish, the rarest game birds, birds' eggs and fruits. Stallholders occupy themselves during slack moments by preparing their produce: trimming artichokes, plucking birds. Crowing cocks and scuttling crabs contribute to the lively atmosphere.

Porta Portese
Ponte Sublicio. Map 9K5. Open 6.30am-2.30pm, Sun only.
This extremely popular clothes market skirts close to the Tiber in a narrow ribbon more than 1km (½ mile) long, from Ponte Sublicio in the N to Ponte Testaccio in the s.

The clothes and accessories are cheap but of poor quality, and you would have to look elsewhere for a real leather handbag. Romans throng here in vast numbers, and it is wise to arrive before 9am.

Via Andrea Doria
Map 4F2. Open 8am-1pm. Closed Sun, Mon.
Ranged along almost the full length of Via Andrea Doria and spilling into the side streets to the s, this large and lively food market may not have all the specialties of **Piazza Vittorio Emanuele** (opposite), but it wins on organization. The vegetable stands are laid out in effortlessly artistic arrangements, draped with strings of onions and chili peppers. The *salumerie* (delicatessen stalls) are packed with cheeses, bottled oils and *prosciutto*, framed by festoons of salami and sausages.

Via Sannio
Map 11J9. Open Mon-Fri 8am-1pm, Sat 8am-7pm. Closed Sun.
Just two stops on the Metropolitana from the larger market at **Piazza Vittorio Emanuele** (opposite), Via Sannio is worth a visit if you are interested in secondhand clothes. Walk down the street past the beads and baubles until you reach a cobbled lane on your right. This is where the clothing stalls begin, but if you want secondhand clothes (in large numbers) you must walk to the open space at the end of the lane. The new clothing is of inferior quality to that at Piazza Vittorio Emanuele, and similar to (if not identical with) that at **Porta Portese** (left). (Some of these stallholders move their wares to Porta Portese on Sun.)

Women's clothes
Rome is not a place for young fashion: for that, you go to London or Paris. However, it is an important center for *alta moda* (high fashion) and chic prêt-à-porter. The keyword is elegance, and even if colors sometimes become adventurous, lines nearly always remain classic. You can find here the very best of Italian fashion, with outlets for Milanese and Florentine as well as local designers. French designers are also well represented: among the old brigade are **Givenchy** (*Via Borgognona 21*), **Courrèges** (*Via Bocca di Leone 84*), **Balenciaga** (*Via Bocca di Leone 83*) and **Céline** (*Via Bocca di Leone 79*).

Expensive ready-to-wear is the Italians' forte, but they also excel at producing knitwear, and Rome is full of shops selling colorful woolen separates at moderate prices.

Shopping

Benetton
Via Condotti 59 ☎ *6797982. Map 6G6* [AE] [⊙] [◎] [VISA]
The most central of several branches, this store sells classic young separates with the Benetton label, in wool and cotton. The clothes are well made and inexpensive, and there is an exciting choice of colors. Other stores selling Benetton are **Merceria** (*Via Frattina*) and **Tagliacozzo** (*Via del Gambero*).

Giorgio Armani
Via del Babuino 102 ☎ *6793777. Map 6G6* [AE] [⊙] [◎] [VISA]
The most talented of the young Milanese designers, Armani has a flair for putting different textures, patterns and colors together, with sensational results. You won't find better Italian prêt-à-porter than this anywhere, and the shop is as delightful as the clothes: flowering plants are packed into every available corner, and the staff is not in the least bit snooty.

Filippo   See *Men's clothes.*

Jap di Kenzo
Via Capo le Case 1 ☎ *6783146. Map 6G6* [AE] [VISA]
Admirers of Kenzo's color genius and wacky ideas will not mind the short uphill walk to this slightly off-center boutique. Prices are the same as in Paris.

Job-Fiorucci
Via della Maddalena 27 ☎ *6569653. Map 6H5* [AE] [⊙] [◎] [VISA]
For comfortable, inexpensive young fashion in bold designs and shocking colors, this Milanese designer is unbeatable. An added bonus here is the collection of highly original children's clothes, from 2yrs upward.

Krizia
Piazza di Spagna 77 ☎ *6793419. Map 6G6* [AE] [⊙] [◎] [VISA]
Designed in Milan by Mariuccia Mandella, Krizia knits have won an international reputation for stylish sophistication. Selling separates as well, this shop will appeal to both the young and the not-so-young.

Linea Lui/Lei/Sport, Play Jeans
Via del Corso 49 ☎ *6786725. Map 6G5* [AE] [⊙] [◎] [VISA]
Four shops in one, this store has good-value clothes for the young, including a big selection of woolen separates.

Missoni
-1Via del Babuino 96 ☎ *6797971. Map 6G6* [AE] [⊙] [◎] [VISA]
King and queen of the knitwear

Clothing sizes
When shops give clothing sizes in centimetres, use the following conversion scale to determine the correct size

12 *in*	16	20	24	28	32	36	40	44	48
30 *cm*	40	50	60	70	80	90	100	110	120

When standardized codes are used, although these may be found to vary considerably, the following provides a useful guide.

Women's clothing sizes
UK/US sizes	8/6	10/8	12/10	14/12	16/14	18/16
Italian sizes	36	38	40	42	44	46
Bust *in/cm*	31/80	32/81	34/86	36/91	38/97	40/102

Men's clothing sizes
European code (suits)	44	46	48	50	52	54	56
Chest *in/cm*	34/86	36/91	38/97	40/102	42/107	44/112	46/117
Collar *in/cm*	13½/34	14/36	14½/37	15/38	15½/39	16/41	16½/42
Waist *in/cm*	28/71	30/76	32/81	34/86	36/91	38/97	40/102
Inside leg *in/cm*	28/71	29/74	30/76	31/79	32/81	33/84	34/86

Men's and women's shoe sizes
UK/US sizes	3/4½	4/5½	5/6½	6/7½	7/8½	8/9½	9/10½	10/11½	11/12½
European	36	37	38	39	40	41	42	43	44

scene, Ottavio and Rosita Missoni continue to produce breathtakingly beautiful designs from their base at Varese, near Milan. Subtle color variations, geometric or flaring patterns and nubbly textures are the elements of the unmistakable Missoni style.

Emilio Pucci
Via Campania 59 ☎ *4758584. Map 7F7* AE ⊙ VISA

A longish walk away from the shops and lights of Via Veneto, a grand mansion contains the prêt-à-porter collection of this classic Florentine designer. Signed scarves and monogrammed ties are the specialties of the house, and Pucci designs all the silks out of which he makes his timeless blouses and dresses.

Yves St Laurent
Via Bocca di Leone 35 ☎ *6795577. Map 6G6* AE ⊙ ⊙ VISA

St Laurent has seven shops in Italy, but this is the only one in Rome. There are no men's clothes (ties excepting) and no perfumes, but the women's prêt-à-porter collection is large, colorful and exciting. Sadly, prices are slightly higher than in Paris.

Luisa Spagnoli
Via Frattina 116 ☎ *6795517. Map 6G6* AE ⊙ ⊙ VISA

A respected doyenne among Italian knitwear designers, Luisa Spagnoli has perhaps failed to keep pace with the times. The quality of the fine woolen knits is still superb, but styling and flair are noticeably absent.

Stefanel
Via Frattina 31 ☎ *6792667. Map 6G6* AE ⊙ ⊙ VISA

A fairly new shop, selling woolen and cotton separates — pullovers, skirts *and* trousers — in a multitude of bright colors. All designed by Stefanel Beppino.

Ungaro
Via Bocca di Leone 24 ☎ *6789931. Map 6G6* AE ⊙ ⊙

Ungaro is probably the most Italian of the French designers. His classic silk dresses and wool suits are made in Italy and cost less here than they do in Paris.

Valentino Boutique
Via Bocca di Leone 15 ☎ *6795862. Map 6G6* AE ⊙ ⊙ VISA

Some people believe that Valentino has lost direction, but it could just be that by sometimes breaking all the rules he offends the Italian ideal of classic elegance. One of the undisputed giants of the Italian fashion scene, he may not appeal to all tastes all of the time, but his prêt-à-porter is always young and original. Couture is elsewhere (*Via Gregoriana 24*).

Gianni Versace
Via Bocca di Leone 27 ☎ *6780521. Map 6G6* AE ⊙ ⊙ VISA

This Milanese designer favors "unmatched" separates in plain, somber colors that work easily together. Prices are in the same range as **Giorgio Armani** (see previous page) or **Valentino** (see above).

Rome environs

The rolling Roman *campagna*, or countryside, is almost as rich in historical associations as the city itself, and offers many areas of outstanding natural beauty. To the SE, the Alban Hills shelter the Castelli Romani, hillside towns famous for their white wines and scenic views across crater-lakes and valleys. To the NW of the city, another volcanic lake, Bracciano, is dominated by the fairy-tale castle of the Orsini. Toward the coast, at Cervéteri and Tarquinia, wide open plains and windswept plateaux conceal fascinating ancient Etruscan tombs — luxurious treasure-houses of this long-vanished civilization.

The following listings also include EUR, Mussolini's almost regimental dream town on the outskirts of the city, and Tivoli, home of two world-famous villas.

Albano Laziale
Map 15D4 ◁€ 25km (15 miles) SE of Rome. Getting there: By train, from Stazione Termini (40 mins); by car, Via Appia Nuova (SS7); by bus, ACOTRAL from Anagnina (on Metropolitana Line A).

The chief attractions of the Castelli Romani — Albano and the other hill towns perched on the extinct volcanoes to the SE of Rome — are their white wines and welcome coolness in the heat of summer. It was probably for the very same reasons that the Emperor Domitian kept a vast estate here with a magnificent villa. Then, at the end of the 2ndC AD, Septimius Severus, wishing to instil a little respect in his Roman subjects, established a permanent legionary camp, known as the Castra Albana.

The nearby civilian settlement outgrew the camp and developed into a small town. In the Middle Ages this became an important bishopric. The modern town, largely rebuilt after World War II, reveals many traces of its varied history: an **amphitheater**, the gateway to the military camp and, most remarkably, a vast Roman **cistern**, still in use for the purpose of irrigation. The **Duomo**, much abused by history, still contains fragments of the 4thC basilica, but is of less interest than the church of **San Pietro**, founded in the 6thC over the ruins of the Roman baths.

⊐ Visitors to the town may eat in the restaurant of the **Miralago** hotel (*Via dei Cappuccini 12* ☎ 9322253 **Ⅲ◻** ◻) or that of **Motel del Mare** (*Via Olivella 100/104* ☎ 9322335 **Ⅱ◻**).

Anzio During the summer months, ferries and hydrofoils link this favorite Roman resort with the even more popular island of Ponza, both described in *Excursions*.

Bracciano
Map 14C3 ◁€ 42km (26 miles) NW of Rome. Getting there: By train, from Stazione Termini (1hr); by car, Via Cassia (SS2) to Madonna di Bracciano, then 493; by bus, ACOTRAL from Via Lepanto (on Metropolitana Line A).

The small town stands high over Lake Bracciano, an almost circular expanse of water that fills a volcanic crater in the Sabatini hills. A drive of 35km (22 miles) takes you right round the lake, passing the picturesque village of **Trevignano** and the popular resort of **Anguillara**. The shores, planted with pine and olive groves, make pleasant picnic spots and swimming areas. Bracciano itself is dominated by the castle of the Orsini, the former landlords of the town.

Sights and places of interest
Castello Orsini 🏛 ☆
Piazza Mazzini ☎ 9024003 ▦ ✗ *compulsory. Open Tues-Sat 9am-noon, 3-6pm (Oct-Mar 3-6pm).*

This magnificent example of a Renaissance private castle was completed about 1485. Its polygonal shape and five slender circular towers give it a certain austere grace, yet its battlemented walls were strong enough to withstand a determined assault carried out by the troops of Alexander VI, the Borgia pope.

Many of the rooms on show still boast their original frescoes and contain a wide assortment of family heirlooms of the Orsini and the Odescalchi (the present owners). These include some good Etruscan relics and a fascinating collection of arms and armor. (Telephone to check that the castle is open — it is a very popular movie set.)

≅ Two reasonably priced restaurants are **Casina del Lago** (*Via Lungolago Argenti 1* ☎ *9024025* ⬛ *closed Tues*) and **Selene** (*Via Claudia 115* ☎ *9024040* ⬛).

Castel Gandolfo
*Map **15**D4 ⇇ 25km (15 miles) SE of Rome. Getting there: By train, from Stazione Termini (35mins); by car, Via Appia Nuova (SS7); by bus, ACOTRAL from Anagnina (on Metropolitana Line A).*

Superbly situated at 426m (1,400ft), overlooking Lake Albano, the summer residence of the Pope enjoys a wonderful view of the wooded slopes that plunge steeply down into the dark green waters of the volcanic crater. Castel Gandolfo is thought to be the site of the legendary Alba Longa, the most powerful city of the Latin League, until superceded by the upstart Rome. The cheerful, but far from prosperous, little town shows no trace of its glorious prehistory, nor do the down-to-earth inhabitants pay much attention to their most illustrious resident.

Sights and places of interest
Palazzo Papale ⯃
Piazza della Libertà.
Built in 1624 by Carlo Maderno on the orders of Urban VIII, the palace was radically altered and enlarged earlier this century by Pius XI. The original facade, however, was left untouched and during the summer and fall, when the Pope is in residence, Swiss Guards stand on duty outside its great central portal. General audiences are held in the modern hall of the Villa Cybo at 11am on Wed, but you must apply to the Vatican for tickets (see *Papal audiences* in *Basic information*). At noon on Sun the Pope gives an address in the courtyard of the palace, for which no permit is required.

☜ ≅ The **Garden** hotel has a decent restaurant, **La Perla** (*Via Spiaggia al Lago 6* ☎ *9360064* ● *616244* ⊗ *4817912* ⬛).

Cervéteri
*Map **14**D3. 46km (28 miles) NW of Rome. Getting there: By train, from Stazione Termini (1hr 10mins) or Roma Tiburtina (50mins) to Cervéteri-Ladíspoli, then local bus; by car, Via Aurelia (SS1) or Autostrada A12; by bus, ACOTRAL from Via Lepanto (on Metropolitana Line A).*

The interest of Cervéteri lies not in the remains of the medieval town, but in the fact that, as Caere, it was one of the wealthiest and most powerful cities of the Etruscan Federation. Etruscan cities are known to have been well planned, with fine temples and public amenities, but hardly anything remains of them, mainly because the houses were built of wood. However, archeological discoveries in the 18th and 19thC opened up a marvelous lost Etruscan world, for this extraordinary civilization built necropolises of stone, with paved streets between the long rows of *tumuli*. Just 2km (1 mile) to the N of Cervéteri, in an area of open country known as the Banditaccia, lies one of the finest of these cities of the dead.

Sights and places of interest
Necropoli della Banditaccia ⯃ ★
☎ *9950003* ▦ ✗ ⇌ *Open Tues-Sun, 9am-1hr before sunset. Closed Mon.*
Do not be disappointed by your first sight of the tombs, which resemble beehives thatched with grass. All the ornamentation was reserved for the inside, where the sarcophagi of the Etruscan nobility were surrounded with worldly goods — food, drink, jewelry and weapons — while the walls were

painted to remind them of the pleasures of this life, with scenes of banquets, dancing, fishing, swimming and all manner of sporting activities. Only a few of the finest tombs are lit and, as tomb-robbing is still a flourishing profession, all their portable relics have been removed to museums.

Many of the tombs are constructed as exact replicas of houses. The **Tomb of the Seats and Shields** has no fewer than seven chambers. The seats after which it is named are carved from the living rock, complete with footrests. Originally they would have supported effigies of the deceased husband and wife.

Unfortunately the most fascinating of all the tombs, the **Tomb of the Reliefs**, is now closed to the public, but special permission to visit it can be obtained in Rome from *Villa Giulia*. One of its painted stucco reliefs depicts beautifully detailed scenes of animal life, and the central pillars are decorated with an invaluable inventory of Etruscan household equipment, including knives, spoons, ladles and axes.

A tour can take 2-4hrs, depending on how many of the major tombs are open, so it is wise to bring some refreshment with you. The spirits of the Etruscan dead will certainly not object: they would be more likely to take it as a mark of respect.

EUR

Map 12E3 ✱ *6km (4 miles) s of Rome. Getting there: By car, Via Cristoforo Colombo (Porta Ardeatina); by Metropolitana, Line B; by bus, 93 from Stazione Termini or 97 from Piazza Sonnino (Trastevere).*

The initials stand for Esposizione Universale Romana, a grandiose project sponsored by Mussolini as a permanent exhibition to the glory of Rome, as renewed by the cleansing power of Fascism. Its intended opening in 1942 was prevented by the war, and work did not begin again in earnest until 1952. The large modern buildings are laid out on an expansive plan, and even today the wide spaces are practically empty of traffic and pedestrians. The structure that will most interest students of modern architecture is the **Palazzo dello Sport**, built for the 1960 Olympics. The dome, with a span of 100m (330ft), is the work of the great engineer, Pier Luigi Nervi.

For children (with a lot of money in their pockets) there is a permanent fairground, **Luna Park**, to the left as you enter EUR along Via Cristoforo Colombo. The central area above the artificial lake consists almost entirely of ministries and museums.

Sights and places of interest
Museo delle Arti e Tradizioni Popolari
Piazza Marconi 8 ☎ *5926148* 🚻 *Open Tues-Sat 9am-2pm. Sun 9am-1pm. Closed Mon.*
A vast collection of artifacts illustrating every aspect of Italian life at the turn of the century. Particularly interesting are the sections on agriculture and traditional costumes.
Museo della Civiltà Romana ✩
Piazzale Giovanni Agnelli 10 ☎ *5926135* 🚻 *Open Tues, Thurs 9am-2pm, 5-8pm, Wed, Fri, Sat 9am-2pm, Sun 9am-1pm. Closed Mon.*
The museum was a gift from FIAT to the city of Rome and houses a large collection of plaster-casts of famous monuments and statues, including the entire series of reliefs from **Trajan's Column**.
Museo Preistorico ed Etnografico Luigi Pigorini
Viale Lincoln 1 ☎ *5910702* 🚻 *Open Tues-Fri 9am-2pm, Sat 9am-6pm, Sun 9am-1pm. Closed Mon.*
One of the most comprehensive collections of its kind in the world, the Museo Preistorico charts the development of the Stone, Bronze and Iron Ages, with particular reference to Italy and the Aegean.

🍽 EUR's eating places tend to be expensive and ostentatious. Less pretentious than some is **Shangri-La** (*Viale Algeria 141* ☎ *5918861* ▥ 🖭 💠 🖂).

Frascati

Map 15D4 ⟨⟨ 22km (14 miles) SE of Rome. Getting there: By train, from Stazione Termini (30mins); by car, Via Tuscolana (SS215); by bus, ACOTRAL from Anagnina (on Metropolitana Line A).

A sizeable town of 22,000 inhabitants, Frascati is the best-known of the Castelli Romani, famous for its white wines and its villas. It suffered heavy damage during bombing in World War II, when it was the German headquarters in the defense of Rome. Several buildings of note, including the cathedral of **San Pietro**, were rebuilt after the war. Nevertheless, it is an ideal place for a day's outing from the city, with splendid views across the Roman *campagna*.

In the sweeping panorama from the town's main square, **Piazza Marconi**, you will see the gardens of the **Villa Torlonia** (now a public park) and the magnificent avenue of clipped trees that sweeps up to the entrance of the **Villa Aldobrandini**. There are several other equally fine estates, but these are the only ones you are allowed to visit.

Sights and places of interest
Villa Aldobrandini ⊞

Via Cardinale Massaia ⊠ Tickets must be obtained from the Azienda di Soggiorno (local tourist office), Piazza G. Marconi ☎ 9420331. Open Mon-Sat 9am-1pm. Closed Sun.

The villa itself is closed to the public, but from the terrace there is a glorious view of the whole city of Rome, stretching away to the NW. The building was begun at the end of the 16thC by Giacomo della Porta, but is not as spectacular as the park, which has dense groves of ilex, ornamental gardens, statues, grottoes and fountains.

≡ After walking, the principal pastimes of visitors to Frascati are eating and drinking. Two of the most popular restaurants are **Cacciani** (*Via Diaz 13* ☎ 9420378 ⫴ ▭ ▬ 🍴 AE) and **Spartaco** (*Viale Letizia Bonaparte 1* ☎ 9420431 ⫴ ▭ ▬ 🍴 ▬ AE ◉).

Grottaferrata

Map 15D4. 21km (13 miles) SE of Rome. Getting there: By car, Via Tuscolana (SS215), then 511; by bus, ACOTRAL from Anagnina (on Metropolitana Line A).

The great attraction of Grottaferrata, which would otherwise be the most peaceful of the Castelli Romani, is its famous abbey. This looks more like a moated castle than a monastery, but the real reason for its celebrity is the fact that the liturgy of its Basilian monks is Greek. Since its foundation in 1004, the Abbey has been a center of Greek scholarship, but it was only 100yrs ago that the pope again allowed the use of a completely Byzantine rite. The services, those in Holy Week in particular, are noted for their color and spectacle.

Sights and places of interest
Grottaferrata Abbey ⊞ †

Corso del Popolo ☎ 945309 ◙ ✗ compulsory. Visitors should make a donation. Open 9am-12.30pm, 4.15-7pm.

On crossing the bridge, you should ring the bell. One of the monks will come to show you round the monastery, with its **library** of rare Greek texts and **museum** of ecclesiastical treasures. Giuliano della Rovere, before he became Pope Julius II, was Abbot of Grottaferrata. The warlike cardinal was responsible for much of the fortification, and the fine portico of the monastery by Sangallo bears his crest.

Returning to the main courtyard of the abbey, you go left to visit the church of **Sant Maria** with its magnificent 12thC campanile. Most of the

interior is Baroque, and in the **Chapel of San Nilo**, dedicated to the
founder of the abbey, there is a series of **frescoes (★)** by Domenichino.

➤ The wine of Grottaferrata is highly regarded by *conoscenti* of the
Castelli vineyards and may be enjoyed under the pine trees of **Al Fico** (*Via
Anagnina 134* ☎ *9459214* ⫪ ☐ ⊒ ⊕ 🆑 ▣). Alternatively, you can
eat at **Taverna dello Spuntino** (*Via Cicerone 20* ☎ *9459336* 🍴 🔧 ⫪⫪)
or **La Cavola d'Oro** (*Via Anagnina 35* ☎ *9459955* 🍴 ⊕ 🆑 🆑 ⫪⫪).

Lido di Roma *(Ostia)*
*Map **14**D3. 30km (18 miles) SW of Rome. Getting there: By
train, from Porta San Paolo (30mins); by car, Via del Mare
(SS8) or Via Cristoforo Colombo; by Metropolitana, from
Termini (see Ostia Antica opposite); by bus, ACOTRAL
from Via Giolitti.*
The nearest and most accessible resort to the city, Ostia — or
Lido di Roma, as it is now more commonly called — becomes
very overcrowded in summer. Private enterprise run riot has
covered all the beaches with restaurants, bars, changing huts and
video games. On Sun seemingly endless traffic jams tail back
along the roads to Rome. Unfortunately it is healthier to remain
ashore and inhale the gasoline fumes than to dip into the
Mediterranean, since pollution there is even higher. Along the
coast to the E, however, at **Castel Fusano**, there are beautiful
pine woods and the sea is much cleaner. Many of the beaches
there are private, but fortunately, by law, the 10m (11yds) of sand
next to the sea itself is public property.

➤ Wiser Romans drive to Ostia not to swim but to eat the seafood.
Mussels, crayfish, *fritto misto di mare* and *spaghetti alle vongole* are on offer
at nearly every restaurant. Two recommended ones are **Ferrantelli** (*Via
Claudio 7* ☎ *5625751* ⫪⫪ 🍴 ☐ 🆑) and **La Nuova Capricciosa** (*Via
Rutilio Namanziano* ☎ *5696250* ⫪⫪ ☐ 🆑).

Marino
*Map **15**D4 ◁ᕲ 22km (14 miles) SE of Rome. Getting there:
By train, from Stazione Termini (30mins); by car, Via Appia
Nuova (SS7), then Via dei Laghi (217); by bus, ACOTRAL
from Cinecittà (on Metropolitana Line A).*
The vineyards of Marino produce excellent white wine,
considerably stronger than one would expect from the Castelli
Romani. On the first Sun in Oct it literally flows in the streets at
the annual *Sagra dell' Uva* (Festival of the Grape). The town is a
favorite spot for outings from Rome, yet comparatively
unspoiled. The beautiful road that climbs from the town in the
direction of Nemi reaches over 600m (2,000ft) and gives a
glorious view across Lake Albano to the hills beyond.

➤ Many of the simple *osterie* serve only wine but, if you ask, they are
only too pleased to let you eat your own food. Try some of the cold pork
on sale at roadside stalls. The pigs are roasted whole and sliced to order.
For a more substantial meal to accompany your drinking, try **Antonio al
Vigneto** (*Via dei Laghi* ☎ *9387034* ⫪⫪ ☐ ⊒ 🍴 🆑 ▣ 🆑 🆑).

Nemi
*Map **15**D4 ◁ᕲ 34km (20 miles) SE of Rome. Getting there:
By car, Via Appia Nuova (SS7), then Via dei Laghi (217); by
bus, ACOTRAL from Cinecittà (on Metropolitana Line A).*
The village of Nemi balances high above the road along an

escarpment that falls away abruptly to the lake below. The lake itself is the loveliest of all the crater-lakes around Rome, its still waters reflecting the colors of the changing seasons on the surrounding wooded hills. These are famous for their wild strawberries, but the strawberries consumed in the village in their millions in early summer are, alas, all cultivated.

The name of the lake and village derives from *Nemus Dianae* (the Grove of Diana), which has been identified with the site of a temple overlooking the lake's NE shore. The primitive cult of the goddess, with its homicidal rite of succession to the priesthood, was the starting point of Frazer's great anthropological treatise *The Golden Bough*.

Throughout Roman times the lake was known as the Mirror of Diana, and festivals in her honor reached such a scale that Caligula built two huge ships to navigate its restricted waters. These, not surprisingly, sank and lay beneath the lake for nearly 1,900yrs. They were eventually raised in 1932, but were then tragically burned in World War II.

If you come to Nemi during the strawberry festival in June, you have little hope of finding somewhere to eat, but at other times of year try **Lo Specchio di Diana** (*Corso Vittorio Emanuele 13* ☎ 9378016 ▯ ▭ ▱), with its terrace overlooking the lake.

Ostia Antica

Map **14**D3. *25km (15 miles) sw of Rome. Getting there: By train, from Porta San Paolo (30mins); by car, Via del Mare (SS8); by Metropolitana, from Termini (only three trains per day — depart 8.03am, 9.03am, 10.03am, return 1.14pm, 5.24pm, 6.24pm); by bus, ACOTRAL from Via Giolitti.*

The ruins of Ostia provide a fascinating insight into daily urban life in Roman times. After the 2ndC AD, the prosperity of Ostia, until then the main port of Rome, began a steady decline. From the time of Constantine, Rome's other port (Portus Romae, on the other side of the Tiber) handled more and more of the city's shipping. The Barbarian invasions and endemic malaria finally killed off the town completely, and its ruins were buried in the sand that has so magically preserved it. As at **Pompeii** (see *Excursions*), you have the sensation that the clock has been turned back nearly 2,000yrs. In summer, a visit in the late afternoon is preferable, as there is little shade among the ruins.

Sights and places of interest
Scavi di Ostia Antica ▥
☎ 5650022 ▨ ▱ *Open Tues-Sun 9am-1hr before sunset. Closed Mon.*

You enter the excavations at the Porta Romana, then follow the long main street, the Decumanus Maximus. The first large public building you will come to is the expertly restored **Theater** (★). From here you overlook the **Piazzale dei Corporazioni**, where the important traders and shippers had their offices, many paved with beautiful mosaics indicating the nature of their business. The chief commodity was corn, but they also imported such luxuries as ivory (which is illustrated by an elephant).

Farther along the Decumanus Maximus you reach the **Capitolium** (★), high above steps that are now brick but were once faced with rich marbles. Sited at the end of the **Forum**, it was a temple dedicated to Jupiter and Minerva, begun during the reign of Hadrian (AD117-138).

Of particular interest at Ostia today are the remains (★) of the **insulae** (apartment blocks), often four or five stories high. Similar blocks are known to have existed in contemporary Rome, but there not one has survived. They were robustly built of brick, well lit, well supplied with running water, and had sanitation on every floor. Most of the population lived in apartments, for only rich merchants could afford to build themselves villas. The larger *insulae* had integrated rows of shops, as did the enormous **horrea** (warehouse). The well-preserved **laundry** and **wine shop** should also be visited.

Two splendid private houses that must be seen are the **House of Cupid and Psyche** (★), w of the Capitolium, and the **House of the Dioscuri** (★), at the sw end of the town. The former has a fine **nymphaeum** (loggia), while in the latter there are mosaics of Castor and Pollux and of Venus, as well as a complete sequence of baths.

≡≡ Most tourists end up eating under the trellis of **Allo Sbarco di Enea** (*Via dei Romagnoli 675* ☎ 5650034 ▥▥ ⬜ 🚗 🚙) or at **Monumento** (*Piazza Umberto I, 8* ☎ 5650021 ▣ 🍴).

Palestrina
*Map **15**D4* ◈ *38km (23 miles)* SE *of Rome. Getting there: By train, from Stazione Termini (40mins), then local bus from Stazione Palestrina to the town, or direct from narrow-gauge railroad from Via Giolitti (on s side of Stazione Termini); by car, Via Casilina (SS6) then 155; by bus, ACOTRAL from Piazza dei Cinquecento.*

Many people today are familiar with Palestrina as the birthplace of the great 16thC composer, who took his name from the town. The reasons for its fame in Classical times date back to prehistory. By the 7thC BC Praeneste, as it was called then, was a thriving community and an important religious center for the Etruscans. Subsequently the Romans also went there to consult its celebrated oracle, and in the 2ndC BC they built the enormous and prestigious **Temple of Fortune**. In a major feat of engineering, great terraces were projected from the hillside, supported on huge arches. Only after the bomb damage of World War II did archeologists realize the full extent of the temple, most of which is concealed by the medieval town.

The heart of the town is **Piazza Regina Margherita**, flanked by the **cathedral** and the weathered facade at the **Sala Absidata**, an impressive assortment of ancient stones and columns. Nobody is certain to what use the Romans put it. Only traces of the original Romanesque exterior of the cathedral remain, while the interior is pleasant, if unoriginal, Baroque. The crypt, however, reveals massive Roman foundation stones, probably for the Sanctuary of Juno.

Even on the hottest summer's day, you will want to make the steep climb up the terraces to where the **Palazzo Colonna Barberini** follows the original lines of the Rotunda of the Temple of Fortune. From the fourth terrace the view out across the valley between the Alban Hills and the Monti Lepini still excites the awe that made Praeneste one of the most revered shrines of Classical Italy. The interior of the palace has been redesigned to house the **Archeological Museum**.

Sights and places of interest
Museo Nazionale Archeologico Prenestino ☆
Piazza della Cortina ☎ 9558100 ▦ *Open Tues-Sat 9am-1.30pm, Sun 9am-noon. Closed Mon.*
Although many of the more valuable finds at this site have been transferred to the *Villa Giulia* in Rome, the museum's collection gives a fascinating picture of the early history of Praeneste. Its prize exhibit is the Roman mosaic of *The Nile in Flood*, which once decorated the floor of the Sala Absidata.

≡≡ If you are suffering from the heat and a surfeit of antiquity, the modern **Hotel Stella** has a very reasonable air-conditioned restaurant, the

Ristorante da Coccia (*Piazzale della Liberazione 3* ☎ *9558172* ▮▮▯ AE ⦿ VISA ▭ ▤).

Rocca di Papa

Map 15D4 ⋞ 27km (16 miles) SE of Rome. Getting there: By car, Via Tuscolana (SS215), then 511 to Grottaferrata, then 218; by bus, ACOTRAL from Anagnina (on Metropolitana Line A).

The town, so-named in the 12thC after a castle built here by the popes, stands at over 680m (2,200ft) and is the highest of all the Castelli Romani. The lower part is modern, but the medieval quarter at the top is still a picturesque maze of crooked stairways and narrow alleys. The countryside around is excellent for walking, which, at this altitude, is agreeable even in midsummer.

Above the town soars the summit of **Monte Cavo** (949m/ 3,113ft), which is visible from the eastern heights of Rome itself. The ascent can be made by road (6km/4 miles) or on foot along a mule track. This follows part of the ancient **Via Triumphalis** or Via Sacra, up which victorious Roman generals carried their spoils to the **Temple of Jupiter Latialis**. No trace remains of the temple, once the rallying point of the entire Latin League. Its place has been taken by a hotel and a television mast. From the summit there are magnificent panoramic views across the Castelli, the lakes of Albano and Nemi and the entire *campagna* as far as the coast. To the E you can even see the snow-capped peaks of the Apennines, while to the S you can follow the coastline beyond the island of Ponza to the promontory of Circeo.

If you take the road to Lake Albano, 4km (2½ miles) SW of Rocca di Papa, you will find a very pleasant restaurant in **Le Mimose** (*Via dei Laghi* ☎ *949195* ▮▮▯ ▭ AE). Alternatively, in Rocca di Papa itself, with a fine view across the countryside, there's **Angolleto** (*Via del Tufo 32* ☎ *949020* ▮▯).

Tarquinia

Map 14C3 ⋞ 96km (58 miles) NW of Rome. Getting there: By train, from Stazione Termini (1hr 10mins); by car, Autostrada A12 to junction with SS1 (12km (7½ miles) S of Tarquinia); by bus, ACOTRAL from Via Lepanto (on Metropolitana Line A).

Unlike nearby *Cervéteri*, Tarquinia is today a town of some substance with many fine medieval and Renaissance buildings. The pleasure of walking round the medieval streets and the view across gently rolling plains toward the sea would be reasons enough for a day excursion from Rome, but, of course, Tarquinia's real attraction lies in its great Etruscan necropolis.

Tarquinii was one of the three major cities of Etruria, the others being Vulci and Caere. The commercial and artistic center of the civilization as a whole, it had a population of over 100,000. The finds here have been, accordingly, more spectacular than at Cervéteri, but the fabulous vases, silverware and jewelry are now scattered throughout the world in museums and private collections. Many fine pieces may be seen in Rome at the *Villa Giulia* and in the *Vatican Museums*.

The Necropolis stands on a high, windy plateau called Monterozzi, 4km (2½ miles) to the E of the town. You can drive straight up to the tombs, but in the morning it is better to go to the **museum** in Tarquinia, which organizes guided tours at regular intervals.

Sights and places of interest
Museo Nazionale Tarquiniese
Palazzo Vitelleschi ☎ (0766) 856036 ▨ Open Tues-Sat 9am-2pm, Sun 9am-1pm. Closed Mon.

The museum is housed in the beautiful 15thC Palazzo Vitelleschi. The **courtyard**, with its fine Gothic arcade, is used to display some of the larger exhibits. Its best-known treasure is the superb pair of **winged horses (★)** placed high on a wall, at which height they once decorated the front of an Etruscan temple. There are also many splendid sarcophagi, on which the effigies of the deceased recline, reflecting their former indulgence in their noticeably generous paunches.

In one room, several tombs have been reconstructed to house precious frescoes under controlled conditions. The dancers and musicians of the **Tomb of the Triclinium (★)** are the work of an exceptional artist, as are the athletes of the **Tomb of the Olympic Games ★**

Necropoli di Monterozzi ▥ ★
Open Tues-Sun 9am-7pm. Closed Mon. Guided tours also start from the museum (see above) ▨ ✗ compulsory.

Many tombs are still undiscovered or unexplored, but over the last 25yrs the excavations have accelerated enormously, thanks to such modern inventions as aerial photography and the probe camera, which does away with the need to investigate each burial chamber. More than a thousand new tombs were discovered between 1958 and 1959. In a tour of about 1½hrs, you will be shown only five or six of the more famous ones. These should certainly include the **Tomb of the Augurs (★)** with its frescoes of a funeral and the attendant games. On the far wall, professional mourners strike their foreheads in attitudes of grief, while on the right, in complete contrast to this solemnity, two naked wrestlers strive vigorously to grab hold of each other. You should also see the **Tomb of the Leopards (★)**, the walls of which depict a variety of scenes from a banquet, a subject close to the Etruscan heart. You will notice that all the men are colored reddish-brown, while the women are always white with blonde hair.

▧ An excellent meal, if not an Etruscan banquet, can be had at **Solengo**, the restaurant of the modern **Hotel Tarconte** (*Via Tuscia 19* ☎ *(0766) 856585* ● *612172* ⠿ ▭ ◢ 〔AE〕〔VISA〕); also **Il Bersagliere** (*Via Benedetto Croce 2* ☎ *856047* ⠿ ◢ 〔AE〕〔◈〕 ✿).

Tivoli
Map 15D4 ◁≋ 38km (23 miles) E of Rome. Getting there: By train, from Stazione Termini (40mins); by car, Via Tiburtina (SS5) — Villa Adriana lies to the right, 6km (3½ miles) before you reach the town; by bus, ACOTRAL from Via Gaeta — inquire which buses go nearest to Villa Adriana.

Modern Tivoli is an attractive, lively town of some 45,000 inhabitants. It stands on the Aniene, a tributary of the Tiber, overlooking Rome from the slopes of the Sabine Hills. In order to prevent flooding, the river has been diverted through a tunnel, from which it emerges in a spectacular cascade. This is enclosed in the park of Villa Gregoriana.

In Classical times called Tibur, it was here that wealthy Romans built their magnificent summer villas. The most splendid of these, Hadrian's Villa, now competes for the considerable tourist trade with the Villa d'Este, world-renowned for its terraced gardens and fountains.

Sights and places of interest
Villa Adriana ▥ ★
Bivio Villa Adriana, 6km (3½ miles) sw of Tivoli ▨ Open Tues-Sun 9am-1hr before sunset. Closed Mon.

Begun in AD125 and completed 10yrs later, this was the largest and most sumptuous villa in the Roman Empire. Hadrian's own enjoyment of it was brief, as he was forced by illness to seek a healthier climate farther s. The Emperor was himself an accomplished architect and on his constant journeys around his dominions was inspired to reproduce his favorite buildings in the grounds of his villa. From Athens came the **Poikile**, the massive colonnade through which one enters the villa, while the **Serapeum** and **Canal of Canopus**, with its delightful caryatids, were based on the Temple of Serapis complex near Alexandria.

The charming circular building that stands surrounded by a moat is the misnamed **Maritime Theater** and was probably a summer-house where Hadrian withdrew to indulge in his favorite relaxations — poetry, music and the study of architecture. Today in the huge grounds, where lizards bask on scattered fragments of masonry, there are plenty of secluded spots to read poetry or simply to have a picnic on the grass.

Villa d'Este ★

Viale delle Cento Fontane 🚻 *Open Tues-Sun 9am-1hr before sunset; May-Sept also open 9-11.30pm with gardens floodlit. Closed Mon.*

The villa itself has reopened to the public after extensive restoration. It was built on the site of a Benedictine convent for Cardinal Ippolito d'Este II in the mid-16thC. Its fountains immediately became one of the wonders of Italy. Montaigne was here in 1580, and was much amused by the **Owl Fountain**, as was John Evelyn, the diarist, in the following century. This no longer emits screeches and birdsong, nor does the **Organ Fountain** produce music, for in the 18thC all the fountains fell into a sad state of decay. Fortunately, in recent years the Italian State has done all it can to maintain the unique display of hydraulic wizardry. From the bottom of the garden, make your way up past the ornamental pools to where three magnificent jets of water soar like silver cypresses to the level of the balustrade above, or stroll along the secluded pathway of the **Terrace of the Hundred Fountains**.

Villa Gregoriana

Largo Sant' Angelo 🚻 *Open 9am-1hr before sunset.*

Besides the *Grande Cascata*, the product of the engineering works ordered in the last century by the public-spirited Gregory XVI, this park has smaller cascades, grottoes and a fine belvedere.

🍴 Tivoli abounds in restaurants, many offering panoramic views of Rome. Popular, but reasonable, is the **Sibilla** (*Via della Sibilla 50* ☎ *(0774)20281* **III]** 🍴).

Biographies

A selection of notable figures associated with Rome.

Agnes, St *(died 304)*

A young Roman girl who consecrated herself to God and was martyred during **Diocletian's** persecutions.

Alexander VI (Rodrigo Borgia) *(1431-1503)*

The most corrupt and worldly of all the Renaissance popes, Alexander disposed of his enemies by poisoning them.

Algardi, Alessandro *(c.1598-1654)*

Bolognese sculptor who represented a graver, more Classical style than his extrovert rival, **Bernini**.

Angelico, Fra (Giovanni da Fiesole) *(c.1387 or c.1400-55)*

Dominican friar who frescoed the Chapel of Nicholas V (in the *Vatican Museums*), but worked mainly in Florence.

Augustus, Caius Octavianus *(63BC-AD14)*

Julius Caesar's great-nephew and designated successor, Augustus enjoyed a long, peaceful and illustrious reign after defeating his former ally, Mark Anthony, at Actium in 31BC.

Barocci, Federico *(c.1535-1612)*

His highly emotional paintings look forward to the Baroque.

Bernini, Gianlorenzo *(1598-1680)*

As both sculptor and architect, a tremendously influential figure of the Baroque. His energy and invention and, above all, his joy in life, were apparently boundless.

Boniface VIII (Benedetto Caetani) (*pope 1294-1301*)
The great villain of Dante's *Inferno*, he used his office to advance the fortunes of his family against the Colonna.

Borromini, Francesco (*1599-1667*)
With **Bernini**, he virtually created the Roman Baroque style in architecture, but the novelty and daring of his ideas were unparalleled.

Bramante, Donato (*1444-1514*)
A fundamental figure of the High Renaissance, Bramante exerted great influence through his designs for *St Peter's*.

Caesar, Caius Julius (*c.101-44BC*)
Roman general and writer who documented his military exploits in Gaul and Britain in *De Bello Gallico*. Having returned to defeat his great rival Pompey at the battle of Pharsalus (48BC), he became sole ruler, but was soon afterward assassinated.

Canova, Antonio (*1757-1822*)
Neoclassical sculptor, best known for his study of *Pauline Borghese*, Napoleon's sister, in the *Borghese Gallery*.

Caracalla (Marcus Aurelius Severus Antoninus) (*186-217*)
An unpopular emperor who murdered his brother and co-ruler, Geta. His nickname derives from the Gaulish coat he wore.

Caravaggio, Michelangelo Merisi da (*1573-1610*)
The violent realism of his paintings was as controversial as his life. After murdering a man in a brawl, he was forced to flee the city and died before a pardon could be obtained.

Carracci, Annibale (*1560-1609*)
Less flamboyant than his rival **Caravaggio**, Carracci exerted a decisive influence on 17thC Classical painting.

Catullus, Caius Valerius (*84-54BC*)
One of the great love poets of all time, whose lyrics are often addressed to his beloved Lesbia.

Cavallini, Pietro (*active 1273-1308*)
Artist whose mosaics and frescoes provide a Classical link between antiquity and the Renaissance.

Cecilia, St (*died 3rd or 4thC*)
Her legend centers around the church of *Santa Cecilia in Trastevere*, where her body was rediscovered in 1599.

Cellini, Benvenuto (*1500-71*)
Florentine sculptor and goldsmith, whose *Autobiography* contains a fascinating account of the Sack of Rome in 1527.

Cicero, Marcus Tullius (*106-43BC*)
Orator, philosopher and prominent political figure of Republican Rome.

Clement VII (Giulio de' Medici) (*1478-1534*)
During the Sack of Rome in 1527, Clement was forced to take refuge in the *Castel Sant' Angelo* — a humiliation from which he never recovered. His dealings with Henry VIII of England led to the triumph of English Protestantism.

Constantine the Great (*c.274-337*)
Following his victory over Maxentius at the Milvian Bridge (312), Constantine became sole ruler in the West, and the first Christian emperor.

Cortona, Pietro Berrettini da (*1596-1669*)
Almost equally distinguished as architect and painter, he is the third great creator of the Roman Baroque after **Bernini** and **Borromini**.

Cosmati (*active 12th to 14thC*)
This was the name originally given to a single family of Roman marble workers — one of whom bore the Christian name

Cosmatus — and thence to all artists working in this medium, notably the Vassalletti family.

Diocletian, Caius Aurelius Valerius *(245-313)*

A notable builder, as the great *Baths of Diocletian* demonstrate, but mainly remembered as a persecutor of Christianity.

Domitian (Titus Flavius Domitianus) *(51-96)*

Despotic emperor who lived in fear of assassination and was duly murdered.

Frances of Rome, St *(1384-1440)*

A roman matron who devoted her life to charitable works.

Garibaldi, Giuseppe *(1807-82)*

Soldier and patriot who, with Mazzini and Cavour, was responsible for the unification of Italy. Earlier, he defended Rome from French attack on the *Janiculum Hill* (1849).

Giulio Romano *(1492 or 1499-1546)*

Pupil of **Raphael** who helped to develop the Mannerist style in both architecture and painting.

Gregory I, St (the Great) *(c.540-604)*

One of the four Doctors of the Church, and the pope who sent St Augustine to England.

Hadrian *(76-138)*

An exceptionally cultivated though sometimes ruthless emperor, best known as the builder of the *Pantheon*.

Horace (Quintus Horatius Flaccus) *(65-8BC)*

Perhaps the greatest of the Roman lyric poets, Horace wrote odes inspired by the beauty of nature and by the philosophy of *Carpe diem* ("Pluck the day" or "Live life to the full").

Innocent X (Giovanni Battista Pamphili) *(1574-1655)*

Although nominally responsible for the redevelopment of *Piazza Navona* into a Baroque showpiece, Innocent was a weak pope, dominated by his sister-in-law, Olimpia Maidalchini.

John XXIII (Angelo Giuseppe Roncalli) *(1881-1963)*

His untiring work to promote Christian unity included the setting up of the Second Vatican Council in 1962.

John Paul II (Karol Wojtyla) *(born 1920)*

The first non-Italian pope for more than 450yrs, he has traveled more widely and spoken out more strongly on issues of human rights than any previous pontiff.

Julius II (Giuliano della Rovere) *(1443-1513)*

The archetypal Renaissance pope, Julius was a great warrior as well as a great churchman, and patron of both **Michelangelo** and **Raphael**. He began the rebuilding of *St Peter's*.

Leo X (Giovanni de' Medici) *(1475-1521)*

Outstanding patron of learning and the arts, he created and sold new offices to finance his grandiose schemes.

Lucretius (Titus Lucretius Carus) *(99-55BC)*

Author of *De Rerum Natura*, a long poem expounding the principles of Epicurean philosophy.

Maderno, Carlo *(1556-1629)*

The first major architect of the Roman Baroque.

Marcus Aurelius Antoninus *(121-180)*

An able general and emperor of high principles and great culture, best remembered for his *Meditations*.

Michelangelo Buonarroti *(1475-1564)*

Painter, sculptor, architect and poet, he was the archetypal genius. His powerful representations of the human figure have never been equaled.

Moravia, Alberto *(born 1907)*

Pen name of the Roman novelist whose work has been dubbed Neo-Realism.

Biographies

Mussolini, Benito (1883-1945)

Fascist dictator of Italy from 1922-43, he significantly altered the appearance of the capital by driving major roads through its historic quarters.

Nero, Claudius Caesar (37-68)

An emperor as monstrous as is popularly supposed. He murdered his mother and his first wife, persecuted Christians, and was held responsible for the great fire of Rome in 64.

Nerva, Marcus Cocceius (c.30-98)

Benevolent but feeble emperor, whose reign brought greater freedom after the tyranny of **Domitian**.

Ovid (Publius Ovidius Naso) (43BC-AD18)

Roman poet, chiefly remembered for his *Metamorphoses*, relating the transformations of the gods in Classical legend. His treatise on love, the *Ars Amatoria*, may have been one cause of his banishment to the Black Sea by **Augustus**.

Palestrina, Giovanni Pierluigi da (1525-94)

Composer of sacred choral music.His lovely *Missa Papae Marcelli* inspired a legend that he had heard angels singing.

Paschal I, St (817-24)

Early medieval pope who founded a number of churches in Rome and had himself depicted in the mosaics therein.

Paul, St (died c.67)

Paul was beheaded at Aquae Salviae (now Tre Fontane), and buried on the spot where **San Paolo fuori le Mura** now stands. Tre Fontane takes its name from the tradition that Paul's severed head bounced upon the ground three times, causing three fountains to spring up.

Paul III (Alessandro Farnese) (1468-1549)

An enlightened patron of the arts, he was also the first Counter-Reformation pope.

Peter, St (died c.64 or 67)

The apostle, whose role as Bishop of Rome made him the first pope, was martyred under **Nero**. **San Pietro in Montorio** is said to mark the place of his crucifixion.

Philip Neri, St (1515-95)

Sometimes called the second apostle of Rome, he founded the Congregation of the Oratorians and built the **Chiesa Nuova**.

Pinturicchio, Bernardino (c.1454-1513)

Artist who frescoed the Borgia Apartments (**Vatican Museums**). He was greatly influenced by Perugino.

Piranesi, Giovanni Battista (1720-78)

Architect turned etcher, he recorded ancient and modern Rome in a series of etchings known as the *Vedute*. These were widely circulated and highly influential in the development of the Neoclassical style.

Pliny the Elder (23-79)

Author of a monumental scientific work, the *Historiae Naturalis*, he died while investigating the eruption of Vesuvius. The *Letters* of his nephew, **Pliny the Younger** (62-113), give a marvelously sharp insight into everyday Roman life.

Raphael (Raffaello Sanzio) (1483-1520)

With Leonardo and **Michelangelo** he was one of the three great creators of the High Renaissance. Because of his early death, his promise as an architect was never really fulfilled and his greatest works are the frescoes of the so-called Raphael Stanze in the **Vatican Museums**.

Rienzo, Cola di (1313-54)

Popular hero and short-lived tribune, he was greatly admired by Petrarch and inspired Wagner's unfinished opera, *Rienzi*.

Sansovino, Andrea (c.1467-1529)

Florentine sculptor whose fascination with the antique brought about a new style in funerary monuments.

Sixtus IV (Francesco della Rovere) (1414-84)

By bringing great artists to Rome to decorate the so-called Sistine Chapel, this pope set a trend of great importance.

Tacitus, Caius Cornelius (c.56-120)

Historian and brilliant stylist, whose *Annals* are vivid accounts of Roman politics in the 1stC AD.

Trajan (c.53-117)

A great soldier and prolific builder, Trajan was also a wise and benevolent administrator.

Urban VIII (Maffeo Barberini) (1568-1644)

His reign as pope was a period of tremendous artistic activity, with **Bernini** in supreme command.

Valadier, Giuseppe (1762-1839)

Architect and town-planner, responsible for the dramatic arrangement of *Piazza del Popolo*.

Vasari, Giorgio (1511-74)

Painter, architect and author of the *Vite dei Più Eccellenti Architetti, Pittori, et Scultori*.

Vassalletto   See Cosmati.

Vespasian (Titus Flavius Vespasianus) (9-79)

A shadowy figure whose greatest achievement was to prevent the dissolution of the Empire after **Nero's** death.

Victor Emanuel II (1820-78)

Proclaimed first King of Italy in 1861, he did not acquire Rome until 1870. He is buried in the *Pantheon*.

Vignola (Jacopo Barozzi) (1507-73)

Important late Renaissance architect who built the *Gesù*, one of the most powerful symbols of the Counter-Reformation.

Virgil (Publius Vergilius Maro) (70-19BC)

Epic poet, author of the *Eclogues* and *Georgics*, and of the *Aeneid*. The latter tells the story of the wanderings of Aeneas, proto-founder of Rome, after the Fall of Troy.

Chronology of Roman emperors

In the later Empire, succession was more often disputed than not. Even in its first 200yrs, assassinations interrupted the Julio-Claudian dynasty (27BC-AD68), the Flavian (69-96) and the Antonine (including Trajan and Hadrian, 98-192).

Augustus 27BC-AD14	Didius Julianus 193	Decius 249-251
Tiberius 14-37	Septimius Severus	Gallus 251-253
Caligula 37-41	193-211	Aemilian 253
Claudius 41-54	Caracalla 198-217	Valerian 253-260
Nero 54-68	Geta 211-212	Gallienus 253-268
Galba 68-69	Macrinus 217-218	Claudius II 268-270
Otho 69	Heliogabalus 218-222	Quintillus 270
Vitellius 69	Alexander Severus	Aurelian 270-275
Vespasian 69-79	222-235	Tacitus 275-276
Titus 79-81	Maximinus the Thracian	Florian 276
Domitian 81-96	235-238	Probus 276-282
Nerva 96-98	Gordian I 238	Carus 282-283
Trajan 98-117	Gordian II 238	Numerianus 283-284
Hadrian 117-138	Pupienus 238	Carinus 283-285
Antoninus Pius 138-161	Balbinus 238	Diocletian 284-305
Marcus Aurelius 161-180	Gordian III 238-244	Maximian 286-305
Commodus 180-192	Philip the Arabian	Constantius I 305-306
Pertinax 193	244-249	Galerius 305-311

Flavius Severus 306-307
Maxentius 306-312
Constantine the Great 306-337
Licinius 308-323
Maximinus Daia 309-313
Constantine II 337-340
Constans 337-350
Constantius II 337-361
Magnentius 350-353

Julian the Apostate 361-363
Jovian 363-364
Valentinian I 364-375
Valens 364-378
Gratian 365-383
Valentinian II 375-392
Theodosius 379-395
Honorius 395-423
John 423-425
Valentinian III 425-455

Petronius Maximus 455
Avitus 455-456
Majorian 457-461
Libius Severus 461-465
Anthemius 467-472
Olybrius 472
Glycerius 473-474
Julius Nepos 474-475
Romulus Augustulus 475-476

Chronology of popes

The dates of the early pontificates cannot be authenticated, and the distinction between pope and antipope was often decided many years later, sometimes rather arbitrarily.

St Peter martyred 64 or 67
St Linus 67-76(?)
St Cletus 76-88(?)
St Clement I 88-97(?)
St Evaristus 97-105(?)
St Alexander I 105-115(?)
St Sixtus I 115-125(?)
St Telesphorus 125-136(?)
St Hyginus 136-140(?)
St Pius I 140-155(?)
St Anicetus 155-166(?)
St Soter 166-175(?)
St Eleutherius 175-189
St Victor I 189-199
St Zephryinus 199-217
St Calixtus I 217-222
St Urban I 222-230
St Pontian 230-235
St Anterus 235-236
St Fabian 236-250
St Cornelius 251-253
St Lucius I 253-254
St Stephen I 254-257
St Sixtus II 257-258
St Dionysius 259-268
St Felix I 269-274
St Eutychian 275-283
St Caius 283-296
St Marcellinus 296-304
St Marcellus I 308-309
St Eusebius 309-310
St Melchiades 311-314
St Sylvester I 314-335
St Marcus 335-336
St Jylius 337-352
St Liberius 352-366
St Felix II 355-365
St Damasus I 365-384
St Siricius 384-399
St Anastasius I 399-401
St Innocent I 401-417
St Zosimus 417-418
St Boniface I 418-422
St Celestine I 422-432
St Sixtus III 432-440

St Leo I (the Great) 440-461
St Hilarius 461-468
St Simplicius 468-483
St Felix III 483-492
St Gelasius I 492-496
St Anastasius II 496-498
St Symmachus 498-514
St Hormisdas 514-523
St John I 523-526
St Felix IV 526-530
Boniface II 530-532
John II 533-535
St Agapetus I 535-536
St Silverius 536-537
Vigilius 537-555
Pelagius I 556-561
John III 561-574
Benedict I 575-579
Pelagius II 579-590
St Gregory I (the great) 590-604
Sabinian 604-606
Boniface III 607
St Boniface IV 608-615
St Deodatus I 615-618
Boniface V 619-625
Honorius I 625-638
Severinus 640
John IV 640-642
Theodore I 642-649
St Martin I 649-655
St Eugenius I 654-657
St Vitalianus 657-672
Deodatus II 672-676
Donus I 676-678
St Agatho 678-681
St Leo II 682-683
St Benedict II 684-685
John V 685-686
Conon 686-687
St Sergius I 687-701
John VI 701-705
John VII 705-707
Sisinnius 708
Constantine I 708-715
St Gregory II 715-731
St Gregory III 731-741

St Zacharias 741-752
Stephen II 752
Stephen III 752-757
St Paul I 757-767
Constantine II 767-768
Philip 768
Stephen IV 768-772
Adrian I 772-795
St Leo III 795-816
St Stephen V 816-817
St Paschal I 817-824
Eugenius II 824-827
Valentinus 827
Gregory IV 827-844
Sergius II 844-847
St Leo IV 847-855
Benedict III 855-858
St Nicholas I 858-867
Adrian II 867-872
John VIII 872-882
Marinus I 882-884
St Adrian II 884-885
Stephen VI 885-891
Formosus 891-896
Boniface VI 896
Stephen VII 896-897
Romanus 897
Theodore II 897
John IX 898-900
Benedict IV 900-903
Leo V 903
Sergius III 904-911
Anastasius III 911-913
Landonius 913-914
John X 914-929
Leo VI 928
Stephen VIII 929-931
John XI 931-935
Leo VII 936-939
Stephen IX 939-942
Marinus II 942-946
Agapetus II 946-955
John XII 955-964
Leo VIII 963-965
Benedict V 964-966
John XIII 965-972
Benedict VI 973-974
Benedict VII 974-983

Boniface VII 974, 984-985	Gregory IX 1227-41	Marcellus II 1555
John XIV 983-984	Celestine IV 1241	Paul IV 1555-59
John XV 985-996	Innocent IV 1243-54	Pius IV 1559-65
Gregory V 996-999	Alexander IV 1254-61	St Pius V 1566-72
John XVI 997-998	Urban IV 1261-64	Gregory XIII 1572-85
Sylvester II 999-1003	Clement IV 1265-68	Sixtus V 1585-90
John XVII 1003	Gregory X 1271-76	Urban VII 1590
John XVIII 1004-09	Innocent V 1276	Gregory XIV 1590-91
Sergius IV 1009-12	Adrian V 1276	Innocent IX 1591
Benedict VIII 1012-24	John XXI 1276-77	Clement VIII 1592-1605
John XIX 1024-32	Nicholas III 1277-80	Leo XI 1605
Benedict IX 1032-48	Martin IV 1281-85	Paul V 1605-21
Sylvester III 1045	Honorius IV 1285-87	Gregory XV 1621-23
Gregory VI 1045-46	Nicholas IV 1288-92	Urban VIII 1623-44
Clement II 1046-47	St Celestine V 1294-96	Innocent X 1644-55
Damasus II 1048	Boniface VIII 1294-1303	Alexander VII 1655-67
St Leo IX 1049-54	Benedict XI 1303-04	Clement IX 1667-69
Victor II 1055-57	Clement V 1305-14	Clement X 1670-76
Stephen X 1057-58	John XXII 1316-34	Innocent XI 1676-89
Benedict X 1058-59	Benedict XII 1334-42	Alexander VIII 1689-91
Nicholas II 1059-61	Clement VI 1342-52	Innocent XII 1691-1700
Alexander II 1061-73	Innocent VI 1352-62	Clement XI 1700-21
St Gregory VII 1073-85	Urban V 1362-70	Innocent XIII 1721-24
Victor III 1086-87	Gregory XI 1370-78	Benedict XIII 1724-30
Urban II 1088-99	Urban VI 1378-89	Clement XII 1730-40
Paschal II 1099-1118	Boniface IX 1389-1404	Benedict XIV 1740-58
Gelasius II 1118-19	Innocent VII 1404-06	Clement XIII 1758-69
Calixtus II 1119-24	Gregory XII 1406-17	Clement XIV 1769-74
Honorius II 1124-30	Martin V 1417-31	Pius VI 1775-99
Innocent II 1130-43	Eugenius IV 1431-47	Pius VII 1800-23
Celestine II 1143-44	Nicholas V 1447-55	Leo XII 1823-29
Lucius II 1144-45	Calixtus III 1455-58	Pius VIII 1829-30
Eugenius III 1145-53	Pius II 1458-64	Gregory XVI 1831-46
Anastasius IV 1153-54	Paul II 1464-71	Pius IX 1846-78
Adrian IV 1154-59	Sixtus IV 1471-84	Leo XIII 1878-1903
Alexander III 1159-81	Innocent VIII 1484-92	St Pius X 1903-14
Lucius III 1181-85	Alexander VI 1492-1503	Benedict XV 1914-22
Urban III 1185-87	Pius III 1503	Pius XI 1922-39
Gregory VIII 1187	Julius II 1503-13	Pius XII 1939-58
Clement III 1187-91	Leo X 1513-21	John XXIII 1958-63
Celestine III 1191-98	Adrian VI 1522-23	Paul VI 1963-78
Innocent III 1198-1216	Clement VII 1523-34	John Paul I 1978
Honorius III 1216-27	Paul III 1534-49	John Paul II 1978-
	Julius III 1550-55	

Rome for children

Italians love children. They tend to spoil their own and, given the opportunity, are equally indulgent toward other people's. This attitude is perhaps most obvious in restaurants and cafés, where small children receive almost regal treatment. Parents who are happy to join in the general spirit of indulgence, or feel called upon to offer the occasional bribe, will find the best ice cream in the world a useful ally. (See *Bars, cafés and ice cream shops*).

A mild climate, large parks and many traffic-free zones mean that children can spend much of the time playing out of doors. Bicycling and roller-skating are favorite pursuits, and there are plenty of safe open spaces for both (see *Parks and zoos* below). Most other activities also center on the parks and pedestrian piazzas, notably the Villa Borghese and Piazza Navona.

Parks and zoos
Villa Borghese (*N of centre*) is Rome's largest park, perfect for roller-skating and cycling. Boats can be rented at the

Giardino del Lago. The small but well-kept zoo, **Giardino Zoologico**, is open from 8.30am to sunset, and feeding times are displayed near the entrance. Other attractions are a fairground and occasional puppet shows (see *Theatre and other events* below).

There are several other parks in Rome, offering the usual facilities — and some with more unusual entertainments. **Villa Ada** (*W of Via Salaria*) is ideal for energetic children, with two well-equipped playgrounds, a roller-skating rink, bicycling areas, ponds and wooded slopes. **Villa Celimontana** (*S of the Colosseum*) also has ponds and a bicycle track. **Villa Glori** (*N of Villa Borghese*) offers pony rides, and **Villa Balestra** (*NW of Villa Borghese*) pony cart-rides. **Villa Sciarra** (*Trastevere*) is one of the smaller parks, but has an aviary. A cannon is fired at noon from the **Gianicolo** park (*W bank of the Tiber*), overlooking the city, and sometimes there are puppet shows.

The **Villaggio Olimpico** (*E of Corso di Francia*) has a roller-skating rink and playground. Merry-go-rounds and a roller-skating rink are the main attractions of the gardens of the **Ministero degli Affari Esteri** (*Piazzale della Farnesina*), and **Parco Oppio** (*N of the Colosseum*) also has a small fairground. But for a really impressive funfair, complete with big dipper and roller coaster, go to the **Luna Park** (*Via delle Tre Fontane, EUR* ☎ *5925933*) and use the boating lake and mini-golf course as well. **Piazza Navona**, in the heart of the old city, is not strictly a park but is sealed off to traffic and makes an attractive play area.

There is a **safari park** near Fiumicino Airport (*Via Portuense, 35km (22 miles) outside Rome* ☎ *6011188, open Wed-Mon 10.30am-1hr before sunset*), and a large **bird sanctuary** at Palo (*about same distance from city, run by the World Wildlife Fund* ☎ *9911641, open Thurs-Sun 9.30am to sunset*).

Museums
There is an intriguing waxwork museum called **Museo della Cere** (*Piazza Santi Apostoli 67* ☎ *6796482*). The **Museo Storico della Motorizzazione Militare** (*Viale dell' Esercito 86 (near Via Laurentina)* ☎ *5011885*), a museum of military vehicles, is about 20mins from the city centre by car — telephone first to organize entry permits. Children with more peaceful tastes might like to visit the **Museo degli Strumenti Musicali** (*Piazza Santa Croce in Gerusalemme 9* ☎ *7575936*), a museum of musical instruments. The **Galleria Nazionale d'Arte Moderna** (*Viale delle Belle Arti 131* ☎ *802751*) has a delightful garden dotted with modern works of art. The moving exhibits inside are equally fascinating. **Museo Civico di Zoologia** (*Via Aldrovandi 18* ☎ *873586*) is a natural-history museum where visitors to the zoo are allowed free admittance.

Theatre and other events
Puppets are an Italian speciality. Shows take place at **Alla Ringhiera** (*Via dei Riari 81, Trastevere* ☎ *6568711*). Irregular open-air shows are given in the **Villa Borghese** and in the **Gianicolo** park. A number of theatres, such as **Teatro Goldoni** (*Vicolo dei Soldati 3* ☎ *6561156*), stage occasional children's productions. For current listings, look in *Il Messaggero* under "Attività per ragazzi".

Other ideas
One of the more exciting ways for a child to see Rome is from a horse-drawn carriage (see *Other transport* in **Basic**

information). In July and Aug you can take a river trip through central Rome organized by the **Amici del Tevere**: see *This Week in Rome* for details.

Many of the major historical sights such as the *Colosseum* and *Castel Sant' Angelo* make fascinating outings for children blessed with vivid imaginations and a stimulating guide. The city's many fountains are another big attraction: the *Trevi Fountain* is a special favourite with children, who delight in the tradition of throwing coins into the water to ensure that they will one day return to Rome.

If the children are running short of reading matter, buy them an Italian comic. *Topolino* (Mickey Mouse) is published weekly, is excellent value and may even help them learn Italian.

Activities for children increase in the weeks leading up to Christmas, and decorations go up in Piazza Navona, Via dei Coronari, Via Frattina and Via Condotti. From mid-Dec until Epiphany (Jan 6), a market is held in **Piazza Navona**, with stalls selling Christmas cribs, figures and decorations, and toys and sweets. The market ends with a carnival on the Eve of Epiphany. Next morning, Italian children traditionally receive presents from *La Befana*, a female version of Santa Claus.

For other annual festivals, see *Calendar of events* in **Planning and walks**.

Toyshops

Piazza Navona has a long association with children, culminating each year in the Christmas market (see above). But the year-round toyshops in the area are best avoided. Competition to attract tourists is fierce, and sizes and prices of the furry animals know no limits. Life-size Alsatians and leopards may make ostentatious presents, but are less likely to please than some of the smaller toy animals found elsewhere.

At **Galleria San Carlo** (*Via del Corso 114* ☎ *6790571*), furry animals on wheels double as rocking-horses, elephants and dogs. There are tiny bamboo rocking chairs for very small children and lace-draped bamboo cradles for very large dolls. Among the cuddly toys, woolly lambs steal the show.

Marina Menasci (*Via del Lavatore 87* ☎ *6781981* [AE] [◎] [VISA]), close to the Trevi Fountain, is a friendly little shop that sells hand-made toys from northern Italy. Pinocchios of all sizes are the speciality, as at **Pinocchio** (*Via Sistina 135* ☎ *4743723*).

Sports and activities

Rome has three major sports centres within easy reach of the city centre: **Tre Fontane** (☎ *5926386 at EUR, about 15mins away on the Metropolitana*); **Foro Italico** (☎ *3964206, on the w bank of the Tiber, beyond Via Flaminia*); and Acqua Acetosa (☎ *879248, N of Villa Ada*). EUR and the Foro Italico were both created by Mussolini, although additions were made to the Foro Italico before the 1960 Olympic Games. Check availability for tourists with **CONI — Italian National Olympic Committee** (*Foro Italico* ☎ *36851*).

Bicycling

Reckless Roman drivers make bicycling hazardous, but many parks have areas where children can cycle in safety (see *Rome for children*). Bicycles may be hired from **R. Collalti** (*Via del*

Sports and activities

Pellegrino 82) — see *Other transport* in **Basic information**. There are racing-tracks for more serious cyclists at **Villa Celimontana** (*s of the Colosseum*) and at **Villa Sciarra** (*Trastevere*). For further information, contact the **Federazione Ciclistica Italiana** (*Via Leopoldo Franchetti 2, 00194 ☎ 36851*).

Boating
Rowing boats can be hired at the Giardino del Lago in the **Villa Borghese**. Farther away, there is the lake at **EUR**, and there are several sailing clubs at **Lake Bracciano** (*about 50km (30 miles) N of Rome*), offering sailing lessons and dinghies for hire. The same facilities are available on the coast at **Fregene** and **Lido di Roma** (*about 35km (21 miles) and 30km (18 miles) w of the city respectively*). International sailing championships are held at **Castel Gandolfo**, on **Lake Albano** (*25km (15 miles) SE of Rome*). For information, contact the **Federazione Italiana Canottaggio** (*Viale Tiziano 70, 00196 ☎ 3966620*).

Bowling
There are two particularly good bowling alleys (*bocciodromi*).
Bowling Brunswick   Lungotevere Acqua Acetosa ☎ 3966696
Bowling Roma   Viale Regina Margherita 181 ☎ 861184

Camping
The most central camp site is **Roma Camping** (*Via Aurelia, sw of the Vatican ☎ 6223018*). For more information, contact:
Centro Nazionale Campeggiatori Stranieri   Casella Postale 649, Florence 50100
EPT (Ente Provinciale per il Turismo)   Via Parigi 11, 00185 ☎ 461851
TCI (Touring Club Italiano)   Via Ovidio 7a, 00187 ☎ 388602

Fishing
For river fishing you must buy a licence from the police and join (for a small charge) the **Federazione Italiana della Pesca Sportiva** (*Piazza Emporio 16a, 00153 ☎ 5755253*). Lakes outside Rome often display signs saying *Lago — Pesca Sportiva*, indicating that you may fish there for a fee.

Football
Football is a popular spectator sport, and Rome is divided in its support of the Lazio and Roma teams, who play on alternate Sun afternoons from Sept-May at the **Stadio Olimpico**. For information apply to the **Associazione Sportiva Lazio** (*Via Col di Lana 8, 00195 ☎ 385141*) or the **Associazione Sportiva Roma** (*Via Circo Massimo 7, 00153 ☎ 575151*).

Golf
There are two 18-hole courses: the **Acqua Santa** (*Via Appia Nuova 716, 00178 ☎ 783407*) and **Olgiata** (*Largo Olgiata 15, 00123 ☎ 3789141*). Apply for guest admission in advance. Both are closed on Mon. There is also a 9-hole course, closed Wed, at **Fioranello a Santa Maria dell Mole** (*☎ 608291*). The "Open Internazionale" tournament is held in spring. For information, apply to the **Federazione Italiana Golf** (*Via Flaminia 388, 00196 ☎ 3963279*).

Greyhound racing
Greyhound events are held at the **Cinodromo** (*Ponte Marconi, Via della Vasca Navale 6 ☎ 5566258*). See local press for details.

Health clubs

Most health clubs require long-term membership, but **Sporting Roma** (*Via Barberini 36* ☎ *483607*) and **The Health Club** (*Largo Somalia 60* ☎ *8394488*) allow you to join for a month. The **Budokan** sports club offers all the facilities needed for a work-out at its two centres in Prati (*Via Stefano Porcari 6 and Via Properzio 4*) and welcomes temporary members.

Horse racing

Flat races and steeplechases are held at the **Ippodromo delle Capanelle** (*Via Appia Nuova (12km/7½ miles)* ☎ *7993143*); and there are trotting races at the **Ippodromo di Tor di Valle** (*Via del Mare (9km/5½ miles)* ☎ *592683*). Look in the local press for details.

Motor racing

Motor racing takes place at the **Valle Lunga** race-track (*Via Cassia (34km)* ☎ *9041417*). See local press for details.

Riding

Riding schools in the city are reluctant to accept short-stay visitors, but **The Riding Club** (*Via di Tor Carbone (near Via Appia Antica), 00178* ☎ *5423998*) will take telephone bookings for single sessions. The major equestrian event is the international horse show, "Concorso Ippico Internazionale", in Piazza Siena at the **Villa Borghese** in May. For information, write to the **Associazione Nazionale Turismo Equestre (ANTE)** (*Largo Messico 13, 00198* ☎ *864053*).

Swimming

The major outdoor pools in Rome are at the **Foro Italico** and **EUR**, open June-Sept. An indoor pool at the Foro Italico is open Nov-May (☎ *3601498 for details*). The **Terme Acque Albule** (*at Bagni di Tivoli*) offers sulphur-water swimming pools for the health-conscious (*on the Via Tiburtina, 22km (13 miles) outside Rome* ☎ *529012*). The best beach is at **Fregene**, less than 1hr's drive w of the city.

Tennis

There are public courts at the following:

EUR	Viale dell' Artigianato 2 ☎ 5924693	
Foro Italico	☎ 3619021	
Tennis Belle Arti	Via Flaminia 158 ☎ 3600602	
Tre Fontane	Via delle Tre Fontane ☎ 5926386	

Reservations are necessary. The major event of the year is the "Campionati Internazionali d'Italia" held at the **Foro Italico** in May. For details, apply to the **Federazione Italiano Tennis** (*Via Eustachio 9, 00161* ☎ *855894*).

Excursions

A general exodus from the city gets underway during the hot summer months, as residents and tourists take to the cool of the hills and beaches in vast numbers. Here, you can take your pick from simple, one-day excursions around Rome to more ambitious sorties into the Neapolitan region that will almost certainly involve an overnight stop. All the inland destinations make good winter breaks, too.

Excursions/Anzio

Anzio

Map 15E4. 62km (39 miles) s of Rome. Population: 23,000.
Getting there: By train, from Stazione Termini (1hr
20mins); by car, SS148 to junction at Aprilia, then 207; by
bus, ACOTRAL from Anagnina (on Metropolitana Line A)
i AAST, Riviera Zanardelli 115 ☎ 9848135.

The town of Anzio suffered extensive damage in World War II
during the course of a combined Anglo-American landing, and
much of the town has been rebuilt. However, the older parts close
to the port have retained some character, and the port itself is lively,
especially in the evenings. Judging by the amount of fish and other
seafood sold from harbour stalls, the local fishing industry is
booming. It is now rare to see fish being sold locally in Italy:
generally it is packed in ice and transported to the big cities. The
harbour has numerous fishing boats and a separate basin for yachts.

Anzio is a favourite Roman holiday resort. The Emperor Nero built
a villa here, now known as **Nero's Villa** (★). You can see the ruins
of this along the coast, not far from the lighthouse. It is an important
archaeological site and is soon to be excavated. The town also has
the large Carmelite church of **Santa Teresa** — a Neo-Romanesque
building dating from 1927 — and the beautifully maintained
British Military Cemetery.

The coast running NW from Anzio has sandy beaches and several
small resorts, the most important of which is **Lavinio-Lido di Enea**,
where there are a number of hotels and *pensioni*. There is good
bathing all along this coast, and a large camping site at **Lido dei
Pini**, 5km (3 miles) NW of Lavinio. On the other side of Anzio, and
running E, is the twin town of **Nettuno**, with long sandy beaches
and, inland, the huge **American Military Cemetery**.

In summer, ferries and hydrofoils leave Anzio daily for **Ponza**
(*June 15-Sept 15*). The chief attraction of this rugged, almost treeless
island is the wonderful clarity of the sea, so different from the
polluted waters along the mainland coast. Ponza is therefore a
favourite place for swimming, snorkelling and sub-aqua fishing. For
a day-visit from Anzio, take the hydrofoil (1hr 10mins) rather than
the ferry (2hrs 30mins), to give more time to explore the island.

Dei Cesari (*Via Ardeatina* ☎ 9844353 Ⅲ) has sea views and a
swimming pool and is open all year; **Lido Garda** (*Piazza Caboto 8*
☎ 9845389 Ⅱ) is open April-Oct.

Flora (*Via Flora 9* ☎ 9846001 ⅢⅡ ▤ ▨ ▣ ▨ ✸); **Al Turcotto**
(*Riviera Mallozzi 44* ☎ 9846340 Ⅲ ➝ ◈).

Capri

Map 16F6. 200km (125 miles) s of Rome. Population: 8,000.
Getting there: By train, from Stazione Termini to Napoli
Centrale (2hrs 30mins), then taxi or bus to Mole Beverello
for ferry or hydrofoil to the island; by car, Autostrada A2 to
Naples, then ferry or hydrofoil from Mole Beverello (tourist
cars are not allowed on the island); by tourist bus, inquire
at CIT, Piazza della Repubblica 68 ☎ 47941 i AAST,
Piazzetta Ignazio Cerio 11 ☎ (081) 370424.

The population of Capri fluctuates perhaps more than any other
island in the world. In the summer months, apart from the
temporary residents enjoying their holidays, there is the daily
invasion of tourists from the mainland. In winter, life reverts to the
dreamy pace that has been so characteristic of Capri over the
centuries until 20thC tourism jolted it from its slumbers.

From **Marina Grande**, the main harbour, take the funicular up to the town of **Capri**, where you can enjoy a memorable view over the **Bay of Naples** from **Piazza Umberto I**, famous meeting place of film and opera stars. On the NE tip of the island is a remarkable relic of ancient Roman times, the ruined **Palace of Tiberius** (✭). It is perched on a dizzying cliff-top from which the Emperor is said to have thrown his enemies. The longish walk from the town of Capri is rewarded by spectacular views. On the s edge of the town is the **Certosa di San Giacomo**, a 14thC Carthusian monastery now largely in ruins. Another atmospheric place is the **Parco Augusto** (✭), with its dramatic series of belvederes and a fine view to the s. From here, a road leads to the **Marina Piccola** (Small Harbour). Between here and the SE tip of the island are many places where you can swim from the rocks in crystal-clear water.

Anacapri is another charming town, perched high up on a rocky plateau, its flat-roofed buildings distinctly Moorish in style. The 18thC church of **San Michele** (✭) is remarkable for its majolica pavement depicting the *Garden of Eden*. Nearby is the romantic **Villa San Michele** (✭), with a beautiful garden and rich collection of Classical sculpture. From Anacapri you can walk or take a chair lift up to **Monte Solaro**, which has amazing views over the entire island and towards **Ischia**.

As for natural features, there is the famous **Grotta Azzurra** or **Blue Grotto**. Visitors are taken from Marina Grande by motor-boat and transferred to rowing boats to enter the grotto. The silver-blue colour of the water is caused by refraction of light entering the grotto from an opening beneath the surface. Equally beautiful are the three limestone rock pinnacles known as the **Faraglioni** that soar almost vertically out of the sea, and the **Arco Naturale**, an arch of rock carved by wind erosion, just off the E shore.

Walking is by far the best way of getting about the island, but horse-drawn carriages and buses operate, the latter linking Capri and Anacapri, and Marina Grande and Marina Piccola.

▱ **Quisisana** (*Via Camerelle 2, Capri* ☎ *(081) 8370788* ● *710520* ●*(081) 8376080* ▥▥ ▤▤ ▢ ▱ 🅰🅴 ⊙ ⬤ ▥▥ 🏊) is ultra-luxurious, with swimming pool and good views; **La Vega** (*Via Occhio Marino 10, Capri* ☎ *(081) 8370481* ● *710531* ▥▢ 🅰🅴 ⊙ ⬤ ▥▥).

⇶ **Da Gemma** (*Via Madre Serafina 6, Capri* ☎ *(081) 8370461* ▥▢ 🅰🅴 ⬤ ▥▥); **La Pigna** (*Via Lo Palazzo 30, Capri* ☎ *(081) 8370280* ▥▥▥ 🅰🅴 ⊙ ⬤ ▥▥).

Orvieto
*Map **14**B3. 100km (62 miles) N of Rome. Population: 23,000. Getting there: By train, from Stazione Termini (1hr 20mins); by car, Autostrada A1* i *AAST, Corso Cavour 36* ☎ *(0763) 35562.*

The town of Orvieto sits proudly on a broad plinth of tufa rock, commanding magnificent views over the surrounding Umbrian countryside. It is equally famous for its cathedral and its white wine, the one a brilliant array of multi-coloured mosaics, the other golden and deliciously smooth. You can savour the delights of both at once by sitting outside a wine bar in **Piazza del Duomo** opposite the cathedral facade.

Originally an Etruscan town, Orvieto became a Roman colony and later, in the Middle Ages, enjoyed mixed fortunes. Its loyalty to the papacy never faltered, and it was rewarded with the motto *Fortis et fidelis* (Strong and faithful) by Adrian IV. The overwhelming impression of the town, with its winding, narrow streets, ancient houses and venerable churches, is still medieval.

Orvieto is noted for its ceramics, and each Sat there is a pottery market in **Piazza del Popolo**.

Cathedral 🏛 ✝ ★
This marvellous blend of Romanesque and Gothic styles is one of the finest cathedrals in the whole of Italy. The sumptuous facade (★), with its exquisite mosaics and complementary low-reliefs, is mainly the work of the Sienese architect Lorenzo Maitani, although completed after his death in 1330 by Andrea Pisano. Inside, the nave and aisles are built in alternating courses of black and white stone. In the N transept, the **Corporal Chapel** houses a finely-wrought **tabernacle** (★) richly studded with precious stones and containing the relics of the Miracle of Bolsena — the phenomenon that inspired Urban IV to build this cathedral. The beautifully-carved and inlaid **choir stalls** and the **stained-glass window** behind them are also 14thC. In the S transept, in the **Chapel of San Brizio**, are frescoes of *The Apocalypse* (★) begun by Fra Angelico and continued by Luca Signorelli.

Other sights
Although the cathedral dominates the town architecturally, there are other buildings that are well worth seeing. The **Papal Palace** (★) is a severe yet handsome structure to the right of the cathedral, dating from the time of **Boniface VIII** (1294-1303). The **Great Hall** on the first floor houses the **Cathedral Museum** (📷 *open Tues-Sun 9am-noon, 2-4pm (summer 6pm), closed Mon*). Also notable are the **Palazzo del Popolo**, begun in the 11thC, modified in 1280 and recently restored, and **San Bernardino**, a charming Baroque monastic church.

🍴 **La Badia** (*at La Badia, 5km (3 miles) outside Orvieto* ☎ *(0763) 90359* ||||| 🚗 🗒 🖭 ⊙ ⓒ ⊡ 🍷) is beautifully situated in a 12thC monastery; **Maitani** (*Via Maitani 5* ☎ *(0763) 42001* ● *564021* ||||| 🖭 ⊙ ⓒ 🗎 🍷) is close to the cathedral, with quiet rooms.

🍽 **Maurizio** (*Via del Duomo 78* ☎ *41114* 🍷), closed Tues, Jan; **Dell' Ancora** (*Via di Piazza del Popolo 7/11* ☎ *42766* 🍴 🖭 ⊙ ⓒ 🗎).

Pompeii and Herculaneum
Map 16F6-7. Pompeii, 237km (147 miles) SE of Rome. Population 23,000. Herculaneum (modern name Ercolano), 224km (140 miles) SE of Rome. Population 58,000. Getting there: By train, from Stazione Termini to Napoli Centrale, then 5mins' walk to Circumvesuviana station for local train to Ercolano or Pompeii Scavi (allow 3-3½hrs for total journey); by car, Autostrada A2 to Naples, then S18, S70; by tourist bus, inquire at CIT. Piazza della Repubblica 68 ☎ 47941. Both sites 📷 ✗ Open Tues-Sun 9am-1hr before sunset, closed Mon i Pompeii: AAST, Via Sacra 1 ☎ (081) 8631041; Herculaneum: EPT, Via Partenope 10a, Naples ☎ (081) 418988.

Pompeii
The eruption of Vesuvius in AD79, which submerged Pompeii, Herculaneum and Stabiae, was a tragedy for the 2,000 inhabitants who died and the thousands more who lost their homes, but a boon for 20thC archaeologists. It created an almost perfect time capsule, sealing in for many centuries an important cross-section of ancient civilization. Before the catastrophe, Pompeii was an old-established city with a polyglot population of about 25,000 that

reflected successive waves of colonization: Oscan, Greek, Samnite and Roman. By 80BC it was a favourite resort of affluent Romans — Cicero, for example had a villa here. Although the ruins were discovered in the 16thC and excavations of a kind began in 1763, systematic excavation did not get under way until 1911. Since then about three-fifths of the site has been revealed.

As you stroll through the narrow lanes of the city now, and walk in and out of the buildings, it is not hard to imagine yourself in the 1stC AD. The walls are covered in *graffiti*, ranging from erotic drawings to political slogans: a local election was taking place when the eruption occurred.

The rich Pompeiians lived in style, as you can tell from the grander houses with their spacious rooms, elegant courtyards and abundant frescoes. The **House of the Faun (★)** and **House of the Vettii (★)** — in the residential area N of the **Forum** — are among the most magnificent examples. The bronze statuette of the *Faun* in the former is a copy of the original, now in the National Archaeological Museum in Naples. The House of the Vettii belonged to a couple of rich Roman merchants; it has some of the finest ancient frescoes in existence, depicting mythological scenes with nymphs and *putti*. Other particularly luxurious residences are the **House of Menander** (to the E of the Forum), which takes its name from the painting of the poet Menander, and the **Villa of the Mysteries (★)**, a suburban residence to the W of the main town, which contains paintings of secret Dionysiac rites. The **House of Pansa** (to the N of the Forum) is a large, symmetrically-planned building that included rented apartments.

The Dionysos cult was only one of many that flourished in the city. The **Temple of Isis**, to the E of the Forum, testifies to the strong following that the Egyptian goddess had here. More important still (and both forming part of the Forum) are the **Temple of Jupiter** and **Temple of Apollo (★)**, the latter with a superb colonnade and dramatic backdrop of Vesuvius. Other public buildings include the **Amphitheatre**, in the E of the city, begun c.80BC and the first in Italy to be built of stone; the **Odeon (★)**, just E of the **Temple of Isis**, a small covered theatre dating from the same period; and the **Basilica (★)**, in the Forum, the largest building in Pompeii, where legal matters were hammered out, judgments pronounced and commercial transactions made. The most up-to-date building in the city at the time of the eruption was the **Stabian Baths (★)**, E of the Forum, with spacious rooms, elaborate bathing facilities and sophisticated heating arrangements.

Herculaneum

Lying 27km (17 miles) to the NE of Pompeii, Herculaneum was a much smaller town, with only 5,000 inhabitants. Unlike Pompeii, it had virtually no commerce and its industry was restricted to fishing. The volcanic mud that flowed through every building and street in Herculaneum was different from that which buried Pompeii; it settled eventually to a depth of 12m (40ft) and set rock-hard, sealing and preserving everything with which it came into contact. The absence of the hail of pumice and hot ash that rained down on Pompeii, smashing and burning its buildings, meant that many of the inhabitants of Herculaneum were able to get away in time, and that complete houses, with their woodwork, household goods and furniture, were preserved.

Although Herculaneum was a relatively unimportant town compared with Pompeii, several of the houses that have been excavated were in the luxury class, their owners perhaps being prosperous Romans seeking to pass their retirement years in the peace of a small seaside town. The most desirable residential area was in the SW, on the edge of the promontory overlooking the ocean, where terraces made the most of the sea view. Here you will find the **House of the Stags** (★), famous for its sculpted stags and drunken figure of Hercules as well as its beautiful frescoes, and to the W of this, the equally fine **House of the Mosaic Atrium** (★).

Farther to the N, the **House of the Wooden Trellis** is named after the building technique used in its construction. Next to this, the **House of the Wooden Partition** (★) is marvellously preserved, one of the most complete examples of a private residence in either town. The partition itself, now in fragments, is a screen separating the atrium from the living room. To the N of this house are the **Baths**, an elaborate complex incorporating a gymnasium and assorted men's and women's baths, and to the E of them, the small but delightful **House of the Charred Furniture**. The few crafts shops that have been discovered were solely for the manufacture of luxury goods. The artisans who worked in them lived in apartment blocks clustered around the **Palestra** to the E.

For those planning to stay overnight, Naples is convenient for both sites, 26km (16 miles) from Pompeii and 9km (6 miles) from Herculaneum. The **Excelsior** (*Via Partenope 48* ☎ *(081) 417111* ☎ *710043* ☎ *(081) 411743* ▮▮▮▮ ▤ ✲ ▯ ▱ 🗚🗚 ▣ ▣ 💳 ✈) is in the luxury class; the **Palace** (*Piazza Garibaldi 9* ☎ *(081) 264575* ☎ *720262* ▮▮▮▮ 🗚🗚 ▣ ▣ 💳 ✈) has first-class amenities.

La Sacrestia (*Via Orazio 116* ☎ *664186* ▮▮▮▮ 🗚🗚 ▣ ▣ 💳 ✈), elegance with a terrace; **La Cantinella** (*Via Cuma 42* ☎ *405375* ▮▮▮▮ 🗚🗚 ▣ ▣ 💳 ✈), specializing in seafood; **Giuseppone a Mare** (*Via Ferdinando Russo 13* ☎ *7696002* ▮▮▮ 🗚🗚 ▣ 💳).

Viterbo

*Map **14C3**. 81km (50 miles) NW of Rome. Population: 57,000. Getting there: By train, from Stazione San Pietro (2hrs); by car, Via Cassia (SS2); by bus, ACOTRAL from Via Lepanto (on Metropolitana Line A) (1hr 30mins)* i *EPT, Piazzale dei Caduti 16* ☎ *(0761) 226161.*

Viterbo was originally an Etruscan town, but was colonized by the Romans in 310BC. By the early Middle Ages it had become an important city and an episcopal see. A number of popes sought refuge here during the recurring conflict between the papacy and the Holy Roman Emperors, and in 1257 Alexander IV was the first of several pontiffs to make Viterbo his official city of residence.

The strong flavour of the Middle Ages is obvious the moment you pass through one of the graceful gateways in the well-preserved medieval walls — an impression reinforced within the quarter of **San Pellegrino**, with its solid-stone, small-windowed buildings and low, dark, archways.

Viterbo is unusually rich in buildings of outstanding architectural interest. Perhaps the most famous is the 13thC **Papal Palace** (★), a fine example of Gothic civil architecture. Beside the Palace is the **Cathedral of San Lorenzo**, its Baroque facade masking an essentially Romanesque structure, largely rebuilt after damage in World War II. The splendid Gothic campanile in striped white and grey stone shows the Sienese influence, and the interior is notable for its delicately carved nave capitals and fine marble floor.

The town has many lovely churches besides the cathedral. **Santa Maria Nuova** (★) in the San Pellegrino quarter dates from the 12thC and has graceful cloisters and an external pulpit from which St Thomas Aquinas once preached. It too has been heavily restored following bomb damage. **Santa Maria in Gradi** has beautiful 13thC cloisters. **San Sisto**, built in the 11thC and enlarged in the 12th and 13thC, has a magnificent campanile. The early 13thC **San Francesco** was also rebuilt after World War II. It contains two fine monuments: the **Tomb of Clement IV** (died 1268) by Pietro di Oderisio and the **Tomb of Adrian V** (died 1276), attributed to Arnolfo di Cambio.

Piazza San Lorenzo (★) is an imposing square, flanked by the cathedral and Papal Palace. It occupies the site of the former Etruscan acropolis. But the real heart of the town is **Piazza del Plebiscito**, overlooked by the 13thC **Palazzo del Podestà** (with 15thC tower) and 15thC **Palazzo Comunale**. The **Municipal Museum** (🏛 *open Tues-Sun 8.30am-1.30pm, 3.30-6pm, closed Mon*) is housed in the former Convent of Santa Maria della Verità and contains Etruscan objects, and a number of fine paintings including works by del Piombo and Salvator Rosa.

🍴 **Balletti Park** (*at San Martino al Cimino, 6km (4 miles) outside Viterbo* ☎ *(0761) 379777* 🖰 *623059* 🅸🅸🅸🅸 🆎 🅾 🆅🅸🆂🅰); **Leon d'Oro** (*Via della Cava 36* ☎ *(0761) 344444* 🅸🅸🅸 🆎 🅾 🆅🅸🆂🅰); **Mini Palace** (*Via Santa Maria della Grotticella 2* ☎ *(0761) 239742* 🖰 *(0761) 341930* 🅸🅸🅸🅸 🆎 🅾 🆅🅸🆂🅰 ✠).

🍽 **Aquilanti** (*at La Quercia, 3km (2 miles) outside Viterbo* ☎ *(0761) 341701* 🅸🅸🅸 ▤▤ 🆎 🆅🅸🆂🅰); **12L** (*Via Carioli 24* ☎ *(0761) 235921* 🅸🅸🅸 🆎).

Glossary of art and architecture

Aedicule   Niche framed by columns
Ambo   Early form of pulpit
Architrave   A supporting beam above a column
Archivolt   Continuous moulding around a door or window
Atrium   Central room or court of pre-Christian house; forecourt of early Christian church
Baldacchino   Canopy, usually over altar, throne, etc.
Basilica   Rectangular Roman civic hall; early Christian church of similar structure
Bottega   An artist's workshop
Campanile   Bell tower
Camposanto   Cemetery
Caryatid   Carved female figure used as column
Chiaroscuro   (Heightened) light and shade effects in painting
Ciborium   Altar canopy; casket for the Host
Crossing   Space in church at intersection of chancel, nave and transepts
Diptych   Work of art on two hinged panels
Ex-voto   Work of art offered in fulfilment of a vow
Fresco   Technique of painting onto wet plaster on a wall
Herm   Sculpted male nude or bust on tapered pillar
Intarsia   Inlay of wood

Loggia   Gallery or balcony open on at least one side
Lunette   Semicircular surface or panel, often painted or carved
Misericord   Ledge or bracket projecting from pew or stall
Ogival   Of a double-curved line, both concave and convex
Piano nobile   Main floor of house, usually raised
Pieve   Parish church
Pietà   Representation of the Virgin lamenting over the dead Christ
Pietradura   Mosaic of semiprecious stone
Predella   One or more small paintings attached to the bottom of an altarpiece
Putto   The plump, naked child, often winged, in works of art
Scagliola   Plaster-work polished to resemble marble
Sgraffiti   Designs scratched into glaze to reveal base colour
Sinopia   Preparatory drawing made beneath a fresco
Stucco   Light, reinforced plaster
Tondo   Circular painting or sculpture
Transept   Transverse arms of a cruciform church
Tribune   Raised area of gallery in a church; the apse of a basilica
Triptych   Work of art on three hinged panels

SPECIAL INFORMATION

A guide to Italian

This glossary covers the basic language needs of the traveler: for essential vocabulary and simple conversation, finding accommodations, visiting the bank, shopping and using public transportation or a car. There is also a special menu decoder, explaining all the most common descriptions of food terms.

Reference words

Monday lunedì	Friday venerdì
Tuesday martedì	Saturday sabato
Wednesday mercoledì	Sunday domenica
Thursday giovedì	

January gennaio	July luglio
February febbraio	August agosto
March marzo	September settembre
April aprile	October ottobre
May maggio	November novembre
June giugno	December dicembre

1	uno	11	undici	21	ventuno
2	due	12	dodici	22	ventidue
3	tre	13	tredici	30	trenta
4	quattro	14	quattordici	40	quaranta
5	cinque	15	quindici	50	cinquanta
6	sei	16	sedici	60	sessanta
7	sette	17	diciassette	70	settanta
8	otto	18	diciotto	80	ottanta
9	nove	19	diciannove	90	novanta
10	dieci	20	venti	100	cento

First primo, -a	Six o'clock le sei
Second secondo, -a	Quarter-past.... ....e un quarto
Third terzo, -a	Half-past.... ....e mezzo
Fourth quarto, -a	Quarter to.... ....meno un quarto
One o'clock l'una	

Mr signor(e)	Ladies signore, donne
Mrs signora	Gents signori, uomini
Miss signorina	

Basic communication

Yes sì	Today oggi
No no	Tomorrow domani
Please per favore/per piacere	Next week la settimana prossima
Thank you grazie	Last week la settimana scorsa
I'm very sorry mi dispiace molto/mi scusi	....days ago ....giorni fa
Excuse me senta! (to attract attention), permesso! (on bus, train, etc.), mi scusi	Month mese (m)
	Year anno
	Here qui
	There lì
Not at all/you're welcome prego	Big grande
Hello ciao (familiar), pronto (on telephone)	Small piccolo, -a
	Hot caldo, -a
Good morning buon giorno	Cold freddo, -a
Good afternoon buona sera	Good buono, -a
Good evening buona sera	Bad cattivo, -a
Good night buona notte	Beautiful bello, -a
Goodbye ciao (familiar), addio (final or familiar), arrivederci	Well bene
	Badly male
Morning mattino	With con
Afternoon pomeriggio	And e, ed
Evening sera	But ma
Night notte (f)	Very molto
Yesterday ieri	All tutto, -a

Open aperto
Closed chiuso
Entrance entrata
Exit uscita
Free libero
On the left a sinistra
On the right a destra
Straight ahead diritto
Near vicino
Far lontano
Up su
Down giù
Early presto
Late tardi
Quickly presto
Pleased to meet you. Molto
lieto/piacere.
How are you? Come sta?
Very well, thank you. Benissimo,
grazie.
Do you speak English? Parla
inglese?
I don't understand. Non capisco.
I don't know. Non lo so.

Please explain. Può spiegare per
favore.
Please speak more slowly. Parli
più lentamente per favore.
My name is.... Mi chiamo....
I am American/English. Sono
americano/inglese, -a.
Where is/are....? Dov'e/dove si
trova/dove sono....?
Is there a....? C'è un, una....?
What? Cosa?
When? Quando?
How much? Quanto?
That's too much. È troppo caro.
Expensive caro
Cheap a buon mercato
I would like.... Vorrei....
Do you have....? Avete....?
Just a minute. Un momento.
That's fine/OK. Va
bene/benissimo/OK
What time is it? Che ore sono?
I don't feel well. Non mi sento
bene/sto male.

Accommodations

Making a reservation by letter

> Dear Sir/Madam,
> *Egregio Signore/Signora,*
> **I would like to reserve one double room (with bathroom) —**
> *Vorrei prenotare una camera doppia (con bagno) —*
> **a twin-bedded room, and one single room (with shower)**
> *— una camera con due letti, e una camera singola (con doccia)*
> **for 7 nights from 12 August. We would like bed and breakfast/half board/full board**
> *per 7 notti dal 12 agosto. Vorremmo una camera con colazione/mezza pensione/pensione completa*
> **and would prefer rooms with a sea view.**
> *e possibilmente camere con vista sul mare.*
> **Please send me details of your terms with the confirmation.**
> *Sarei lieto di ricevere dettagli del prezzo e la conferma.*
> **Yours sincerely,**
> *Cordiali saluti,*

Arriving at the hotel

I have a reservation. My name is....
Ho già prenotato. Sono il signor/la signora....
A quiet room with bath/shower/WC/wash basin
Una camera tranquilla con bagno/doccia/WC/lavandino
....overlooking the sea/park/street/the back.
....con vista sul mare/sul parco/sulla strada/sul retro
Does the price include breakfast/tax/service?
E'tutto compreso/colazione/tasse/servizio?
This room is too large/small/cold/hot/noisy.
Questa camera è troppo grande/piccola/fredda/calda/rumorosa.
That's too expensive. Have you anything cheaper?
Costa troppo. Avete qualcosa meno caro?

Floor/story piano
Dining room/restaurant sala da pranzo/ristorante (m)
Manager direttore, -trice
Porter portiere
Have you got a room? Avete una camera?
What time is breakfast/dinner? A che ora è la prima colazione/la cena?
Is there a laundry service? C'è il servizio lavanderia?
What time does the hotel close? A che ora chiude l'albergo?
Will I need a key? Avrò bisogno della chiave?

Words and phrases

Is there a night porter?   C'è un portiere di notte?
I'll be leaving tomorrow morning.   Parto domani mattina.
Please give me a call at....   Mi può chiamare alle....
Come in!   Avanti!

Shopping (La Spesa)

Where is the nearest/a good....?   Dov'è il più vicino/la più vicina....?
   Dov'è un buon/una buona....?
Can you help me/show me....?   Mi può aiutare/Può mostrarmi....?
I'm just looking.   Sto soltanto guardando.
Do you accept credit cards/travelers cheques?   Accettate carte di
   credito/travelers cheques?
Can you deliver to....?   Può consegnare a....?
I'll take it.   Lo prendo.
I'll leave it.   Lo lascio.
Can I have it tax-free for export?   Posso averlo senza tasse per
   l'esportazione?
This is faulty. Can I have a replacement/refund?   C'è difetto. Me lo
   potrebbe cambiare/rimborsare?
I don't want to spend more than....   Non voglio spendere più di....
Can I have a stamp for....?   Vorrei un francobollo per....

Shops

Antique store   negozio di
   antiquariato
Art gallery   galleria d'arte
Bakery   panificio, forno
Bank   banca
Beauty parlor   istituto di bellezza
Bookstore   libreria
Butcher   macelleria
Cake shop   pasticceria
Clothes store   negozio di
   abbigliamento, di confezioni
Dairy   latteria
Delicatessen   salumeria, pizzicheria
Fish store   pescheria
Florist   fioraio
Greengrocer   ortolano,
   erbivendolo, fruttivendolo
Grocer   drogheria
Haberdasher   merciaio
Hairdresser   parrucchiere, -a

Jeweler   gioielleria
Market   mercato
Newsstand   giornalaio, edicola
   (kiosk)
Optician   ottico
Perfumery   profumeria
Pharmacy/drugstore   farmacia
Photographic store   negozio
   fotografico
Post office   ufficio postale
Shoe store   negozio di calzature
Stationers   cartoleria
Supermarket   supermercato
Tailor   sarto
Tobacconist   tabaccheria (also sells
   stamps)
Tourist office   ente del turismo
Toy store   negozio di giocattoli
Travel agent   agenzia di
   viaggio

At the bank

I would like to change some dollars/pounds/travelers cheques
Vorrei cambiare dei dollari/delle sterline/dei travelers cheques
What is the exchange rate?
Com'è il cambio?
Can you cash a personal check?
Può cambiare un assegno?
Can I obtain cash with this credit card?
Posso avere soldi in contanti con questa carta di credito?
Do you need to see my passport?
Ha bisogno del mio passaporto?

Some useful goods

Antiseptic cream   crema antisettica
Aspirin   aspirina
Bandages   fasciature
Band-Aid   cerotto
Cotton   cotone idrofilo (m)
Diarrhea/upset stomach pills
   pillole anti-coliche
Indigestion tablets   pillole per
   l'indigestione
Insect repellant   insettifugo
Laxative   lassativo
Sanitary napkins   assorbenti igienici

Shampoo   shampoo
Shaving cream   crema da barba
Soap   sapone (m)
Sunburn cream   crema antisolare
Sunglasses   occhiali da sole
Suntan cream/oil   crema/olio solare
Tampons   tamponi
Tissues   fazzoletti di carta
Toothbrush   spazzolino da denti
Toothpaste   dentifricio
Travel sickness pills   pillole contro
   il mal di viaggio

Bra	reggiseno	Shirt	camicia
Coat	cappotto	Shoes	scarpe
Dress	vestito	Skirt	gonna
Jacket	giacca	Stockings/tights	calze/collants
Pants	pantaloni	Swimsuit	costume da bagno (m)
Pullover	maglione (m)	Underpants	mutande

Film	pellicola	Postcard	cartolina
Letter	lettera	Stamp	francobollo
Money order	vaglia	Telegram	telegramma (m)

Driving

Service station   stazione di rifornimento (f), distributore (m)
Fill it up.   Faccia il pieno, per favore.
Give me....lire worth.   Mi dia....lire.
I would like....liters of gasoline.   Vorrei....litri di benzina.
Can you check the....?   Può controllare....?
There is something wrong with the....   C'e un difetto nel/nella....

Accelerator	acceleratore (m)	Lights	fanali, fari, luci
Axle	l'asse (m)	Oil	olio
Battery	batteria	Spares	i pezzi di ricambio
Brakes	freni	Spark plugs	le candele
Exhaust	lo scarico, scappamento	Tires	gomme
Fan belt	la cinghia del ventilatore	Water	acqua
Gear box	la scatola del cambio	Windshield	parabrezza (m)

My car won't start.   La mia macchina non s'accende.
My car has broken down/had a flat tire.   La macchina è guasta/la gomma è forata.
The engine is overheating.   Il motore si scalda.
How long will it take to repair?   Quanto tempo ci vorrà per la riparazione?
I need it as soon as possible.   Ne ho bisogno il più presto possibile.

Car rental

Where can I rent a car?   Dove posso noleggiare una macchina?
Is full/comprehensive insurance included?   E'completamente assicurata?
Is it insured for another driver?   E'assicurata per un altro guidatore?
Does the price include mileage?   Il kilometraggio è compreso?
Unlimited mileage   kilometraggio illimitato
Deposit   deposito
By what time must I return it?   A che ora devo consegnarla?
Can I return it to another depot?   Posso riportarla ad un altro deposito?
Is the gas tank full?   E'il serbatoio pieno?

Road signs

Accendere le luci in galleria	lights on in tunnel	Divieto di sosta	no stopping
Autostrada	highway	Lavori in corso	roadworks ahead
Caduta di massi	falling stones	Passaggio a livello	level crossing
Casello	toll gate	Pedaggio	toll road
Dare la precedenza	yield	Raccordo anulare	beltway
Divieto di accesso, senso vietato	no entry	Rallentare	slow down
		Senso unico	one-way street
Divieto di parcheggio	no parking	Tangenziale	bypass
Divieto di sorpasso	no passing	Tenersi in corsia	keep in lane
		Uscita (autocarri)	exit (for trucks)

Other methods of transportation

Aircraft	aeroplano	Train	treno
Airport	aeroporto	ticket	biglietto
Bus	autobus (m)	Ticket office	biglietteria
Bus stop	fermata	One-way	andata
Coach	corriera	Round trip	andata e ritorno
Ferry/boat	traghetto	Half fare	metà prezzo
Ferry port	porto	First/second/economy	prima classe/seconda classe/turistico
Hovercraft	aliscafo		
Station	stazione (f)	Sleeper/couchette	cuccetta

When is the next....for....?   Quando parte il prossimo....per....?
What time does it arrive?   A che ora arriva?
What time does the last....for....leave?   Quando parte l'ultimo....per....?

Words and phrases

Which track/quay/gate? Quale binario/molo/uscita?
Is this the....for....? E'questo il....per....?
Is it direct? Where does it stop? E'diretto? Dove si ferma?
Do I need to change anywhere? Devo cambiare?
Please tell me where to get off. Mi può dire dove devo scendere.
Take me to.... Mi vuol portare a....
Is there a dining car? C'è un vagone ristorante?

Food and drink

Have you a table for....? Avete un tavolo per....?
I want to reserve a table for....at.... Vorrei prenotare un tavolo per....alle....
A quiet table. Un tavolo tranquillo.
A table near the window. Un tavolo vicino alla finestra.
Could we have another table? Potremmo spostarci?
I did not order this. Non ho ordinato questo.
Breakfast/lunch/dinner prima colazione/pranzo/cena
Bring me another.... Un altro....per favore.
The check please. Il conto per favore.
Is service included? Il servizio è incluso?

Hot	caldo	Dry	secco
Cold	freddo	Sweet	dolce, amabile
Glass	bicchiere (m)	Salt	sale (m)
Bottle	bottiglia	Pepper	pepe (m)
Half-bottle	mezza bottiglia	Oil	olio
Beer/lager (draft)	birra (alla spina)	Vinegar	aceto
		Mustard	senape (f)
Fruit juice	succo di frutta	Bread	pane (m)
Mineral water	acqua minerale	Butter	burro
Orangeade/lemonade	aranciata/limonata	Cheese	formaggio
		Milk	latte (m)
Carbonated/noncarbonated	gassata/non gassata	Coffee	caffè (m)
		Tea	tè (m)
Flask/carafe	fiasco/caraffa	Chocolate	cioccolato
Red wine	vino rosso, vino nero	Sugar	zucchero
		Steak	bistecca
White wine	vino bianco	well done	ben cotto
Rosé wine	vino rosé	medium	medio
Vintage	di annata	rare	al sangue

Menu decoder

Abbacchio baby lamb
Acciughe anchovies
Acqua cotta thick bread and vegetable soup with egg
Affettati sliced cold meats
Affumicato smoked
Aglio garlic
Agnello lamb
Agnolotti pasta envelopes
Agro sour
Albicocche apricots
Amaro bitter
Ananas pineapple
Anatra/anitra duck
Anguilla eel
Animelle sweetbreads
Antipasto hors d'oeuvre
Aragosta langouste, lobster
Arancia orange
Aringa herring
Arrosto roast meat
Arselle baby clams
Asparagi asparagus
Baccalà dried salt cod
Basilico basil
Bianchetti whitebait
Bianco plain, boiled
Bietola Swiss chard

Biscottini di Prato small, hard almond biscuits
Bistecca alla fiorentina grilled T-bone steak
Bollito misto boiled meats
Brace (alla) charcoal grilled
Braciola chop
Branzino sea bass
Bresaola dried salt beef
Brodetto fish soup
Brodo consommé
Bruschetta garlic bread
Burrida fish stew
Burro (al) (cooked in) butter
Cacciagione game
Cacciucco fish stew
Calamaretti baby squid
Calamari squid
Calzone half-moon-shaped pizza
Cannelloni stuffed pasta tubes
Capitone large conger eel
Cappelletti stuffed pasta hats
Cappe sante scallops
Capretto kid
Carciofi alla giudia artichokes fried in oil and lemon
Carne meat

Words and phrases

Carote carrots
Carpa carp
Carpaccio raw lean beef fillet
Carrello (al) from the trolley
Casa (della) of the restaurant
Cassalingo, -a homemade
Castagnaccio chestnut cake
Castagne chestnuts
Castrato mutton
Cavolfiore cauliflower
Cavolini di Bruxelles sprouts
Cavolo cabbage
Ceci chick peas
Cenci fried pastry twists
Cervella brains
Cervo venison
Cetriolo cucumber
Cicoria chicory
Ciliege cherries
Cima cold stuffed veal
Cinghiale wild boar
Cipolle onions
Cocomero watermelon
Coda di bue oxtail
Coniglio rabbit
Contorno vegetable side-dish
Controfiletto sirloin steak
Coppa cooked pressed neck of
  pork or an ice cream sundae
Cosciotto di agnello leg of lamb
Costata di bue entrecôte steak
Costolette cutlets
Cotto cooked
Cozze mussels
Crema custard, cream soup
Crespolini savory pancakes
Crostacei shellfish
Crostini small savory toasts
Crudo raw
Diavola (alla) in a spicy sauce
Dolci desserts, sweets
Espresso small black coffee
Fagiano pheasant
Fagioli all'uccelletto beans with
  tomatoes and garlic
Fagiolini French beans
Faraona guinea fowl
Farcito stuffed
Fatto in casa homemade
Fave broad beans
Fegatini chicken livers
Fegato liver
Ferri (ai) grilled
Fesa di vitello leg of veal
Fettina slice
Fettuccine thin flat pasta
Fettunta garlic bread
Fichi figs
Filetto fillet
Finocchio fennel
Finocchiona fennel-flavored
  salami
Focaccia dimpled savory bread
Formaggio cheese
Forno (al) cooked in the oven
Fragole strawberries
Fresco fresh
Frittata omelet

Frittelle fritters
Fritto fried
Frutta fruit
Frutti di mare shellfish
Funghi mushrooms
Gamberetti shrimps
Gamberi big prawns
Gelato ice cream
Giorno (del) of the day
Girarrosto (al) spit-roasted
Girello topside of beef
Gnocchi small pasta dumplings
Grana Parmesan cheese
Granchio crab
Granita water ice
Graticola (alla) grilled
Griglia (alla) grilled
Indivia endive
Insalata salad
Involtini skewered veal and ham
Lamponi raspberries
Lampreda lamprey
Lasagne baked flat pasta
Lenticchie lentils
Lepre hare
Lesso boiled (meat)
Limone lemon
Lingua di bue ox tongue
Lombata, -ina loin, loin chop
Lonza cured fillet of pork
Luccio pike
Lumache snails
Macedonia di frutta fruit salad
Magro lean
Maiale pork
Mandorle almonds
Manzo beef
Marmellata jam
Medaglioni rounds of meat
Mela apple
Melagrana pomegranate
Melanzane eggplant
Melone melon
Merluzzo cod
Miele honey
Minestra soup
Minestrone vegetable soup
Misto mixed
Mostarda pickle
Muscolo alla fiorentina beef
  casserole with beans
Naturale (al) plain
Nocciole hazelnuts
Noci nuts
Nodino di vitello veal chop
Nostrale, nostrano local
Oca goose
Ombrina black umber
Orata gilt-head bream
Osso buco veal knuckle
Ostriche oysters
Paglia e fieno green and white
  tagliatelle
Paillard thin grilled steak
Palombo dogfish
Panforte di Siena hard cake with
  honey, fruit and almonds
Panino imbottito roll

Words and phrases

Panna   cream
Panzanella   salad of soaked bread and fresh vegetables
Pappa al pomodoro   thick tomato and bread soup
Pappardelle   long flat pasta
Parmigiano-Reggiano   Parmesan
Passato   purée
Pasta e fagioli   bean and pasta soup
Pasticcio   layered pasta pie
Pasto   meal
Patate   potatoes
Pecorino   hard ewes' milk cheese
Penne all'arrabbiata   short pasta tubes with a fiery sauce
Peperoni   sweet peppers
Pera   pear
Pernice   partridge
Pesca   peach
Pesce   fish
Pesce persico   perch
Pesce spada   swordfish
Pesciolini   small fry
Pesto   green basil sauce
Petto di pollo   chicken breast
Pezzo   piece
Piacere   according to taste
Piatto del giorno   today's dish
Piccante   spicy, piquant
Piccata   thin escalope
Piccione   pigeon
Pinzimonio   oily vegetable dip
Piselli   peas
Polenta   maize porridge
Pollame   poultry
Pollo   chicken
Polpette   meatballs
Polpettone   meatloaf
Polpo   octopus
Pomodoro   tomato
Pompelmo   grapefruit
Porchetta   roast sucking pig
Primizie   spring vegetables
Prosciutto   ham
Prugne   plums
Quaglie   quails
Radicchio   red bitter lettuce
Ragù   meat and tomato sauce
Rane   frogs
Ravanelli   radishes
Ravioli   stuffed pasta squares
Razza   skate
Ribollita   thick vegetable soup
Ricciarelli   almond biscuits
Ricotta   cheese — similar to cottage cheese
Rigatoni   ridged pasta tubes
Ripieno   stuffed
Risi e bisi   pea and rice soup
Riso   rice
Risotto   savory rice dish
Rognoni   kidneys
Rombo maggiore   turbot
Rosmarino   rosemary
Rospo   angler fish
Salsa (verde)   (green) sauce
Salsiccia   sausage
Saltimbocca alla romana   veal escalopes with ham and sage
Salvia   sage
Sarde   sardines
Scaloppine   escalopes
Scelta (a)   of your choice
Schiacciata alla fiorentina   vanilla sponge cake
Scottadito   grilled lamb cutlets
Selvaggina   game, venison
Semifreddo   frozen dessert
Semplice   plain
Seppie   cuttlefish
Sgombro   mackerel
Sogliola   sole
Sottaceti   pickled vegetables
Spaghetti
   all'amatriciana   spaghetti with bacon, tomatoes
   alla bolognese   with *ragù*
   alla carbonara   with bacon, eggs
   alla napoletana   with tomato
Spezzatino   meat stew
Spiedini   skewers, kebabs
Spiedo (allo)   on the spit
Spigola   sea bass
Spinaci   spinach
Squadro   monkfish
Stagionato   hung, well-aged
Stagione (di)   in season
Stoccafisso   stockfish
Stracciatella   clear egg soup
Stracotto   beef in red wine
Stufato   braised, stew(ed)
Sugo   sauce
Supplì   rice croquettes
Susina   plum
Tacchino   turkey
Tagliatelle   thin flat pasta
Tartufi   truffles
Tegame (al)   fried or baked
Telline   cockles
Timballo   savory pasta pie
Tinca   tench
Tonno   tuna
Tordi   thrushes
Torta   flan, tart
Tortellini   small stuffed pasta
Tost   toasted sandwich
Totano   squid
Tramezzino   sandwich
Trancia   slice
Trenette   flat, thinnish pasta
Trifolato   fried in garlic
Triglia   red mullet
Trippa   tripe
Trota   trout
Uccelletti   grilled beef on skewers
Umido (in)   stewed
Uova   eggs
Uva   grapes
Verdure   green vegetables
Vitello   veal
Vongole   clams
Zabaglione   egg yolks and Marsala whip
Zuccotto   ice cream liqueur cake
Zuppa   soup
Zuppa inglese   trifle

Index

General index: 211   Gazetteer of street names: 221

Individual hotels, restaurants, cafés, nightclubs and shops are not generally indexed, because they appear in alphabetical order within their appropriate sections. However, the sections themselves are indexed. Streets and squares are listed in the gazetteer and not the index.

Page numbers in **bold** type indicate the main entries. *Italic* page numbers refer to the illustrations and plans.

Index

Index

Index

Index

Index

Index

Index

Index

Gazetteer of street names

Numbers after each street refer to pages on which it is mentioned in the text. Map references relate to the maps that follow this gazetteer.

It has not been possible to label every street drawn on the maps, although all major roads and squares are indicated. Some unlabeled streets still appear in the gazetteer, however, to give an idea of their approximate location.

A

Acciaioli, V., 41; Map 5H4

Acqua Acetosa, Lungotev., 196; Map 3B-C5-6

Aelius, Pons, 87; Map 5H4

Agonale, Corsia, 40; Map 6H5

Allessandria, V., 16; Map 7F8-9

Amba Aradam, V., 17; Map 11J-K8

Andrea Doria, V., 175; Map 4F2

Angelico, Borgo, 162; Map 4G3

Anima, V. dell', 105; Map 5H5

Appia, Porta, 88; Map 11L8

Appia Antica, V., 61, 197; Map 13D4

Appia Nuova, V., 196, 197; Map 11J-K9-10

Appio, Pzle., 170; Map 11J9

Aracoeli, Pza. d', 106; Map 9I6

Aracoeli, V. di, 39; Map 10I6

Arco della Pace, V., 109; Map 6H5

Argentario, Clivio (Clivus Argentarius), 116; Map 10I6

Argentina, Largo, 45, 148, 166; Map 5I5

Augusto Imperatore, Pza., 149; Map 5G5

Aurelia, Porta, 88; Map 8J3

Aurelia Antica, V., 88; Map 8J2-3

Aurora, V., 155; Map 7G7

B

Babuino, V. del, 16, 85, 86, 167, 168, 169, 170, 176; Map 6F-G5-6

Barberini, Pza., 17, 37, 67, 125, 138, 157; Map 7G7

Barberini, V., 172, 197; Map 7G7

Baullari, V. dei, 43-4; Map 5I5

Belle Arti, Vle. delle, 69, 133, 194; Map 6E5-6

Benaco, V., 162; Map 7D9

Biscione, Pza. del, 155; Map 5I5

Bissolati, V., 12; Map 7G7

Bocca di Leone, V., 43, 141, 172, 173, 174, 175, 177; Map 6G6

Bocca della Verità, Pza., 46, 84, 107, 122, 123; Map 9J6

Boezio, V., 137; Map 5G4

Bollette, Vic. delle, 154; Map 6H6

Bolzano, V., 161; Map 13C4

Boncompagni, V., 16, 164; Map 7G7-8

Borghese, Pza., 77; Map 6G5

Borgognona, V., 43, 167, 171, 173, 175; Map 6G6

Borsi, V., 166; Map 3D7

Bufalo, V. del, 43; Map 6G6

C

Cadlolo, V., 138, 163; Map 12C3

Caio Cestio, V., 88; Map 9L5-6

Cairoli, Pza., 97; Map 5I5

Campana, Vic. della, 151; Map 5G5

Campania, V., 50, 143, 153, 177; Map 7F7

Campidoglio, Pza. del, 23, 34, 39, 55, 56, 81, 84; Map 10I6

Campidoglio, V. del, 90; Map 10I6

Campo dei Fiori, Pza., 43-4, 55, 84, 162, 167, 174; Map 5I5

Capena, Porta, 88; Map 10J7

Capo di Ferro, Pza., 44, 81; Map 5I5

Capo le Case, V., 176; Map 6G6

Cappuccini, V. dei, 168; Map 6G6

Capranica, Pza., 42; Map 5H5

Carrozze, V. delle, 86, 168; Map 6G6

Cartari, V. de', 41; Map 5H4

Cassia, V., 197; Map 2A-B4

Castro Pretorio, Vle, 15; Map 13C4

Cavalieri di Malta, Pza. dei, 26, 46, 50; Map 9K5

Cavour, V., 12, 17, 142; Map 10I7

Cenci, Lungotev. dei, 16; Map 9I5

Cestari, V. dei, 45; Map 5H-I5

Cestio, Ponte, 44, 71; Map 9J5

Chiesa Nuova, Pza. della, 75; Map 5H4

Chigi, Largo, 169, 170; Map 6H6

Cinque, Vic. del, 44; Map 8I4

Cinquecento, Pza. dei, 10, 52, 122; Map 7H8

Circo Massimo, V. del, 46, 63, 196; Map 10J6

Col di Lana, V., 196; Map 2E4

Cola di Rienzo, V., 17, 34, 38, 157, 167; Map 4G3-4

Collegio Romano, Pza. del, 79; Map 6H6

Colonna, Pza., 39, 43, 64, 78, 84; Map 6H6

Colosseo, Pza. del, 49, 63, 122; Map 10I-J7

Colosseo, Pzle. del, 34; Map 10I-J7

Conciliazione, V. della, 26, 39, 55, 133, 138, 161; Map 4H3

Condotti, V., 43, 86, 159, 166, 167, 168, 169, 170, 171, 172, 173, 176, 195; Map 6G6

Coronari, V. dei, 34, 40, 168, 195; Map 5H5

Corso, V. del, 42, 55, 78, 79, 85, 124, 158, 166, 167, 170, 173, 176, 195; Map 6G-H5-6

Crescenzi, Salita de', 40; Map 5H5

Crescenzio, V., 137; Map 4G3

Gazetteer

Gazetteer

ROME

1

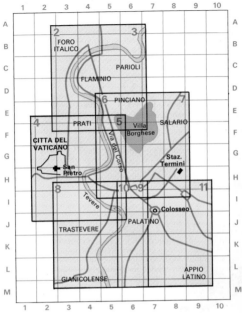

LEGEND

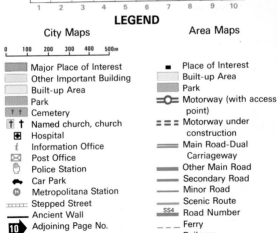

City Maps

0 100 200 300 400 500m

Major Place of Interest
Other Important Building
Built-up Area
Park
†† Cemetery
† † Named church, church
✚ Hospital
i Information Office
⊠ Post Office
✋ Police Station
🅟 Car Park
Ⓜ Metropolitana Station
▭▭▭ Stepped Street
▬▬ Ancient Wall
10 Adjoining Page No.

Area Maps

■ Place of Interest
Built-up Area
Park
=O= Motorway (with access point)
= = = Motorway under construction
▬▬ Main Road-Dual Carriageway
▬▬ Other Main Road
▬▬ Secondary Road
▬ Minor Road
▬ Scenic Route
SS4 Road Number
– – – Ferry
▬▬ Railway
✈ Airport
✦ Airfield
⚑ Abbey, monastery
∴ Ancient site, ruin
☂ Good Beach
15 Adjoining Page No.

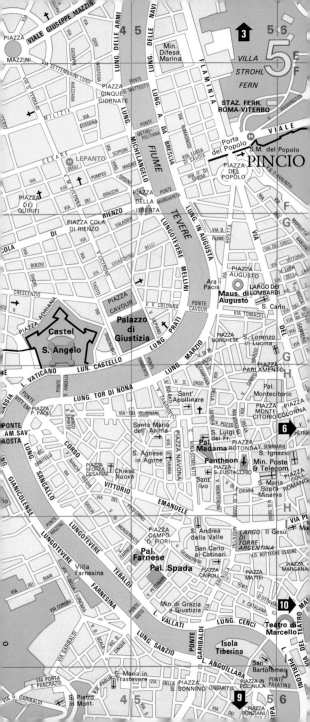

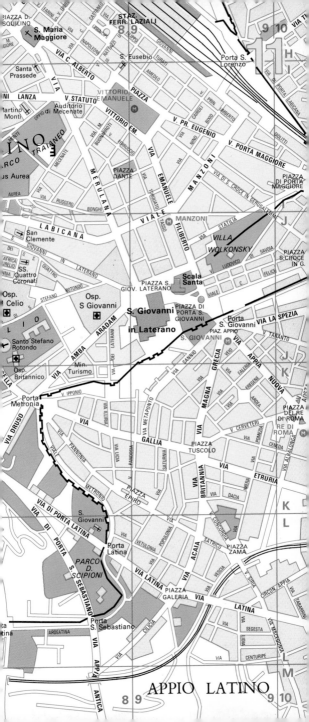

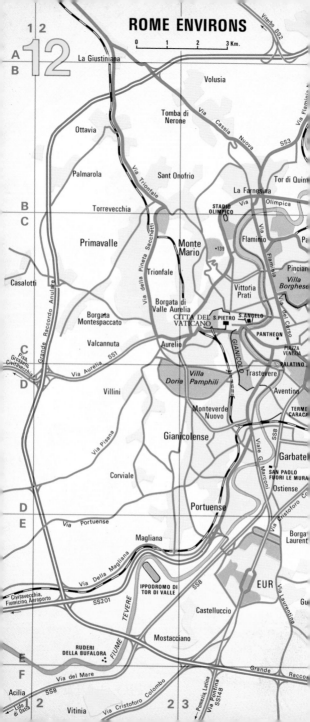

ROME ENVIRONS

0 1 2 3 Km.

A
B

1 2
12

La Giustiniana

Volusia

Tomba di Nerone

Ottavia

Via Cassia Nuova

SS3

Via Flaminia

Palmarola

Sant Onofrio

Via Trionfale

Tor di Quin

La Farnesina

Via Olimpica

B
C

Torrevecchia

STADIO OLIMPICO

Flaminio

Pa

Primavalle

Via della Pineta Sacchetti

Monte Mario

•139

Via Flaminia

Pincian

Villa Borghese

Casalotti

Trionfale

Vittoria Prati

Grande Raccordo Anulare

Borgata Montespaccato

Borgata di Valle Aurelia

CITTA DEL VATICANO

S.PIETRO

S.ANGELO

Via del Corso

PANTHEON

Pisa Grosseto Civitavecchia

Valcannuta

Aurelio

GIANICOLO

PIAZZA VENEZIA

C
D

Via Aurelia SS1

Villa Doria Pamphili

Trastevere

PALATINO

Villini

Monteverde Nuovo

Aventino

TERME CARACA

Via Pisana

Gianicolense

Viale G. Marconi

SS8

Garbate

SAN PAOLO FUORI LE MURA

Corviale

Ostiense

D
E

Via Portuense

Portuense

Via Cristoforo Co

Borga Laurent

Magliana

Via Della Magliana

IPPODROMO DI TOR DI VALLE

SS8

EUR

Via Laurentina

Gu

Civitavecchia, Fiumicino Aeroporto

SS201

FIUME TEVERE

Castelluccio

E
F

RUDERI DELLA BUFALORA

Mostacciano

Via del Mare

Grande

Racco

Acilia

SS8

Lido di Ostia

Vitinia

Via Cristoforo Colombo

Pomezia Latina SS148

Via Pontina

2

3

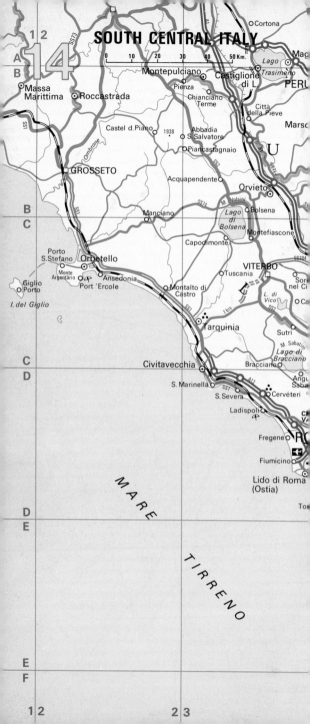

monday 9th Oct

CHURCH of GESU.

FORUM de TEMPIO (Roman buildings)

PANTHEON.

PIAZZA

PIAZZA NAVONA. I CAVOUR

ST PETER'S PIAZZA BUS

(49) VATICAN

(87) COLOSEUM.